MAPPING REGION IN EARLY AMERICAN WRITING

Mapping Region in Early American Writing

EDITED BY

EDWARD WATTS, KERI HOLT,

AND JOHN FUNCHION

THE UNIVERSITY OF GEORGIA PRESS   ATHENS AND LONDON

Paperback edition, 2018
© 2015 by the University of Georgia Press
Athens, Georgia 30602
www.ugapress.org
All rights reserved
Set in Adobe Garamond Pro by Graphic Composition, Inc.

Most University of Georgia Press titles are
available from popular e-book vendors.

Printed digitally

The Library of Congress has cataloged the
hardcover edition of this book as follows:

Mapping region in early American writing / edited by Edward Watts,
Keri Holt, and John Funchion.
vii, 310 pages : map ; 24 cm
  Includes bibliographical references and index.
  ISBN 978-0-8203-4822-3 (hardcover : alkaline paper) —
  ISBN 978-0-8203-4823-0 (ebook)
1. American literature—Colonial period, ca. 1600–1775—
History and criticism. 2. American literature—Revolutionary
period, 1775–1783—History and criticism. 3. American
literature—1783–1850—History and criticism. 4. Regionalism
in literature. 5. Space perception in literature. 6. Landscapes in
literature. 7. Geographical perception in literature.
8. Community life in literature. I. Watts, Edward, 1964–
II. Holt, Keri. III. Funchion, John.
  PS186.B67 2015
  810.9'001—dc23

                                            2015005757

British Library Cataloging-in-Publication Data available

Paperback ISBN 978-0-8203-5383-8

CONTENTS

Acknowledgments   vii

INTRODUCTION. Bordering Establishments: Mapping and Charting Region before 1860   1
Edward Watts and Keri Holt

Section 1. Chartings: Colonies and Countries

CHAPTER 1. "To plant himself in with soveranity": Welsh Indians and the Early West, 1576–1812   25
Edward Watts

CHAPTER 2. Reading the Routes: Early American Nature Writing and Critical Regionalism before the "Postfrontier"   45
William V. Lombardi

CHAPTER 3. The "Humor of the Old Southwest" and National Regionality   62
Robert Gunn

CHAPTER 4. West Indian Emancipation and the Time of Regionalism in the Hemispheric 1850s   81
Martha Schoolman

Section 2. Mappings: Creating Places

CHAPTER 5. The Labor of Regions: A Comparative Analysis of the Economic and Literary Production of Three Southern Regions in the Eighteenth-Century Atlantic World   99
Steven W. Thomas

CHAPTER 6. Captive in Mexico: Zebulon Pike and the New American Regionalism   121
Andy Doolen

CHAPTER 7. On the Hudson River Line: Postrevolutionary Regionalism, Neo-Tory Sympathy, and "A Lady of the State of New York"   138
Duncan Faherty

CHAPTER 8. "I Was Now Living in a New World": Frederick Douglass, Herman Melville, and New Bedford's Cosmopolitan Locality   160
Jennifer Schell

Section 3. *Countermappings: New Spaces in Old Places*

CHAPTER 9. Tribal Christianity: The Second Great Awakening and William Apess's Backwoods Methodism   181
Harry Brown

CHAPTER 10. "We, Too, the People": Rewriting Resistance in the Cherokee Nation   199
Keri Holt

CHAPTER 11. African American Literature of the Gold Rush   226
Janet Neary and Hollis Robbins

POSTSCRIPT. Creole Adjudication: Governing New Orleans and Regional Provisionality in the Long Nineteenth Century   249
John Funchion

Works Cited   269

Contributors   295

Index   299

ACKNOWLEDGMENTS

A PROJECT LIKE THIS would not exist without the able assistance and contributions of a great number of people. First, we would like to thank the following at the University of Georgia Press: Walter Biggins, Beth Snead, and John Joerschke. Their consistent professionalism, cheerfulness, and efficiency are the marks of true professionals. The copyeditor, Lori Rider, made the book better in innumerable ways and reminded us of just how little we know about the work of our own lives.

Second, thanks to our contributors. Meeting deadlines, responding to emails, being receptive to suggestions for revisions, and performing other chores associated with collaboration and cooperation are all essential to producing a book such as this. And, of course, we express our gratitude for their willingness to share their work at many stages of its development.

Third, each of us would like to acknowledge our own support systems, without whom and which the work could not have been done.

Edward Watts would like to thank the Newberry Library and its Darcy McNickle Seminar Series for allowing him to present a version of chapter 1 in the fall of 2013 and the Department of English at Michigan State University for allowing him to present that version as a faculty talk in 2012. Thanks as well to MSU for a sabbatical in fall 2014, during which much of the book's production work was undertaken. Finally, thanks to Stephanie, Tony, and Alex for their continued tolerance.

Keri Holt would like to thank George Frizzell, archivist at Western Carolina University, and Bo Taylor, director of the Museum of the Cherokee Indian, who gave her access to archival resources regarding Cherokee print culture that enabled her to write her chapter for this book. Thanks also to the Utah State University English Department for their continued support, as well as to her family and friends who help her get through all the tough stuff.

John Funchion would like to thank his department chair, Pam Hammons, for championing his research, and Ned Watts for his generous collegiality and for showing him and Keri how edited collections get done. Immeasurable gratitude is due to Melanie for sharing her love and knowledge of U.S. legal history. And he thanks his young daughter Dorothy for showing her two midwestern parents how to map Miami's possibilities through her joyful eyes.

MAPPING REGION IN EARLY AMERICAN WRITING

INTRODUCTION

Bordering Establishments
Mapping and Charting Region before 1860

Edward Watts and Keri Holt

THIS COLLECTION TAKES its title from Thomas Jefferson's intriguing turn of phrase in an 1803 letter to John Breckenridge, senator from Kentucky: "The future inhabitants of the Atlantic and Mississippi states will be our sons. We leave them in distinct but bordering establishments. We think we see their happiness in their union, and we wish it. Events may prove it otherwise; and if they see their interest in separation, why should we take side with our Atlantic rather than our Mississippi descendants?"[1] Ironically, in the year of the Louisiana Purchase, Jefferson contemplated a future mapping for North America in which the United States did not stretch across the continent or even into the Mississippi valley. Instead, he accedes that the as-yet-unsettled west may be filled more appropriately with countries or communities—establishments—not suited for membership in the eastern republic. Perhaps his concerns about the overextension of the republic—more often a Federalist fear—made such extranational developments seem only "natural."[2] Perhaps he thought lifeways in the two watersheds would diverge to an extent that political union could be infeasible. Either way, while continental aspirations ran rampant in the early republic, so did more particularized and local projections and conjectures, ones in which the continental American nation was neither unified, dominant, nor even inevitable.

On a broader scale, Jefferson's concession reveals the tremendous instability of states, borders, and countries in a pre-industrial America where geophysical features such as watersheds—Atlantic and Mississippi—still factored into place and identity.[3] Moreover, given the newly emergent concept of *nation* itself, Jefferson's use of "establishments"—instead of more ordinary terms such as republics or kingdoms—points to an open-ended process of state building, even while the narrative of white expansion itself remains unchallenged.[4] In this environment, the unsettled relation of smaller places—specific locales or regions—to larger ones such as nation or empires engendered the imagining of vastly different American establishments than the ones that have since ossified.

As we think about the establishments that might have been, as we reimagine sets of borders and identities other than what seem to be the unchanging spatial divisions of an immemorial nation, we engage in a process Denis N. Cosgrove labels *mapping*, "The measure of mapping is not restricted to the mathematical; it may be equally spiritual, political, or moral. By the same token, the mapping's record is not confined to the archival; it includes the remembered, the imagined, and the contemplated."[5] Cosgrove defines mapping as an internalized process entangled with the externalized practices of moving and creating in time and space, as opposed to charting, a process of defining space based on borders and closure. Studies of archival American maps have flourished in the past twenty years in the work of Martin Brückner, Thomas Hallock, Peter Mancall, and many others. Yet the study of American *mappings*—of instances when writers imagined and contemplated places that, like Jefferson's divergent Atlantic and Mississippi watershed-based communities, alternative nations, places, and futures—has been underserved.

However, just as Jefferson's open-ended Louisiana Purchase engaged the national imaginary to *map* that unbordered space, his 1784 Land Ordinance (fig. 1) *charted* a more proscribed process of prefabricated place making. In contrast to mapping, charting involves a more calculated and controlling process of defining space, one that tends to foreclose alternative mappings by establishing or asserting proscriptive narratives prior to settlement. The 1784 Land Ordinance was intended to chart, first, the Old Northwest, and, presumably, western areas yet to be annexed, as a rigidly ordered space of reason and productivity.[6] The implicit paranoia of Jefferson's rage for order also demonstrates the presence of alternative, perhaps less U.S.-based and undoubtedly less orderly, mappings that might have disrupted or redirected the new nation's orderly colonization of the territory. In fact, as the United States expanded, dozens of early American texts mapped new establishments and communities, many of them studied here, and many of them at odds with eastern versions of the nation and its formative values. Contrarily, other writers and policy makers simultaneously charted the frontier by maintaining the older narratives: rewriting and imposing narratives that disciplined divergent places and maps to meet a single imperial standard. Either way, early American writing continually queried the meaning of local distinctiveness in a post-Enlightenment moment defined by globalizing developments such as emergent industrialism, new transportation technologies, romantic nationalism, and republican ideologies, all discouraging localization and promulgating larger narratives.[7]

The essays collected in *Mapping Region in Early American Writing* document the debates surrounding the role of regions in the establishment of North American communities during the late eighteenth and early nineteenth centuries:

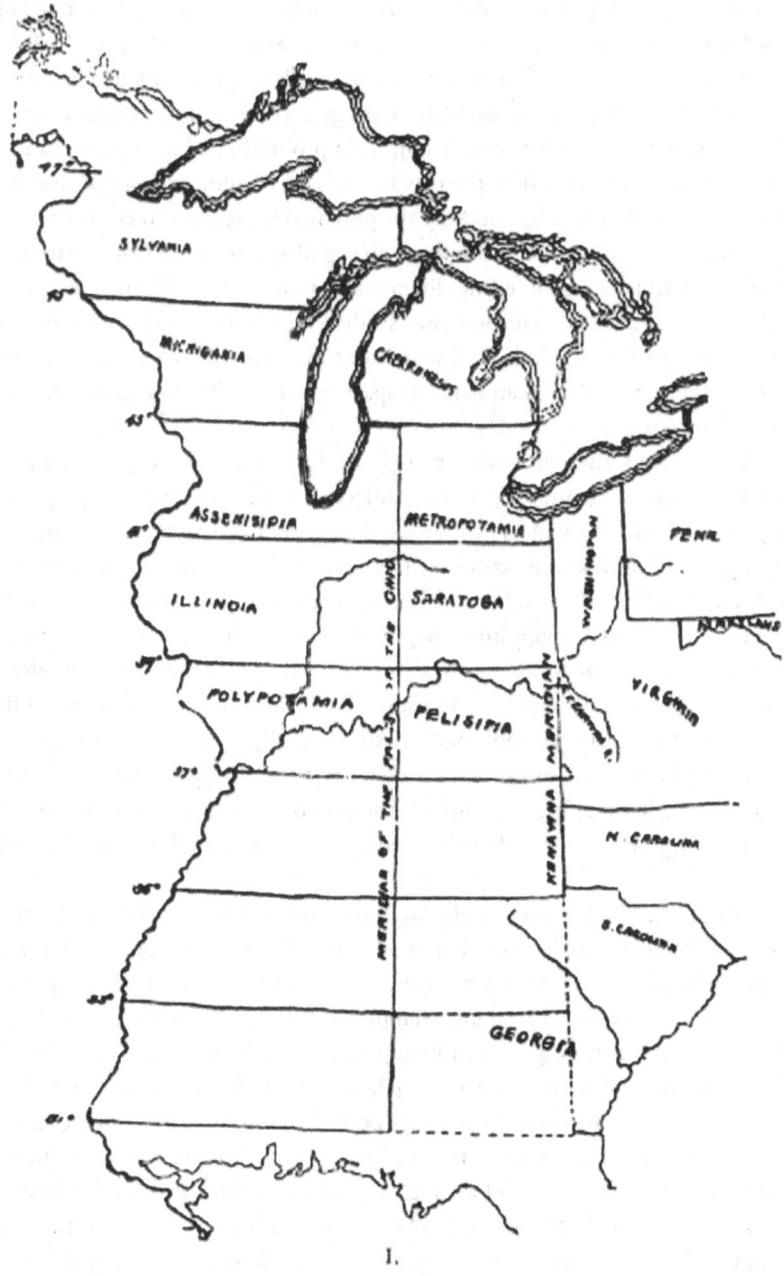

I.

PROPOSED DIVISION OF THE WEST IN THE
PLAN OF MARCH 1, 1784.

Figure 1. Map of the Land Ordinance of 1784. Jay Amos Barrett, *The Evolution of the Ordinance of 1787*. New York: Putnam's, 1891.

Americans—and not just white Americans—contemplated alternatives to the oft-charted sea-to-shining-sea narrative of inevitable continental white nationhood. Challenges to that monolith were articulated in place-specific counternarratives that stand apart from the increasingly homogenized and homogenizing aspects of the emergent consumer culture's simplistic promotion of a singular national identity. These essays track how the new nation's print culture struggled over how to represent its differences by checking the potential for regions to erode the unity of the nation: anxieties concerning these divergent spatial projections were transformed into narratives—sometimes literary, but more often polemic, journalistic, or otherwise narrativized—in processes studied by scholars such as Hsuan Hsu, John Seelye, and Susan Schulten. The tensions that arise in studies of the operating preconceptions of American national space transcend the usual geographic and political oppositions.

By transcending the narratives created and imposed by both geography and politics and by foregrounding more subjective means of imagining space—divergent, though not wholly opposed—Cosgrove's concepts of charting and mapping help illuminate the complexities at stake. While chart makers imagine a centralized nation wherein the local or the regional is subordinated to the national or the universal, mappings imagine just the reverse: a decentered nation that accommodates the local and the divergent. These differences are revealed in opposed temporal and spatial orientations. First, the temporal: while mappings are, on the whole, forward-looking, chartings usually look to the past, projecting American narratives as extensions of inherited models and myths. Second, the spatial: while mappings operate on the subcontinental and the subnational levels, chartings articulate macrocosmic national, continental, and global ambitions.

The mapping of new regions, although resembling a covert gesture of empire building disguised as liberatory, is not intrinsically expansionist or colonizing. Mapped places—as projections or alternatives—usually exclude the oppressive presences that alienated the writers. Mappings, as Cosgrove concedes, are largely fantasies, and the mappings traced here project American places less defined by such exclusions and more open to racial, gender, and socioeconomic fluidity. More important, chartings and mappings both demonstrate a preoccupation with the stresses between the national and the local in early American writing. In later periods this stress was expressed through the terms "region" and "regionalism" to evoke spaces not bound by political definition but rather by cultural commonalities and their relationship to the nation. As such, these terms—usually absent from conversations about antebellum writing—reflect the stresses between maps and charts. By addressing how these ideas reveal a previously underexamined aspect of early American textuality, this collection unites scholars who recognize that the temporal boundaries of region and regionalism must be continuously rethought.

REGIONS AND REGIONALISMS IN ANTEBELLUM AMERICA

From the start, imaginings of American regions at the microhistorical level were challenged by macrohistorical cartographies evoking biblical, racial, and imperial destinies on a world-historical scale. Susan Schulten begins her study of "History and Cartography in Nineteenth-Century America" with two observations. First, early republic historiography defined the nation as the only endpoint of colonial history: "writers of history began the study of American history as that which explained the emergence of the United States, particularly in political and territorial terms." Second, she traces the subsequent popularity of nation-based maps:

> In fact historical cartography presented a self-fulfilling prophecy: by explaining "the rise of the nation," maps and atlases ordered the past around this narrative. As a result, maps structured around American history as territorial growth. . . . For the United States, unlike France or Germany, the present could be framed as the fulfillment of the past struggles. The past was never the story of loss, only gain. Historical maps, timelines, graphs, and charts transformed the unpredictable and contingent into orderly stages of inevitable growth.[8]

Furthermore, also unlike France or Germany, millennial foundations undergirded this a priori and exceptionalist nationalism from 1630 forward. John Winthrop's "city on the hill" or "new Canaan" charts Massachusetts as a space that extends and completes Christian history.[9] As Protestant millennialism melded with Enlightenment universalism, this "always already" cartography accelerated, phrased here ironically by Hector St. John de Crèvecoeur: "Americans are the western pilgrims who are carrying along with them that great mass of arts, sciences, vigour, and industry which began long since in the east; they will complete the great circle."[10] The American farmer ventriloquizes the *translatio imperii* narrative to chart the territorial expansion of Anglo-America to the Pacific, making the establishment of a white transcontinental civilization the final chapter in Europe's history and thereby depriving it of any history of its own. Within this model, regional or local history must somehow serve the master narrative of westward expansion with any divergence erased or trivialized.

By addressing a sampling of the many texts that operate on a more microhistorical level, however, the essays here insist that regionalism was present and important in American writing from the eighteenth century forward, albeit in a form different than that constructed by William Dean Howells, Hamlin Garland, and others of the postwar generation.[11] By marking 1865 as the end of how earlier Americans imagined regions, we share Paul Giles's claim that, before the Civil War, "the country's sense of national identity was as uncertain, as provisional as its cartography," and that the war "consolidated the geography of the nation by ensuring it would henceforth be integrated into one political territory," no longer to be mapped as a series of distinct, divergent, or bordering establishments.[12] By focusing on this earlier period, like Brückner and Hsu, these essays confirm that early American writing describes "fictional worlds" that "transform the literary stage from the homogeneous space of an expansive democratic empire to a multitude of qualitatively different spaces that varied significantly from prominent discourses."[13] Brückner and Hsu's collection, however, addresses almost exclusively what we call chartings by tracking a shaping narrative of "the long historical trajectory that has taken the United States from colonialism to uneven development and global empire" between 1500 and 1900.[14] In contrast, *Mapping Region in Early American Writing*'s insistence that region might decenter nation in our conversations about American places challenges that trajectory by identifying divergent local counternarratives.

These essays rethink "region" by considering how Americans before the Civil War imagined arrangements of territory in ways that were detached from narratives undergirded by national membership or destiny. Departing from more conventional ways of thinking about regions, these essays do not treat regions simply as precursors to, components of, or alternatives to the nation, although the specter of national homogenization haunts even the mostly wildly divergent mappings. The "regions" they address might be those awaiting settlement on the empty spaces on the edges of maps, or, just as important, settled places in need of reimagining as the images of those places no longer aligned with their identities. These regions may also have been imagined in relation to nation—or just as often not—but their integration or absorption was by no means a *fait accompli* or an "always-already" inevitability.[15] This volume, then, doesn't simply find an earlier, prewar backstory in Caroline Kirkland or John Kennedy Pendleton for the familiar postwar regionalism; instead, it explores the role of alternative mappings of American places to develop ways of rethinking American culture, literally, from the ground up. Moreover, because labels such as northern, southern, western, or midwestern pertain to a national frame of reference, we largely dispense with them, especially in the essays describing mappings. Following these, in terms of cultural history, then, this volume breaks from the usual uses of "region" in four important ways.

First, region often figures as the epitome or symbol of nation in its manifestation of characteristically national qualities. In contrast, the essays here detach region from its destination as or component of the nation, finding a consistent and intriguing tendency for writers to imagine destinies other than national membership. This challenges the master narrative later articulated by Frederick Jackson Turner: "By this peaceful process of colonization a whole continent has been filled with free and orderly commonwealths so quietly, so naturally, that we can only appreciate the profound significance of the process by contrasting it with the violent spread of European nations through conquest and oppression."[16] For Turner, each region's distinctiveness is subordinated to its fulfilling a role in the nation in a "natural" and "peaceful" process.[17] Turner's racial myopia notwithstanding, this argument positions the regional beneath the national, and, in turn, the hemispheric and the cosmopolitan, as well. Attendance to any localized deviation has been dismissed as a serious or autonomous subject of sustained scholarly attention.[18] "Region"—or its other subnational cognates "area," "section," or "state" (in the administrative sense)—has become a cul-de-sac, a way of referring to places that become meaningful only in their affirmation (or momentary contradiction) of the larger multiregional, national, or global narratives at stake. The cosmopolitan ambit of most scholarship subsumes the potential offered by the local or the regional. By approaching region as a concept that can be both entangled with and independent from the nation, this collection brings these critical possibilities to the fore.

Turner's use of "colonization" in its benign administrative guise also bears notice as it charts a nation based on interregional equality and intranational coherence. But even in the 1890s, "colonization" was a weighted term. Throughout the late nineteenth-century Anglophone world, "region" was directly linked to "colony." For British colonial theorist Richard Jebb, Canada and New Zealand were British imperial "regions" that would transition to "colonial nations" while maintaining their economic and cultural subordination to the Commonwealth.[19] For Jebb, the assimilation of the colony or region into the nation or the empire describes a controlled process of replication, cultivation, and dominion that mirrors the child/parent relationship. Given the rejection of the nation's relegation to child status in the revolutionary rhetoric—Thomas Paine's "Common Sense," for example—Americans resist the notion that they "colonized" everything west of the Appalachians in the same sense that Europeans had "colonized" everywhere else. Nonetheless, the expansionist chartings of the 1780s—the Land Ordinances of 1784 and 1785 and the Northwest Ordinance of 1787—prescribed a process of colonization designed to suppress regional difference, whose effectiveness Turner would simply narrate.

In their sublimation of intercolonial regional differences, both Turnerian and counter-Turnerian historiographies posit the East, specifically New England, as the model of and for the nation, where the local is nationalized when it conforms to the nationalist chart.[20] This narrative cherry-picked local phenomena to reposition them as national. For example, Jonathan Arac's observation of how the "American Renaissance" lost its New England origins at the hands of F. O. Matthiesson, rewritten as "no longer local, regional, or sectional" but supposedly "shared among 'All the people,'" demonstrates the nationalization of the local.[21] Between 1840 and 1900, Arac argues, the Emerson-centered efflorescence was "regional." Academic scholarship to serve imperial America, however, demanded a larger stage, a macrohistory to compete with European macrohistories, and the renaissance's local flavor was dissolved into the national. The patterns continue, albeit in purportedly counterimperial methodologies: hemispheric, transatlantic, postcolonial, and "deep time" narratives value the local mostly only as it emblematizes the larger nonregional narratives constructed to counter national and imperial linkages.[22]

Second, as American literature gained institutional status, "regionalism" became sequestered in anthologies and literary histories to the late, long nineteenth century. Moreover, it has been applied mostly to middle-class white writers from peripheral American places who perpetuated the subordination of the local to the national. According to the received narrative, regionalism—sometimes mistakenly identified as local color—generally appears after the Civil War, coinciding with the "closing of the frontier" announced by the 1890 U.S. Census and its internment by Turner. No longer drawn west by open lands, white Americans looked more closely at the local places their ancestors had created from the spatial territory of the North American wilderness. These writers thought about how to connect these places—often left behind by the urbanizing and industrializing nation—to the accelerated culture of the cities. But there had to be limits. The Confederate privileging of the sectional over the national set a dangerous precedent. Too much localism led to regionalism, which led to sectionalism, and then on to secession. Whatever diversity or divergence they found was usually trivialized, integrated, or locked in a museum of the past. The goal became the containment of difference, especially as massive immigration was redefining the nation demographically, just as urbanization was transforming it geographically.

As writers sought to accommodate diversity without disunion, the postbellum decades saw the ascendance of the harmless nostalgia of local color writing. Local color preserved those few special places not yet absorbed into the incorporation of America by removing them from relevance.[23] Marjorie Pryse and Judith Fetterley describe "the commodification of regions in local color as a destructive form of cultural entertainment that reifies not only the subordinate status of regions but also the hierarchical structures of gender, race, class, and nation."[24] Ironically, then, regional literature developed only when actual regions as distinct cultural entities vanished. Regional literature was then granted a small presence in the national canon, but only as it recited its own elegy. As different regions or subregions came into contact with the vortex of industrialism and commercial consumer capitalism, they could either forfeit local distinctiveness to join the mass culture or cling to local identity, but only so long as it remained safely in the past. Regionalism was still confined to memory and recovery, a form of curatorship rather than creativity, limited by its backward-looking imprimatur and by its inability to comment on extraregional issues or to attract an audience beyond the boundaries of the region in question. By resituating regionalism in the years before the Civil War—when divergence was less restrained by the unilateral nationalism of the later nineteenth century—these essays address the materials that construct earlier regionalisms, which were more than mere reaction to the absorption of the local into the imperial or the industrial.

Third, then, is the reconsideration of early American literature to include regionalism and the reconsideration of regionalism to include the early American. For many of the same reasons regionalist texts were marginalized in American literary history, so, too, were many early American texts. Each testified to a diversity that challenged the singularity demanded by the cultural nationalism that instigated the institutionalization of an American canon a century ago. As such, pre-1860 texts resisting the cultural politics of millennial, nationalist, and other subnarratives of the nation's literature were doubly ignored and left to molder in the archive alongside texts by women and members of racially marginalized populations—all voices less likely to conform to the unilateral representations of gender, race, and, we argue, *place*, set forth as criteria for canonization.[25] In fact, during these decades "region" increasingly appeared throughout the nation's print culture, suggesting a growing awareness of a need for describing a sub- or nonnational space separate from the "state" as a political unit or "section" as a national subdivision.[26] Simultaneously, "region" itself can be hard to pin down. The term is general enough to encompass half the nation (the West) and a space smaller than a state (the Bay Area). Because it has no established governmental designation to restrict its usage or to link it inevitably to nation, it describes a variety of conditions, relationships, economies, and communities that apply to both interconnected and independent localities.

As such, "region" in early America mediates between micro- and macrohistorical narratives, territories whose only meaningful boundaries are those imagined and projected by those who set the region off from their own locale. John R. Eperjesi contends that "regions are myths, stories about space circulated by and through various institutions that help make sense out of a diffuse and chaotic world."[27] The essays here study stories about space in American culture before 1865, all of which reflect a preoccupation with the regional, a term usually held in reserve until the postbellum period. Perhaps spurred on by the Missouri Compromise's unofficial fissure of the nation in 1820, the terms "region" and "regional" saw expanded and more specific usage in the 1830s and 1840s. For example, Constantine Rafinesque begins his *New Flora and Botany of North America* (1836) by rejecting the earlier division on the continent into only two or three regions: "I have rectified these views since 1832 by increasing our regions to seven: to which I have given the names of the Boreal, Canadian, Alleghenian, Floridean, Louisianian, Texan, and Origonian."[28] As topographic and climatological knowledge expanded and diversified public understandings of regional spaces, the development of steam and rail transportation technologies, which bound the nation together more tightly, also catalyzed a stronger attendance to the now-threatened local.

Andrew R. L. Cayton and Susan E. Grey connect the emergence of regional thinking to the excessive nationalism after the War of 1812: "Alienation from the center engendered regionality. . . . The power of exclusions based on race and gender is well known; no less important was exclusion based on place. 'Mainstream' America may have been white and male, but it was also about where one lived."[29] Or, the writers examined here might add, mapping a place where one *wanted* to live, both as a goal for transforming existing regions or by mapping new communities in spaces where "Indian title" may or may not have been "extinguished" in the terms of the Northwest Ordinance. Not surprisingly, many of the texts addressed here originate from the pens of women and nonwhites. The work of diversifying early American writing must be ongoing, and the next important step in redefining early American studies has to do with place and region: the local.

Early American texts foregrounding specific locales—cities, states, watersheds, etc.—have not yet been sufficiently excavated. As the essays here show, this effort begins with both rereading well-known texts with an eye toward their local, as illustrated by Thomas, Schell, and Brown, *and* with recovering texts "lost" on account of their incompatibility with the master narratives of American literary history, as seen in the essays by Schoolman, Faherty, and Neary and Robbins. Despite their diversity of methods and subjects, these essays approach and express the same localist sensibility: when Americans wrote about regions before 1860, the narrative was progressive rather than regressive, projecting what they hoped to create in a region rather than (mis)remembering an idealized past. Furthermore, the mappings and the responding chartings that these essays excavate and address often diverge from the more orthodox cartographies of a monolithic "American" nation usually etched onto the empty spaces on the continent's maps. In other words, they fit neither the triumphalist nationalism of Turner nor the reactionary critical regionalism of Pryse and Fetterley, insisting instead that local distinctiveness be detached from both extremes to attend, directly, to the local *as* the local, not as components of nation-based narrative or counternarrative.

Whether a local text resists or accommodates or whether it occupies a space between the two or ignores them altogether, its preoccupation with an immediate locale identifies it as regional, prioritizing space-specific information, conditions, and subjectivities for their own sake. Necessarily, then, difficult and internalized contradictions have always already prevented regional texts from identification with one ideological position or another on the national scale required for sustained literary or historiographical scrutiny. Local distinctiveness demands place-specific, microhistorical textuality. Likewise, the more recent division in early American studies over the role of print culture in unifying the new nation—binding the nation more closely (for Michael Warner, et seq., following Benedict Anderson) or extending its complex differences (Trish Loughran, following Walter Benjamin) perpetuates the neglect of regional or local subjects *for their own sake*, outside of the nation-based parameters of conventional scholarship, as is discussed below.[30]

In contrast, the authors here employ—and often recover or excavate—texts that describe distinct places in early America as apart from, or even contemplating an escape from, the delocalizing coercions of the changing nation. From a place outside the coercions of a nationalism or cosmopolitanism, they reposition the regional as something other than parochial, self-referential, or provincial, articulating an important nexus between geography and subjectivity. Paul Giles describes regionalism as "the opening up of other kinds of cartographies so as to avoid both the more positivistic emphasis of traditional maps and the top-heavy superstructures of social science theory."[31] Philip Joseph links regionalism to rapid change, a constant in pre-industrial America: "Informed by such principles, regionalist literature can help us to realize more porous and historically adaptive communities. Such communities, in turn, ensure that the conversation on locality goes on in dynamic and unpredictable ways."[32] While Joseph studies texts after 1870, *Mapping Region in Early American Writing* identifies this "unpredictability" as informing American writing for at least a century beforehand. Even in the opening section's focus on literary cartographies, the texts at hand mean to discipline a regionalist sensibility that they mean to reintegrate into the national conversation, demonstrating the presence of a regionalist sensibility in early America.

Fourth, and finally, in this process of retrieving and localizing regionalist texts in the early American literary archive is the repositioning and inclusion of texts from the most disciplined and discouraged communities: racial minorities. A number of the essays here recover and, if necessary, re-place African American or Indian texts to establish their regional origins. Texts by minority authors have often suffered the ultimate delocalization by an externally coerced racialization: nonwhite intellectuals were compelled to work on the universalist stages of race and history to counter white racism and violence. Of New England African American antebellum writers, Patrick Rael observes: "black elites found themselves challenged to develop rhetorical strategies rooted in the American tradition. They sought not to revolutionize existing discourse but instead to appeal to its core values in changing the 'public mind' on racial matters."[33] Given the national or universalist—and therefore placeless—scale of those "core values," Frederick Douglass was (and is) first considered as an African American, and traditionally only incidentally as a New England writer, an oversight Hollis Robbins and Janet Neary overturn in their essay. Likewise, as Vine Deloria Jr. has claimed, "Straddling worlds is irrelevant to straddling small pieces of land and trying to earn a living."[34] Keri Holt's work on the Cherokee and Harry Brown's on William Apess recover that regional resistance to the assigned burden of speaking for an entire race, when, in fact, these writers were more concerned with representing the immediate needs of their tribes, themselves, and their specific locations. While these communities straddled the worlds of race and nation, they also addressed the boundaries and characteristics of the small pieces of land they claimed as their own regions.

On these grounds, this collection rediscovers local and regional voices in early American writing by unlinking them from the narratives that engendered their erasure, marginalization, and obscurity. Along the way, it also addresses misreadings of some better-known texts that drained the vitality of their place-based energies having been burdened by an unfair scope of national articulation and responsibility. However, the complex role of print culture in the creation, distribution, and reading of these texts—as alluded to above—raises larger questions about the fact of and desire for national cohesion and coherence, despite so many factors contributing to its diversity and divergence.

REDRAWING THE MAP:
REORIENTING U.S. REGIONAL STUDIES

In offering a revised premise and practice for regional literary studies, this collection challenges long-standing arguments about the relationship between print culture and nationalism, presenting new models for understanding how people imagined and represented the United States in the early nineteenth century. In doing so, *Mapping Region in Early American Writing* also asks us to reconsider the conventional categories used to define U.S. regions in relation to the North, East, South, and West, reimagining regional writing not just as a representation of a particular place but also as a mode of political, social, and aesthetic practice. The existence of clear regional identities and differences defined the British American colonies, each of which was founded by different groups for various religious, social, and economic reasons. When the colonists declared independence in 1776, this diversity immediately posed a problem for conventional ideas of national unity. Defined by variations in topography and climate, as well as differences in local laws, governing practices, industries, religious views, educational systems, currencies, and social customs, the citizens of this newly independent republic were more likely to identify themselves in relation to their home states than their new home country, and the dominance of these local ties raised concerns about the future stability of the nation. "In a period such as this . . . when thirteen colonies unacquainted in a great measure with each other are rushing together in one Mass," noted John Adams, "it would be a miracle if such heterogeneous ingredients did not at first produce violent fermentations."[35]

As the United States transitioned from an association of colonies to a united republic, its citizens became preoccupied with finding ways to unite these "heterogeneous ingredients" without producing divisive conflicts and competition. The federal structure of the nation—originally imagined under the Articles of Confederation and established in more formal terms under the Constitution—was specifically designed to foster a workable model of a plural and locally oriented union.[36] By representing a diverse range of local interests, conditions, and affiliations, the federal United States challenged traditional models of national unity, which were founded on a more homogeneous understanding of the body politic. Instead of defining the nation in terms of a common set of experiences, interests, and practices, the United States became defined as a diverse yet cohesive union of local and regional communities.[37] Within this model, regional and local distinctions were perceived not as obstacles to union but as a central means of expressing and producing nationalist sentiments. Under this federal model, citizens consistently represented the nation in local and regional terms over the course of the late eighteenth and early nineteenth centuries, contributing to the practice of a regionalist nationalism where local and national sentiments were seen as interdependent and mutually constitutive, rather than antithetical and antagonistic. In contrast, then, to post-1865 regionalism, which developed alongside an imperial nationalism made paranoid by the legacy of southern sectionalism, pre-1860 regionalism developed in the context of a more heterogeneous version of nationalism and more supple concepts of national membership.

Within literary studies, print has long been viewed as a crucial medium for binding this early heterogeneous nation together.[38] While the essays in this collection agree that print played a crucial role in promoting and imagining a unified sense of nationalism, however, they ultimately argue for a new understanding of the kind of union that printed texts helped citizens to imagine. For the past thirty years, scholars have argued that print culture helped imagine the nation by enabling citizens to transcend or overcome their sense of local and regional differences. According to this argument—exemplified by the work of Benedict Anderson and Michael Warner—the process of reading and circulating printed texts made it possible for citizens to experience a sense of shared time and shared sentiments, which allowed them to see themselves as part of an imagined national community, despite the many differences and distances that separated them.[39] This model of print nationalism has been enormously influential, particularly with regard to asserting the political importance of early American literary texts. The dominance of this print culture thesis, however, has been challenged in recent years, largely because of its inability to account for the important role local and regional communities and affiliations played in imagining the early United States. As Loughran writes, "we might more usefully think of print culture as a factory that produced the nation called regions and sections, rather than as the great unionizer and unifier is it so often remembered as."[40] Loughran's work, which delves into the material conditions of early American print culture, has drawn new attention to the strong local production, emphases, and audiences of early American writing, transforming the way that scholars understand public recognition and expression of early American nationalism itself. "Though we frequently forget it," writes Loughran, "1776 produced not a nation, but a confederation—a compact among former colonial units (each one dubbed a 'state'). The nation, such as it was, was simply less legible—more literally speaking, less *available*—as a mode of affective affiliation than were the state, the county, the village."[41]

Building on this argument, the essays in this collection pay serious attention to the role that the local communities of the state, region, and village played in early U.S. print culture, examining how these categories both informed and resisted the process of imagining a unified nation.[42] In doing so, *Mapping Region in Early American Writing* actively participates in reshaping critical understandings of print nationalism in the early United States, delving into the archive and reexamining canonical texts to illuminate the extent to which early American print made readers more aware of the distinct local interests and characteristics that comprised the nation, rather than providing them with a means of overlooking or transcending those differences. Contrary to the assumption that awareness of such differences made it harder to imagine a unified nation, these essays suggest that the regional dimensions of these literary texts helped citizens embrace the United States in and for its diverse terms, as a union of distinct local communities rather than a union of contrived sentiments and cultural similarity.

These essays offer multiple approaches for reassessing the relationships among early American regionalism, nationalism, and print culture in ways that foreground diversity. Faherty's analysis of the regional dimensions of "anonymous" authorship in the case of "A Lady of New York," for instance, draws new attention to the ways that print culture served regional and nationalist ends simultaneously by exploring this literary representation of urban New York. Holt and Neary and Robbins likewise focus on the diverse dimensions of regional writing from Cherokees in Appalachia and African Americans on the Pacific Coast to explore the close relationship between regional identities and the assertions of national belonging by examining how communities excluded from the nation drew on the logic and rhetoric of regionalist nationalism to assert their simultaneous desires for both independence and national membership in the 1830s and 1840s. Other essays focus not so much on the close relationship between regionalism and nationalism but on how U.S. writers actively emphasized regional definitions and distinctions as they exported national ideals through the practice of imperialist expansion, as evident in the work of Doolen and Schoolman.

In addition to rehistoricizing the relationships between region, locality, and nationalism, this collection also challenges the conventional categories used to define regions and regional studies. The localities of the United States have traditionally been grouped and interpreted in relation to the geographic locations of the North, South, East, and West.[43] Early national geography books identified these regional cartographies as the primary framework for understanding the distinctive geographic, social, and political characteristics within the United States. As Jedidiah Morse stated in *Geography Made Easy*, one of the most influential geography textbooks of the late eighteenth and early nineteenth centuries, "The American Republic . . . consists of three Grand Divisions, denominated the Northern, or more properly Eastern, Middle, and Southern States."[44] This list of "Grand Divisions" would be expanded in the nineteenth century to include the ever-growing territory of the "Western States," and other geography textbooks and atlases readily copied and codified these regional designations.

These chartings have been extremely powerful, helping define communal identities and consolidate political power among states that shared similar conditions and interests. At the same time, though, these categories are also problematic, defining regional spaces in terms that are, at times, too nebulous and imprecise to be useful. Where, for instance, might we define the regional space of the "West"? Beyond the Appalachians? the Mississippi River? the Rocky Mountains? In other cases, relying so heavily on temporally shifting geographic orientations of east/west or north/south may not always reflect the relationships and orientations experienced by regional communities, particularly for Native American and other marginalized groups. Referring back to the critical terms of this collection, the use of East, West, North, and South to define our definitions and understandings of regional communities creates a proscriptive chart for approaching U.S. regional studies, a chart that precludes and forecloses other ways of mapping the regions that emerge in early American writing.[45] Studies of regional literature, for example, have typically focused on a specific regional orientation, examining how literary texts can be positioned within a northern, eastern, western, or southern set of traditions and practices—political, cultural, or aesthetic.[46] While these place-centered approaches have offered productive critical frameworks, this collection offers an alternative model for organizing and reorienting early American regional studies.

These essays cover a broad range of regional communities. In presenting this material, however, we have not organized these essays according to geographic categories or conventional regional locations. Instead, to emphasize how regions and localities can be read and interpreted as a mode of political and aesthetic practice—rather than focusing on what these texts reveal or convey about a specific place—this collection foregrounds how literary and textual representations of place can be used as a strategy for conveying larger arguments about race, class, imperialism, nationalism, and cosmopolitanism, displacing the oppositional politics of some of the other recent scholarly "regionalisms."

The essays that examine the place that would become the "West," for instance, demonstrate our emphasis on orientation as well as geography—figurative as well as physical. The variety of western locations explored in this collection, which extend from Watts's analysis of the western Welsh Indian legends to Hollis and Neary's exploration of African American settlement during the California gold rush to Gunn's study of the southwestern humor tradition, expose the limits of using this geographic category to link these studies together. Although these essays do focus on the western areas of the geographic United States, they address extremely different communities, landscapes, and critical agendas that draw on the representation of regional and local spaces in radically different ways. Rather than grouping these essays in relation to place, this collection is arranged to emphasize how writers imagine regional and local spaces, as opposed to how they base them in someone's charts. These three sections—"Chartings," "Mappings," and "Countermappings"—provide new ways of mapping regional studies, such that the critical *use* of region in the rendering of appropriate place-specific utterances becomes a method for exploring the relation of place, nation, and text.

* * *

The essays here almost always intervene in the imposition of charts—representations of space that forecast and attempt to instill particular boundaries and uses for a given area, exemplified by Crèvecoeur's Farmer James's Enlightenment millennialism, Manifest Destiny, or the ever-receding "line" of the frontier between the civilized and the savage. Other charts are queried as well. Chronology itself charts the past. Certain temporal markers—1608, 1776, 1815, 1820, 1860—chart history from the singular perspective of a universal, nationalist narrative. As such, the collection is structured by three distinct yet thematically overlapping strategies that early American writers used to reimagine the territory around them.

The first section, "Chartings: Colonies and Countries," engages specifically with the process of charting U.S. expansion—from the westward, transcontinental growth of the nation to its more global, transnational, and transoceanic development. Edward Watts, William Lombardi, and Robert Gunn each examine how certain writers charted the lands located at the western and southern boundaries of the nation. In contrast to the standard ideological push to chart these regions as simply open for white settlement and ripe for the transplantation of Enlightenment ideals and a sense of fixed cultural homogeneity, these essays show how early American writers sought to challenge and disrupt these projections by insisting on the complexities and problematics of western expansion on account of preexisting regional ideas and institutions—the illusory nature of the earlier maps' use of *terra nullius* or *tabula rasa* labels. Watts, for example, examines how early republic visions of a seamless westward extension of the new nation were troubled by narratives invoking the legend of the Welsh Prince Madoc, whose white yet also indigenous—and, ultimately, fictional—descendants raised questions about the origins, cultural history, and legal entitlement of the lands located in the western borders of the United States.

Lombardi likewise investigates the chartings of the west imposed by Manifest Destiny, focusing specifically on early nature writing to explore how the scientific aspirations of early American nature writing interacted with human communities to define regions in paradigmatically different ways. Through his analysis of *The Journals of Lewis and Clark* (1803–6) and John Kirk Townsend's *Narrative of a*

Journey across the Rocky Mountains to the Columbia River (1839), Lombardi studies how "natural history," as represented within these works, queries both local distinctiveness and Enlightenment universality in ways that offer alternative ways of mapping any given frontier space. Shifting focus to the southwestern regions of the United States, Gunn turns to the literary genre of "old Southwest humor" to examine and, ultimately, challenge the way that these writings have been used to chart the southern United States as a space that is separate and distinct from the rest of the nation. In contrast, Gunn rereads these works as a means of mapping a "national regionality" where the relationship between local, national, and imperial identity can be more clearly recognized and analyzed in the fields of literary and historical study. In all, these essays debunk the idea of the West as a premapped *tabula rasa* awaiting Anglo-American settlement.

Moving outside the national boundaries of the United States, the final essay in this section builds on the imperial chartings explored by Watts, Lombardi, and Gunn in relation to westward expansion by examining American narratives of emigration and colonization involving Jamaica in the early 1850s. Schoolman's examination of postemancipation Jamaica and efforts of one writer to colonize the island culturally through an imposition of pre-industrial New England lifeways anticipates the global and imperial ambits of American noncontiguous expansionism—a form of empire building where colonies are assimilated by being reimagined as regions, as was already happening in many areas contiguous to the growing nation.

The next section, "Mappings: Creating Places," focuses on the complex processes of defining, imagining, and maintaining regional spaces, beginning in the colonial period and continuing through the projected U.S. expansion into Mexican territory in the mid-nineteenth century and the opening forays into conversations about the cosmopolitan transition wrought by the United States' increasingly global ambitions. These essays find very different regional backstories, both with regard to place and time. Steven Thomas begins with an analysis of the colonial "South," disrupting traditional understandings of this region as a single entity, or even its inclusion in the "global south" by identifying specific subregional variations based on the cash crops grown in each place. In doing so, Thomas shows how the activities within these colonies helped produce a much more complex and diversified map of the American "South," one that embraced the representation and recognition of regional differences. By recovering both the existence and the possibilities set forth by this colonial mapping of the South, Thomas's essay lays a strong foundation for examining how regional spaces and regional diversity were mapped in the early United States, at times complementing and at other times challenging the emergence of a national cartography.

Essays by Andy Doolen and Duncan Faherty intervene in this process of mapping the new nation, focusing specifically on the way writers sought to develop new models and methods for defining and situating already-populated spaces. Faherty examines how regionally specific forms of discourse were used to imagine and map a new national identity by turning his attention to the local dimensions of early American literary texts. Through his analysis of two novels published in New York in 1798 and 1801, Faherty illuminates how the literary genre of the novel, combined with the anonymous yet also regionally specific representation of authorship, allowed citizens to map a postrevolutionary nation that was nevertheless still tied to prerevolutionary class structures and ideological concerns. While the local focus of early American novels did provide citizens with a means to map the new nation in distinctive and original terms, Faherty's essay shows how these new maps remained irrevocably tied to prenational structures of place, class, and culture. Meanwhile, Doolen's essay explores a more radical attempt to create a new map. In his reading of Zebulon Pike's journals of an expedition to a region that was four decades from national incorporation (and whose inclusion is still problematic), Doolen explores how different nonindigenous societies were remapped to redefine the nature and scope of American expansionism. In his efforts to replace these inherited maps with an "American" chart, Pike also had to contend with the intransigence of the Spanish colonial presence, which had their own designs on mapping the borderlands, presciently looking ahead to when colonization would mean more than the erasure of savages, and when regional identity would incorporate local cultures and languages, not just annihilate them.

In the final essay in this section, Jennifer Schell explores how writers remapped New England as a space of cosmopolitan diversity. By re-regionalizing Herman Melville and Frederick Douglass, Schell examines work from a more canonical literary locale, that of antebellum New England. By studying New Bedford, Massachusetts, as the most cosmopolitan of all American places in the antebellum decades, she remaps an established hierarchy that equated urbanity with global consciousness. In doing so, her essay provides a compelling rereading of the way that works by Douglass and Melville use regionalist reading strategies to undermine and redefine the coherence of the new nation by identifying gaps between the perception and reality of experiences in specific locales.

The third section, "Countermappings: New Spaces in Old Places," takes notice that for three hundred years, charts of North America were made exclusively by white people and so reflected their values of the exploring, conquering, colonizing, and settling narratives they imposed on the land and its peoples. By focusing on Native American and African American writers, these essays define regional spaces in ways that resist the dominant boundaries that had perpetuated the oppression, displacement, removal, and erasure of these historically marginalized groups. The essays by Harry Brown, Keri Holt, and Janet Neary and Hollis Robbins each explore countermappings whereby nonwhite communities reimagine and take control of spaces designated as "empty" by white authorities. For Brown, William Apess's imagining of the creation of a place in the wilderness for Christian Indians runs counter to both integrationist and removalist mappings of race in the 1830s. His reimagining of a frontier space available to Indian refugees and their fellow-traveling white Methodists maps a hope for expansion based on not just material growth but also moral improvement.

Holt explores a different strategy of countermapping in her analysis of the Cherokee's resistant redefinition of tribal land during the late 1820s and 1830s when the Cherokee nation engaged in aggressive and, at times, conflicted efforts to assert their sovereignty and independence. By invoking the same language and arguments used to justify the transformation of British colonial space into an independent nation, these Cherokee arguments represent a unique method of resistance where the language of early U.S. nationalism counteracts the same nation's evocation by the Cherokee as a model for their own independence. Likewise, Neary and Robbins study African American writing of the Gold Rush to find nonwhite writers hoping to find the language to map a new American region more open to multiracial cohabitation. In the texts they address, black writers hope California can be a region unlike any other, a place where African Americans can be free and equal citizens.

Finally, John Funchion's postscript, "New Orleans and the Regionalizing of the Globe after the Civil War," considers how the issues taken up by this collection compel us to rethink the way we understand regionalism and local color writing after 1865. Instead of reading this body of writing in relation to American literary realism, Funchion argues that we might instead examine how postwar writers extended or responded to the ways antebellum writers mapped localities. Rather than casting regional writing produced after the Civil War as either serving or undermining the aims of Howells's realist project, Funchion explores how postbellum writers instead continued to imagine spaces in their own terms to imagine new social and political possibilities. Specifically, the postscript revisits one of the classic texts of postwar local color writing, George Washington Cable's *The Grandissimes*, to show how microlocalities such as New Orleans remained contested cultural spaces both before and after the Civil War. Cable's novel and other postwar representations of New Orleans establish how this collection radically alters the genealogy of place-based literature and textuality in America.

Taken as a whole, the essays in this collection continually push us to examine region and regionalism, not just as representations of place but also as critical strategies or practices, ones that enabled writers to criticize, undermine, revise, and resist modes and methods for representing forms of local, national, and imperial identity. They allow revisionist readings that localize and integrate these divergent forces to reimagine the tension between the distant and the immediate as less intimidating. Either way, the persistence and insistence of place—either as a *locus* of difference or a *nexus* of absorption—cannot be denied as a shaping site for reorganizing our understanding of the constantly evolving relation of specific yet dynamic local communities to the ever-changing nation. By foregrounding the extent to which early American writing was involved in charting and mapping its many regional spaces, this collection opens the door for more aggressive and challenging studies of region and regionalisms in American literature and culture as a whole.

NOTES

1. Jefferson, "Letter to John C. Breckinridge, Aug. 12, 1803," in *Portable Thomas Jefferson*, 55.
2. See esp. Onuf, *Jefferson's Empire*; Browne, *Jefferson's Call for Nationhood*.
3. See esp. Seelye, *Beautiful Machine*; Irwin, *Continental Congress*; Ed White, *Backcountry and the City*. In pre-industrial America, "drainage was destiny," as the saying went.
4. Histories of the term "nation" consulted here include Anthony D. Smith in both *National Identity* and *Nationalism and Modernism*; Hobsbawm and Ranger, *Invention of Tradition*; and many of the essays in Bhabha's *Nation and Narration*.
5. Cosgrove, *Mappings*, 14.
6. See as well Joel Kovarsky's *True Geography of Our Country*, 65–85.
7. These narratives of scale, anticipating the continental and finally global ambit of American expansion, are traced out by John Carlos Rowe's *Literary Culture and U.S. Imperialism*; Wilentz, *Rise of American Democracy*; and Howe, *What God Hath Wrought*, expanding a tradition begun with George Bancroft, *History of the United States*, and Parkman, *France and England*.
8. Schulten, *Mapping the Nation*, 11.
9. There is a long history of milliennialist and destinarian rhetorics in early America. See esp. Bloch, *Visionary Republic*; Jehlen, "Literature of Colonization," 109–25; Elliott, "New England Puritan Literature," 255–378. Nordholt offers a unique version from a European perspective in *Myth of the West*, 54–69. See Woodworth on the cultural contexts of Manifest Destiny. *Manifest Destinies*, 40–47.
10. Crèvecoeur, *Letters*, 55.
11. Bell, *Development of American Realism*, and Cady, *Light of Common Day*, offer the standard historiographies, as does almost every late twentieth-century anthology of American literature. More recent students of postbellum regionalism define their own work as responding to that narrative. See Fetterley and Pryse, *Writing Out of Place*; Foote, *Regional Fictions*; Joseph, *American Literary Regionalism*; Lutz, *Cosmopolitan Vistas*; McCullough, *Regions of Identity*.
12. Giles, *Global Remapping*, 5, 9.
13. Brückner and Hsu, introduction to *American Literary Geographies*, 13.
14. Ibid., 22.
15. See Greeson, *Our South*; Grant, *North over South*; and Watts, *American Colony*, for discussions of how both the "South" and the Old Northwest contemplated regional destinies separate from national membership. Texas's independence prior to joining the nation enacts a similar non-U.S. regional identity.

16. Turner, *Frontier in American History*, 169–70.

17. Critics of Turner emerged almost immediately, as did generations of followers. See Steiner, "From Frontier to Region," for a succinct overview of the debates.

18. See Dorman, *Revolt of the Provinces*, including his section on the agrarians, 105–43.

19. See esp. Jebb, *Studies in Colonial Nationalism*, 61–86. See also Belich, *Replenishing the Earth*, 177–98; Eddy and Schreuder, introduction to *Rise of Colonial Nationalism*.

20. The story of the academy's appropriation and transformation of American literature between 1880 and 1920 has been told many times. See in particular Gross and Kelley, *History of the Book in America*, 2:1–52, and Philip Fisher, *Still the New World*, 3–14.

21. Arac, "F. O. Matthiessen," 94, which summarizes the politics of canonization, 93–101. See also Jay, *American Literature*; Pease, *Revisionist Interventions*.

22. See Arac, "F. O. Matthiessen"; Foote, *Regional Fictions*; Joseph, *American Literary Regionalism*; Lutz, *Cosmopolitan Vistas*. From a historical perspective, see Cayton and Gray, *American Midwest*, and Shortridge, *Middle West*. Goldman, in *Continental Divides*, sums up the phenomenon, 21–38.

23. As early as 1894, Hamlin Garland was aware of this process as he wrote *Crumbling Idols*. More recently, Fetterley and Pryse have pursued this line of argument in *Writing Out of Place*.

24. Fetterley and Pryse, *Writing Out of Place*, 6.

25. See in particular the essays by Grey Gundaker and Barry O'Connell in Gross and Kelley, *History of the Book in America*.

26. Grey's *Yankee West* adumbrates this narrative as it was worked out in the specific locality of three townships in antebellum Kalamazoo County, Michigan.

27. Eperjesi, *Imperialist Imaginary*, 4.

28. Rafinesque, *New Flora and Botany*, 24.

29. Cayton and Gray, *American Midwest*, 9.

30. By employing Benjaminian subjectivities, Loughran's *Republic in Print* sees early nineteenth-century print culture as exposing interregional differences, thus diminishing the role of print culture in the spread of a singularized national identity. This breaks from Warner's assertion in *Letters of the Republic*, following Benedict Anderson's claim in *Imagined Communities* that early republic print culture, in its central role in imagining the national community, forged postrevolutionary nationalism.

31. Giles, *Global Remapping*, 223.

32. Joseph, *American Literary Regionalism*, 22.

33. Rael, *Black Identity and Black Protest*, 5.

34. Deloria, *Custer Died for Your Sins*, 86.

35. Adams, "Letter to Samuel Osgood, 14 November 1775," in *Letters of Delegates*, 342.

36. See Hallock, *From the Fallen Tree*; Drake, *Nation's Nature*; Lawson-Peebles, *Landscape and Written Expression*; and Linklater, *Measuring America*, for discussions of Federalism's unwillingness to pursue a monolithic national culture.

37. See Slaughter, "Dividing Line," 61–88.

38. See Gross, "Reading for an Extensive Republic," and McGill, *American Literature*.

39. See Anderson, *Imagined Communities*, 36–46.

40. Loughran, *Republic in Print*, xx.

41. Ibid., 12.

42. See Gruenwald, *River of Enterprise*; Irwin, *Robes of Sovereignty*; Loughran, *Republic in Print*; Nellis, *Empire of Regions*; Richard White, The *Middle Ground*.

43. See Ayers et al., *All over the Map,* wherein even revisionist historians such as Limerick maintain these boundaries. Larson's "Pigs in Space" historicizes these boundaries.

44. Morse, *Geography Made Easy*, 106.

45. While regionalist scholars such as Foote and Holman maintain these distinctions, the crossover of these oversimplifications to mass-market media has been seamless. Institutions such as national sports competitions and election rhetoric are deeply informed by these four cardinal directions, charting a system of regions largely detached from experience on the ground.

46. The prevalence of scholarly and professional organizations such as the Western Literature Association, the Society for the Study of Midwestern Literature, and the Society for the Study of Southern Literature highlight the place-centered emphasis of regional studies, and regional scholarship tends to be supported and published in place-focused journals such as the *New England Quarterly*, *Western American Literature,* and *Southern Literary Journal* or regionally oriented book series such as *New Directions in Southern Studies* (University of North Carolina Press), *Place Matters: New Directions in Appalachian Studies* (University of Kentucky Press), and *The Modern American West* (University of Arizona Press).

SECTION I

Chartings
Colonies and Countries

CHAPTER ONE

"To plant himself in with soveranity"
Welsh Indians and the Early West, 1576–1812

Edward Watts

IN BOTH THE 1590s and the 1790s, powerful, English-speaking white men were looking west. In the 1590s, the Spanish Armada defeated, Elizabethan courtiers plotted their late entry into the land grab for American territories already undertaken by Spain, Portugal, and France. In the 1790s, the British—in theory—defeated and their constrictive Proclamation Line of 1763 erased, early republic Americans gazed westward. Prospective colonies and empires there were imagined to fill in the blank spaces on the left sides of their maps with new towns, plantations, mines, and cities replicating their own communities, all sources of wealth to be shipped eastward. However, in both decades doubts about the legal and moral legitimacy of the seizure of the western lands catalyzed a process of self-examination: by what right could Christians and republicans (to varying degrees) claim lands already occupied by indigenous inhabitants? For the Elizabethans, conquest for wealth alone called to mind the "Black Legend" of the Spanish pillaging of South and Central America; for the Americans, a more vexing paradox awaited: how could a nation born of rejecting colonial subordination plan and plant its own colonies? How could it claim legitimate dominion in subordinated territories so soon after they had accused the British of abdicating theirs?

For both, the same old legend—retold and updated in the 1790s—was unearthed to legitimize the westward-lying colonial and imperial ambitions: the legend of Prince Madoc and the Welsh Indians. This legend, as described below, established a white presence in the American West that established a narrative of primordial whiteness in the continent—predating the written record—that both denied the isolation and thus the otherness of indigenous populations and constructed a deeper, romantically tinged history for white people in North America, further grounding their occupation in the authenticating mists of legend. This rehearses Philip Deloria's concept of "playing Indian": "Americans wanted to feel a natural affinity with the continent,

25

and it was Indians who could teach them such aboriginal closeness. Yet in order to control the landscape they had to destroy the original inhabitants."[1] By diminishing the "firstness" of the inhabitants and vesting themselves with "aboriginal closeness," fantasies such as the Madoc legend became central to the propaganda and rhetoric of national expansion in both the 1590s and the 1790s. In its latter iteration, however, the legend contributed more directly to the colonization and conceptualization of the regional "West"—not as a specific space on a map, but as a site for constructing a mythic past—and thus as a location for defining both ambitions and anxieties of the nation throughout the first decades of its history.

Of course the Madoc legend was not the only fantasy of European inhabitation used to romanticize and whiten pre-Columbian American history. Time and again, legends and flimsy archaeological evidence would be trotted forth to shift that continental affinity from the Indians to the Anglo-Americans. As the nation spread west after the War of 1812, an appropriate primordial ancestor would be found in the Mound Builders. As described by Caleb Atwater in 1818, actual Indians are parvenus, destroyers of an ancient white "civilization" based on advanced technology, organized communities, and agricultural planning. White Americans then claimed the Mound Builders as moral and intellectual ancestors. While there were few claims that the Mound Builders were biologically "white," the consensus was that they were not "Indian." The narrative soon shifted to their destruction: how they had been defeated and supplanted by "our" Indians, as William Cullen Bryant's "The Prairie" imagined in 1832, a narrative of a civilization crushed by barbarism whose revival and continuation would be taken up by avenging whites who would justifiably remove the late-coming Indians. Later, a vogue for all things Viking—bolstered by the "discovery" of eleventh-century Norse settlements in New England in the 1830s—more directly established whites in North American prehistory.[2] Moreover, the Vikings were refashioned to reflect "American" values. Annette Kolodny's *In Search of First Contact* documents how Henry Wadsworth Longfellow's "A Skeleton in Armor" (1841) imagines a berserker Viking turned docile New England farmer. His subsequent domestication in Victorian America enacts the method of primordial nationalism: their paganism, savagery, and nomadism forgotten, Vikings become models for the white nation.

But before those seized the public imagination, there were the Welsh Indians, a prefabricated prehistory suited to the absorption of the West into the nation. Here is the core of the story: in 1170 a Prince Madoc supposedly fled internecine warfare and sailed west, never to be seen again. Four centuries later, a new version emerged that told of Madoc's landing in Mobile Bay and his broad travels across the Mississippi valley, before leading a meandering series of settlements from North Carolina to Tennessee and finally up the Missouri River to become the Mandans. By way of corroboration, the expansionists of the 1790s cited French explorers Du Pratz, La Hanton, Bossu, and Charlevoix, who all reported light-skinned people along the Mississippi in the seventeenth century. In 1740 London's *Gentleman's Magazine* published a series of reports that the Tuscarora Indians were speaking Welsh; in 1768 Charles Beaty reported accounts of a Welsh village near New Orleans, reflecting similar accounts in 1752 and 1791, when the Conestoga Indians of western Pennsylvania were also said to be Welsh. Like Jonathan Carver, George Croghan offered a similar narrative in 1753 and even claimed, secondhand, that Welsh Indians still had Bibles in their possession.[3] This culminated in British poet Robert Southey's 1805 epic *Madoc,* in which Madoc defeats the Mayans in Florida and then the Welsh *become* the Aztecs.[4]

However, the legend of Prince Madoc and the Welsh Indians saw a momentous heyday between 1780 and 1815, when stories and speculations about Welsh "Indians" proliferated on both sides of the Atlantic to justify land grabs—the British even used it against Russia to claim the Nootka Sound. Its American usages, however, were far more extensive and complex. Soon after the revolution, as a component of the new nation's obsession with expansion, the number of reports multiplied, and a consensus coalesced that the Welsh had moved up the Missouri as the Padoucas, or the white Padoucas, also known as the Mandans, conveniently beyond the reach of confirmable reporting. Gwyn Williams reports that "by the 1780s a tidal wave of Welsh Indian stories was breaking on English-speaking America. Literally scores of people reported direct conversations in Welsh with Indians, several Indian chiefs swore that their ancestors had been Welsh. . . . At least thirteen real tribes were identified as Welsh, eight others invented to fit. . . . In the last years of the century, something of a Madoc fever broke in the USA and belief in Welsh Indians became universal."[5] And it lingered: in the nineteenth century William Richards, C. S. Rafinesque, George Catlin, and many others reported meetings with Welsh-speaking Indians. These versions held that the Welsh were still living up the Missouri, speaking Welsh, fishing in Welsh corracles (leather-hulled boats), and building Welsh villages.[6] "Proof" was delivered in Welsh-style fortifications along the Tennessee River, purportedly Welsh remnants in the language of the "lighter skinned" Tuscaroras of North Carolina, copper and iron arrowheads indicative of metallurgic skills unknown to "red" Indians, and fragments of books and Bibles.

This wave of publications coincided with—or perhaps created—a national debate about the relation of the coastal nation and its western hinterlands. The American frontier borderlands during these decades were highly unstable: devastating wars with Indians, disputes concerning British and American land claims in the Treaty of Paris (1783) and the Jay Treaty (1794), and conflicts over the loyalty and suitability of white frontiersmen—the failure of the militias in the Indian Wars and the Whiskey Rebellion (1793–94) were signs of trouble. Claiming, colonizing, and settling the left side of the map would be more complicated than had been imagined. The controversy over the Welsh came to serve as crucible for addressing the nation's anxieties concerning these lands. In the end, however, the Madoc legend *charted* the Mississippi and Ohio watersheds in the interest of

American expansionism not only to erase Indian presence from American history but also to discipline the region by portraying resistance to eastern nation-building as indicating a potential loss of whiteness among the settlers, as the Welsh came to be depicted as having regressed to savagery. The region's future, then, was charted to preclude both Indian persistence and regional deviation among white settlers.

THE DOCTRINE OF DISCOVERY AND THE CANT OF COLONIZATION

Proof of Welsh presence in the territorial United States, it was thought in both the 1590s and the 1790s, would allow the application of the long-standing Doctrine of Discovery to erase Indian land rights. Shawnee legal scholar Robert J. Miller has traced the concept back to the Crusades and its use to "claim" lands held by non-Christians. Conquest alone was considered barbaric, so a legal rubric was needed to legitimize their seizure and occupation of the Holy Land. When the New World became an issue, an element of habitation was added: "England and France thus added to the Doctrine the element of actual occupation and possession as a requirement to establish European claims to title by Discovery" to claim North America, even though the Spanish and Portuguese had hit the beaches first.[7]

In 1576 Elizabethan courtier Sir John Dee first deployed Madoc to establish British legal title to North America. In a privately circulated memo, noting that England had absorbed Wales in 1289 and thus all its rights and properties, Dee wrote: "The Lord Madoc, sonne of Owen Gwyndd prince of North Wales, leaving his brothers in contention, and warre for their inheritance south, by sea (westerly from Irland), for some foein, and—Region to plant himself in with soveranity: with Region he had found, he returned to Wales againe and hym selfe with Shipps, vituals, and men and women sufficient for the coliniy, with speedily he leed into the peninsula; then named Farquara; but of late Florida . . . nowe named America."[8] Dee's memo found its way to George Peckham, Thomas Powell, and Richard Hakluyt, whose texts influenced Samuel Purchas and Thomas Heriot. Peckham made the crucial link to the Doctrine of Discovery: Madoc's settlement "doth shew the lawful tytle, which the Queen's most excellent Majestie hath unto those countries" and that the English were entitled to "restore her [America] to her Highness's right and interest." Dee's claim that Madoc meant "to plant himself in with soveranity" distinguished him from nomadic Indians, traders, or explorers. Hakluyt's expanded discussion of the Welsh from a brief note in his 1582 *Divers Voyages* to a full chapter in his 1589 *Principle Navigations*—published after the defeat of the Spanish Armada—reveals the legend's use as propaganda rather than as reliable history.[9]

Miller also identifies missionary work as validating the doctrine, and the pilgrims deployed it in 1626 as such. After trivializing the doctrine alone as flimsy—"Letting pass the ancient Discoveries"—Robert Cushman wrote in *Mourt's Relation*:

> And first, seeing we daily pray for the conversion of the heathens. . . . This then is a sufficient reason to prove our going thither and live lawful: their land is spacious and void and there are but few and do but run over the grass, as do also the foxes and wild beasts. They are not industrious, neither have art, science, skill or faculty to use either the land or the commodities of it; . . . As the ancient patriarchs, therefore removed from straiter places into more roomy, where the land lay idle and waste, and none used it though there dwelt inhabitants by them (as Gen. 13:6, 11, 12 and 34:21 and 41:20) so it is lawful now to take a land which none useth, and make use of it.[10]

Cushman here articulates the doctrine's most important codicil: the discoverers' claim to forward the values of the home culture. When proselytization ends, commodification begins. Under this reading of the doctrine, only virtuous Christianity and commercial agriculture could legitimize the seizure of Indian lands. In addition, the need to defend the pilgrim migration and settlement bespeaks an implicit counterargument that had been both heard and anticipated as delegitimizing colonization.

Similarly, the same debates about the West characterized early republican culture in the United States. Accordingly, the legend's contestation reveals the same anxieties as the Elizabethans' but now played out in a more public forum. More important, debates over the legend were more than just historiographic. Contestations over Madoc revealed deeper fissures concerning how the new nation would position itself as the Enlightenment faded and a less restrained era began. Ultimately, the split reveals two opposed nationalisms split mostly along party lines. While Federalists believed in a civic nation and dismissed Madoc, Jeffersonians projected a romantic nation that embraced him. Lloyd Kramer distinguishes the forms of nationalism: "The first form of nationalism, which is often called liberal [civic] nationalism, typically includes individual rights in its definition of the nation's fundamental ideals. The second form of nationalism, often called integral [romantic] nationalism, typically subsumes the individual into a national community and identifies the nation in terms of race, ethnicity or culture rather than politics or individual rights."[11] The Doctrine of Discovery is irrelevant in a civic nation with its focus on individualism and immediacy, yet it is foundational in a romantic nation and its focus on larger collectivities and historic continuity. One must only keep in mind that the Federalist Party ended in 1816 to conceive which philosophy predominated. Still, the Federalist skepticism toward the Madoc legend represents a crucial and lost episode in the history of alternative and competing American nationalisms.

DOUBTING DEE: FEDERALISM AND CIVIC NATIONALISM

After the revolution, masses of western squatters could no longer be ignored or evicted, necessitating their incorporation into a coherent national narrative.

Worse yet, more settlers were streaming across the mountains without bringing the republic's preexisting social, cultural, economic, and religious institutions with them, nor did any such structures await their arrival. Federalists feared the diverse and little-known populations of the region and responded by minimizing the damages to the nation their inevitable assimilation would incur. White "frontiersmen"—living in the woods, eating wild game, and interacting with the "savages"—had become "new-made Indians," in the terms of Hector St. John de Crèvecoeur.[12] Gouverneur Morris worried that the borderlands "would not be able to furnish men equally enlightened to share in the administration of our common interests." Squatters had already resisted eastern versions of law and order in the Paxton, Shays, and Whiskey uprisings. Yet George Mason stated the need for balancing these interests: if the states to be formed from these territories and peoples were not equally represented they "will either not unite or will speedily revolt from the Union."[13]

The result was the Northwest Ordinance of 1787, a model for integrating the area north of the Ohio and east of the Mississippi into the nation. The ordinance defines the office of the governor, who is appointed by Congress and empowered to form a general assembly when five thousand white males petition for one. However, local assemblymen must own their land "fee simple": given that most early settlers were squatters, this assured power to late-coming eastern immigrants. At the same time, the ordinance proceeds under a narrative of an honorably managed transition, with no mention of the Doctrine of Discovery: "The utmost good faith shall always be observed towards the Indians, their lands, and property shall never be taken from them without their consent."[14] In brief, the ordinance codifies a process whereby the region would re-create not only eastern models of law and governance but also the economic and social hierarchy that sustained it, based on the "consent" of both the white land-owners and the indigenous population now willingly removed. Its emphasis on rights, order, and sustainability extended the notion that such principles were "self-evident" in decades after the revolution, and not in need of support by fables of medieval Welsh princes.

Here's where the legend of the Welsh became a stand-in for debates about the expansion of the new nation more generally. The Federalists simply did not need the Welsh or the primordial legacy of white occupation and sovereignty they supplied. However, because expansionists kept dredging up Madoc and his descendants, the Federalists had to rebut repeatedly what they viewed as a dangerous narrative that contaminated the rule of law with fabulation and race-based mythologies. Most prominent among the doubters was Jeremy Belknap in *American Biography* (1794). Here, Belknap not only refuted the legend as unfounded and chimeric but also identified it as corrupt for its link to pro-expansionist propaganda going back to Dee. Citing Dee's memo, Belknap accuses Hakluyt of being a pawn. Belknap's rejection of Hakluyt, then, might also be read as a critique of the Jeffersonian expansionists: "National prejudice might prevail, even with so honest a writer, to convert a Welsh fable into a political argument to support, against a powerful rival, the claim of his sovereign to the dominion of the continent."[15] For Belknap, the promulgation of the legend was a front for land speculation, not a basis for historical knowledge or national identity. Had he lived so long, Belknap, like most New England Federalists, would have challenged the Louisiana Purchase and other indications of unchecked ambitions in the West, as he had in his political satire *The Foresters* (1787).[16] At the same time, Belknap's encyclopedic *American Biography* (1794–98) lists no Indians among subtitle's claim to be "Historical Account of those People who have been Distinguished in America," implying that only whites qualified as "people" capable of distinguishing themselves. The use of Madoc to justify expansion was, to Belknap, emblematic of a larger ambition to stretch the nation beyond the ability of any republic to administer without degenerating into demagoguery, dictatorship, or democracy. For him, Welsh Indians represented a primordial history fabricated to bolster corrupt ends: romanticism imagined a nation defined by race and identity rather than reason or law. A secondhand legend about a medieval prince based in obscure sources and substantiated by flimsy material proof compelled other Federalist writers to echo the same sentiment, reflecting their Enlightenment values. Benjamin Franklin's "Edict by the King of Prussia" (1773) mocks British claims to the rights of discovery of America as assuring ownership in perpetuity by having a German ruler invoke sovereignty in Great Britain eight hundred years after its Saxon "Discovery."[17] In 1805 Charles Brockden Brown reprinted a scathing review of Southey's *Madoc* that assaults not only the poem itself but also its theft of Spanish conquest history to invent an epic scale missing from the real legend.[18]

Washington Irving's *A History of New York* (1809) annihilates "the question which has thus suddenly arisen, is, what right had the first discoverers of America to land, and take possession of a country, without asking the consent of its inhabitants, or yielding them an adequate compensation for their territory?" First, Irving reduces the doctrine to its true essence: "the Right of Extermination, or, in other words, the Right by Gunpowder." Then, he then imagines "Moon-Men" landing in New York and restating some very familiar assumptions. A "profound philosopher of the Moon's culture" expostulates: "That—whereas a certain crew of Lunatics have lately taken possession of that dirty little planet, called the earth—and that it is inhabited by none but a race of two legged animals, . . . of a horrible whiteness instead of pea green—therefore and for a variety of other excellent reasons—they are considered incapable of possessing any property in the planet they infest, and the right and title to it are confirmed to its original discoverers."[19] Irving's legal training shows here. His parody of the language underpinning the doctrine strikes at its core: extermination and gunpowder lurk behind its façade. To the Federalists, it mattered little if there were Welsh Indians, or whether an archaic legal fiction such as the Doctrine of Discovery legalized expansion: primordial events are irrelevant to a nation based on the firmer ground and forward-looking aspect of a civic nation.

Finally, Henry Marie Brackenridge's rejection of Madoc reflects his actual practice of civic nationalism. The son of novelist Hugh Henry Brackenridge, Henry was raised in Missouri and western Pennsylvania, fluent in Spanish and French. In *Views of Louisiana* (1814), he affirms: "That no Welsh nation exists at present on this continent is beyond a doubt. . . . We are often tempted by a fondness for the marvelous to seek out remote or improbable causes for that which may be explained by the most obvious."[20] Three years later, Henry was in the Maryland legislature when the Jew Bill banned Jews from public office, legislation typical of racial nationalism. He fought it and lost, resigning in protest. Later, as emissary to South America, he insisted on recognizing the indigene-based governments in Bolivia and Venezuela, costing him his job.[21] To a civic nationalist, ethnic identity—Jew or indigenous—had nothing to do with citizenship or legitimacy. Of course he had no use for Madoc.

CLAIMING MADOC, CLAIMING THE WEST

Despite such efforts, the legend persisted. Before the War of 1812, the Welsh legend repeatedly provided both the continental scope and the racial precedent for colonization and was brought to mind time and again in Jeffersonian propaganda. However, later accounts shifted from dubious twelfth-century artifacts and fragments to testimony from more recent Welsh immigrants who claimed to have conversed with their long-lost cousins. For example, land speculator John Filson in his *Discovery, Settlement, and Present State of Kentucky* (1784) accedes that the Welsh presence "is universally believed to be fact," a sentiment echoed by Gilbert Imlay in his *Topographical Description* (1793).[22]

Its ubiquity and presumed universal acceptance was such that the Madoc legend was put to direct use to establish land claims during the 1790s: British empire-builders resurrected Madoc's "Discovery" of North America and the lingering presence of his descendants to press claims against Russia for mineral rights in the Pacific Northwest. George Burder's *The Welch Indians* (1797) collected about twenty accounts of living Welshmen in the American wilderness. Welsh clergyman Morgan John Rhys, observing that "Tis to be lamented that the frontiers of America have been peopled in many places with people of bad morals," purchased land along the Ohio River with his partner Benjamin Rush and, citing Madoc as his predecessor, founded the city of Beulah in 1794 as a new Welsh homeland where, away from the pressure of English dominion, Welsh culture might be revived.[23]

In essence, "Welsh" became not only a part of the medievalist revival associated with the trend toward romantic nationalism that made Sir Walter Scott so popular, but also the infiltration of such ideas into actual legal policy making. Eric Hobsbawm viewed such efforts skeptically: "It is clear that plenty of political institutions, ideological movements and groups—not least in nationalism—were so unprecedented that even historic continuity had to be invented, for example by creating an ancient past beyond effective historical continuity."[24] For expansionists, the lack of historical continuity compelled the invocation of transcendent categories that exist beyond the boundaries of empirical evidence; in this case, race, a somewhat new cultural construction of the eighteenth century. It had been five hundred years since England had absorbed Wales, there was no proof of Madoc's crossing, and there were no white Indians. To fill this gap, in the late eighteenth century, according to Robert Young and Bruce Dain, among others, "race" was repositioned as a biological category that transcended nation to provide the "historical continuity" lacking from the inconvenient historical record.[25]

This was especially crucial, as almost every account of the supposed Welsh Indians noted that, aside from their language, the Welsh Indians had become just that—Indians. One 1792 account reported that "the people subsist by the produce of the chase; that the instruments they use on the occasion are generally bows and arrows." Another observed "they had several books which were most religiously preserved in skins and were considered by them as mysteries."[26] Last, the expansionists could not claim the Welsh as forefathers, only as fore-uncles, relying on an indirect familial lineage. Aside from their biological status as "white," then, there seemed to be very little on which to base the grand claims of the expansionists. As such, "race" alone was left to establish Madoc as foundational forefather in the United States. Expansionists were working from a presumption of white ownership established by the Welsh, a racial claim on geographic space based on the Doctrine of Discovery, now stripped of its static, moral, and theological authority. Therefore, it was very important, in all the accounts, that the Welsh had not interbred with the Indians but maintained a genetic whiteness.

Because race had been by the 1780s defined as a primordial biological category, its invocation reveals the power of romantic nationalism to overwhelm Enlightenment-era ideas about civic membership being (in theory) blind to its members' identities. Anthony Smith's definition of primordial nationalism might then be applied: "[Primordial] nationalism holds that the world consists of natural nations, and has always done so; that nations are the bedrock of history and the chief actors in the historical drama . . . ; that the members of nations may, and frequently have, lost their national self-consciousness along with their independence; and that the duty of nationalists is to restore that self-consciousness and independence to the 're-awakened' organic nation."[27] For romantic nationalists, then, the proof of the continental destiny begins with the Doctrine of Discovery established by the Welsh. Next, the Welsh—regardless of their degeneration—and subsequent white Americans in general would need to be "re-awakened" to the legacy and meaning of their whiteness.

This would be the function of a romantic national literature. In 1845, in reference to evidence of Viking ties to U.S. territory, William Gilmore Simms contemplated: "It is something, surely, to be able to boast that we have an American antiquity.... The more rude the annals, the more susceptible of an original polish—the more imperfect the history, the more encouraging to the genius which adventures boldly."[28] Simms recognizes here that even a "rude annal" about whites in North America supplants any materials generated by or about indigenous populations in the white nation's quest for national legitimacy based in the needed deep-time frame. A primordial white history would give the new nation, anxious about its authenticity and its coherence, a feeling of "natural" legitimacy that would "awaken" the historically based mission of millennial nationhood it was their duty to realize, a feeling later restated as Manifest Destiny. Moreover, the Welsh had supposedly been sighted everywhere—landing in Alabama, east to North Carolina, north to Ohio, and finally west to the Dakotas. At a time when the nation was flirting with sectionalism and secession, the Madoc myth provided a binding narrative, a romantic link to an epic of white survival and racial unity that transcended specific regional affiliation.

THE WELSH AND THE REPUBLICAN SYNTHESIS

As much as the legend spread virally, it was also challenged and in ways more direct than Belknap's ideological and historiographical excision. In 1792 John Evans, a Welsh explorer, traveled to the Mandans to test their authenticity as Welshmen.[29] On his return, he reported finding none: "In respect to the Welsh Indians, I have only to inform you that I could not meet with such a people, and from intercourse I have had with Indians ... I think you may with safety inform our friends that they have no existence."[30] Nonetheless, the expansionists denied him: Evans was immediately denounced as a Spanish agent tasked with discouraging Anglo interest in the West, and Jefferson told Meriwether Lewis—son of Welsh immigrants—to seek the Welsh up the Missouri.[31] In brief, Evans's testimony notwithstanding, the Welsh had degenerated, having lost all the markers of whiteness but their skin color and their language. Such a regression embodied the Federalist fears of the frontier's threatening corruptions in their arguments against expansion.

However, as much as Federalists feared the uncontained energies of the frontier, and as much as Jeffersonians embraced them, each would learn to live with the other, in what historians call "the republican synthesis."[32] In a series of compromises Federalists and Republicans selectively back-burnered their differences in the name of national cohesion until the War of 1812. The synthesis bears consideration as it reflects an effort to put national needs above partisan ideologies. Anthony Smith writes: "The severely practical aspects of nation here join hands with the purely symbolic. Nationalism is about 'land,' both in terms of possession and (literal) rebuilding, and of belonging where forefathers lived and where history demarcates a 'homeland.'"[33] The Federalist demand for the "severely practical" is seen in the Northwest Ordinance, while the romantic Jeffersonians trafficked more in the symbolic and the essential.

The Madoc myth, then, integrated the Federalist need to control the behavior of western settlers without violating the romantic narrative of the white destiny to possess the continent, refitted to merge the Welsh presence with a corrective narrative of white regression, a cautionary tale equating the lack of racial discipline on the frontier with a loss of whiteness, awakening early republic readers to the threat posed by unstructured, unregulated colonization. Ultimately the controversy over the Madoc legend epitomized the debate over *how* the region would be colonized by the nation, not *if*. The Welsh became a stand-in for white frontiersmen; each was welcome in the new nation if and only if they performed "white" behaviors that validated the seizure of Indian land via the Doctrine of Discovery. Out of a broad archive, the narrative of Maurice Griffiths (1792) and Amos Stoddard's *Sketches Historical and Descriptive of Louisiana* (1812) best represent efforts to wed Jeffersonian fantasies of expansion with the Federalist rage for order.

In December of 1792, the same year Evans rejected the Mandans as Welsh, *the Kentucky Palladium* published an extended account of another Welshman, Maurice Griffiths, as provided by Judge Henry Toulmin. This account would subsequently enjoy broad circulation. After Hugh Henry Brackenridge, in the early 1790s Toulmin was the most prominent western man of letters. Later, he strongly advocated the Louisiana Purchase and the removal of the Spanish to clear the way for Protestant white settlement.[34] Toulmin reported having heard Griffiths's account from a John Childs and offered his personal endorsement of Childs's reliability. Griffiths's account would be reprinted at least a dozen times and on both sides of the Atlantic; moreover, the Filson Society reprinted Griffiths's account at least twice in the late nineteenth and early twentieth centuries. In the 1792 publication Toulmin introduces the account by addressing the doubters: "Sir,—No circumstance relating to the history of the Western country probably has excited, at different times, more general attention and anxious curiosity than the opinion that a nation of white men speaking the Welsh language reside high up the Missouri. By some the idea is treated as nothing but the suggestion of a bold imposture and easy credulity; whilst others regard it as a fact fully authenticated by Indian testimony and the report of various travellers worthy of credit."[35] Subsequently, Toulmin refers to the Welsh as "white Americans" and offers proof that, like latter-day white Americans, they were "an agricultural people," and their relics reveal the "genius of who relied more on their military skill than their numbers"—craftsmen and farmers, Jeffersonian yeomanry. Griffiths's own account, however, reveals a more complex situation.[36]

Toulmin records that Griffiths was sixteen when he migrated to Ohio from Wales and was promptly captured by the Shawnee and subsequently spent a number of years as an adopted warrior.[37] When the Shawnee undertook their own expedition up the Missouri, Griffiths accompanied them. Like the fictional Alonso de Calves in John Trumbull's *New Travels to the Westward* (1786), Griffiths describes finding an all-white tribe close to the headwaters of the Columbia and Missouri Rivers. After traveling for a month, past the Sandhills of Nebraska, the Shawnee adopted a policy of rotating the role of intermediary with the other tribes they met. Finally, the landscape shifts: "After passing the mountains they entered a fine fertile tract of land which having traveled through for several days they accidentally met with three white men in the Indian dress. Griffiths immediately understood their language, as it was pure Welsh."[38] However, as it is not Griffiths's turn as intermediary, he says nothing.

Griffiths and the Shawnee are then taken to "the village of these white men" where "the whole nation was of the same color, having all the European complexion" where they are taken before "the king and chief men of the nation." The council then deliberates the fate of Griffiths and the Shawnee and decides that their "fire-arms, their knives, and their tomahawks" indicate that they were "a war-like people" who would likely come back with "a powerful body of invaders" if they were allowed to return downriver. When a death sentence is pronounced to protect the isolation of the tribe, "Griffiths then thought it was time for him to speak. *He addressed the council in the Welsh language*" and assured his captors that "it was their wish to trace the Missouri to its sources; and that they should return to their country satisfied with the discoveries they had made without any wish to disturb the repose of their new acquaintances." Subsequently, "An instant astonishment glowed in the countenances, not only of the council, but of his Shawnee companions," and they were released.[39]

Griffiths and the Shawnee stayed among the Welsh for eight months, during which time he learned of their degenerated state:

> As to the history of this people he could learn nothing satisfactory. The only account they could give was, that their forefathers had come up the river from a very distant country. They had no books, no records, no writings. They intermixed with no other people by marriage: there was not a dark-skinned man in the nation.... Their clothing was skins well dressed. Their houses were made of upright posts and barks of trees. The only implements they had to cut them were stone tomahawks; they had no iron. Their arms were bows and arrows.... They had neither horses, cattle, sheep, hogs, nor any domestic or tame animals. They lived by hunting.[40]

Having lost the technology, faith, and literacy that define civilized society, only their biological whiteness defines them as Welsh; otherwise, they are wholly degenerated to a state of savagery, just as the Federalists feared. The next year, Toulmin would excerpt Crèvecoeur's essay "What Is an American?" in his anthology of promotional tracts, *A Description of Kentucky*. Crèvecoeur writes, "Now we arrive near the great woods, near the last inhabited districts; there men seem to be placed still farther beyond the reach of government. . . . There men appear to be no better than carnivorous animals of a superior rank, living on the flesh of wild animals when they can catch them, and when they are not able, they subsist on grain. He who wishes to see America in its proper light, and have a true idea of its feeble beginnings' barbarous rudiments, must visit our extended line of frontiers where the last settlers dwell."[41] The similar descriptions of old Welsh and new frontiersmen project the logical extension of Federalist fears concerning white degeneration: in fact, neither is "an agricultural people" and the virtues of yeomanry have been lost. In the spring Griffiths and the Shawnee are released—on promising not to reveal the secret of the Welsh Indians—and travel back down the settlements. Subsequently as well, Griffiths becomes a farmer and records his account for posterity, not bound by promises made to savages, regardless of their technical whiteness. Unlike the Welsh, Griffiths had survived both adoption by a Native tribe and exposure to the frontier, yet he emerged with his cultural identity as a civilized white man intact. By this reckoning, the Welsh, like the Shawnee—who vanish once the Welsh are discovered—become paths not taken, and Griffiths takes his place as yeoman in the republican hierarchy on the frontier, culturally subordinate to men such as Childs and Toulmin.

Likewise, Crèvecoeur's narrator describes his own father's redemption from captivity and return to yeomanry. Moreover, in the "Andrew the Hebridian" section, Andrew learns to live on the frontier without regressing from white values and lifeways. However, for both Toulmin and Crèvecoeur, the threat of regression looms. Toulmin acknowledges the Federalist demand for more stable means of securing the frontier: whiteness alone is not enough. Griffiths's narrative shows that whites can lose those characteristics that distinguish them from other races, threatening the power of the doctrine both to claim the land and erase the indigenes. By implication, if settlement and expansion continue without discipline and oversight—the synthesis of romantic primordialism and civic order—disaster will follow.

Only a few writers speculated that the Indian mounds spread throughout the Mississippi and Ohio basins had been built by the Welsh; Amos Stoddard, a decorated military veteran and territorial governor who represented the United States at the ceremony symbolizing Saint Louis's transition to American city in 1804, was among them. Stoddard's *Sketches Historical and Descriptive of Louisiana* (1812) anticipates American victory in the War of 1812 and presents his compendium of information concerning the space his countrymen would soon occupy.[42] Its final chapter, "A Welsh Nation in America," indulges his fascination with primordial whites: for decades he gathered information concerning the global sources of pre-Columbian North American populations from the Phoenicians to the Polynesians.

When viewing the premodern era, he posits the continent as thoroughly connected to a number of ancient civilizations, though he concedes these had all melted into a single "Indian" race by 1492. Stoddard's North America had never been awaiting white settlement in the silence of prehistory but rather had been a global crossroads for millennia prior to the three-hundred-year disruption that began after the Welsh arrived. As such, Stoddard's Welsh stand out mostly as representing the final external presence prior to centuries of isolation. This final chapter binds together the other four hundred pages, linking the pre- and post-Columbian Americas through the transformational nature of the Welsh presence. However, unlike others, Stoddard addresses at length the influence of the Welsh on Indian culture during those three centuries and finds that, in fact, the most advanced elements of "Indian" culture in 1492 were based in Welsh traditions.

To begin, Stoddard domesticates the Madoc legend by drawing parallels between it and pilgrim history. Stoddard's narrative, in a sense, transplants by 430 years the standard founding rhetoric of European refugees seeking a haven for liberty and autonomy. Like Jefferson in his "A Summary View" (1774), Stoddard begins in 1066 by establishing Wales as "the last refuge of British liberty" after the Norman invasion and creates a narrative that mostly substitutes the Welsh for pilgrim, Puritan, and colonial legends and better-known histories: "Invaded from without and convulsed within, the Welsh had strong motives to abandon their country, and to hazard their lives in pursuit of another, especially at a time when they had nearly lost all hope of maintaining their liberties."[43] Like the pilgrims, the Welsh migrated for liberty when their rights in Europe had been extinguished. This positions them as refugees, not invaders, coming to a locale known for diversity and multiracial cohabitation.

Next, Stoddard conducts a thorough review of the available sources, starting with Hakluyt's contemporary David Powell (1584) and ending with a refutation of Belknap and a corroboration of Griffiths. Of particular interest is his reference, when revisiting the text of Charles Beaty, an eighteenth-century British "witness" to Welsh Indians in Arkansas, to "a Welsh Bible [which] they kept carefully wrapped up in a skin because they could not read it." Nonetheless, "both men and women observed the rites and ceremonies prescribed by Mosaic law" (477). In all these cases, Stoddard describes Welsh Indians behaving like postrevolutionary Americans: jealous of their liberty and generally Christian. Next, Stoddard confronts Evans's and Belknap's accusation that legends of the Welsh in so many places proved their actual presence in none. To address this, Stoddard breaks from the standard narrative in intriguing and expansive ways. When refuting these doubters, he writes: "Against these authorities several plausible objections may be urged, calculated at first blush to weaken their validity. In the first place it may be said that, if they prove anything, they prove too much" (479). Then he demonstrates a Welsh presence as saturating thirteenth- and fourteenth-century North America with a Malthusian study of population growth. From an original base of eleven hundred, he calculates a doubling every fifty years, so that by the time of the first recorded sighting of Welsh Indians in 1660, there would have been 1.26 million Welsh in North America.

He also supposes that a third Welsh fleet in Virginia—no longer just ships, but fleets now—landed separately from the first two in Alabama. Finally, he presumes universal military superiority for the Welsh in their conflicts with the previous inhabitants: "Hence we are led to believe, that population was rapid among them; and perhaps the moreso as they had exchanged a foggy and barren country, for one of a serene atmosphere, and more prolific in the necessaries of life, both vegetable and animal. No doubt they preserved many of the useful arts a long time, particularly the art of war, which enabled them to reside in regions of their choice, and to multiply in security" (480–81). Again, this is a palimpsest of seventeenth-century colonial history, simply transferred six centuries into the past and a thousand miles farther west. Next, Stoddard builds on Southey's narrative that the Welsh either conquered the Aztecs in Florida and then supplanted them in Mexico, or that they *were* the Aztecs, citing Montezuma's shield's similarity to the Welsh coat of arms: "a griffin with expanded wings, holding a tiger in his talons" (481). Presumably, then, as the Spaniards erased Aztec culture, so they also erased other evidence of its Welsh origins.

Other groups of Stoddard's Welsh, however, diverged from this core. Stoddard reproduces a letter from Tennessee governor John Sevier in which he remembers a thirty-year-old conversation with a Cherokee chief. In reference to the remains of a fort in Tennessee, "the Cherokee" recalled:

> It is handed down by our forefathers, that the works were made by *white people*, who had formerly inhabited the country. . . . At length it was discovered that the *whites* were making a number of large boats which induced the Cherokees to suppose, that they intended to descend the Tennessee River [and attack the Cherokees]. At length, the whites proposed to the Indians that if they would exchange prisoners and cease hostilities, they would leave the country, and never more return; which was acceded to, and, after the exchange, parted in friendship. The whites then [went] up the Muddy River (Missouri) then up that river to a very great distance. They are now on some of its branches: But they are no longer a *white people*; they are now become like all Indians; and look like the other red people of the country. (484)

In their surrender to the Cherokee, the Welsh colonists lost more than their land. By conceding to Indians, they seemed to lose their sense of difference and superiority, beginning to become "like all Indians." In addition to this concession, Stoddard admits that the Welsh, like other pre-Columbian populations, had been nearly decimated in the intervening three centuries of European incursion, leaving only various fragments.

Despite this, Stoddard concludes with a portentous paragraph in which he links the Welsh to the fundamentals of republican government and the practices of Freemasonry so prevalent among the Founders and the signers of the ordinance: "Travellers describe certain private societies among the Indians which apparently resemble our lodges of Freemasons. Their rules of government, and the admission of members, are said to be nearly the same. No one can be received as a member of the fraternity, except by ballot, and the concurrence of the whole is necessary to a choice. They have different degrees in the order. The ceremonies of initiation, and the mode of passing from one degree to another, would create astonishment in the mind of an *enlightened* spectator. Is not this practice of European origin?" (488, emphasis in original). This passage serves two functions. First, it completes the Welsh-icization of Indian culture, suggesting that the few "civilized" aspects of pre-Columbian culture were rooted in Welsh tradition. The ubiquity and dispersal of Welsh people and culture over a vast mass of the continent, coupled with their exogenous dominance (Aztec) and endogenous influence (secret societies), simply models the white dominance of Indian culture in the nineteenth century. Seizing North America, then, was simply a matter of reincorporating a variant on European culture, and by no means the destruction of anything genuinely different, indigenous, or aboriginal because, by Stoddard's logic, no such thing had existed in six centuries.

Second, Stoddard shifts the focus away from the degenerated Welsh to identify Freemasonry as the deeper and more lasting source of transforming "Indian" culture. In the early republic, Freemasonry was at its apex. Steven C. Bullock analyzes Dewitt Clinton's Masonic claims: "The new language of Masonic science first placed the fraternity into the accepted genealogy of learning and civilization, giving it a central role in the lineage of progress. The scientific principles that underlay these changes, furthermore, had continuing significance at a time when Americans had embarked on an unprecedented experiment in liberty and equality."[44] Following this reasoning, Stoddard parallels Madoc's historical moment and his own, at the precipice of the U.S. realization of its continental ambitions through its imagined victory in the War of 1812. In both instances, communities founded on fair-minded principles of liberty and Freemasonry were attacked by tyranny and ignorance: "In the early periods of English history, the knowledge of freemasonry was mostly confined to the druids; and Wales was more fruitful of this description of men, than any other part of Europe. They were almost the only men of learning in those days. They executed the functions of priest, historians, and legislators. Those in Wales in particular animated their countrymen to a noble defense of their liberties, and afforded so much trouble to the first Edward that he ordered them to be barbarously massacred" (488). Writing on the eve of a second war with England, Stoddard—a writer, soldier, and legislator, and so likely a Freemason himself—makes the cause of the Welsh the cause of the new nation in 1812 with the threat of recolonization by the British tyrants. By reminding early nineteenth-century white Americans of the long history of the frontier as the place where freedom has long resisted tyranny, Stoddard would reawaken in them a nationalist pride concerning their own legacy handed down from the Welsh, the first American whites.

* * *

After the War of 1812 granted easy access to the western regions white Americans considered both legally and transcendentally *theirs*, the story of the Welsh Indians faded, as the claim on the land turned from abstract to material. While the Welsh still provided a primordial link to a distant white past, both the accounts of their degeneration and the continued inability of even the most pro-Welsh expansionists to provide material proof reduced their legend to irrelevance as the era of hyper-colonization and global capitalism called forth new fables of primordial parents better suited to the changing nation, such as Mound Builders and Vikings. In this new era, Federalist resistance to wholesale expansion likewise faded in the cacophony of claims louder than the rights granted by Doctrine of Discovery. From this point forward, romantic ideas of imperial nationhood and raced citizenship predominated.

Nonetheless, while it circulated, the Madoc legend provided a chimeric legacy of white primordialism imagined to unify the nation around the continental and racial ambitions of the expansionists. During the early republic, its competition with Federalism's insistence on the pragmatic, however, established the frontier as site of both fantastic projection and anxious self-reflection that has outlasted any leftover quests for Welsh Indians. The idea that the living descendants of Madoc's people awaited them up the Missouri both excited the imaginations of travelers and colonizers. However, the simultaneous threat of regression inhered as well. The ever-shape-shifting western frontier, then, began at the headwaters of the Ohio in the years after the revolution and was always more about the projection of eastern and national fears and needs than about actual local conditions, histories, or demographics. As a series of regions, the various "wests" of the left edge of the maps have always absorbed the "offcasts" of the eastern nation—its hopes, fears, and fantasies—all created to suit the needs of the cities, not the settlements.

As the nineteenth century moved on, the Madoc legend did not entirely vanish: it persisted in a minor key, especially in descriptions of the doomed Mandans. Nonetheless, the Madoc legend has lasted well into the twenty-first century, spawning a new book "proving" its truth about every decade and a lovely monument on the shores of Mobile Bay.[45] The Internet as well has proven a fertile site for all manner of speculative history and combative argumentation, most of which simply rehashes the older disputes between Belknap and Stoddard. The function of the legend remains the same: to undermine the uniqueness and indigenousness of American Indians, thereby both assuaging white guilt concerning the conquest and near genocide of the Indians by Europeans in the last half millennium and establishing whites as primordial—and hence authentic—North Americans. In both 1812 and today, the dream of finding primordial whites reveals a deep and racist impulse: white America's quest for indigenous ancestors, a national authenticity proven by a primordial paternity.

NOTES

1. See Philip Deloria, *Playing Indian*, 5.
2. See Kolodny, *In Search of First Contact*, 103–50.
3. I have used Benjamin Bowen's 1876 collection *America Discovered by the Welsh in 1170* for the preceding account. Bowen reprinted a great number of accounts of Welsh Indians, including Griffiths's. I have used this version instead of the Filson Society reprints due to its proximity to other narratives. Earlier eighteenth-century accounts are available in Burder, *Welch Indians*.
4. Southey's *Madoc* is a sprawling and incoherent account of Madoc leading the Welsh against the armies of Montezuma in Florida. Encouraged by Samuel Taylor Coleridge, Southey hoped that profits from the verse epic would fund a pantisocratic community somewhere in America. The book sold poorly, and the community was never founded. See Catherine Franklin, "The Welsh American Dream," and Craig, *Robert Southey*.
5. Gwyn A. Williams, *Madoc*, 37.
6. These are all excerpted and summarized in Armstrong, *Who Discovered America?*; Bowen, *America Discovered by the Welsh*; Burder, *Welch Indians*; Deacon, *Madoc*; Olson, *Legend of Prince Madoc*; Stoddard, *Sketches Historical*; Traxel, *Footprints*; Gwyn A. Williams, *Madoc*.
7. Miller, *Discovering Indigenous Lands*, 19.
8. Quoted in Barone, "Madoc and John Dee," 1.
9. Ibid., 2–4. The best reviews of the politics of Hakluyt's and Powell's late sixteenth-century versions of the story appear in Traxel, *Footprints*; Gwyn A. Williams, *Madoc*.
10. Cushman, *Mourt's Relation*, 91–92.
11. Kramer, *Nationalism*, 24.
12. Crèvecoeur, *Letters*, 72. See Letter III, "What Is an American?" In it, Crèvecoeur's fictional narrator James the farmer twice returns to the "back-settlers," unable to incorporate them into his otherwise Edenic vision, thus expressing Crèvecoeur's profound skepticism. Charles Brockden Brown's *Edgar Huntly*'s transformation also internalizes the frontier's regressive properties.

13. Quoted in Rakove, "Northwest Ordinance," 14.
14. See "Northwest Ordinance," in Frederick Williams, *Old Northwest*, 135.
15. Belknap, *American Biography*, 1:137.
16. Philip Gould's "Representative Men" links Belknap and Federalist expansion policies. My comments on romantic nationalism are based in Anthony D. Smith's *Nationalism and Modernism*, 63–79.
17. Benjamin Franklin, "Edict," 226.
18. Charles Brockden Brown, "For the Literary Magazine," 342.
19. Irving, *History*, 412, 419, 423.
20. Brackenridge, *Views*, 169, 170.
21. See Keller, *Nation's Advocate*, for biographical information on Brackenridge.
22. See Filson, *Description*, 75; Imlay, *Topographical Description*, 143.
23. See Rhys, "Oration on Liberty," 57.
24. Hobsbawm and Ranger, *Invention of Tradition*, 7.
25. See Young, *White Mythologies*, and Dain, *Hideous Monster*. Dain writes, "Self-evident, visible, perceptible truths would not be able to capture this thing called race. Race itself was a monster if ever Americans conceived one, but a monster hidden in their minds, not, as many of them came to think, in the reality of a nature behind the appearances" (vii).
26. See Bowen, *America Discovered by the Welch*, 88, 89.
27. Anthony D. Smith, *Nationalism and Modernism*, 146.
28. Simms, *Views and Reviews*, 137. Simms's "American Sagas of the Northmen" reviewed the literature of the Vikings in North America from the 1770 translation of the Eddas up through Longfellow's work.
29. The best accounts of Evans's travels are Deacon, *Madoc*, 137–50, and Gwyn A. Williams, *Madoc*, 179–93.
30. Quoted in Gwyn A. Williams, *Madoc*, 148.
31. Ibid., 84, 121–53.
32. The best overview of the "republican synthesis" are the essays collected in Klein et al., *Republican Synthesis Revisited*.
33. Anthony D. Smith, *Nationalism and Modernism*, 70.
34. Thomas Clark's introduction to Toulmin's 1792 collection of promotional materials, *A Description of Kentucky in North America*, is the best source of biographical information on Toulmin.
35. See Benjamin Bowen's reprint in *America Discovered by the Welch*, 96–131. This version corrects a number of errors that had entered the text through its numerous reprintings.
36. Ibid., 97.
37. See Axtell's *Invasion Within* for a discussion of how early republic spokesmen from Crèvecoeur to Franklin struggled with the pattern of "rescued" white captives returning to their captors' tribes and lifeways, 165–72.
38. Quoted in Bowen, *America Discovered by the Welch*, 101.
39. Ibid., 102, emphasis in original.
40. Ibid., 104.
41. Crèvecoeur, *Letters*, 59–60.

42. Aron's *American Confluence* addresses Stoddard, 186–97. Stoddard embodied the republican idea of the literate gentleman. He also wrote on racial difference and national history.

43. Stoddard, *Sketches*, 467. Subsequent references will be given parenthetically.

44. Bullock, *Revolutionary Brotherhood*, 143.

45. This pattern is demonstrated in Armstrong, *Who Discovered America?* (1950); Deacon, *Madoc* (1966); Olson, *Legend of Prince Madoc* (1987); Gwyn A. Williams, *Madoc* (1979); and Traxel, *Footprints* (2004).

CHAPTER TWO

Reading the Routes
Early American Nature Writing and Critical Regionalism before the "Postfrontier"

William V. Lombardi

FORT MANDAN, 1805

Late in March 1805, near Fort Mandan, spring thaws broke apart the frozen Missouri River, sending ice floes downstream. Having spent his first winter in the newly acquired American lands of the Upper Missouri, William Clark recorded scenes of industrious Indians capturing the dead buffalo that floated with the ice, and setting fire to the plains around their villages as part of an annual fuel reduction and game management program. At the same time, Clark writes that he was sending a barge to President Jefferson containing the specimens that the Corps of Discovery had collected on the central and northern prairies. Its cargo included skeletons and skins of the birds and mammals they had encountered, Indian clothing and implements, and parcels of plants and roots. By early spring the corps was ready to depart Fort Mandan for what has sometimes been described as "unknown" country;[1] indeed, on April 7, the hazards of the Continental Divide still before him, Meriwether Lewis writes: "we were now about to penetrate a country at least two thousand miles in width, on which the foot of *civilized* man had never trodden."[2] In this utterance, which invokes the imperial dichotomy of savage and civilized races, Lewis performs an erasure of Indian inhabitation and stewardship that helped enable American nationalism in the West. Lewis's erasure likewise extends to the long-present French, the Spanish to the south, and the British and Russians farther west.

   This scene draws attention to two aspects of the American western discovery narrative that are of concern to both critical regionalism and ecocriticism. First, to be sure, contemporary scholarship has had to recover the turbulent political landscape the Corps of Discovery traveled through, reinstating the lands west of the Mississippi as a place of diverse inhabitation and established global economic exchange, rather than a *tabula rasa* on which the American narrative would be inscribed. Second, and more fundamentally, the Mandan interlude reveals the postmodern paradox underpinning "discovery" itself: while Lewis injudiciously but perfunctorily obscured Indian and European presences, the corps' venture nonetheless produced geographic, demographic, anthropologic, and Linnaean taxonomic certainty in the region through its maps, collections, and ethnopolitical intelligence. The trope of "discovery," then, positioned at the very heart of early American literature, in fact proves itself a problematic "production of the real," as Nathaniel Lewis, after Jean Baudrillard, claims in the final chapter of *Unsettling the Literary West: Authenticity and Authorship* (2003).[3] Incongruously, the discovery narrative invented a textual, wholly constructed western "wilderness"—an open, heterotopic space William Cronon has called "the creation of very particular human cultures at very particular moments in human history"[4]— even as it empirically established the West's specific ecological, geographical, and political boundaries.

Bold as it is, however, Nathaniel Lewis's sensitivity to the literature of the American West as a two-hundred-year-long "record of creative imagining" representative of "the first and best example of postmodern writing in American literary history"[5] is complicated by the figure of the naturalist in early frontier literature, and by the role of nature writing more generally in the western tradition. While Lewis argues for recognition of the discursive, rather than the customary geographic/historical production of the West even in its earliest documents, the naturalist's central position in the genre and his vocation alone seem to preclude the purely social construction of western space. Naturalists from around the globe in this period were feverishly establishing an empirical record of the American West. Still, Michael P. Branch, in his introduction to *Reading the Roots: American Nature Writing before Walden* (2004)—from which this essay derives its title—concedes "the wonderful, fallible lens of language"[6] that early naturalists used to describe what they saw, and Edward Watts has written recently on the literary "varnishing" employed by prominent naturalists in their western narratives in order to generate sales.[7] In short, as Enlightenment projects, naturalists' scientific precision demystified the frontier by cataloguing western species and classifying western spaces, even as their literary accounts of travel and adventure fueled eastern and continental imaginations. Early American nature writing, which Branch locates loosely across several subgenres of nonfiction,[8] thus displays an intricate both/and, or "real-and-imagined,"[9] sensibility that suggests environment and postmodernity as coextensive. By this I mean that early American nature writing, both for its accuracy *and* its intertextuality and embellishments, was instrumental in the creation of a western or frontier imaginary, one of plenitude and anticipated loss that was shaped through the combined and shifting rhetorics of imperialism and colonialism, as well as by popular, literary, and material artifacts that reached the world at large. The paradox is that the figure of the naturalist both enchanted and disenchanted the landscape simultaneously, unintentionally confounding the intersection between nature and culture. The early naturalist stands at the crossroads of our conceptions of a material and a socially constructed U.S. West.

With a few notable exceptions, recent literary critiques that reconsider early economic and intercultural exchanges in the West fail to establish the era's canonical, historical continuum with the cosmopolitanism and literatures of the present day, while contemporary critiques of the region, by contrast, omit the formative years of trans-Mississippi American expansionism in the late eighteenth and early nineteenth centuries altogether, as if a routed West was a new or somehow separate phenomenon.[10] Critical regionalism, to paraphrase Douglas Reichert Powell, seeks to articulate what is unique about a given place even as it acknowledges its interconnections with broader aspects of history, politics, and culture.[11] However, critical regionalism is informed largely by "posts": postmodern, postregion, postwest, and postfrontier,[12] and therefore critical regionalists to date have focused mainly on late twentieth- and early twenty-first-century issues and texts, despite acknowledging, as Neil Campbell does, that the West "has always had a global dimension as a geographical, cultural, and economic crossroads defined by complex connectivity, multidimensionality, and imagination."[13] Additionally, critical regionalism has yet to confront the ongoing influence of the natural world on western American culture, or to adapt ecocritical approaches to a socially constructed West.[14] Therefore, it is necessary to include early American nature writing in the critical regionalist discourse because it allows us to view the literature and culture of the U.S. West before the postfrontier as diverse, as opposed to homogeneous, and to recognize its emplotment as global in scale and rhizomatic, rather than nationalist and linear, in its construction. In order to read the routes constituting a transnational West before the postfrontier just as after, we need to read their roots in the natural history tradition and recognize the inseparability of western nature and western culture.

My goal is to demonstrate the usefulness of critical regionalism in an early nineteenth-century context, with the aim of establishing a rapport between critical regionalism and ecocriticism that will allow critics to expand and enrich their approach to these early documents. Within this framework, I look for traces of transnationalism in the spatial productions of the quintessential epic *The Journals of Lewis and Clark* and the lesser known and rarely studied *Narrative of a Journey across the Rocky Mountains to the Columbia River* (1839), by ornithologist and botanist John Kirk Townsend. With an eye toward reading the West as a real-and-imagined space of natural environment and mythical composition, this essay highlights the culture of transnational exchange already embedded in the western "wilderness" in 1803 and beyond, and interrogates the routes taken by Lewis and Clark and John Kirk Townsend as less isolated, more interconnected and multidimensional, than is usually accepted. Together, ecocriticism and critical regionalism both expose and renegotiate the complex interrelations of nationalism, commerce, and environment at the heart of meaning making in the U.S. West.

"A CROWDED WILDERNESS": READING THE ROUTES/ROOTS

The "wild" spaces of Lewis and Clark's *Journal* and Townsend's *Narrative* can be read as social spaces, forming a web of global exchange that aligns with postwestern thought. To reject the "blank page" paradigm of the period is not simply to acknowledge the region's cultural and commercial infrastructure; it is to witness a long-standing Native land use ethic, and in the process to elevate nature to more than mere setting—an impulse with which ecocriticism has concerned itself since its inception. Therefore, it is imperative to recognize that the West was not simply "a crowded wilderness"[15] in a cultural sense, but a conspicuously maintained environment as well. Reconstructing what Lewis and Clark saw, James P. Ronda tells of a region of "astounding human diversity" and "large-scale economic development" that was "crisscrossed with trading trails and exchange routes,"[16] and Colin G. Calloway, in his introduction to *Our Hearts Fell to the Ground: Plains Indian Views of How the West Was Lost*, states, "When Lewis and Clark crossed the continent they entered an Indian world with ancient roots but one that was already changed and continually changing as a result of contact with both Indian and non-Indian outsiders."[17] In these and other histories, the recurrent rhetorical imposition of commercial *routes* aligned against a fixed sense of regional *roots* is remarkable; rather than a single historical narrative pathway, this "Old" West appears to bear the chaotic, rhizomatic hallmarks of "exchange, movement, relations, and hybridization"[18] ascribed to more recent literature and culture. Yet however productive—and surely correct—a West recast as cosmopolitan rather than vacant may seem, theorizing it carries its own pitfalls. Critical regionalism and ecocriticism have complex affinities. Just as traditional frontier mythology would empty the landscape of people, conversely, critical regionalism minimizes the affective role of the physical environment. When routes/roots collide conceptually in postwestern criticism, nature is often lost in the analysis of its discursive production. Because global networks are driven by resource extraction if not outright exploitation, ecocritical concerns *must* shadow any examination of globalization's complex connectivity.

"For the Purposes of Commerce": Jefferson's Instructions

Early in 1803 Jefferson wrote a set of instructions to Lewis directing him regarding his purpose, duties, and comportment in the western lands. His instructions stated that the corps' mission was to find a practicable water route to the Pacific Ocean "for the purposes of commerce."[19] The very act of establishing such a route announces Jefferson's intended interventions within the region, if not his global trade designs. Furthermore, despite Lewis's subsequent distinction between civilized and savage peoples and the imperialist erasures it signified, Jefferson's orders make clear that successful navigation in the West—and, indeed, successful commerce—depended on knowledge of organized tribal infrastructures. It seems that Jefferson's goal was not to usurp "savage" influence but to ensure an American share in existing international trade systems that already recognized Indians as pivotal.[20] Nor did Jefferson view the tribes monolithically; instead, diplomatic parcels were conspicuously packaged based on his foreknowledge of specific tribal biases and desires, thus acknowledging the diversity of Indian cultures. Kathleen DuVal comments that Indian and European relations of the period did not disqualify constructions of Us and Them, but rather that "these categories were never as simple as *Indians* and *Europeans*. . . . All were mindful of the differences between, for example, French and English, and the Osages and the Shawnees."[21] Though not precisely egalitarian, difference was forged by political alliances and *realpolitik* rather than solely by ethnicity. From Jefferson's instructions it is already possible to posit a regional Indian arbiter playing a decisive role in a system of intense local, regional, and international exchange in the Far West who was key to the movement of local resources worldwide in a manner specific to his particular tribal, commercial affiliations.

Still, the details of Jefferson's instructions appear peculiar if the natural history tradition is not accounted for in the configuration of commerce and nationalism. His pragmatic admonition to carefully observe and record the features of the corps' route becomes a series of ethnographic inquiries; in part to cement regional knowledge for commercial advantage, his orders seem to digress into purely scientific curiosity. Jefferson's list includes six objectives regarding the natural history of the land. Ranging from instructing Lewis and Clark to note soil and vegetation, observe mineral wealth, and the keeping of careful climatological records, his instructions likewise include the almost banal directive to mark the leafing of the trees and the return of birds and insects to a locale. In this light, Jefferson's commercial aim is both nationalist *and* scientific. Yet such are the collections' utility that he writes to Lewis: "in the loss of yourselves, we should lose also the information you will have acquired. by returning safely with that, you may enable us to renew the essay with better calculated means."[22] That is, Jefferson deemed it crucial that Lewis and Clark return to the American government with intelligence about Indian laws and customs, *the remains of extinct animals*, and *knowledge of the prevailing winds at different seasons*. As strange as it may seem, the agglomeration of the corps' objectives exhibits how impossible it was to extricate commerce from natural history, or natural history from nationalism.

In addition to Jefferson's plural sense of the Indian nations, his acknowledgment of the Indians' position in transnational exchange, and his naturalist's interest in the landscape, his instructions further disclose his foreknowledge of continental political and physical geography. He writes, for example, "The Northern waters of the Missouri are less to be enquired after, because they have been ascertained to a considerable degree, and are still in a course of ascertainment by English traders and travelers."[23] Moreover, he outlines the probable routes of communication for the corps to employ while on the trail, citing "an intercourse" between "white settlements" on the Missouri and "Spanish posts at St. Louis," as well as between the Indian settlements at Cahokia and Kaskaskia, and the French town of Sainte Genevieve. He notes further that traders and Indians might carry letters, "a copy of [the] journal, notes and observations of every kind" from the corps to American outposts.[24] Also, Ronda verifies that Jefferson was conversant with at least six transcontinental maps of varying reliability and conjecture produced in Britain, Spain, France, and America, as well as French and Spanish accounts of the terrain.[25] Far from being unknown, as nearly as was possible, Jefferson's route for the corps took a calculated course through contested space. Finally, the planning underlying Jefferson's instructions to Lewis intimates a transnational network of American exchange that reaches from the Philadelphia tradespersons who outfitted the corps, through transactions with Indians, Frenchmen, and Englishmen, to trade routes that sent raw western materials around the globe. A reassessment of Jefferson's instructions thus destabilizes the heroic "blank page" narrative while opening a more fluid, multicultural view of the region. Jefferson had to instill a global sense of regional place in Lewis and Clark if they were to be successful. Branch reminds us, though, of the almost purely "utilitarian ethic" this awareness proscribed, and he suggests that the study of early American nature writing helps us "better understand how certain misguided and destructive ideas gained prominence in our culture";[26] thus, in Jefferson's instructions we see a concise but conflicted portrait of the meaning of environment at the time, and its problematic resonance within this global imaginary and commercial system.

"The Countrey and Its Productions": Lewis and Clark en Route

Cultural critic Hsuan L. Hsu calls for "a fluid and flexible understanding of regions," and Stephen Tatum remarks that the recovery of "subaltern voices and alternate histories" is the primary goal of postfrontier studies.[27] These and other contemporary western literary scholars invested in critical regionalism draw broadly from Arjun Appadurai's sense that modern subjectivity is imaginatively derived from media and migration,[28] and that the transferability of this imaginary undergirds the construction of place. That is, an evolving, mutable geographical and historical imagination is remade constantly by everyday social practice. With these claims in mind, the region as real-and-imagined space as it plays out in exploration narratives reveals that the early frontier was not as culturally uniform as is sometimes supposed. In the *Journals* we can track the effects of a landscape that was partly known but rarely described, and which was daily exposed to the imaginative influence of the simultaneous charting and emptying—the both/and mixture of taxonomizing and "varnishing" mentioned above—that compelled the pens of Lewis and Clark as informed nonspecialists in the field of natural history.

Traveling northwest on the trail along the Missouri, two things were apparent to the corps: the transregional, transnational flow of goods and people on established trade routes, and the bounty of the prairie ecosystem. As amateur naturalists, both Lewis and Clark reported amazement at large herds of bison and elk, and they described many new mammals and birds with which they, and the scientific community, were unfamiliar. As ambassadors, they carefully transcribed the names of tribes they encountered, tribal populations, and the names of tribal leaders. By late September 1804 they logged their first experiences with diverse bands of Sioux. Clark reported that "the greater part of [the Sioux] make use of Bows & arrows," but that a number of them carry guns."[29] The combination of traditional weapons and guns displays the globally determined cultural flux experienced in the region, but it also makes clear that transregional trade was not a simple matter of whites bringing technology—civilization—to a premodern people. Rather, among the Yankton band, Clark describes a large council house whose interior was decorated with "the flags of Spain & the Flag we gave them," in addition to scattered swan's down and a ceremonial peace pipe that was later used to make "a Sacrefise to the flag."[30] The blending of Sioux, Spanish, and American iconography in the Yankton lodge and the incorporation of international emblems into Yankton ceremony is evidence of competing national imaginaries already in circulation on the plains, and Clark's involvement shows that the exchange between explorer and Native American was dialogic. In this scene we see a flexibility of regional cultures so often represented as fixed or stable, and we see a fluidity of regional meaning and boundaries that refuses to be branded as parochial. The irony of American nationalism in this scene is that it records and performs transnational participation despite its ultimate imperial erasure in the interest of conquest.

Approaching the northern plains, when Clark writes that "Capt. Lewis went out with a View to See the Countrey and its productions,"[31] he means that Lewis intended to survey the region's natural wealth and ultimately to bring back dinner. However, then as now, the subtext of "production" is resource use. Indeed, production on the plains did not even necessarily mean "wild": corn, squash, and beans were farmed by several tribes, and tobacco and whiskey, as well as trinkets and furs, were all part of the social and economic exchange the corps witnessed and participated in. Women, too, were part of the bargain. These elements taken together, the *Journals* furnished a script for other narratives that followed in the ensuing decades. The corps was participating in a hybrid culture—indeed, depended on it for their survival—while experiencing personal freedoms they were not accustomed to in the East. It is this libratory, imaginative sense within the

Journals that was transferable, that became part of the imperial and the popular imaginative register. The corps was subjected to and producing—and, in the *Journals*, reproducing—a western American cultural imaginary established on newness and wonder. Plenitude, danger, and exoticism became mainstays of western myth after Lewis and Clark, an admixture of natural, material, and textual production.

Still, the exploration narrative was a mode of inquiry as much as it was a narrative of conquest or a vehicle of commerce,[32] which is why the delivery at spring thaw of the natural history collections from Fort Mandan to President Jefferson is so significant. Until Lewis and Clark, science and trade in the West were not yet so intermingled as to be indistinguishable. The pirogues that went back down the Missouri that day carried a message in cipher of taxonomy *and* opportunity. Yet in the historical moment, scholars depict the several international rivalries in the West as "borderless," their claims to the land defined by blurry boundaries, thus allowing the frontier to be a place of "intercultural relations" productive of "mixing and accommodation as opposed to unambiguous triumph."[33] This complex mixture of imperialism, commerce, and accommodation is of acute interest to critical regionalists because it expands Stephanie LeMenager's point that "it was trade, more than any other activity, that gave imaginative definition to the North American West."[34]

So, in many ways the Lewis and Clark expedition drained the region of its ambiguity by forcing the clarification of those territorial boundaries and imposing a narrative of American triumphalism that unbalanced the cultural and political as well as the physical landscape of the region by producing its first, conclusive narrative. By "opening" the West to American interests, the corps figuratively narrowed the region's meaning. Alternately, as the impetus of what he calls a "premature" closure of the West, historian Richard Slotkin writes that within two decades after Lewis and Clark, in the period from 1820 to 1845, American expansionism was stalled by a combination of natural obstacles and politics, seemingly codifying international borders indefinitely.[35] In a real sense, this is the moment that the West became "territory," the basis for acknowledgment that western lands and resources were finite, and so foretelling of a postwestern future. As the region became "known," and a distinctly American narrative was established, conceptions of the frontier became more rigid in the national consciousness.

This premature postwestern era spanning the 1830s, as both Slotkin and LeMenager label it, should not be undervalued. In fact, it was not as premature as might be supposed. The strategic nostalgia and anxiety of authenticity expressed in firsthand accounts by an army of scientific and literary tourists—from Washington Irving to John Kirk Townsend to George Catlin to Francis Parkman—should be registered as the complaints of an expected, real closure, as the pangs of a shifting frontier attitude from the muse of possibility and plenitude to that of loss, and not merely the "cultural capital" wrought by authorial competition.[36] Representing the end, albeit not immediately, of the centuries-long "middle ground," after Lewis and Clark borderlands were organized into bordered spaces, and indigenous cultures and natural resources were finally hemmed in by political, geographical, and biological limitations. As these paradigms were absorbed by Townsend and others, and the landscape was described, classified, and scientifically and creatively circulated, a new and abiding American, western, regional imagined community was formed. And so, it is essential to recognize that this bounded sense of the West imparted by the corps is what makes a critical regionalist approach to this period so necessary. Critical regionalism reminds us that all borders are permeable and no narrative is totalizing. We need to acknowledge that, however subsumed into the conquest narrative, there were nonetheless real, self-serving differences between nationalist narratives promoting what was codified into Manifest Destiny as a type of closure, the tourists' senses of a passing place and way of life, and that of the naturalist, rushing to become the first to find, describe, and catalog new flora and fauna. Winter at Fort Mandan, then, is symbolic of American national imagination and desire, of nature as impasse and resource, and of the actual consolidation of territories that produced the premature postwestern.

We should be conscious that social interaction is determined by resource extraction. The raw materials harvested on the frontier and traded at Fort Mandan and other frontier settlements are the foundation for the various social "scapes" derived from them. The Enlightenment science driving exploration and natural history ordered its world in hierarchies of utility; by highlighting the relevance of environmental contributions to and impacts on these narratives, an ecocritical perspective recognizes that without abundant natural resources, Indian, French, British, and American would likely not have shared the landscape at all. Therefore, the more fluid understanding of region that Hsu prescribes rewards cultural critics with a maze of alternate histories, including the complex environmentality charging Lewis and Clark's imaginative range that undercuts static representations of wildness in their time and our own.

JOHN KIRK TOWNSEND: NEW ROUTES WEST

Two threads regarding the regional/global production of the U.S. West should be evident: first, through the movement of diverse people and goods in and out of the region a cultural imaginary was discursively produced and then continuously reproduced through literary, scientific, economic, and political iteration and interaction worldwide; and second, in its constant reproduction and interconnection, this regional identity was dynamic and multivalent in a rhizomatic sense, neither fixed nor essentializing as the linear narrative of expansionism would insist. And yet, the West salubrious, the West of vast herds of prairie megafauna and wandering wolves and grizzlies, the West of untrustworthy, alternately picturesque or drunken Indians, were ubiquitous by the mid-1830s. With each iteration these tropes became more stable, more rigid rather than fluid. In this way, the imperial erasures in the *Journals* that assured mastery and promised plenitude nevertheless enabled a rhetoric of loss, what can be thought of as elegiac imperialism, that accompanies those same images in the generation of texts that followed.

As I turn my attention to Townsend's exceptional but rarely read *Narrative*, it is vital to point out that western narratives after Lewis and Clark also persist in their erasures and reflect their imperial impulse. Just as Lewis and Clark's journals cite antecedents in the voyages of Columbus and Cook to establish this ethos,[37] so too does Townsend, like many of his contemporaries, trace his own lineage through Lewis and Clark's *Journals*. Therefore, Townsend's *Narrative* is one of many texts that participates in what Nathaniel Lewis calls "a repetition compulsion,"[38] which he tracks through frontier literature produced during the 1820s and 1830s that cements a normalized, American geography and plot line. Not only does Townsend recall the corps' expedition throughout his text, he likewise remarks widely on the works of Irving, James Fenimore Cooper, Izaak Walton, and Percy Bysshe Shelley to emplot a collectively historical, romantic, and scientific narration that is decidedly literary. In the same manner, Irving, Cooper, and others relied on firsthand accounts before Townsend's for episodic content and narrative verisimilitude. In this way the regional ethos was popularly formed and disseminated textually just as it was being distributed materially through buffalo robes and beaver pelts on the world market. Notably, though, this is ultimately a decentralized production of Westness, mutually shaped both from within and outside of the region, and with no single source. The combined textual-experiential-material composition of the West highlights the exchange of produced and received images driving the culture and literature of the era identifying the West as a real-and-imagined space.

Townsend's *Narrative* is unique, however, for several reasons. Most importantly, he was the first trained naturalist and zoologist to cross overland to the Pacific Coast,[39] and the *Narrative* included on its publication an appendix cataloging the mammals he recorded while in Oregon Territory. Further, the skins Townsend preserved from his trip became the basis for John James Audubon's western addition to his classic *Birds of America* (1827–38).[40] Townsend traveled in the company of eminent botanist Thomas Nuttall, whom Thomas J. Lyon calls "the most knowledgeable of the all-purpose naturalists of the early period in this country," and though Lyon is less impressed with Townsend's observational skill, Branch calls *Narrative* one of the "most engaging and interesting nineteenth-century accounts of landscapes and fauna of the American West."[41] Also noteworthy is the fact that Nuttall figures briefly in Irving's *Astoria* (1836) and Richard Henry Dana's *Two Years before the Mast* (1840), so that Nuttall essentially passes from Irving, through Townsend, only to reappear in Dana as a figure not entirely unlike Cooper's naturalist, Dr. Obed Battius, whose dedication to his craft lends comic relief to *The*

Prairie (1827). As scientifically influential as Nuttall is in Townsend's narrative, his presence forges a literary link between Irving's popular histories, Townsend's scientific endeavor, and Dana's transcendentalist-inspired, class-conscious western individualism. Lastly, because Townsend was connected to Nathaniel Wyeth's second attempt at forming an outpost in Oregon Territory, his *Narrative* functions similarly to Wyeth's nephew John's account of the earlier attempt to establish a trade route, in that Townsend's is a "prophetic linkage of global capitalism and imperialism with the books that fuel such enterprises."[42] In other words, Townsend's *Narrative* toes that line between "the transmutation of the facts" that Steven Watts isolates for its richness when comparing the rhetoric of various imperial and local concerns.[43] Therefore, Townsend's "blank page" is conceptually "scientifically unexplored" as opposed to merely strategically vacant, and yet it marks a precise intersection of real-and-imagined Westness circulating globally in this era.[44] Accordingly, the wonder and elegiac imperialism Townsend registers throughout the *Narrative* problematizes the pre-postwestern trope that predicts the extinction of the buffalo and the end of tribal life; he gestures toward a less stylized, more empirical and ethical interpretation that counteracts the myth of endless abundance without unduly romanticizing the Old West's passing.

Equally as important to the study of western regionalism, Townsend did not stop at the Pacific Coast. Between collecting trips in the Columbia and Willamette watersheds, traveling the routes that Wyeth, and John Jacob Astor before him, had envisioned, Townsend made two trips from the Pacific Northwest to Hawaii to continue his work, finally returning around Cape Horn to the States three years later. Townsend's journey effectively transcends the geographic borders of the West while expanding its conceptual boundaries.[45] As scholars consider hemispheric American studies and critical regionalists seek to envision the West beyond a closed geographic locale, the *Narrative* betokens a useful alternate history to regional political and cultural normalization. Townsend offers a compelling early model of how far the regional imaginary actually extended in theory and in practice.[46]

Elegiac Imperialism and the Global Beaver:
The Western Regional Imaginary in the South Seas

Although the *Narrative* is of tremendous value for marking changes in the political, cultural, and environmental composition of the West between Townsend's time and the corps', for the purposes of my project I have chosen to focus on a later scene during Townsend's stay in Hawaii depicting the formal mourning of the royal court because it exemplifies "how the global is always being localized and the local is always being globalized."[47] In "Nineteenth-Century United States Culture and Transnationality," John Carlos Rowe argues, "No reconsideration of nineteenth-century United States culture from a transnational perspective should ignore the importance of the Pacific Islands . . . in the formation of national identity."[48] In fact, Townsend's *Narrative* is full of the same odd combinations and surprising juxtapositions of regional and international products and iconography that made up the affinities of the continental West in the *Journals*. Similar to the routes crisscrossing the continental West, the routes between the islands, South America, China, and the American interior moved goods, people, and ideas from the local to the global and back, so that just as Townsend records the death by drowning of "eight Sandwich Islanders" (165), a white man, and an Indian woman at the mouth of the Columbia River when their canoe loaded with salmon bound for Boston capsizes in a truly emblematic transnational moment, so too does he remark in Hawaii on the presence of Spanish vaqueros herding cattle into the hold of a ship sailing for the mainland (209). The Pacific, commensurate with the West, was likewise a contested but blurry space of imperial opportunity. As was the case on the mainland, Rob Wilson describes it as "a nexus of global commercial and strategic relations" that served "the economic and national interests of London, Paris, Madrid, and Washington."[49]

While he was on Oahu, Townsend attended the funeral of Hawaiian princess Harieta Nahienaena, who had died from complications after childbirth. In what can be read as an allegory of local and global exchange, Townsend presents a scene framed by commentary that is strikingly in the same vein as the rhetoric of loss conveyed toward resource depletion and Native American decline in the continental West. Expressing a similar, elegiac imperialism in his description of the circumstances of the princess's death, Townsend remarks: "Should Harieta die, the royal Hawaiian line will be broken for ever, the insignia of Sandwich Island rank will be buried in her tomb, and the children of her reigning brother will not inherit their father's rank" (197). Thus, the Native or local line dies and the region succumbs to imperial desire; Townsend can afford to appear personally saddened, but the consequences of the princess's death contain a subtext of local upheaval and imperial opportunity.[50] And yet, despite the allegory the critical regionalist perspective proposes, Townsend nonetheless communicates an overarching dialogic exchange expressed through the material culture of the palace and the truly cosmopolitan gathering of people in attendance to pay their respects to the deceased. Here, Townsend takes considerable care to describe the king's dress in particular on this occasion, which he says was a gift from the foreign residents of the island: "He was most magnificently attired in a fine blue regimental coat, richly embroidered with gold and silver lace, and two splendid gold epaulets on the shoulders. His pantaloons were of very delicate white cassimere, embroidered down the seams with gold lace, and from a crimson sash depended a beautiful, and highly ornamented dress sword, the scabbard of which was of fine gold, His *chapeau bras* was in keeping with the rest of his attire, being of black beaver, ornamented with broad bands of gold fiber" (202). Though the king perhaps cuts what might be seen as an ironic figure of colonial influence to today's reader, the scene itself exhibits the tremendous transregional exchange underpinning the service. Dressed as a proper Victorian diplomat, King Tamehameha III [*sic*; the correct name is Kamehameha] is the very embodiment of the global culture of the era. Stressing the profoundly international flavor of the event, Townsend provides a footnote to the above passage, stating that the uniform was "presented some years ago to the king, by the subscription of the foreign residents at Oahu. It was made in Lima" (202). The strands of globalism in this ritual moment are astounding; among the most intriguing of those materials expressive of transnational routes intersecting in Hawaii is the king's black beaver *chapeau bras*. Demonstrating the range of what might be described as the "global beaver"—a totemic western animal emblematic of environmental-cultural-commercial interconnectivities—the raw material for the king's hat was perhaps gotten somewhere in a remote stream in the Rocky Mountains by a lone French Indian trapper and sold at a rendezvous in Colorado, the beaver pelt could have been processed in the Pacific Northwest by Canadians in the employ of the Hudson's Bay Company, then shipped on either a British or American brig to Lima, Peru, where it, along with the uniform, would have been cut in the English style at the expense of foreign dignitaries, only to be sent to the South Pacific to be worn by a Hawaiian king, dressed to mourn the loss of his sister, the last of her line.[51]

Townsend's description of the funeral services continues: "The procession was headed by a band of very good music, most of the performers being negroes" (202). Lastly, he remarks, "The service was opened by an address in the native language by the Re. Mr. Bingham; this was followed by hymns, short addresses, and prayers alternately, by several other missionaries who were present" (203). Not only is this scene reminiscent of the incorporated national iconography in the Yankton Sioux council house in Lewis and Clark, the ever-widening wilderness here appears less rustic, more cosmopolitan, and more filled with transnational routes tracing ever more rhizomatic, hidden histories than we have yet presumed.

IN THE RUINS OF FORT CLATSOP, 1836

Townsend had been surprised by the "improvements" he had found when his party first reached Fort Vancouver. Later, he would remark of the fort his company built in the Willamette watershed: "the whole scene looked so like the entrance to a country village, that it was difficult to fancy oneself in a howling wilderness inhabited by the wild and improvident Indian" (128). Of course, Townsend's "wilderness" was perhaps little more than fancy, and it was only by the aid of the "improvident" Indian that his company survived the inhospitable sagebrush plains of present-day eastern Oregon at all (287). In fact, in a cruel demonstration of the dark side of encounter, as had been the case on the prairies, Columbia River tribes were rapidly being decimated by diseases the traders had brought to the coast decades before, and tribal populations would be reduced by half before the mid-1830s, making Townsend's elegiac imperialism all the more pronounced. Too, the Indians in the neighborhood of both forts were an integral part of trade in the region, and they had been crucial to traders' survival since before Lewis and Clark built their winter quarters on the coast at Fort Clatsop.

Shortly after his arrival on the coast, and at nearly the same time Irving was writing *Astoria* in New York, Townsend was paying a visit to the ruins of the actual site of Astor's abandoned fort. He saw the ruins' cultural and dramatic potential, describing its lone remaining chimney as "a melancholy monument of American enterprise and domestic misrule," which was now so "overgrown with weeds and bushes, [it] can scarce be distinguished from the primeval forest which surrounds it on every side" (132). In its sublimity, the reabsorption of Fort Astoria into the primeval forest provides a *memento mori* quite different from Townsend's depictions of the active forts above. If those forts symbolize a settled present, one that promises to overtake the "howling wilderness," the ruins of Astoria refer to an "uncivilized" age Townsend sensed was passing, one that aesthetic tradition already compelled him to consolidate into a paradox of environmental loss, Edenic expression, and wilderness adventure.

Shortly before he left the coast for his final trip to Hawaii, and from there home to Boston, Townsend made a similar pilgrimage to the ruins of Fort Clatsop. There, he encountered the same romantic scene, "the whole vicinity [of which had] overgrown with thorn and wild currant bushes" (189). Only at Clatsop, he tells of a neighboring child who found, just "a few days since, a large silver medal, which had been brought here by Lewis and Clark, and had probably been presented to some chief, who lost it." Because Townsend's *Narrative* is written as a journal, and each segment is dated, his use of the adverb "since" is problematic. It smacks of editorial hindsight, implying that just a few days *after* Townsend had been there, a child found the coin—impossible for him to know if his journal is a faithful recording of the events of the day. Interpreted this way, the coin is distinctly literary and its appearance in the hand of a child is a portentous amendment after the fact: the coin of empire, which, through its speculative loss by the unknown chief, insinuates Native American forfeiture. The coin, in the hands of a child, implies the promise of a bright commercial future, rather than a reminder of failure. But to be sure, just as Astoria's ruins convey a lesson against "domestic misrule," the ruins of Fort Clatsop impart unambiguous American nationalism.

I conclude in the ruins of Fort Clatsop because, juxtaposed with Fort Mandan, Clatsop was for Lewis and Clark in many ways the nadir of their journey; it was a place of discomfort and privation, unyielding dampness, and exorbitant trade prices that threatened the viability of their return home, despite the fact that it symbolizes the success of their transcontinental aspirations. I conclude in its ruins because, for Townsend instead, Clatsop and Astoria had already become the sites of American western mythos, innocence and experience combined; his retrospective triumphalism, predicated on the romantic sublime, is fraught with authorial "varnish" and overt intertextuality with the most popular western narratives of the period. Indeed, in spite of itself, Townsend's representation of primordial wilderness in the above scenes is tantamount to Meriwether Lewis's erasure. If early American nature writing and critical regionalism require of us a reconsideration of what texts before the "postfrontier" accomplish, we should recognize how the real-and-imagined West is produced, how it travels, and the manner in which this movement is, in anthropologist James Clifford's words, constantly emergent.[52] In the West's act of becoming, critical regionalist thought should revisit the lessons of the rhizome, of "successive lateral offshoots in immediate connection with an outside," where the American West is the pivot point between route and root,[53] and apply those lessons to an undertheorized "Old" West. To convey a broader definition of the West as a cosmopolitan place is not the least we can do. While Townsend's sense of environmental loss epitomizes a premature postwest, his trajectory promises an expanding nexus of postnational critique. Ultimately, Townsend's *Narrative* is provocative because it opens the West outward, rather than containing it geographically or imaginatively, or ensnaring it entirely in masculine or nationalist ideology the way Krista Comer, after William Cronon, suggests such narratives do.[54] Such a configuration of the West is necessary because, in what I have attempted to reveal as the inherent inseparability of its nature and culture, it enlarges how we think about today's conversations regarding an environmentally responsible sense of planet and the slow violence of global environmental crises in relation to our own materialism. Looking ahead, the critical regionalist's rhizomatic West enables ecocritical studies engaged in what Lawrence Buell calls "experiments in planetary belonging."[55] The earlier we can shift this focus in the legacy of western American literature, the better equipped we are to contend with the West's global environmental legacy.

NOTES

1. See Lewis and Clark, *Journals*, 95; Ronda, *Lewis and Clark*, 14; Furtwangler, *Acts of Discovery*, 2.
2. Lewis and Clark, *Journals*, 99, emphasis added.
3. Nathaniel Lewis, *Unsettling*, 192.
4. Cronon, "Trouble with Wilderness," 69.
5. N. Lewis, *Unsettling*, 192.
6. Branch, *Reading the Roots*, xiv.
7. Watts, "Exploring," 14.
8. Branch, *Reading the Roots*, xxiii.

9. Soja, *Thirdspace*, 6.

10. See Giles, *Global Remapping*; Ronda, *Lewis and Clark*; Rowe, *Literary Culture*; Watts, *American Colony*.

11. Power, *Critical Regionalism*, 18.

12. See Neil Campbell's *Rhizomatic West* and *Post-Westerns: Cinema, Region, West* for concise literature reviews of critical regionalism.

13. Campbell, *Rhizomatic West*, 3.

14. The exception being Krista Comer's *Landscapes of the New West* and *Surfer Girls in the New World Order*, which examine "critical localisms" revealing "from below" ecofeminist activism. See also Heise, *Sense of Place*, and Nixon, *Slow Violence*, which are sympathetic to and seem to practice, but not invoke, critical regionalism.

15. Ronda, *Lewis and Clark*, 1.

16. Ronda, *Finding the West*, 68, 69.

17. Calloway, *Our Hearts Fell to the Ground*, 3.

18. Campbell, *Cultures*, 3.

19. Lewis and Clark, *Journals*, xxiv.

20. Ronda, *Lewis and Clark*, 3.

21. DuVal, *Native Ground*, 4. Emphasis in original.

22. Lewis and Clark, *Journals*, xxvii; unless otherwise noted, all quotations related to Lewis and Clark's journey are reproduced as they appear in the edition of their journals listed in the bibliography.

23. Ibid., xxvi.

24. Ibid., xxvii.

25. Ronda, *Finding the West*, 39–55.

26. Branch, *Reading the Roots*, xxiii.

27. Hsu, "Literature and Regional Production," xi; Kollin, *Postwestern Cultures*, xiv.

28. Appadurai, *Modernity*, 3.

29. Lewis and Clark, *Journals*, 40.

30. Ibid., 54–55.

31. Ibid., 47.

32. Ronda, *Finding the West*, 26.

33. Adelman and Aron, *Borderlands to Borders*, 816; see also DuVal, *Native Ground*; Janin, *Claiming the American Wilderness*; Richard White, *Middle Ground*. LeMenager investigates the obstacles to nationalism this ambiguity presented after Lewis and Clark until the Mexican-American War.

34. LeMenager, "Trading Stories," 683.

35. Slotkin, *Fatal Environment*, 111.

36. Nathaniel Lewis, *Unsettling*, 19. Nonliterary texts are vital to studies of the early American West. LeMenager writes, "I use ... canonical literature as well as newspapers, dime novels, exploration journals, and political tracts" (*Manifest*, 5–6). Notably, she overlooks the valuable archive of natural history writing produced during this period, as does N. Lewis (19–31). Branch, on the other hand, calls for ecocritics to "closely examine environmental writing in many literary genres and rhetorical forms, from various periods, and organized according to a range of ideological assumptions" (*Reading the Roots*, xxi).

37. Townsend, *Narrative*, 99. Subsequent references will be given parenthetically.
38. Nathaniel Lewis, *Unsettling*, 46.
39. Bown, *Naturalists*, 170.
40. Branch, "John Kirk Townsend," 377. Branch characterizes this development—unwittingly enabled by Nuttall on his return from the Far West—as an oversight for which Townsend was never properly recognized or compensated.
41. Lyon, *This Incomparable Land*, 60, 63; Branch, "John Kirk Townsend," 373.
42. Watts, *Republic Reborn*, 22.
43. Ibid., 14.
44. Bown, *Naturalists*, 123.
45. See Rob Wilson, *Reimagining the American Pacific*, for a concise critical regionalist discussion of the West/Pacific as similar imperial constructs (60). Notably, Catlin, in "Letter 9" of his *Letters and Notes* (1844), contends with the notion and location of the "West." Catlin attempts to confront how perception and preconception shaped Westness, as well as its ever-receding tendency the closer one got to it. However, he makes no mention of Hawaii. See also Hsu's discussion of "The Circumpacific West" in "Chronotopes of the Asian American West" (152–55), which acknowledges the larger meaning of western spaces.
46. See Giles, "Transnationalism" and "Reconstructing American Studies"; Levander and Levine, "Hemispheric Literary History." While Irving's *Astoria* delineates the role Hawaii played on the commerce of this era, and Dana perhaps better depicts "Kanakas" on the mainland, the fact that Townsend's route took him from Saint Louis overland and finally to the islands makes it singular among contemporaneous accounts.
47. Tatum, "Spectrality," 7.
48. Rowe, *Literary Culture*, 87.
49. Wilson, *Reimagining*, 59.
50. In the language of the contact zone, Townsend—and his elegiac imperialism—here becomes Mary Louise Pratt's bourgeois, enacting what she calls "anti-conquest," in which the strategies of representation by the European subject seeks to secure his innocence in the same moment as he asserts European hegemony (*Imperial Eyes*, 7).
51. See Timothy Brooks, *Vermeer's Hat*. Brooks depicts an exchange of European weapons, South American silver, and Chinese porcelain driven by trade in North American beaver pelts, on routes typifying the complex connectivity between the West and even the least significant European community. Dana, too, posits a similar connection to the cattle hides generated in the California trade that were loaded by sailors and sent around the horn to eastern manufacturers, who then sent them back to California as shoes, bought by the sailors to replace their worn-out boots. Dana prefigures the abstract "world steer" Stephen Tatum traces on the commodity futures market from which I derive my concept of the global beaver (7).
52. In Campbell, *Rhizomatic*, 1.
53. Deleuze and Guattari, *Thousand Plateaus*, 19–20.
54. Comer, *Landscapes of the New West*, 129–30.
55. Buell, *Future of Environmental Criticism*, 77.

CHAPTER THREE

The "Humor of the Old Southwest" and National Regionality

Robert Gunn

HOW MIGHT WE understand the relationship between the globalization of American studies over the last two decades, a broad trend that encompasses transnational, transatlantic, transpacific, and hemispheric models of scholarly work, and the more recent emergence and future promise of a critical regionalization of American studies? From one point of view, regionalization might seem to render explicit a central aspect of the globalizing turn. After all, transnational spaces are types of regions, as are oceans and hemispheres. In this light, one promise of a critical regionalization of American studies would be to serve as a natural complement of the global turn, a strategic posture of critical balancing that emphasizes the need for ongoing reflection on the meaning of large, postnational regional entities in relation to other practices and purposes of local mapping as they unfolded historically and as fashioned in the topographies of critical scholarship.[1]

But from another point of view, when understood as descriptions of space-oriented processes that entail movements in time, globalization and regionalization would seem to point in opposite directions: as a process, globalization imagines something like "globalism" as a point of open and fully integrated arrival; by contrast, regionalization suggests processes of division and enclosure, the conditions and cultural circumstances through which the local becomes legible (as in the production of literary "regionalism"), and a concern for how geographically bounded identities are made and become politically salient for different constituencies across time (often pointedly in resistance to the forces of globalization itself).

In this essay, I approach regionalization from the standpoint of literary studies as a double-sided process that reflects some of the competing energies expressed above, considering the manner in which emergent cultural representations of the local in the mid-nineteenth-century United States reflect the centralizing work of American empire in the production of what I call national regionality. Whereas literary regionalization might be thought to consist of a set of historical, cultural, and imaginative processes through which localities emerge as distinct representational spaces within literary discourse, national regionality designates a style of regional representation of borderland spaces that is premised on their incorporation into the national body of the United States in the project of nineteenth-century westward expansion.

As a corollary, I consider the secondary uses of national regionality to characterize an entrenched strain of Americanist historiography devoted to a nationally developmental narrative for the emergence of U.S. literary regionalism in the latter part of the nineteenth century. For my case studies here, I consider some texts that may seem counterintuitive for this end: popular examples of the so-called Humor of the Old Southwest, often regarded as the first regionally specific fictional subgenre in the United States. But what, exactly, is "regional" about old southwestern humor? Twenty-first-century readers approaching this antebellum literary subgenre face a perplexing task in reconciling a regionally specific order of literary classification with a catalogue of writers and texts that, on any cursory view, projects a remarkably incongruous image of geographic dispersion.

By way of illustration, consider this short list of some prominent exemplars of the genre, indexed by regional focus: David Crockett (western Tennessee), Thomas Bangs Thorpe (Louisiana, Arkansas), Augustus Baldwin Longstreet (Georgia), Johnson J. Hooper (Alabama), John S. Robb (Missouri), George Wilkins Kendall (Texas, Louisiana again), Morgan Neville (Mike Fink's Ohio Valley), George Washington Harris (southern Appalachia), and Albert Pike (Texas, New Mexico, Mexico).[2] Allowing additionally for the fact that the sketches and "tall tales" of early southwestern humor were often recirculated through regional newspapers such as the *St. Louis Reveille* and the *New Orleans Picayune*, and national periodicals such as (most famously) William T. Porter's weekly *Spirit of the Times* out of New York, the commonplace view of the genre as fanciful varieties of "local color" is complicated further in light of wider systems of print culture that effected regional and national integration.

Yet if this preliminary accounting seems to challenge the utility of "the regional" as an explanatory designation of a particular literary subgenre, my purpose here is not to reject it as inaccurate in the present case but to underscore the degree to which its coherence for literary historiography relies on its coordination with two additional conceptual axes: temporality ("old") and modality ("humor"). Here, temporality entails both past and future orientations. While "southwest" is a regional term, its common designation as "old" suggests a geography that is obsolete. Residing in that temporal qualification is an implicit recognition of historical processes of regional transformation through which what is "south" or "west" (or "southwest") constituted a shifting physical and imaginative horizon vis-à-vis local, regional, and national frames of reference. At the same time, "old" carries a preliminary meaning that looks ahead to later trends in literary history (a sense made explicit in the other most common designation of this body of literature, as "early southwestern humor"). Indeed, despite a significant body of literary scholarship that treats it seriously on its own terms and situates it within antebellum U.S. culture, the final significance of early southwestern humor is seen predominantly to reside not within itself but to the extent that its concerns with locality, vernacular dialect, and "tall-tale" storytelling anticipate the documentary modes of American literary regionalism in the latter part of the nineteenth century.[3] Given that he was both a southerner and a westerner, it is perhaps inevitable that Mark Twain should stand as the adaptive prototype for this phenomenon of cultural reception and literary innovation—an assessment that has become virtually axiomatic in both Twain studies and studies of southwestern humor.[4] According to one distinguished Twain scholar in a recent essay, "almost every critic sees Twain as a unique culmination of nineteenth-century American traditions of humor."[5] Reflecting on this enduring valuation in a recent edited collection that leapfrogs Twain to consider the influence of early southwestern humor on later cultural contexts, Ed Piacentino notes that the authoritative view was that "the Southwestern humorists might have been consigned to oblivion" were it not for the recognition of their importance to Twain.[6]

As a consensus marker for literary history, this critical commonplace is particularly useful to the developmental narratives of literary periodicity, serving to elevate Twain for the realization of a more realistic program of literary regionalism that departs markedly and in kind from the past, even as it works to define his early nineteenth-century antecedents as primitive and quasi-literary. To the extent that it remains caught up in the backstory of the emergence of late nineteenth-century regionalism, the humor of the Old Southwest is foreshortened retrospectively in a manner that obfuscates the particular kinds of cultural and ideological work it performed in distinct historical settings for specific readerships and privileges instead matters of storytelling craft—a catalogue of stock local types and backwoods storytelling techniques that serve as the raw material from which more serious and technically proficient literary achievements can later be made.

To put the matters above somewhat differently, the "regions" of Old Southwest humor are not only geographical but historiographical also. Consigned to an inchoate, noncanonical space for which legibility and literary completion are provided by later writers such as Twain (or Faulkner, O'Connor, or Welty, et al.), a wide range of geographically dispersed and ideologically forceful texts are clustered by common convention within an unfolding narrative of national literary development. In the following sections, I read against this commonplace teleology by considering a few popular examples of the genre in terms of an expansionist discourse of the 1840s, a decade that culminated politically in the U.S. war with Mexico, and in which the federal policy of Indian removal was a momentous issue.

Doing so entails both a historicization of the climate of literary reception and a reorientation of examples of southwestern humor toward the print networks that shaped readerly understandings of the kinds of issues and anxieties humor served to manage and defuse. Rather than view "humor" as autochthonous expressions of distinct localities, then, I argue for an approach to reading humor that emphasizes its productivity for national regionality, in two primary senses: first, as a conventionalized and regionally transcendent literary strategy for bringing nonproximate geographic locations into common relation, and second, as the intentional readerly effect of that strategy, a mode of consensus-building transacted between writer, reader, and textual medium that fashions and clarifies social, political, and cultural attitudes toward westwardly shifting frontiers, borderlands, and zones of conquest.

WILLIAM T. PORTER'S *SPIRIT OF THE TIMES*: NETWORK COMEDIES

Although William T. Porter's New York weekly, *Spirit of the Times* (1835–61), was the most prominent national showcase for works of southwestern humor in the antebellum United States, its identification with a peculiarly American literary style in the 1840s was dictated more by economic circumstance than Porter's later professions of cultural nationalism might otherwise suggest. Modeling his magazine on British sporting journals such as *Bell's Life of London*, Porter reported on and reprinted news of horse racing from England as well as the United States, catering particularly (though by no means exclusively) to a plantation-owning readership in the slave states of the American South that identified with the cultural trappings of the English gentry class. As Norris W. Yates illustrated in his biography of Porter, one consequence of the Panic of 1837 and the six-year depression that ensued was the cratering of the southern horse racing circuit and the posh sensationalism of its lavish purses; consequently, Porter was forced to broaden his readership beyond the neo-aristocratic planter class that had previously formed his aspirational standard even as he relied increasingly on a growing body of moderately Whiggish middle-class correspondents (predominantly lawyers and journalists) to supply original content about the social and cultural margins of southern and western localities.[7]

A benchmark figure in this transformation is Thomas Bangs Thorpe, whose first contribution to the *Spirit*, "Tom Owen, the Bee-Hunter," in July 1839, thematizes this shift in editorial emphasis. While "heroes of the Turf and the common chase have been lauded to the skies," and names such as "Nimrod" and Davy Crockett are familiar to most readers, the "backwoods fraternity" of "Bee-hunters" are, Thorpe suggests, "comparatively unknown." In bringing this class of mythical figures to light in the form of his title character, Thorpe announces a fictional documentary vista onto the process whereby "a country becomes cleared up and settled."[8] In the form of its original publication in the *Spirit*, Thorpe's authorial identity was masked by an attribution of regionality—"By a New Yorker in Louisiana"—with his initials appearing at the end of the sketch. This form of regional, rather than personal, attribution for the *Spirit*'s correspondents was foundational to its new national identity (even as Thorpe's first story would prove paradigmatic in its simultaneous invocation and displacement of Native Americans from expansionist storylines, which I will discuss in greater detail below).

Relying on newfound talent such as Thorpe, Porter quickly converted his shift of editorial emphasis onto western correspondents into a positive marker of cosmopolitan purpose for the magazine, boasting in 1837 of "our thousand and one private correspondents scattered over the Union, the Canadas, and from beyond the seas."[9] The key element of that large network of correspondents was that it was preponderantly "private." Although he would later often advertise the works of Thorpe, George Wilkins Kendall, C. F. M. Noland, and others by name, Porter also emphasized that the larger share of his writers contributed their works anonymously. Indeed, Porter's emphasis on a vast, private network of interconnected correspondents formed a core component of readers' experience of the *Spirit* and inflects centrally the national profile of the dispersed forms of regionality its backwoods sketches collectively produced. Inaugurated as a weekly entry in 1836, the section "To Correspondents" began as a forum for succinct acknowledgment of letters received, noting chiefly new subscriptions (identified by subscriber initials), acknowledging the receipt of submissions, and answering discreet inquiries into racing dates, horse pedigrees, and the like.

By the 1840s that section of the weekly had evolved to a routine showcase of private jokes, knowing innuendo, and vernacular exaggeration characteristic of the backwoods humor featured in the *Spirit*'s articles but shared with private addressees in a public forum. The entry from September 11, 1841, provides a representative illustration of this style of address: "R. S. P. of B., is apprised that a suite of rooms in P. Place is now occupied by the two 'sons of a gun.' The eldest will write when the 'fixins' are in apple-pie order, and send 'an invite' for the first *soiree* of the season. There is 'A bright, wild, wicked, diamond pair' of eyes opposite, and as it is 'the longest pole that knocks down the persimmons,' it is hardly to be expected that the shorter Pilgarlic will be able to 'shine in this crowd.'"[10] This communiqué may, perhaps, have provided "R. S. P. of B." with something like actionable intelligence on the respective romantic prospects of two competing suitors (one tall, one short) with a bright and charismatic young woman in the autumn's social season. But for the *Spirit*'s tens of thousands of other readers, this notice provided something else—an entertaining palimpsest of backwoods speech overlaid onto an elite urban setting (a "suite of rooms" on "P. Place" serving as the clue that this news, ostensibly provided by Porter, refers to New York), and a sense of virtual participa-

The "Humor of the Old Southwest"

tion in a vivid game of social intrigue. Comedically, this sketch turns on the interplay of two dichotomies—urban/rural and insider/outsider—cleverly upending expectations by correlating rural speech patterns with the status of the knowing social insider. In doing so, it provides a nested insight into the *Spirit*'s construction of regionality for its readers, offering a sort of internal confirmation that the verbal play of backwoods vernacular marked as regionally distinct elsewhere in the journal functioned as an insider's linguistic code betokening membership in a knowing masculine fraternity. Because Porter's network of correspondents was organized through the nodal point of the *Spirit*, the image of regional projection Porter enacted through his journal's pages had a centralizing dynamic.

But Porter also emphasized the interconnection of that network; the image of regionality regular features such as "To Correspondents" projected was one of sociality, and not only of national centralization. Another entry from the same column above begins by noting that, "Y. N. O., in his personal allusions, is not wide awake to a circumstance connected with the fire at L., that would have turned him wrong side out with laughter had he heard of it: Ask J. R. T., or Geo. C. of V. The latter made a display that interrupted the fun, though it convulsed the spectators."[11] Although somewhat tantalizing in its mode of allusive disclosure, there's nothing particularly funny about this on its own terms; indeed, nothing very particular is offered here at all. What fire? What display? Where is "L."? or "V."? Veiled behind anonymous initials and oblique details, the existence of a joke is announced and then deferred to a future moment of social revelation for a singular party in an unspecified region elsewhere. Readers may have been left wondering at such games, but notices of this kind do not serve to create, and then frustrate, readerly expectations in any individual circumstance. That is to say, the punch lines were not the point. Instead, the purpose of the weekly "To Correspondents" column as it assumed its more expansive form in the early 1840s was implicit in its sheer volume of perpetually unfolding private allusion. Collectively, what they performed was not humor as such but rather the appearance of a bustling epistolary commerce that effected wide regional integration as a function of a common humorous sensibility.

"A GENEROUS FEELING OF EMULATION": CHARACTERIZING PORTER'S "NOVEL AND ORIGINAL WALK OF LITERATURE"

Capitalizing on the popularity of the works of backwoods humor with which the *Spirit* was increasingly identified in the 1840s, Porter published a compendium titled *The Big Bear of Arkansas, and Other Sketches, Illustrative of Characters and Incidents, in the South and Southwest*, with Carey and Hart in 1845, featuring as its title story the popular tale by Thomas Bangs Thorpe now widely regarded as the representative masterwork of the genre. In his "Preface," Porter makes a vigorous case for the national significance of the new style of works the volume contained: "a new vein of literature, as original as it is inexhaustible in its source," produced by a class of writers unrivaled in conferring "signal honour on the rising literature of America."[12] Central to Porter's case for the national distinction of this "new vein of literature" was its correlation to the network of correspondents he had cultivated through the *Spirit of the Times*—indeed, Porter attributes that literature's origination and development to "the novel design and scope" of the *Spirit*, which "became the nucleus of a new order of literary talent" (vii). Citing the early work of correspondents who documented the "strange language and habitudes, and the peculiar, sometimes fearful characteristics of the 'squatters' and early settlers" of the West, Porter suggests that "in the course of a few years a generous feeling of emulation sprung up in the south and south-west . . . until at length the correspondents of the 'Spirit of the Times' comprised a large majority of those who have subsequently distinguished themselves in this novel and original walk of literature" (viii).

What stands out in this characterization is the idea that a "generous feeling of emulation" can result in a "novel and original walk of literature"—one nominally devoted to the documentation of the diverse and hitherto unknown regions of the West and its distinct examples of local human types. Emulation as originality is outwardly an oxymoronic equation; but this notion is key to understanding national regionality as a style of representation in which regionality is premised on cultural processes of national incorporation. That is to say, national regionality depends not on the specificity of the local but on the evacuation of specificity from it, on the cultural standardization of regional variety and local type. This process turns on the largely anonymous character of Porter's network of correspondents, which remains here a central point of emphasis. Although he cites a number of exemplary figures by name (including some, like Caroline Kirkland, who have only a passing association with the *Spirit*), three times in the span of his short preface he asserts that he is not at liberty to disclose the identities of the majority of his correspondents, claiming in the last of these that he is "utterly precluded, by repeated injunctions of secresy [sic], from giving the 'name' or 'local habitation'" of any writer not expressly identified in the book's pages (xii).

NATIONAL REGIONALITY AND NATIVE DISPLACEMENT

If "secresy" of authorial identity and "'local habitation'" is an indispensable precondition of the development of a novel yet emulative regional literature, it is also central to the image of national regionality that literature collectively projects, one that reflects the material conditions of continental territoriality and looks beyond the geopolitical boundaries of the United States in 1845 to a new era of expansion. Its novel orientation is seen as a marked departure from the old. Crediting Cooper and Paulding as "the first to excite the imagination of the world by their inimitable delineations of back-woodsmen, trappers, and boatmen of the West," Porter consigns them also to "an earlier period—before the genius of Fulton had covered the mighty rivers of the new world in the West with a substitute for the 'broad horns' and flat boats, which took the place of the frail canoes of the aboriginal inhabitants of those 'happy hunting grounds'" (viii). In this, technology is the marker not only of epochal transition but of fundamental regional character. By Porter's reckoning, steamboats have displaced the "broad horns" and flatboats of a previous era, which once displaced the "frail canoes" of Native American peoples. But the "genius of Fulton" represents a technological revolution, an innovation of scale and of kind from the nonmechanized modes of river transport of previous eras, evidence "of the highest civilization, and . . . the enjoyment of all those social, moral, and intellectual blessings engendered by an enlightened public mind, a populous region, and generally diffused wealth and prosperity" (viii–ix). In the following paragraph, Porter is even more explicit in connecting the triumphal march of civilization of this new literary era to an ongoing project of westward territorial expansionism, one that has already taken hold "in regions so distant as rather to overlook the Pacific than the acknowledged boundaries of the Federal Union" (ix). Included in the volume is a sketch titled "A Yankee That Couldn't Talk Spanish," written by John A. Stuart, which exemplifies for the volume most pointedly the acquisitive orientation of the United States toward California while demonstrating a logic of expansionist humor.

Taking as its chauvinistic subject the disabling of Mexican guns at San Diego by Captain W. D. Phelps of the *Alert* following news of the 1842 capture of Monterey by U.S. forces, Stuart's odd sketch fictionalizes the Mexican response as a kind of impotent linguistic discomfiture. Avoiding retaliation for an overt act of war, Mexican officials are reduced by Stuart to hyperbolic expressions of outrage at Phelps's laconic statement that "*he couldn't talk Spanish*" and therefore had no explanation (or apology) to make for hostile military actions outside a declared state of war.[13] In a ridiculing contrast between the exaggerated linguistic dudgeon of Mexican officials and the terse statement of Phelps, Stuart equates Mexican failure of national resolve with their incapacity to appreciate the American style of speech-based humor.

Moreover, in his displacement of aggressive actions onto comedic speech acts, Stuart exemplifies a signal representational strategy of southwestern humor that served to elide the political contexts of conquered frontier spaces. This is particularly true of texts that issue from scenes of Indian removal and the federal management of displaced Native peoples, which constitute a central strain of the *Spirit*'s regional focus. Indeed, in the opening pages of *The Big Bear of Arkansas and Other Sketches*, Porter announces the deep involvement of this literature not only in looming military matters with the republic of Mexico but in representing the spaces of Indian removal as well. In addition to identifying eight U.S. Army officers by name and rank ("and a troop of other gallant officers of the U.S. Army, whom we are not permitted to name"), Porter boasts the contributions of "ex-Gov Butler and Mr. Sibley, the Indian agents" (x–xi). In many respects, the acts of narrative displacement that characterize the *Spirit*'s treatment of Indian removal proved more congenial to its storytelling style than did more homogeneous depictions of regimental life in western frontier spaces. Although the *Spirit* excerpted popular expeditionary narratives by Frémont and Emory, and published dispatches from military officers detailing active regimental life, such as Lieutenant J. Henry Carleton's "Dragoon Expedition to the Rocky Mountains" and "Return of the Dragoons from the Rocky Mountains" in 1845, these works, in the words of Norris Yates, "waxed dull and prosaic."[14] In contrast stand the humorous sketches belonging to what Yates labeled the "Fort Gibson cluster." During the 1830s and early 1840s Fort Gibson stood at the center of the federal administration of Indian removal and relocation in Indian Territory, processing tens of thousands of displaced Native peoples, and housed the largest military garrison in the United States.

Yet in the humorous sketches of life at Fort Gibson that best fit the profile of the *Spirit*, Native Americans are routinely vanished from representations of Indian Territory in favor of horse racing, animal fables, tall tales of wild game hunting, and send-ups of the cultural backwardness of white squatters. Pierce Mason Butler, former governor of South Carolina and federal Indian agent to the Cherokee Nation stationed at Fort Gibson from 1841 to 1845, contributed several sketches to the *Spirit*, including one titled "Western Life and Manners" that was later redacted in telling fashion by Porter for inclusion in *The Big Bear of Arkansas*. Presented in a mock-epistolary style that opens "Dear P—," the transparent framing device consists of an unidentified correspondent reporting that he had met "Governor B—," "a tall, stalwart, manly, and gentlemanly fellow, (about your build and height,) full of fun and humor," during a recent trip to Washington.

Couching himself behind the third person, Butler writes that "Governor B— [was] on his return from a council with the Cumanches, and other Indians of the Prairie, held west of the Cross Timbers." But rather than a story about Indian diplomacy and official duties one might expect, the narrator instead chooses to repeat a story told by the governor, "after a glass or two of potent old liquor," about a trip through the backwoods of the Washita River in which he takes liberties with his untutored white hosts by kissing all of the women and girls present at a backcountry wedding on the pretext that this is customary elsewhere.[15] Although the details of his diplomatic activities as Indian agent are provided as encoded clues to the sketch's actual authorship, the supplantation of Native diplomacy by backwoods farce is nevertheless striking. In his reprinting of the story for *The Big Bear of Arkansas*, Porter elides the Indian presence further by redacting the framing device altogether—beginning with the words of the embedded tale as narrated by the writer, and providing the clue of authorship in his own headnote, which states the author is "one of the most distinguished men in the Union," who, though unnamed, "will be recognized by most readers of the South and West."[16]

Another suggestive story in this vein is a fish-out-of-water tale from 1843 titled "A Sporting Adventure in Arkansas," contributed to the *Spirit* by "An Officer of the U.S. Army." The story depicts a hair-raising hunting expedition that originates on Cherokee land in Indian Territory and features a primly mannered naïf, "very genteelly dressed, but bearing a certain air about him, that spoke the money speculator." Bearing paper money from the "United States Bank" he hopes to exchange for specie, the stranger ("Mr. Knight") accepts from a tavern keeper an offer of sassafras tea. The exchange that follows neatly encapsulates several key tensions in the production of national regionality in wordplay that figures a relationship between commerce, indigenousness, and national belonging:

"That's genuine tea, and I'll swear it—planted it, grew it, gathered it, and drank it."
"Why it *has* a peculiar flavor, sir, and not unpleasant."
"I'm glad you like it, stranger. Take another cup—I reckon if this tea was *im-*ported to some other country, it would bring a fair value."
"Excuse me, sir, for correcting you but you mean *ex*ported."
"So you know what I mean, stranger, its no use correcting. But you're larnt, and I an't, that's the difference.
"Will you inform me, if you please, the manner of cultivating this tea?—for I was not aware of there being any raised in the United States."
"There's things raised in the Cherokee nation, stranger that ain't dreamed of in the States. As to the raisin', we plough deep, so light, and harrow in; after that there's no trouble—just use the roots."
This took the stranger all aback—muttering the word "roots" several times to himself, he arose from the table.[17]

The baffled and repeated muttering of the word "roots" that concludes this scene suggests play with the meaning of "roots" itself, an idea that here could refer to a number of things—practices of agriculture; descent-based claims of identity; the indigenous properties of persons and crops (things "raised in the Cherokee nation . . . that ain't dreamed of in the States"); and, homonymically, the expansionist "routes" that connect Indian Territory and treaty lands both to unlettered squatters like the tavern keeper ("Briggs") and risible speculators such as Knight.

In *The Black Atlantic*, Paul Gilroy explored in a different context the interplay of the routes/roots homonym. Pointing out that traditional accounts of racial identity are constructed on the basis of "roots" and "rootedness," Gilroy argued for an expanded view of racial ontology that also recognizes the "routes" of identity as comprising a space-oriented "process of movement and mediation."[18] In this

Spirit story set in the heart of Indian country, we see something like the colonial inverse of Gilroy's approach; where Gilroy is figuring an emancipatory model of diasporic critical consciousness, the story models a form of expansionist consciousness through light wordplay, making claims of "rootedness" in land subject to the "routes" and networks of settler colonialism.

Cultivating sassafras by leaving "the roots" alone, Briggs in effect lays claim to a vested rootedness in the soil of Indian Territory. The ideological availability of this land for white-settler claims of indigenous possession depends within the story on a metonymic substitution of a native plant (sassafras) for Native peoples (the Cherokee), and more broadly on the ambiguity of Indian Territory as a zone of national regionality. In this, the phonetic doubling and repetition of the "roots"/"routes" wordplay has an additional valence that underscores the earlier perplexity about the meaning of importation/exportation for the exchange of indigenous commodities and the nature of the trade routes that exit and enter Indian Territory. Are the "routes" connecting Indian Territory to the United States foreign or domestic?

The answer this story suggests is that they are both—foreign and domestic, regionally apart and nationally bounded—in a manner that echoes Justice Marshall's famously oxymoronic definition of Indian sovereignty, "domestic dependent nations," as established in *Cherokee Nation vs. Georgia* (1831). Of course, the Cherokee people whose "nation" this nominally is, and for whom sassafras was a traditional remedy and foodstuff, are entirely absent. In the metonymic substitution of a native plant for Native peoples, the story displaces profound questions about race, removal, and political sovereignty with a genial comedic setting of backwoods hospitality in which indigenousness is evacuated of meaning and the "routes" of Cherokee removal are figuratively erased. In that space of absence, Briggs appropriates indigenousness for himself.

As an outside interloper bearing paper money appraised as worthless by the white inhabitants of Cherokee national territory, Mr. Knight represents a monetary system that seeks, but is refused, integration into the economy of Indian Territory. Instead, the story figures the routes of national incorporation on social and cultural grounds. Within the frame of the story, the former is accomplished with the conversion of indigenousness into the exchange value of the commodity form, backed not by paper but by a local system of social relations. Refusing Knight's paper money in offer of payment after a hunt turned practical joke, Briggs proclaims, "Here's my hand—now's all right. The next time you want to hunt panthers, fish, or drink tea, come see me, and I'll treat you well." But, more broadly, the form of printed currency this story endorses is that of the *Spirit* itself, a textually circulating medium through which regionally generated humor completes a national circuit of identification by the implied assent of readerly appreciation. Readers in New York may have carried paper currency, but (unlike, say, the Mexican officials lampooned in Stuart's tale of California) they know when to laugh.

Although "A Sporting Adventure in Arkansas" and Pierce Butler's "Western Life and Manners" are now obscure texts, they carry significance in demonstrating the "generous feeling of emulation" that characterize for Porter the fulfillment of a "new vein of literature." Their broad prototype is provided in the works of the *Spirit*'s most famous contributor, Thomas Bangs Thorpe, and the pattern of Native American regional displacement he had established in expansionist tales such as "Tom Owen, the Bee-Hunter" and "The Big Bear of Arkansas." These stories are often seen as nostalgic lamentations on the passing of American wilderness that are more mythic than political in character; but as Richard Slotkin has suggested, the identities of the Indian killer and that of Thorpe's backwoods figures who represent the transformation of wilderness regions are deeply interconnected.[19] Both tales feature an unnamed outsider whose first-person narration brings to public notice an extraordinary frontier type whose phenomenal destructive powers (Tom Owen, insatiable feller of ancient trees that contain honey hives; Jim Doggett, prodigious hunter of a mythical bear) figure the wholesale transformation of wild borderland regions. Both stories also function explicitly as metonymies for the disappearance of Native peoples.

In "Tom Owen," Thorpe amplifies a by-then widely reprinted legend that held that the presence of honeybees foretold the advance of white civilization. In one of her letters promoting emigration to Austin's Colony in Texas, published in 1833, Mary Austin Holley speaks enthusiastically of the abundance of honey trees in the vicinity of Bolivar, their excellence of quality, and the high price that can be obtained for honey and wax in local markets. She then adds these lines: "It is a very curious fact, in the natural history of the bee, that it is never found in a wild country, but always precedes civilization, forming a kind of advance guard between the white man and the savage. The Indians, at least, are perfectly convinced of the truth of this fact, for it is a common remark among them, when they observe these happy insects, 'there come the white men.'"[20] These lines are reprinted almost verbatim in the spurious *Col. Crockett's Exploits and Adventures in Texas* and recirculated in several posthumous versions of Crockett's *Life* detailing his journey into Texas and death at the Alamo.[21] In the reprinting of this legend in the Crockett texts, the view of Texas on Crockett's arrival is lush and inviting, game is abundant, and Native Americans are virtually absent as a hostile presence.

That Thorpe intended this allusion is made clear by the multiple references to Crockett by name in the original "Tom Owen," along with his mention of Paulding's fictional namesake for Crockett, Nimrod Wildfire. But whereas the bee hunter in *Col. Crockett's Exploits and Adventures* is a cheerful and peaceful presence, a portent of the easy settlement guaranteed by Crockett's national martyrdom at the Alamo, Thorpe's Tom Owen is a merciless killer that recalls the nonfictional Crockett who burned alive forty-six Muscogee warriors trapped in an Alabama house in 1813: a "conqueror among his spoils" who smokes out the "enraged mob" of bees until "his enemies are destroyed." Moreover, while the association of bees with an "advance guard between the white man and the savage" is central to the legend in its earlier tellings, Native Americans are entirely absent in Thorpe's story. In their place is a metaphorical excess of violence in an unfolding series: the "spoils" "soon to be devoured, and replaced by the destruction of another tree, and another government of bees" (247). Native Americans, in other words, are displaced from Thorpe's story; but the process of settlement that honeybees, and bee hunters, announce is, in Thorpe's telling, irremediably violent; and even as Tom Owen calls to mind the Crockett who committed atrocities during the Creek War, the personification of the bees Thorpe performs with such phrases as an "enraged mob," "enemies," and "government" invites us to imagine the objects of that violence as human.

The slaughter of Native Americans casts a shadow over "The Big Bear of Arkansas" as well, though Native Americans are (as in the case of "Tom Owen") absent as a personified presence in the story itself. In a text most famous for the rich vernacular and storytelling prowess of Jim Doggett, the first human sound that is heard is an "Indian war whoop"—an exotic phonetic event that belongs not to a Native American but to "The Big Bear of Arkansaw" himself, who uses that sound as a sort of prelude to his virtuosic tale.[22] When read in the context of Thorpe's 1846 collection, *The Mysteries of the Backwoods*, though, the meaning of the "Indian war whoop" and its relation to acts of storytelling takes on a violent dimension.

In "The Disgraced Scalp-Lock," Thorpe offers something of a valedictory on the career of Mike Fink, the "'last of the flat boat-men,'" and relates the story of his "last and best shot."[23] Mike Fink's "last best shot"—an unprovoked potshot that severs the scalp-lock of a Cherokee named "Proud Joe," deeply humiliating him, and setting in motion events that lead to violent death—is presented in the story as a percussive repetition of a previous act of insulting speech. Approaching Louisville on the Ohio River, Fink discovers a group of Native Americans Thorpe paints as the type of "renegade Indians who lived about the settlements, and which is still the case in the extreme south-west," and who "generally are the most degraded of their tribe—outcasts, who, for crime or dissipation, are no longer allowed to associate with their people": "Without ceremony, [Fink] gave a terrific war-whoop; and then mixing the language of the aborigines and his own together, he went on in savage fashion and bragged of his triumphs and victories on the war path, with all the seeming earnestness of a real 'brave.' Nor were taunting words spared to exasperate the poor creatures, who, perfectly helpless, listened to the tales of their own greatness, and their own shame, until wound up to the highest pitch of impotent exasperation" (123). As in the case of "The Big Bear," a "war whoop" commences a powerful performance of verbal mastery; here, Fink combines Native languages and his own hyperbolic English in order to taunt and humiliate his Native audience (including Proud Joe), an act that inspires other insults from passers-by and forces the "renegade Indians" to "retreat ashore, amid the hooting and jeering of an unfeeling crowd" (123). Seeing Proud Joe farther downstream sometime later, now on the Mississippi, Fink casually shoots the scalp-lock from the base of Proud Joe's skull from a great distance—a virtuosic act of marksmanship that, like his previous act of verbal ridicule, is entirely unprovoked and which is here figured as a form of speech.

When a group of white witnesses attempt to apprehend Fink for what they assume at first to be an act of murder, Fink warns them off by raising his rifle muzzle, which, "if it *spoke* hostilely . . . was certain to send a *messenger* of death" (126, emphasis added). Setting this story some thirty years in the past, Thorpe posits Fink as the exemplary representative of a frontier age prior to the advent of the steamboat and men such as Jim Doggett of "The Big Bear," and in doing so casts Doggett as Fink's storytelling heir. But where speech is explicitly coded as a form of violence for men such as Fink, the anti-Indian animus of backwoods oral performance is elided for a later generation of storytelling. Indeed, when the image of dead Indians is raised in "The Big Bear of Arkansas," Doggett is quick to quash the inference. In response to an Arkansas settler who complains that the bottom soil surrounding Doggett's cabin is unfit for cultivation, because "it's full of cedar stumps and Indian mounds" (an image that also recalls the stumps created by the likes of Tom Owen), Doggett reports to have replied, "'them ar 'cedar stumps' is beets, and them ar 'Indian mounds' ar tater hills'" (22). Like "A Sporting Adventure in Arkansas" and Butler's "Western Life and Manners," the production of national regionality in "The Big Bear of Arkansas" turns on the erasure of Native American inhabitation.

Tall-tale storytelling is the modular template that operates in the space of that erasure, providing in the very form of its hyperbolic exaggerations of regional exoticism and difference the ironic fulfillment of national conventionality. In the substitution of "tater hills" for "Indian mounds," the political and territorial space of Indian removal is fictionally and figuratively remapped, in Doggett's words, as "the creation state, the finishing-up country—a state where the *sile* runs down to the centre of the 'arth, and government gives you a title to every inch of it" (17, emphasis in original).

THE U.S. WAR WITH MEXICO:
SOUTHWESTERN HUMOR AND MALE SENTIMENTALISM

By way of conclusion, I want to consider briefly one last form of cultural work southwestern humor performed in the production of national regionality, specifically with respect to the U.S. war with Mexico (1846–48), and its relationship to what Dana D. Nelson has called the "unfinished business of male sentimentalism."

In an essay that connects her figure of national manhood to the idea of presidential representativity, Nelson suggests that the U.S. president "stands in a symbolic space of loss in the democratic imaginary . . . teaching us to desire from representation not politicalness but the strong sensation of unconflicted recognition, and indeed a protection from politicalness." In this, the model of republican political representation is eclipsed in national experience by an "aestheticizing relation" she calls "representativity," in which a male sentimental ideal is offered "*as* the subjectivity of citizenship."[24] For Nelson, the subjective form of the president's idealized body, beginning with Washington, is both "hard" and "soft"—masculine and impassive on one hand, sentimental and empathetic on the other—an equation that assumed particular "hardness" with the campaign of Indian killer William Henry Harrison in 1840 (334). Following the U.S. war with Mexico, I would suggest that southwestern humor provides an additional regional component to Nelson's model of presidential representativity, providing a well-rehearsed cultural repertoire through which the representativity of Zachary Taylor could be imagined as the embodiment of national regionality.

In August 1848 the *American Whig Review* commended for its readers the recent publication of *The Taylor Anecdote Book* as a worthy illustration of Zachary Taylor's credentials for president: "After they have read the capital anecdotes of the war, of which there is a large assortment, let them peruse the letters of the General himself, and consider the virtue of honesty, and whether it would do the country any material harm to have an honest man for President."[25] The author of *The Taylor Anecdote Book* was identified as "Tom Owen, the Bee-Hunter," a pseudonym that would have been instantly recognizable not only to readers of the *Spirit* but also to American readers who had been following events of the war. During the war Thorpe had traveled extensively with U.S. forces and had published fairly conventional volumes of reportage (*Our Army on the Rio Grande* [1846] and *Our Army at Monterey* [1848]) that received wide readerships; but, at war's victorious end, *The Taylor Anecdote Book* provided Thorpe with an opportunity to try something new. As an example of presidential campaign literature, *The Taylor Anecdote Book* presents an unusual readerly experience. Prefaced by a four-page "Biographical Sketch" of Taylor and concluding with an eleven-page "Appendix" titled "General Taylor's Letters in Reference to the Presidency," the bulk of the volume consists of some three hundred brief sketches of Taylor's campaign in the U.S. war with Mexico.

Composed largely of testimonies of U.S. military valor and masculine fortitude, denigrations of Mexican national character and military competence, effusions of patriotic sentimentality, and sensational descriptions of battle, the book also includes many humorous depictions of life in the war zone, such as the following speech attributed to a "Western volunteer" recently returned from the Battle of Monterey:

"Thunder!" said he, "you may talk about your yearthquakes and sich; but I can tell you what, boys, one real, ginewine scrimmage, like we had at Mounterey, is worth all the Fourth of Julys that ever knocked into one. Thar ain't nothin' in creation like it. Getting' tight on brandy smashers makes a man feel pretty considerable elevated for a while—it's very inspirin' for a man of lively imagination—but if you want to feel taller than a shot-tower, bigger than an elephant, and stronger than a jackass—if you want to feel like you could pull up a tree by the roots, and sweep all creation into kingdom come with the brush end—if you want to see further, hear better, holler louder, jump higher, and step further and quicker, than you ever did in your life—all you've got to do is jest take a hand with Old Zack at them infernal Mexicans, and be ordered up to the pints of their lances and bayonets, like we was at Mounterey."[26]

As this exuberant vernacular showcase makes clear, *The Taylor Anecdote Book* signaled in one sense Thorpe's return to the exaggerated forms of white backwoods speech that had made him famous before the war. But the purpose of that vernacular here, as the *Review*'s endorsement suggests, now had a different character. To follow the *Review*'s recommended sequence of reading *The Taylor Anecdote Book* is to undergo a culturally synthetic process of national identification in which the "virtue of honesty" evidenced by General Taylor's letters is primed for revelation by an experience of wartime documentation that is fragmentary, frequently burlesqued, and populated by figures recognizable as stock regional types, such as the "Western volunteer" whose ventriloquization of Mike Fink's brag is "quoted" above.

Rather than serving as the counterweight to such exaggerations, the image of Taylor is intimately integrated as a presence within them. Indeed, in this sketch, titled "High Pressure Description," the "Western" speaker asserts his pride as a veteran by vouching for Taylor; Taylor, in turn, is unironically validated as a stalwart leader by a forthrightly hyperbolic style of comedic performance. The force of this equation is emphasized in the text by virtue of its placement immediately prior to a sketch titled "General Taylor Taking Leave of the Veterans," which recounts Taylor's farewell to the veterans of Matamoros and Monterey, prior to their redeployment for the Battle of Vera Cruz.

Narrated in a more straightforwardly patriotic and sentimental vein, the sketch concludes with a transcript of Taylor's remarks on that occasion. Professing "'deep sensibility that the commanding general finds himself separated from the troops he so long commanded,'" Taylor "'extends his heartfelt wishes for their continued success and happiness, confident that their achievements on another theatre will redound to the credit of their country and its arms.'" Speaking in the formally impersonal third person, Taylor voices here an openly sentimental tribute of esteem to veteran soldiers—including, to follow the scheme of Thorpe's larger representation, the fictional "Western volunteer" of the previous sketch whose own sentimental admiration for Taylor completes an emotional circuit of identification. What Taylor's formal language lacks in personalized character the linguistic fulsomeness of the "Westerner" fills. Displacing any excess of emotional ardor and rudeness of speech onto a fictional type, the image of Taylor presented here nevertheless assimilates those qualities into a comprehensive and comprehending figure that is both hard and soft, embodying national regionality and elevating it as victorious image of presidential command.

If it is difficult to imagine this style of wartime exaggeration serving the presidential ambitions of, say, John Kerry, it is in part because of the different relationship humor has to national dialogue today; but it is also because the politics of regional belonging inflect national representativity in a manner that has proved remarkably enduring since the 1840s. While it is widely accepted that Kerry's obvious linguistic marking as a New Englander impeded his chances for the presidency (signifying both cultural peculiarity and elevated class station), George W. Bush was largely perceived to have benefited in his presidential campaigns from a Texan style of swagger and drawl that belied his own privileged upbringing and Ivy League education. If Bush might be thought of in this sense as a latter-day type of a Crockett or a Jackson, Kerry's stiff but earnest manner was more akin to Thorpe's portrayal of Taylor's sentimental but featureless formality—but minus the earthy specificity of Thorpe's linguistically marked "Westerner" necessary to complete the circuit of national representativity as stock regional type. In the end, what is perhaps most noteworthy about southwestern humor is not the explanatory utility its stock types may have for interpreting the popular appeal of political figures such as Kerry and Bush, or literary inheritors such as Twain and Faulkner, but its purpose in constructing national regionality on the basis of social consensus building in periodical print discourse. In this, the point of humor is not the gratification provided by the punch line but an alignment of social sensibilities such that the joke may simply be understood—the completion of an ideological and literary circuit that binds the development of national print networks to the conquest of western regions, and fictions of regional role-playing to an expansionist imagination of national fulfillment.

NOTES

1. The emergence of critical regionalism is tied closely to postwestern and postfrontier literary studies, particularly in work by such critics as Campbell, Comer, Kollin, and Stephen Tatum, and also important recent works on geography and space in the American long nineteenth century. See Kollin's influential edited collection for the University of Nebraska Press, *Postwestern Cultures*, and particularly Comer's contribution to that volume, "Everyday Regionalisms in Contemporary Critical Practice" (30–58); Campbell, *Rhizomatic West*; see also Brückner and Hsu, *American Literary Geographies*; Hsu, *Geography and the Production of Space*.

2. Of course, if this accounting projects geographic incoherence, it is partly the result of my fashioning it as such; even so, any regional survey of these texts would become even more vexed in view of the genre's basis in a style of humor. Indeed, from the standpoint of Thomas Chandler Haliburton, the Canadian comic writer and first major anthologizer of several of the writers mentioned here, the dialect-driven "tall tales" now associated most readily with the Southwest would need also to include works from Down East, such as Seba Smith's "Jack Downing" stories (Maine) and Haliburton's own "Sam Slick" tales (Nova Scotia). See Haliburton, *Traits of Western Humor*.

3. Walter Blair stands at the forefront of early critics to devote serious attention to the genre; his works, beginning in the 1930s and updated and expanded through the 1970s, remain indispensable sources. For the most significant and comprehensive recent treatment of the genre, see Justus, *Fetching the Old Southwest*. See also Budd, "Gentlemen Humorists"; James M. Cox, "Humor of the Old Southwest"; Inge and Piacentino, *Humor of the Old South*; Rickels, *Thomas Bangs Thorpe*.

4. De Voto is generally cited as the originator of this trend with his 1932 book, *Mark Twain's America*; for a later and influential affirmation of this equation, see also Lynn, *Mark Twain and Southwestern Humor*; Covici, "Mark Twain and the Humor of the Old Southwest."

5. Sloane, "Mark Twain and the American Short Story."

6. Piacentino, "Intersecting Paths," 9.

7. Yates, *William T. Porter*, 13–28; see also Arac, *Emergence of American Literary Narrative*, 32–34.

8. [Thomas Bangs Thorpe,] "Tom Owen, the Bee-Hunter. By a New Yorker in Louisiana," 247.

9. Quoted in Yates, *William T. Porter*, 14.

10. "To Correspondents," *Spirit of the Times* 11, no. 28 (September 11, 1841): 325.

11. Ibid.

12. Porter, "Preface," *Big Bear of Arkansas*, vii. Additional quotations will be cited parenthetically.

13. Stuart, "A Yankee That Couldn't Talk Spanish," in *Big Bear of Arkansas*, 141.

14. See Yates, *William T. Porter*, 75–77, quotation on 76.

15. [Pierce Mason Butler,] "Western Life and Manners. By a New Arkansas Correspondent of the 'Spirit of the Times,'" *Spirit of the Times* 14, no. 3 (March 16, 1844): 25.

16. Porter, "Life and Manners in Arkansas, By an Ex-Governor of a Cotton-Growing State," in *Big Bear of Arkansas*, 154.

17. "A Sporting Adventure in Arkansas. By an Officer of the U.S. Army," *Spirit of the Times* 12, no. 45 (January 7, 1843): 531.

18. Gilroy, *Black Atlantic*, 19.

19. Slotkin, *Fatal Environment*, 131; on Thorpe as a writer of wilderness nostalgia, see Littlefield, "Thomas Bangs Thorpe."

20. Holley, *Texas*, 44.

21. [Richard Penn Smith,] *Col. Crockett's Exploits*, 79. The text was originally published in Philadelphia by T. K. and P. G. Collins. The attribution of authorship to Richard Penn Smith is made by James Atkins Shackleford, whose research on the many different texts associated with Crockett is indispensable. See Shackleford, *David Crockett*, 253–81.

22. Thorpe, "The Big Bear of Arkansas," 15.
23. Thorpe, "The Disgraced Scalp-Lock," 119, 136. Additional quotations cited parenthetically.
24. Nelson, "Representative/Democracy," 327.
25. Review of "*The Taylor Anecdote Book. Anecdotes of Zachary Taylor, and the Mexican War.* By Tom Owen, the Bee-Hunter. Together with a brief Life of General Taylor, and his Letters," *American Whig Review* 2, no. 2 (August 1848): 220.
26. [Thorpe], *Taylor Anecdote Book*, 136.

CHAPTER FOUR

West Indian Emancipation and the Time of Regionalism in the Hemispheric 1850s
Martha Schoolman

AS AN AESTHETIC and an identity formation, regionalism is traditionally understood in terms of spatial and temporal exemption. What is regionally distinctive grows and develops on a small scale and expands—if at all—ever so slowly and slightly outward. And, despite regionalism's typical identification with the U.S. literary culture of the 1890s, region's claims on place are generally aligned with persistence rather than novelty. Emerging as if from a fathomless past, regional identity appears to offer stubborn resistance to the forces of modernity and homogenization arriving from without. In contrast to this traditional account, more recent critical refigurations of region and regionalism, in the manner of similar deconstructions of nationalism, have attended to the production of regional identity as a project invested not simply in conserving traditional ways but as an ideologically conservative project that aims to invent tradition and cover over contention, demote less desirable identities, and repress less flattering histories.[1] Such critical interventions focused on reading regionalisms for what they spatially exclude and temporally repress have proven enormously productive as contributions toward the "worlding" of regionalism, especially in their efforts to discern a relation between regionalism as a deliberately bounded tradition of intranational self-description and the resistant porosity of a transnational and multiethnic United States.

However, as Hsuan L. Hsu has recently demonstrated, interventions of this latter sort do appear to have the limitation of aiming to deconstruct regional-*ism* as a cultural project while giving a perhaps unwarranted epistemic priority to the region itself as a stable entity that has somehow survived to occlude the material conditions of its own invention. As a solution to this problem, Hsu proposes that critics shift their understanding of the regional from a category premised on the mythic stability of regions toward a focus on the connection between aesthetic regionalism and the dynamic material process of what he calls "regional production." Such an approach, as Hsu demonstrates, both offers us the possibility of broadening our understanding of regional aesthetics and allows us better to attend to literature's place in the workings of capital that make regional distinctiveness legible in the first place.

In this essay, I intend to develop the implications of Hsu's insistence on reading the region as a space of capital by turning critical attention to an early and ultimately ephemeral project of attempted literary and economic regionalization. This project emerged and briefly claimed broader hemispheric public attention as part of the literary and political debates within the United States and around the Anglophone world over the likely and desired shape of postemancipation Jamaica in the early 1850s. By focusing on postemancipation Jamaica at midcentury, I wish to build on Hsu's insight into literary regionalism as a discursive development in concert with the market transformations of the late nineteenth century in order to examine the literary significance of a particular north-south conversation publicized by the Scottish-Jamaican reformer William Wemyss Anderson and advocating the export of a New England ethos marked as culturally and economically regional as the solution to Jamaica's perceived economic ills. By translating Hsu's retheorizing of region from the 1890s to the 1850s, and from the United States to Jamaica, I aim to read this early instance of New England regional identity offered for transnational export as a way of thinking about literary regionalization not only as a realist reflection of economic transformation but also as a discursive site where literature's powers of both fabulation and anachronism may be pressed into service as solutions to perceived economic crisis.

EMANCIPATION AND THE PRODUCTION OF ANTEBELLUM REGIONS

Hsu's work provides an alternative to the tautological dangers attending the study of literary regions by redescribing regionalization in terms borrowed from the discipline of cultural geography that theorize the region not as a stable essence but rather as an epiphenomenon of the development of capitalism. For, as Hsu argues, advancing capitalism not only produces the need for (or the appearance of) the large-scale interchangeability among locales routinely lamented as a condition of globalizing modernity; it also produces the need for new types of geographically located specialization and, therefore, uneven development. As a matter of literary critical practice, Hsu takes his insight into the economic logic of regional variety as an impetus to read region from the perspective of capital itself rather than from the perspective of any one place. For Hsu, a region is not simply—or not only—a stable entity *recruited to* the needs of capital but rather a materially and therefore culturally discernible unit *created by* the needs of capital, "from the outside in." As a way of theorizing the role of literature in the making and remaking of regions, furthermore, Hsu attends to "the ways in which literary works produce, reimagine, and actively restructure regional identities in the minds and hearts of readers."[2] Hsu offers this formulation as a way of first highlighting the global investments of the period-specific literary genre known as regionalism, and then positing a broader investment in the regional in late nineteenth-century U.S. literature more generally. By doing so, he suggests that regionalism as an aesthetic category may be reframed as a style of literary engagement with and commentary on the process of regionalization.

Thus, to summarize Hsu's take on aesthetic regionalism's arguable *locus classicus*—although Sarah Orne Jewett's stories of the fictional town of Dunnet Landing, Maine, describe regional identity in terms of spatial autochthony and temporal stability—Hsu's materialist approach attends to the details Jewett's work offers surrounding the region's "prior cosmopolitanism" that Captain Littlepage of *Country of the Pointed Firs* so bitterly laments.[3] Before Dunnet Landing was rendered aesthetically regional as the seemingly static and affectively nostalgic tourist destination that attracts the novel's narrator (and thus the new market relation that she embodies as tourist), it held a specialized place in the global marketplace, secured by its export of lumber—white pines, but also at times those eponymous pointed firs—for the construction of wooden schooners, the demand for which receded rapidly in the age of steam.[4] The seagoing people of Dunnet Landing became global citizens, that is, by ushering their desirable regional product into the global marketplace. That product, in turn, provided for a time the seemingly indispensible material substrate for the market's functioning. These emissaries of the cosmopolitan then brought the global marketplace back home in the form of the repeatedly remarked-over domestic objects relating to preparation and consumption of tea, that quintessential product of long-distance trade in the West.

In both salient phases of the town's life, that is, region is produced in relation to capital—first drawn in and hastened toward modern trade relations with the larger world, and then spatially isolated and temporally "left behind" by external economic changes. For Hsu, in other words, regionalism is to be understood as a reflection on this oscillation, rather than as the expression of any stable, rooted essence. In Hsu's hands, in other words, historical changes in market-driven human mobility (as opposed, indeed, to the work of staving them off) are very much the subject of *Country of the Pointed Firs*.

By recasting region as a matter of markets as much as of identities, Hsu furthermore expands the definition of regionalism beyond a short list of aesthetic characteristics, and toward a broader project—under way according to Hsu in Booker T. Washington's accounts of the Tuskegee Institute and Frank Norris's meditations on the global wheat market—of making sense of the particular shifting relations of capital in the late nineteenth century. However, in Hsu's work the temporal horizon of this broadened generic definition of regionalism remains nonetheless familiar. The literature of regional production remains a product of the period roughly spanning the end of Reconstruction and the first decade of the twentieth century. I would like to propose here that we build on Hsu's conceptual work on regionalism, capital, and temporality toward a second, diachronic expansion. Developing further his notion of regionalism as a literature of market transformation, I suggest that we make central what is presumed but goes largely unarticulated in Hsu's work, as in most other critical treatments of region: namely, the instrumentality of the century-long process of the emancipation of enslaved Africans in the Western Hemisphere in the making and unmaking of regions. For I contend that the geographically variable and temporally staggered transition from enslaved to compensated agricultural labor is the site where the regionalization process—a process that, to recast Hsu's point somewhat, may be understood to flare up as a cultural problematic at the real or perceived historical hinge between economic ruin and redevelopment—is perhaps not surprisingly laid bare by the intensity of discursive focus on what kinds of social and economic relations could, or should, follow the dismantling of chattel slavery.

A version of this point is already available within the traditional protocols of American studies. For despite regionalism's habitual focus on matters of land rather than labor, the standard periodization of regionalism typically aligns it with nostalgia for a regional distinctiveness marked chiefly as antebellum. And, as the long career of Jewett's acknowledged literary forebear Harriet Beecher Stowe should make especially clear, it is only a very partial view of the archive that would make it possible to separate her tripartite literary engagement with the regional particularities of New England, the South, and the West from her long-standing (if still shamefully underestimated) commitment to emancipation. Speaking more broadly, the spatial and temporal unevenness of emancipation is of course central to the traditional Americanist understanding of the political production of regions, which is often said to emerge from the north-south dichotomy created by the wave of voluntary, gradual emancipations in the northern states along the Eastern Seaboard in the late eighteenth and early nineteenth centuries, in contrast to the emancipation process imposed on the South following the Emancipation Proclamation and during the era of Reconstruction. The West, though archetypally "free territory," of course underwent periods of rapid transformation between the Louisiana Purchase and the Civil War, as the states covered by the Northwest Ordinance remained free, the trans-Mississippi West became the new center of agricultural production and thus forced labor, and the political shape of the western territories was increasingly determined by the eastern states' desire to "balance out" their conflicts as pre- and postemancipation regional economies through westward expansion.

However, this traditional understanding of the intersection between region and emancipation does not acknowledge that slavery and the emancipation process, as economic systems and as economic theories, did not operate solely with regard to the nation. Rather, the hemispheric unfolding of the emancipation process prompts us to ask how the concept of region might be changed spatially as well as temporally when it is examined in relation to the longer transnational nineteenth-century history of slavery and abolition.

NEW ENGLAND ABOLITION AND THE "PROBLEM" OF JAMAICA

If one is to take the long view, the nineteenth century as a whole, from Haitian independence in 1804 to Brazilian emancipation in 1888, could be described as the "age of emancipation." Narrowing the temporal frame somewhat, we could view the period from 1833, the year of the passage of the British Emancipation Act, to 1863, the year of the U.S. Emancipation Proclamation, as the "era of uneven emancipation," that span of time during which the frequency of state-administered transitions in the Americas from chattel slavery to some form of officially designated freedom rendered transnational comparisons among labor arrangements especially salient. As the first of these emancipations-from-above, British emancipation attracted particular interest in the United States as evidence of the practicability of emancipation without war, effected moreover within what was, from the U.S. perspective, the familiar frame of the transnational Anglophone world. The Emancipation Act, as historian Gale Kenny notes, "decreed that on August 1, 1834, all slaves under the age of six would be freed. All other slaves would become apprentices—until 1838 for those nonpraedial, or domestic slaves, and until 1840 for praedials, or those who worked in the fields."[5] The Emancipation Act, it should be added, included compensation in the amount of £20 million sterling for the masters for their "lost property." The "apprenticeship" plan was also designed for their benefit, intended to teach the enslaved to adapt to their designated new role as wage laborers on the sugar estates and the masters to retain their control over land and labor.

In practice, of course, the program did not quite proceed as planned. The planters of Antigua and Barbados chose to forego apprenticeship in favor of an immediate transition to paid agricultural labor, and in the places where it was adopted, the apprenticeship arrangement caused such tension between planters and the formerly enslaved and such outrage among reform activists within Britain that it was abolished on August 1, 1838. Jamaica, the largest, most economically significant, and most geographically varied of the British West Indies, became a particular focus of defenders and critics of the emancipation process. Agrarian unrest in Jamaica in December 1831 and January 1832, the so-called Baptist War, helped force Parliament's hand toward emancipation.[6] Furthermore, established land use practices among the enslaved proved especially incompatible with the administrative fantasy of a population of emancipated Africans for whom freedom would be synonymous with wage labor on the estates oriented to the international sugar market. Under slavery, planters had furnished the enslaved with housing and land on the estates for their own use in feeding themselves and their families without the planters' direct financial support. The produce of these lands, known as provision grounds, became the center of a local peasant economy among the enslaved, and the lands themselves became the locus of kinship relations and patterns of inheritance that had little to do with either the export economy or the imperial property relations in which they were embedded. Under slavery, the enslaved's "other lives" on the provision grounds existed more or less symbiotically with the needs of the sugar estates.

After slavery, work on the provision grounds came to be viewed as competition for the freed people's time and attention, and the planters often retaliated against the formerly enslaved for withholding their free labor by charging rent for use of land the people worked and the homes they had inhabited, in order to coerce them into joining the cash economy. Taking advantage of Jamaica's particular topography, as well as the increasing number of abandoned estates, the formerly enslaved often responded by leaving their former homes entirely and establishing subsistence farming on other lands.[7]

Keeping in mind Hsu's insight that late nineteenth-century regionalism should be understood as a literature of market transformation, what is perhaps most notable about the transnational literature of British West Indian emancipation is its collective dual character as a document of failure and a fable of success. As Thomas Holt notes, historians of slavery have long debated the profitability of slavery and the economic imperatives behind emancipation, as well as the extent to which British imperial markets continued to need West Indian sugar.[8] However, the contemporary conversation about what came to be regarded as the "problem of Jamaica" that in the Anglophone North shadowed the emancipation process was, initially at least, only minimally engaged with the question of what the formerly enslaved were doing with their time. More prominent by far was the question of what they were *not* doing, and perhaps more particularly, with what the estates were *not* producing. Indeed, understood in its moment principally as a voluntary bureaucratic process of emancipation from above—rather than as an unstoppable convulsion from below as in Haiti—British emancipation was widely described in terms of a social experiment, the results of which were watched and debated from a range of ideological positions in the United States and Britain. Statistics about the export of sugar, rum, and coffee, the price of real estate, and the wages commanded by the formerly enslaved were consumed eagerly on both sides of the Atlantic. Those who weren't satisfied with mere data traveled to the British Caribbean to see for themselves, often contributing to the growing, oddly hybrid genre of the West Indian travelogue-cum-agricultural report, in which the authors would provide traveler's recommendations about accommodations, health, and hygiene, along with descriptions of life on the now free-labor plantations, and transcriptions of interviews with planters and the formerly enslaved.[9]

In view of the economic disappointment that Jamaica appeared to represent, a key element of the transnational conversation about the British Caribbean turned therefore to debates about how to interpret Jamaica's lackluster performance as a *free-labor* sugar colony and what to do about it. Perhaps the best-known literary response to Jamaica's woes then as now was Carlyle's series of racist rants "on the negro question," advising among other things the restoration of slavery to exact labor from those who "would not work" otherwise.[10] The best-known policy response, offered more or less on the same logic, was the decision by Parliament to allow the importation of indentured labor from Africa and Asia to compensate for the widely reported reluctance of the formerly enslaved to perform plantation labor of a kind otherwise indistinguishable from their previous work, and often for their former masters, apparently regardless of the level of wages offered. There were, however, other responses, and responses that did not so precisely retrace the lines of imperial markets and governance, nor did they focus exclusively on the sugar market. West Indian emancipation became, for example, an important discursive locale for U.S. political debate in the antebellum period, as various metrics for the success or failure of British emancipation were recruited by proslavery southerners and Free-Soil northerners to bolster their own forecasts for the shape of emancipation in the United States.

As I discuss in greater detail elsewhere, the U.S. abolitionist reception of British emancipation was itself highly ambivalent. On the one hand, the bare historical fact of British emancipation helped galvanize the U.S. abolitionist movement by offering incontrovertible proof that slavery could in fact be abolished on a large scale and in the agricultural context of the global South, without the feared acts of retributive violence against the master class. The legislative achievements of the British antislavery movement furthermore served to solidify ties among abolitionists on both sides of the Atlantic, as well as to present African Americans in particular with a threefold sense of Great Britain as free soil. Especially in the wake of the Fugitive Slave Act, formerly enslaved African Americans visited, wrote about, and in some cases permanently expatriated themselves to Canada, the British Caribbean, and Britain itself with growing frequency. In both mixed-race and majority African American contexts, furthermore, August 1, the day of transition in the British West Indies, was increasingly adopted through the 1840s as an abolitionist holiday, a British "Emancipation Day" (still celebrated in the Caribbean today) offered as ironic rejoinder to the hollow claims of "Independence Day" celebrated in the United States one month earlier.[11]

However, the emphasis within the broader transatlantic intellectual culture on the economics of emancipation seemed increasingly to be a source of something like ennui to those U.S. activists motivated more by what we might today recognize as Christian social justice radicalism than by the dubious moral claims of classical liberalism. We can see this, for example, in the most committed of radical abolitionists' recourse to sarcastic scare quotes where conversations over the economics of West Indian emancipation were concerned, as in Wendell Phillips's introduction to Frederick Douglass's 1845 autobiography, in which he recalls that, "in 1838, many were waiting for the results of the West India experiment, before they could come into our ranks. Those 'results' have come long ago; but, alas! Few of that number have come with them, as converts."[12] Or indeed in the title of Richard Hildreth's 1855 exposé of Jamaica's ongoing reliance on the slave trade after 1808, called *The "Ruin" of Jamaica*.[13]

The dominant literary conversation about the British West Indies in the antebellum period, particularly in the 1840s, is, as I have suggested, one of negation and failure. However, an intriguing minor chord within the broader field of abolitionist/anti-abolitionist dispute is the collection of texts that we might designate as West Indian regionalist fiction. I refer here to those books, pamphlets, and letters engaged in inventing a New England regional economic identity on West Indian soil—precisely on the principle adumbrated by Hsu's account of regionalization—that new land and labor arrangements can indeed be imposed from without. For just as the New England abolitionist exasperation with the counterproductive recirculation of West Indian news did not temper their growing enthusiasm for annual August 1 celebrations, it furthermore did not forecast an end to abolitionist internationalism, whether initiated from New England, Great Britain, or indeed the much discussed and diagnosed British Caribbean itself. Rather, whereas the British West Indies became a kind of unstable signifier for U.S. politics, it would appear that New England's self-understanding as regional could itself be put into circulation and pressed into service by and for the benefit of the British West Indies in general, or Jamaica in particular, as a site whose broader economic and geopolitical affiliations were regarded as themselves up for renegotiation. For it appears that while the British West Indies were being assessed as a possible future for the U.S. South, at least one peripatetic West Indian intellectual was using his familiarity with the emergent mythos of New England cultural and economic self-representation in service of a reverse operation. Whereas the northern view of the emancipation process read the temporality of emancipation in relation to geographic contiguity, Anderson proposed to read emancipation as enabling new affiliations among places that were to be understood as regional, even though they were clearly noncontiguous. Offering his own particular combination of the economic languages of ruin and redevelopment, Anderson offers a prospective redescription of Jamaica as a Caribbean copy of New England, and one that was to invent itself with the combined help of emigrant African Americans and white northern patronage.

A HEMISPHERIC REGIONALISM?

William Wemyss Anderson's footprint on the historiography of transnational abolition is vanishingly small.[14] Yet he enjoyed a long career in transnational abolitionism and postemancipation land reform, spanning from the 1830s, when he apparently relocated to Jamaica during the early stages of West Indian apprenticeship, to his death in Kingston in 1877.[15] If our still somewhat obstructed view of the world of the transnational circuits of nineteenth-century print among the United States, Great Britain, and the West Indies is to be trusted, he appears to have cut a briefly ubiquitous figure in the North Atlantic world around 1850 as an advocate for emigration to Jamaica among both African Americans and certain categories of Euro-American whites. Various U.S. abolitionist press outlets recorded his presence at antislavery meetings in New York, London, Buffalo, and Toronto—as well as in Kingston—promoting Jamaica as a prospective "home of the colored man . . . the place in which he can train his children virtuously and prosecute without hindrance any branch of industry he may please to select."[16] That effort at recruitment, furthermore, was clearly part of a larger postemancipation project of social and economic reorganization in the West Indies, a project that we might wish to understand as his life's work given the timing of his initial emigration.

Emigration and colonization schemes often have a quality of ephemerality given their speculative nature, the ambivalent investments and ambiguous motives of even their most voluble proponents, their well-documented failure to take hold on a large scale, and their tendency to be discussed in private or public meetings rather than in print. However, Anderson left evidence of his tenacity in published books and pamphlets, as well as through his epistolary and reported presence in the news. Two lengthy letters from Anderson appear in the travelogue *Jamaica in 1850*, published in 1851 by the Free-Soil partisan and *New York Evening Post* editor John Bigelow. Anderson himself published three pamphlet-length works in 1851 promoting Jamaican emigration to different audiences. *Jamaica and the Americans*, first presented as a lecture to the Colonial Literary Society in Jamaica, was published as a book dedicated "To Americans, whose state of health renders it desirable to have, during the winter months, a place of residence in a genial climate, in the vicinity of their own magnificent country, without involving the painful necessity of wholly abandoning it." A pair of lectures cocredited to the British abolitionist John Scoble, and titled *Canada and Jamaica: Two Addresses Addressed to the Colored Citizens of New York*, was issued by the same publisher. The third is a heavily annotated and liberally supplemented reprint of a 1671 Jamaican emigration pamphlet, *A Description and History of the Island of Jamaica, Comprising an*

Account of Its Soil, Climate, and Productions, Shewing Its Value and Importance as an Agricultural Country, and a Desirable Place of Residence for Certain Classes of Settlers, which Anderson reports having discovered in the library at Yale, intending rather surprisingly to use the almost two-hundred-year-old information as a means to entice new settlers, as if Jamaica could reasonably be described as the blank slate of agrarian possibility imagined by the pamphlet's original Irish author, John Ogilby.

Each text, from the title forward, is at least bilateral in its geographical orientation. *Jamaica and the Americans* is presented as a speech to Jamaicans *about* Americans, but its published form—printed as it was by the religious publisher Stanford and Swords in New York—functions to describe Jamaicans *to* Americans in the familiar locutions of U.S.-American literary expression. No copies of *Canada and Jamaica* appear to be available in the United States, but a colloquy among Anderson, Scoble, and Douglass carried in *Frederick Douglass' Paper* suggests that the lectures are meant to persuade "the colored citizens of New York" that Jamaica is a superior destination for prospective emigrants. In that conversation, Anderson and Scoble responded to a resolution offered apparently by Douglass that "the home of the free black man is most emphatically where his black brother is still held as a slave" with a description of Jamaica as a place where free African Americans would have the opportunity to succeed as individuals—especially within the professional classes—in ways that are impossible in the United States or in Canada. In view of the increasing southern exclusion of free African Americans and continuing northern segregation, Anderson and Scoble propose Jamaica as something of an integrationist paradise, where African Americans can, alongside a multiracial postemancipation Creole population, live out those foundational yet elusive American values of equality and free access.

Anderson's version of Ogilby's *Description and History of the Island of Jamaica* not only repackages a text written by an Irishman for English and Irish readers as one written by a Jamaican for U.S. readers; in the process it also performs several additional feats of spatiotemporal synthesis. The pamphlet's title page declares the British West Indies as "the true and final homes of the civilized colored races." Anderson's prefatory statement then goes on to specify a second kind of climate-based determinism that manages to somehow both racialize illness and medicalize race by adding that "there are two classes who can never be comfortable in a northern climate: the one comprises those whose delicate natural structure needs the aid of dry warm weather to soothe and protect it; the other, the descendants from a stock, which having had its origin in a hot country, and imbibed in consequence certain constitutional peculiarities, can only have perfect development in a similar country."[17] Anderson then concludes the pamphlet with the striking suggestion that the United States consider annexing Jamaica because its climate and its agricultural potential are so well suited to the needs and aspirations of these two sectors of the U.S. population who, as we saw in the dedication to *Jamaica and the Americans*, should be expected to desire both a genial climate and *geographic proximity* to the continental United States.

Taken together, then, Anderson's writings are notable for the range of seemingly contradictory climate determinisms they bundle together into one overarching argument for Jamaican emigration. At one level is the materiality of the interaction between the particular interior conditions of a single person's body and the temperature and moisture of the outside air. People suffering from tuberculosis did indeed find it painful to breathe in cold and damp conditions and thus felt some of the collateral symptoms of tuberculosis, such as pleurisy, alleviated by warmer weather.[18] People in this category often did choose to relocate and so would be asked to choose Jamaica after comparing it to other locations in the U.S. South, the Caribbean, and southern Europe. At another level is the very different kind of assumption that a person's particular genealogical origins determine one's ideal habitat. By this reasoning, Jamaica would be a more natural destination for African Americans than either Canada or the U.S. North. Based on the conversation in *Frederick Douglass' Paper*, however, it would appear that Anderson is at some level aware that African Americans perceive themselves more inconvenienced by social and legal barriers than by the weather, so he has tailored his arguments to include inducement to emigration based on the kind of social and economic arguments that underpinned, for example, the disbursement of western lands in the United States, alongside the racialist claims of the traditional colonization movement.[19] At a third level lies Anderson's insistence on the variability of Jamaican agricultural zones such that typically tropical crops such as sugar and coffee can be grown in the same general geographical area—though at different elevations—as crops more typically favored in temperate areas such as "corn, wheat, potatoes and flax."[20] Thus, Anderson appears committed to viewing the ideal residence of human beings as determined by individual circumstances—such as health status or simple preference—as well as by a racialized destiny that should be taken as transcending health status or preference. At the same time, when he comes to consider those living organisms that really do thrive on particular kinds of soil and require particular kinds of air, Anderson appears committed to understanding plants as more adaptable than humans, and the soil itself as a passive receptor of human effort rather than a living, shifting organism in itself.

Anderson's studiously partial understanding of the adaptability of people and plants would seem logically to suggest a certain essential hostility to the traditional idea of region as a bounded contiguity whose distinctiveness can be discerned from within as well as without. After all, the very notion that Jamaica could be remade by swapping out plants and personnel suggests an imperial vision of Jamaica as a node in long-distance trade, distinctive for its weather rather than its culture, with the implication that the economic prostration of Jamaica could thus be recouped by an infusion of fresh personnel. Such an imperial view of the marketplace is, it should be noted, very much aligned with Hsu's idea of regionalization as a function of large-scale market relations. However, on closer examination, it does appear that Anderson's particular approach to land reform partakes not simply in a reassertion of regional significance as a fixed point in a shifting world system but moreover in a metadiscourse of regionalization according to which a developing cultural language of New England regionalism is imagined as an available blueprint for a future Jamaica whose cultural and economic life is to be defined by neither imperial monoculture—with the cultivation of sugar and coffee for export—nor the extreme locality of already-existing trade and land use practices developed among the formerly enslaved and oriented toward subsistence rather than capital accumulation.

In the pairing of Anderson's *Jamaica and the Americans* and Bigelow's *Jamaica in 1850* the complex discursive interaction between region as an economic and geographic unit and regionalization as a superstructural cultural project of what might be called popular economics emerges with particular clarity. At a certain level, Anderson's and Bigelow's shared belief that Jamaica should be annexed to the United States as the first postemancipation southern state could itself be viewed as a species of regionalization. Mixing Free-Soil republicanism and the hemispheric logic of the Monroe Doctrine, Bigelow suggests that, as a matter of both culture and contiguity, the United States, for all of its own internal turmoil at midcentury, is nonetheless poised to extract maximum profit from the Jamaican soil:

> I will not attempt to conjecture what a change in the revenue policy of Great Britain might effect for her colonies, nor how far a restoration of slavery would contribute to repair the losses which its abolition is supposed by some to have caused; but of two things I am clear. I am clear that neither course would have saved them from bankruptcy, for they were all mortgaged for more than they were worth at the time slavery was abolished and when their staples were protected in the English markets by prohibitory duties. I am also clear that if Jamaica was an American State, she would speedily be more productive and valuable than any agricultural portion of the United States of the same dimensions, and that neither the Emancipation Bill of '33, nor the Sugar Duties Bill of '46, are fatal obstacles to a prosperity far exceeding anything which Jamaica has ever known.[21]

Bigelow then goes on to underline that the economics of annexation are as cultural as they are agricultural. Whereas the members of the British mercantile and political classes look on Jamaica with despair, Bigelow writes, "An American has but to glance his eye over the industry of this island, to discern ample causes for its declining condition, which are quite independent of those to which it has been charged."[22]

As Bigelow develops his argument further, it becomes increasingly clear that the "Americanization" of Jamaica is more precisely to be imagined as its "New Englandification." The former sugar estates, he argues, are too large and should be subdivided into plots such as could be owned, managed, and worked locally by a version of the New England yeoman farmer, described here as "the intelligent *white* operative with no capital but his muscles, his character, and his ambition" (emphasis added). These small farms, he furthermore argues, should be laid out on the New England plan, arrayed around central sugar mills that would enable small landholders to prepare raw material for export more affordably, precisely on the model of the Maine lumber business so central to the prehistory of Jewett's work. Indeed, Bigelow here laments that "the people [of Jamaica] will send to Maine for lumber, and pay $25 a thousand feet for it, rather than be at the trouble of cutting down their own magnificent forests. There is not a single saw mill upon the island."[23]

It is moreover abundantly clear that read again alongside Anderson, this arguably postcolonial economic vision depends on the realignment of Jamaica away from not only the traditional assumptions of British mercantilism but moreover from those economic relations based on geographic contiguity that would definitively fix Jamaica's regional status as Caribbean. Indeed, Anderson states quite baldly what Bigelow mostly implies about the careful work of regionalization that their shared economic vision imagines. Anderson constructs *Jamaica and the Americans* around three main tropes. First, he adopts familiar discourse of U.S. westward migration to encourage Jamaicans to reject both the city and the plantation and to reattach themselves to the idea of the small family farm. Representing rural Jamaica as unspoiled wilderness, Anderson writes, "Would that the day had arrived in Jamaica, when a leader for her youth should arise (too many of whom are now prostrated under a long-continued depression) who, resolving to achieve independence at any cost for himself and them, and to vanquish the apathy that has so long borne down the energies of the country, would call to his fellows, 'A home in the woods! Who will follow?'" In addition to giving Caroline Kirkland's titular phrase a rather more earnest spin than she likely intended, Anderson appears furthermore to channel the literary ideal of Cooper's Leatherstocking when he writes, "A man of that class, with his fowling piece and small supply of provisions in a bag, fearlessly enters the woods and makes his log-house, and subdues the land around him, until he is surrounded by fertility and abundance and beauty."[24]

Anderson's second main argument concerns a way of life that seemed by 1851 to be on the wane in New England, what Horace Bushnell, whom Anderson may very well have encountered during his visit to Connecticut, named "the age of homespun."[25] Implicitly attacking the white female idleness associated with the plantation, and calling indeed on the "woman of valor" of Proverbs 31 ("She seeketh wool and flax, and worketh willingly with her hands"[26]), Anderson praises the domestic industry of women in New England: "I cannot leave this important topic without seeking further to acquaint you with the nature and extent of the industry of American females. They are occupied in all the business of the dairy—the small stock, the spinning wheel, the loom, and the knitting wires.... Now what value of home manufactures could such a body of workers send to market?"[27]

Indeed, as if to underline the literalism of Anderson's position, an 1851 item in the "Foreign Intelligence" department of the *Liverpool Mercury* noted the following:

JAMAICA.

We have files of Jamaica papers to the 10th ultimo. There is no news of importance since our last advices. The cholera is nearly disappeared from the island.

Mr. Wemyss Anderson had imported two spinning wheels from the United States, one for cotton and the other for flax, for the purpose of endeavoring, if possible, to draw attention to the manufacture of home-made yarns, for knitting stockings and other articles of domestic use, such as are used in the farm-houses of the United States and Canada. The subject of immigration of free labourers from the United States and Canada continued to attract the attention of the inhabitants of Jamaica.[28]

Anderson then extends his discussion of female home manufacture into praise for the women of the Lowell mills, singling out for special notice Harriet Farley, editor of the *Lowell Offering*, as providing a model for socially useful female productivity that would in turn energize the cultural life of Jamaica if her example were to be emulated.

At a certain level, what Anderson has to offer here is mere anachronism. When combined with his interest in the seventeenth-century promotional literature of Jamaica as a site of laborless abundance, his prescription that Jamaican men and women rediscover their own connection to the Protestant ethic indicates a particular species of imperialist delusion of the endless availability of "virgin" land.[29] Indeed, it is interesting to note that Anderson's discussion is so fully unexceptional to the ears of U.S. readers then and now that it takes a moment to recognize that he is essentially appealing for racial regeneration among a demographically small group of waning power, when the transnational abolitionist movement more broadly had by this point taken to articulating its vision of Jamaica's future as a place of *African* self-help. When Anderson calls for a "leader for her youth" to lead a prostrate Jamaica to self-sufficiency and imagines such a youth on a New England model, he echoes Emerson's own yearning after the same mythical creature as articulated in "Self-Reliance": "A sturdy lad from New Hampshire or Vermont, who in turn tries all the professions, who *teams it, farms it, peddles*, keeps a school, preaches, edits a newspaper, goes to Congress, buys a township, and so forth, in successive years, and always, like a cat, falls on his feet, is worth a hundred of these city dolls."[30] For Anderson, that "sturdy lad" seems of necessity a white person, an assumption that Bigelow appears to share. At another level, however, and one that may perhaps speak to the neoagrarian and neoartisanal proclivities of the popular economics of the twenty-first century, Anderson's conception of Jamaica as a ruin that can be redeveloped through a certain ethos adjustment toward simplicity, craft, *and* profitability is perhaps especially recognizable today as economic regionalism's classic gambit. As anachronistic as it may initially seem, Anderson's thinking may also be read as a precursor to widely discussed phenomena such as the re-regionalization of postautomotive Detroit by those always-white urban "pioneers" of the small-batch distillery and the conscientiously small but investor-friendly urban organic farm.[31]

NOTES

1. Examples of this large critical corpus especially formative for the present project include Renan, "What Is a Nation?"; Benedict Anderson, *Imagined Communities*; Zagarell, "*Country*'s Portrayal of Community"; Loughran, *Republic in Print*.

2. Hsu, "Literature and Regional Production," 37, 38.

3. Ibid., 39.

4. Ibid., 42.

5. Kenny, *Contentious Liberties*, 56.

6. Holt, *Problem of Freedom*, 13–21.

7. This account draws on Holt, *Problem of Freedom*, and Kenny, *Contentious Liberties*, as well as Paton, "Flight from the Fields."

8. Holt, *Problem of Freedom*, 22–33.

9. Examples of this genre include Thome and Kimball, *Emancipation in the West Indies*; Gurney, *Winter in the West Indies*; Phillippo, *Jamaica*; Bigelow, *Jamaica in 1850*. Bigelow's book will be discussed in greater detail below.

10. Thomas Carlyle, "Occasional Discourse on the Negro Question" (1849); *Latter Day Pamphlets* (1850); and *Occasional Discourse on the Nigger Question* (1853). I discuss this material in a different context in Schoolman, "Violent Places," 13–14.

11. See Katchun, *Festivals of Freedom*; Kerr-Ritchie, *Rites of August First*; Rugemer, *Problem of Emancipation*; Schoolman, *Abolitionist Geographies*.

12. Douglass, *Narrative*, 43.

13. Hildreth, *"Ruin" of Jamaica*.

14. Magness and Page, *Colonization after Emancipation*, 29–33, 137 n. 19; Kenny, "Manliness and Manifest Racial Destiny," 151–78.

15. In an 1849 letter to the *National Era* newspaper, Anderson refers to himself as having "resided [in Jamaica] for the last fifteen years." "The British West Indies," *National Era*, October 25, 1849, via Accessible Archives (accessed December 18, 2014). The unpublished "Sermon on the Death of W. Wemyss Anderson, Delivered July 21, 1877, in the Scotch Kirk, Kingston, Jamaica" delivered by a Rev. John Radcliffe is listed in the catalogue of the British Library. I have not had the opportunity to examine this document.

16. "Reported for Frederick Douglass' Paper. Remarks of John Scoble," *Frederick Douglass' Paper*. October 2, 1851, via Accessible Archives (accessed December 18, 2014).

17. William Wemyss Anderson, *Description*, 11.

18. Sheila M. Rothman, *Living in the Shadow of Death*.

19. On the equivalence between colonization and westward expansion, see Freehling, *Reintegration of American History*, esp. 138–57.

20. "Reported for Frederick Douglass Paper. Remarks of John Scoble," *Frederick Douglass' Paper*, October 2, 1851.

21. Bigelow, *Jamaica in 1850*, 74.

22. Ibid., 75.

23. Bigelow, *Jamaica in 1850*, 109.

24. Anderson, *Jamaica and the Americans*, 16.

25. Bushnell, "Age of Homespun"; Ulrich, *Age of Homespun*, 12–40.

26. Anderson, *Jamaica and the Americans*, 18.

27. Ibid., 18–19.

28. "Foreign Intelligence," *Liverpool Mercury*, May 6, 1851, 354, Gale British Library Newspapers Collection.

29. As Gale Kenny notes, "Although New England and Jamaica shared a common heritage as British colonies, they were separated by a social and cultural gulf as well as geographical distance. As the forefathers of the American missionaries [of Oberlin College] built up their city on a hill in Massachusetts, another Puritan, Oliver Cromwell, oversaw the British Navy's capture of Jamaica from the Catholic Spanish in 1655." Kenny, *Contentious Liberties*, 65.

30. Emerson, "Self-Reliance," 275.

31. Leary's recent work on the regional economic aesthetic of "Detroitism" has been especially helpful for my thinking on this matter.

SECTION 2

Mappings
Creating Places

CHAPTER FIVE

The Labor of Regions
A Comparative Analysis of the Economic and Literary Production of Three Southern Regions in the Eighteenth-Century Atlantic World

Steven W. Thomas

THE MARLBORO MAN, Uncle Ben, and Captain Morgan, among other famous cultural icons invented by advertising agencies, sell both a product and a place: tobacco, rice, and rum are the products; the places are the West, the South, and the Caribbean. The metonymic relationship between commodity and region, one standing in for the other, has been commonplace in popular as well as literary culture for centuries. In contrast to such essentializing symbolizations of regional identity, an art installation by Kara Walker in 2014 presented a different, more critical vision. The setting for her art was the former Domino Sugar refinery in Brooklyn, New York. Once the largest sugar refinery in North America, it was shut down in 2004, just a few years after one of the longest labor strikes in New York history, and will soon be turned into posh apartments and condominiums with a harbor view.[1] Inside one of the factory buildings, Walker's provocative 75-foot-long, 35-foot-tall statue of a sphinx, whose features evoke stereotypes of the slave mammy, is coated in white sugar. Also on the factory floor, as if to serve the viewing public, are several human-sized statues of slave boys made out of brown sugar and molasses. For a few months, before her installation was dismantled and construction of the apartment complex began, Walker's controversial art presented its audience with an uncanny sense of the labor that produces sweetness, the racist sexualization of that labor, and the complex Atlantic economy that connects Caribbean bodies with New York machinery.

Like Walker's installation, recent scholarship on region and regionalism raises the question of how location matters for literature by considering each location's economic and cultural relationship to larger national, Atlantic, hemispheric, and/or global dynamics. I address this very issue by establishing how the aestheticization of local differences ideologically represses and displaces the unique problems of the different economic conditions of particular regions. I argue that a critical approach to the region ought to address literature's relationship to labor, not simply in terms of class conflict and slavery but also in terms of the complex social configurations around particular forms of labor management within a transatlantic economy. In order to understand the uniqueness of each region, one cannot analyze only the literature from that region; rather, one must compare and contrast the symbolic repressions and displacements that differ in relation to the different ways that agrarian capitalism organized itself.

My essay will focus on the literature of three regional economies and the cash crops that drove those economies in the eighteenth century: Tidewater tobacco, Lowcountry rice, and Caribbean sugar. Though my conclusions about regional differences are based on a wide range of literary and nonliterary texts, for this essay I focus my analysis on those texts most likely to be assigned in a literature class: Thomas Jefferson's *Notes on the State of Virginia* (published 1787) and Ebenezer Cooke's poem *Sotweed Redivivus* (1730) about tobacco; George Ogilvie's poem *Carolina; Or, the Planter* (1791) about rice; and James Grainger's poem *Sugar Cane* (1764) about sugar. My comparative analysis emphasizes the very different organizations of labor in each of those three regions. By emphasizing the labor and economic production of cash crops, I dislodge the more traditional division of America's regions along sectarian lines of North versus South and East versus West. Even though much of the recent scholarship on region and regionalism aims to radically revise the mapping of American literary history in terms of a global South in ways that critically pluralize the history of southern culture's many intimate connections to the Caribbean, Europe, and Africa, much of the scholarship on the regional literature of the late nineteenth and early twentieth centuries (when regional literatures were conscious of themselves as such and when regionalism actually became an "ism") persists in assuming a "South" created as a political response to the Missouri Compromise, the Dred Scott decision, the Civil War, Reconstruction, Jim Crow, and *Plessy v. Ferguson*.[2]

Instead, moving away from the paradigm of a divided nation-state, a comparative trans-Atlantic analysis of the different locations of economic and cultural production reveals how the Tidewater, Lowcountry, and Caribbean regions were all part of the same economic world system but related to that system in very different ways. David Armitage distinguishes among three historiographic approaches: circum-Atlantic (analyzing the movement of people, commodities, and culture), cis-Atlantic (analyzing a single location's relationship to a world system), and trans-Atlantic (comparative analysis of different locations within a world system). Armitage borrows the distinction between cis-Atlantic and trans-Atlantic from Jefferson's *Notes on the State of Virginia*, which also reflects on how one writes about the relation between local cultures and Atlantic commerce. Of the three, Armitage advocates for the trans-Atlantic (with the hyphen, emphasizing the metalevel of comparative analysis, distinct from the word "transatlantic" without the hyphen, which simply indicates the crossing of an ocean) as the most illuminating.[3] Comparing the literature from different cash crop economies that were part of an integrated mercantile system highlights how authors anxiously responded to the specific forms of slave management on their plantations and imagined reforms. What this essay will show is that the literature from the tobacco colonies expressed embarrassment over the nature of their crop, the close day-to-day proximity to slave labor, and chronic debt due in part to an unpredictable market; to redeem and reform their economies, they imagined the figure of the virtuous yeoman wheat farmer and movement west. In contrast, literature from rice colonies expressed pride in their slave economies but were disconnected from the day-to-day labor and the technical knowledge and skill possessed by their slaves; they focused on the preservation of almost feudal family structures and class distinction. In the eighteenth century, sugar colonies were the most modern and industrial form of agriculture with a high rate of death and disease that writers attempted to reform through detailed techniques of management and stronger social bonds between Britain and her colonies.

REGIONAL DIFFERENCES, CASH CROP ECONOMIES

Slave labor was not managed the same way throughout the Atlantic world. Philip Morgan's *Slave Counterpoint: Black Culture in the Eighteenth-Century Chesapeake and Lowcountry* describes how organizations of slave labor in the Chesapeake tobacco plantations and the Lowcountry rice plantations differed. A tobacco farm required relatively little startup capital, so anyone who could buy a little land could start growing tobacco. Consequently, although many large plantations existed, the majority of tobacco farms were relatively small with only a few slaves, and whites often worked alongside blacks in a form of labor called gang labor. Gang labor was organized in groups that worked from sunup to sundown at a pace set by the lead hand, under constant supervision by the driver, the overseer, or the planter himself. Because quality tobacco required close attention, everyone was involved in the careful monitoring of the crop. Tobacco cultivation encouraged westward expansion and land speculation because it depletes the soil, and its cultivation in the Tidewater region discouraged urbanization because the crop is lightweight and requires relatively little processing for storage. This problematic dynamic of westward expansion, land speculation, and anxious attention to the crop's quality in the context of a volatile, transatlantic market lay beneath Thomas Jefferson's ideology of yeoman agrarian virtue, an ideology that so influenced and troubled later authors of the early American republic, such as James Fenimore Cooper.[4]

In contrast, rice plantations required a huge capital investment, a minimum of thirty slaves at the outset, and an architecturally sophisticated development of the land, so all rice plantations were very large and had a large number of slaves whose organization was called tasking. Tasking assigned rice plots to individual slaves, and there were other tasks such as the laborious processing of the rice (e.g., milling); work quotas were premeasured so slaves required relatively little supervision.[5] Slaves always lived in self-contained compounds quite a distance from the house of the owner, in contrast to Virginia, which had a mix of large and small farms and where, on small farms, field slaves might even live in the same house as their owner. In addition, the cultivation of rice encouraged coastal development and urbanization because it is heavy and difficult to transport and because it is best grown in the swampy, flat land near the ocean. Unlike tobacco, a significant amount of the rice trade was exempted from the mercantilist Navigation Acts before the Revolutionary War.[6] As a result, planters had diverse opportunities for trade—notably with southern Europe and the Caribbean—but at the same time overall demand was relatively inelastic.[7] In sum, rice farming was a more capital-intensive but also more financially secure and profitable venture than tobacco. Because the economies were different, the cultures that emerged among the slaves in these two regions were also. What Morgan does not consider is the hypothesis that the literary imaginations of the Anglo-American elite would likewise reflect the difference in labor organization.

Morgan's book, published in 1998, compared two regions within the United States, but it did not consider regions outside the framework of the nation-state—notably the Caribbean, which since the late 1990s has been explored by Atlantic, hemispheric, and global approaches to regional literatures. Interestingly, South Carolina was originally colonized at the end of the seventeenth century by people from Barbados and some of the other Caribbean colonies when those colonies became too crowded.[8] Unlike most other colonies where slavery developed gradually after a commercially viable crop had been tested, Carolina settlers brought large numbers of slaves with them at the outset and "expected a suitable crop to materialize."[9] The high ratio of blacks to whites in South Carolina more closely resembled the Caribbean, and hence one might expect the form of labor to be similar, but it was not. Caribbean labor was a mixture of gang labor and complex industrial organization; the stages of sugar economy included clearing, weeding, digging, manuring, planting, harvesting, milling, compressing, boiling, scumming, striking, and curing; moreover, the boiling and scumming often happened at night.[10] The sugar planter was a "combination farmer-manufacturer," and each stage of the sugar-making process required close supervision and careful timing.[11] Although colonial sugar cultivation was in some ways proto-industrial and modern, plantation management insisted that slaves use the less efficient hoe rather than more advanced farming methods in order to keep the process on schedule and the slaves busy so as to deter insurrection, which would more likely occur if they had leisure.[12] The contradiction between the industrial scale and the surprising lack of agricultural innovation is an example of the dichotomous *colonial/Creole* dynamic that Kamau Brathwaite argues emerged within the culture of the elite planter class.[13]

Brathwaite suggests that the transatlantic *colonial* repression of local *Creole development* is one way the Caribbean sugar colonies differed from the United States, though Sean Goudie has recently complicated Brathwaite's conceptualization of that difference by revealing the fundamental dynamic of cultural and economic relations between them.[14] Also significant is the high mortality and low fertility rates on sugar plantations, which required a doctor to keep an exact log of the fitness of each slave as well as necessitating a constant importation of new slaves.[15] Hence, if Morgan's hypothesis is extended to include the Caribbean, clearly the organization of slave labor there was quite different from the Tidewater and Lowcountry regions.

Returning to the question with which I began my essay, did this difference in labor organization matter at all for the literature written in each location? Scholars have vigorously debated how to theorize literature's relation to the economy for more than a century. Many critics of regionalist literature have focused on the genre of the pastoral as the nostalgic literary expression of an ideological false consciousness.[16] Timothy Sweet, however, has instead argued for a renewed attention to the genre of the georgic—a poetics of farming and the management of land and labor that I also focus on here.[17] If all literature involves fantasy, repression, and displacement, as well as critique, recovery, and hopeful transformation, then we might expect the literature from each region to repress and displace their different forms of agricultural labor through very different symbolic and stylistic sublimations as they attempted to critically reform the economic basis of their culture through their art.

TIDEWATER TOBACCO

The Tidewater economy was tobacco. According to McCusker and Menard, at the end of the eighteenth century, tobacco accounted for 72 percent of all of Virginia's exports, and for Atlantic trade, it functioned as a cash crop, meaning that it was used as a medium for settling accounts. Before the governments of Virginia, Maryland, and North Carolina began to secure bank notes, tobacco was not just the primary means to make money; it actually was money. Like the literary response to tobacco trade regulation, the question of how to overcome a recession in the tobacco market dominated the region in the 1720s and 1730s as authors and politicians struggled to articulate a position of virtue and authority within a perilous market and among contentious constituencies.[18] Arguments over tobacco laws would sometimes become so violent as to require the intervention of the local militia. Curiously, however, even literature about the region that purported to be about the local economy such as Jefferson's *Notes on the State of Virginia* and Ebenezer Cooke's *Sotweed Redivivus* almost pathologically avoided mention of it, and when they do, they refer to the cultivation of tobacco and the importation of slave labor dismissively, as if the Tidewater colonies were embarrassed by their own way of life.

Jefferson's *Notes on the State of Virginia* was originally composed shortly after the Revolutionary War in answer to a series of questions posed by the French consulate. It includes chapters on the geography, laws, flora, and fauna of the newly independent state. In its longest chapter, titled "Productions Mineral, Vegetable and Animal," Jefferson's literary classic is remarkable for how little it has to say about tobacco and equally remarkable for how much he has to say about the remains of extinct mammoths. The chapter begins with some lengthy paragraphs about lead and limestone but only one short sentence mentioning all of its staple crops: tobacco, hemp, flax, and cotton.[19] He then proceeds to digress for more than thirty pages about the fossils of mammoths, the virility of Indians, and the peculiar case of an albino slave, all of which is part of his diatribe against the French natural historian Buffon. Jefferson's later chapter "Subjects of Commerce" is one of the shortest in the book, and here again he has little to say about tobacco, despite his own data that tobacco was central to Virginia's economy. His only comment on tobacco in the entire book is dismissive: "It is a culture productive of infinite wretchedness. Those employed in it are in a continued state of exertion beyond the powers of nature to support. Little food of any kind is raised by them; so that the men and animals on these farms are badly fed, and the earth is rapidly impoverished. The cultivation of wheat is the reverse in every circumstance."[20] As Charles Miller has observed, "when Jefferson wrote of agriculture to his friends, he preferred to avoid speaking of his chief cash crop."[21] For instance, one of Jefferson's often-quoted letters has Jefferson exclaiming, "I never saw a leaf of tobacco packed in my life." However, Miller's assessment is not quite right. In that letter, written to one of Jefferson's tobacco agents, Jefferson was in the midst of a protracted epistolary conversation in which he felt put upon to defend his own honor and the reputation of the quality of the tobacco produced on his plantation against a complaining factor (or buyer). In earlier letters, he expressed pride in his diligence and skill as a farmer. Moreover, Jefferson's view after the revolution differs from his view before, in his *Summary View of the Rights of British America* (1774), which does emphasize the importance of the trade in tobacco and slaves for the British empire but represents slavery, not tobacco, as the "toxic commodity."[22] Might Jefferson's contradictory statements on tobacco have something to do with its manner of production? Tobacco and slave labor obviously do not fit the classic image of the yeoman farmer of wholesome crops such as wheat that Jefferson is so famous for promoting.

Jefferson's strangely dismissive comments about the very thing that made him rich and his fantasy about virtuous wheat farmers was nothing new. Like Jefferson, Ebenezer Cooke's satirical poem *Sotweed Redivivus*, published in Maryland in 1730, rails against tobacco, calling it at various instances a poisonous drug, a nauseous vegetive, a nauseous weed, a stinking Indian weed, and a Stinkebus that has caused Maryland to become sick. The supposed topic of *Sotweed Redivivus* was how to revive the tobacco trade, which was in the midst of a crisis because the rapidly increasing supply was driving down prices. It is told with a false naïveté from the point of view of a character wandering about Annapolis talking with randomly encountered people about the recession. Among various proposals entertained in his poem to cure the body politic, one character's prescription prefigures Jefferson's recommendation: "First, let the swamps and marshes drain, / Fit to receive all sorts of grain."[23] To summarize, the poem begins with a lengthy dedication that compares tobacco farmers to their own slaves and invokes the muse of a virtuous girl in homespun clothing who inspires young men to work hard.

In the first canto, the narrator arrives in town and discovers a debate about the money bill intended to improve the economy. The narrator argues for paper money as a medium of exchange, but this conversation is interrupted by noise from the tavern, and then the characters go drink, so we never see the whole argument. In the second canto, after finding lodging for the night, the narrator talks with a character from Cooke's earlier poem, *The Sotweed Factor* (1708), about a tobacco merchant who arrives in Maryland and, after hilarious misadventure, loses his shirt (literally and figuratively) and then returns to England. In the new poem, this character lectures drunkenly about the history of Maryland's economy and complains about slavery and mercantilism before falling asleep. In the third canto, the next morning, the same person prescribes economic diversification in hopes that Maryland will one day rival England as a commercial center, but the narrator counters that economic success cannot be legislated; rather, it depends on the industriousness of the people. The clear moral of the story is that thrift and virtue, alongside a more wholesome grain-based economy and state-backed currency, will help Maryland out of its recession.

Two aspects of Jefferson's and Cooke's writings—both of which, though quite different in literary genre, purport to be about the economy—are significant here. First is the agrarian fantasy that the economy can be rescued by a more virtuous crop (wheat). What is ironic about this imagined economy of supposedly small yeoman farmers is that, unlike tobacco, the processing and export of grain requires urban centers. Urban growth contributed to the development of a functional grain market in the Tidewater region. Noticeably, cities are not part of Jefferson's conceptualization of the yeoman farmer, but westward expansion is; tobacco's deleterious effect on the soil was one of the causes for its cultivation to move westward, as Jefferson himself happily remarks.[24]

The second cause of westward expansion was land speculation. Consequently, the high land prices due to speculation encouraged large plantations and slave labor rather than the small independent farms that both Cooke and Jefferson seem to desire. This aspect of Cooke's and Jefferson's literary works is important for a scholarly conversation about regionalism because the yeoman farmer ideal served as the centerpiece of the regionalist Agrarian movement in the 1930s, which adopted policy recommendations that resembled those Jefferson made in 1776. In early drafts of revolutionary Virginia's new state constitution (not the constitution that was actually ratified), Jefferson proposed granting fifty acres of land to individuals who did not yet own any.[25] In today's "critical regionalism" in a global context, the yeoman farmer ideal (and today, the local organic farm) has been put forward as an oppositional figure against the hegemony of multinational capitalism and industrial-scale farms. Along those lines, Mary Weaks-Baxter argues that both white and black writers in the early twentieth century looked to the yeoman farmer as an ideal democratic figure for reforming the image of the South against the mythos of the racist, cavalier plantation aristocracy.[26] What is problematic about Baxter's argument is that economic analysis of early America has shown that the "fully self-sufficient yeoman farmer of colonial America is largely mythical: almost all colonists were tied to overseas trade," and the deployment of that mythos often served the interests of capitalist land speculators more than it did small family farms.[27]

Second, part of the fantasy of the yeoman farmer requires the repression of the real economic conditions of production, and, in the case of an economy based mostly on tobacco, that means a very specific form of slave labor. In the case of Jefferson, his strange avoidance of tobacco culture in a book that is so detailed about everything else, and his defensive pride in his plantation in his letters to agents and friends, speak to the peculiar anxieties of the tobacco planter analyzed by Mechal Sobel in her seminal work, *The World They Made Together*, and by T. H. Breen in his classic *Tobacco Culture*. According to Breen, the Tidewater planters' belief that their virtue—their continence, rectitude, incorruptibility, and vigilance—secured a profitable crop was an incoherent response to the fluctuations of the market price of tobacco that often left them in chronic debt.[28] Similarly, focusing on time management, Sobel details the planters' anxiety over slave labor and the often hysterical frustration expressed by wealthy planters such as Landon Carter about the laziness of slaves. As Carter wrote in his diary, "I find it almost impossible to make a negro do his work well."[29] According to Morgan's *Slave Counterpoint*, this was typical of the grueling sunup-to-sundown modality of gang labor that presented every incentive to work slowly and no incentive to work hard. But importantly, tobacco planter anxieties about work ethic applied not only to slaves but also to each other.

Carter, Jefferson, and George Washington had the same difficulty motivating their own children to do work, and they complained about them dancing and drinking with the slaves. The result was an obsession with time and productivity, symbolized by the many clocks and bells in Jefferson's home at Monticello.[30] Indeed, given the frustration with the organization of labor and with the fluctuating commodity price, Jefferson's reluctance to talk about labor management in public is understandable.

The cultivation of tobacco also required white and black laborers to work side by side. On small farms, this often meant the owner of the farm worked alongside his slaves, and some farms were owned by free blacks. Cooke's poem begins with the concern that white planters are so focused on quick profits from tobacco that they destroy the land and become "like Negroe Asses" in order to "glut the Market with a poisonous drug" (v). Cooke's racism is strongly articulated in this stanza (the first stanza in the poem), as he seems more troubled that planters have to "head a Troop of Æthiopian Hands, / Worse Villains are, than Forward's Newgate Bands" than he is by the low market price of the tobacco crop (even though the low price of the crop is the stated subject of the poem). What Cooke's poem hopes for instead is the independent and virtuous yeoman farmer:

> Bright Ceres, whom the poets feign
> To till the ground, instructs the swain,
> By Industry t'improve his Lands,
> Without the help of Savage Hands. (15)

If the goddess Ceres is not sufficient, Cooke also suggests that a stable currency might facilitate such industriousness and purge the colony of African slaves. Tobacco's functionality as a cash crop actually impedes economic development because it is a poor medium for purchasing labor. Cooke writes, "But to be paid with Indian weed, / In Parcels will not answer need" (13). In other words, one can better pay laborers with paper money than with a cash crop, and therefore paper money is better for facilitating diversification and prudent investment. Cooke is echoing Benjamin Franklin's argument for state-backed paper money, published the year before Cooke's poem, which bears some resemblance to Adam Smith's argument years later for a free labor force, and of course, the use of tobacco for cash and the lack of coin is precisely why slave and indentured labor were the de facto choice for the colony—that is, because planters had no ready currency, they looked for a labor force they did not have to pay with currency.[31] However, in contrast to Franklin and Cooke, Smith actually complicates this theory, explaining that, in addition to such liberal notions of a free work force, the commodity price depends on the cost of labor and land, and hence the wealthy will do everything in their power to minimize and control this cost. It is precisely the real economic contradiction between freedom and control that Cooke sublimates through the image of an industrious wheat farmer. The literature of the Tidewater economy avoided talking about its crop's production and instead fantasized about another crop. In contrast, literature from the Lowcountry and

Caribbean celebrated their crop and the labor that produced it, though not in the same way.

LOWCOUNTRY RICE

The content and style of Ogilvie's poem *Carolina; Or, the Planter* and John Drayton's history *A View of South-Carolina* bear significant similarities to—and differences from—Jefferson's and Cooke's writings, and these similarities and differences are symptomatic of the uniqueness of each crop and therefore also the culture and aesthetics of each region. Literature from both the Tidewater and Lowcountry regions celebrates industry, improvement, and republican virtue; both participate in what Jefferson called a transatlantic "republic of letters" that values the exchange of knowledge and ideas. Drayton's work, for instance, is an imitation of both Jefferson's *State of Virginia* and Edward Long's *History of Jamaica*, and Drayton's work discusses and agrees with Jefferson's commentary on Buffon and similarly argues for the whiteness of Carolinians against Buffon's climactic theories of racial degeneracy. But in contrast to Virginian literature's embarrassed and sometimes hysterical attitudes toward African slaves, South Carolinian literature celebrates slavery as part of the natural order of things. Also contrasting Virginia's symbolic displacement of its anxieties about its cash crop onto a virtuous, independent wheat farmer, Carolina's dominant metaphor is the extended family unit, a gentlemanly country estate with a beautiful garden and a chivalrous ethos. Stylistically, Carolina's writing is more lush and romantically pastoral.

George Ogilvie's poem *Carolina; Or, the Planter* illustrates one of the problematics of regionalism within the context of national literature. First composed in South Carolina in 1776 but completed in 1791 in England, the poem has received little critical attention, except for David Shields's effort to recuperate it from the dustbin of history. It does not easily fit within traditional, nation-centered narratives of America or English literature because the poem affiliates with Carolina planters but was published in England after Ogilvie fled America during the revolution due to his Loyalist politics. As Shields has argued, much of the poem's discussion of family and the filial obligation of children to their parents served as an allegory for political unity that was a standard British metaphor against the revolution.[32] Considering that the commercial networks for the rice trade usually included extended family relations, the metaphor for the family may have also had an economic component to it.[33] The poem was published shortly after Ogilvie's lawsuit to regain property lost during the war; he won the suit but was unable to force postrevoluntary Carolinians to follow the letter of the law. We might easily read his poem, published at this particular moment, as a plea to his American friends to help him retrieve his losses. Another reason for the poem's neglect might be its cavalier ethos and unapologetic attitude toward slavery. Unlike the

Tidewater tobacco authors such as Jefferson and Cooke, who appear conflicted by slavery and sublimate that conflict by promoting the virtuous image of the independent yeoman farmer, the Lowcountry rice authors evoke a European gentility and contentment with slavery that few readers today would find acceptable or even readable.

Ogilvie is similar to Jefferson and Cooke in that he also avoids his own subject, but rather than repressing the work of the plantation as the Tidewater planters do, what Ogilvie represses is the technical skill and knowledge of his slaves. The poem is a Virgilian georgic in two cantos, each a little over seven hundred lines. As was typical in colonial literature, the first canto begins with a description of the geography and history of the region, including advice on where to live and an extensive description of the various kinds of trees. This description transitions into the history of Native Americans there, including a lengthy monologue of a lone Santee Indian mourning the demise of his tribe due to factions and infighting. This monologue is clearly intended as an allegory against the political separation of North America from Britain. Although the poem's stated topic is the plantation, Ogilvie's avoidance of the actual production of rice and indigo is striking. About halfway into this first canto, the poem abruptly raises the subject of rice production.[34] Surprisingly, this is the first and only time the word "rice" is used in the poem, even though one might assume from its title that this is ostensibly what the poem is about. Ogilvie briefly details a number of other important commercial products such as maize, cotton, oak, and pine before he ever so briefly mentions happy slaves.

One might expect the rest of the canto to proceed with an explanation of rice production, considering that this is what the poetic line promises to do, but instead there is a sudden shift to a sad romantic story that dominates the rest of the canto. Such bucolic digressions are a standard feature of Virgilian georgic poetry, providing the personal, emotional aspect of the farmer's life, but they usually supplement rather than interrupt the poem's subject matter. Ogilvie's tragic character, a young Antonio, apparently does not care for work on the rice plantation, because he was in love with a woman named Fanny who was promised by her father to a wealthier man. Overcome with a dangerously transgressive passion, Antonio and Fanny secretly have sex, causing Fanny to feel such a severe degree of shame that she dies. The moral of the story is for men to respect the institution of the family and not to lose their virtue by abusing their power over women (l. 642). The canto ends with Fanny dead and Antonio depressed.

The second canto begins, "Once more, my Garden, come and bring along / Thy kind indulgence to an artless song," so we might anticipate again that the poem will finally get to its subject. After some lengthy discussion of various kinds of snakes (always a threat to any Edenic garden), the poem digresses about a gentlemanly stag hunt. Then, at long last, the poem finally returns to its subject to describe the construction of an enormous and sophisticated system of mounds, trenches, drains, and floodgates. Indeed, the architecture of rice production is extraordinarily massive and complex, rivaling the Egyptian pyramids in size and scope. According to Shields, Ogilvie's poem has one of the first accounts published detailing the mechanics of a rice plantation. As soon as the poem reaches a point where it must describe the actual labor of this construction, the tone shifts from the matter-of-fact detailing of measurements and mechanics to lofty, neoclassical images of nymphs, dryads, and Greek deities. Such aesthetic sublimation is significant, as the poem never fully returns to the subject of rice, so the reader never finds out how the planters of Carolina learned to construct such massive architecture or how the crop is planted, cultivated, harvested, or milled.

The second section of the second canto is an encomium to his friends' homes and families, and here the poem follows the genre of the country house poem, celebrating the tasteful arrangement of diverse and exotic flora on a gentleman's estate. The estate's library is full of texts both classical (e.g., Horace and Terence) and modern (Locke and Buffon) that celebrate an ordered world, listed in exhaustive detail. Nymphs and Greek gods briefly reappear in this section, and then Ogilvie praises the industrious attempt to invent new labor-saving water-powered milling technology and expresses hope that it will someday be realized. (This milling technology would be successfully invented shortly after Ogilvie published his poem.) Poetically, the lack of information about labor is here displaced in favor of copious information about other kinds of knowledge. The poem narrates a tragedy of death in the family, and then, as if suddenly reminded of its subject matter, it concludes with a summary of all the candidates for "rural fame"—including hemp and tobacco among many others, but notably not ever mentioning rice explicitly. In sum, the poem's displacement of labor onto romantic love, deer hunts, nymphs, lush gardens, a beautiful library full of classics, and extended family loyalty is in a sense one of the earliest examples of a "pastoral scene of the gallant south," as Billie Holiday so sarcastically and bitterly put it in her famous 1939 song about lynching, "Strange Fruit."

A View of South-Carolina (1802), a history written by the nascent state's governor, John Drayton, is interestingly similar to Ogilvie's poem, despite the obvious differences in genre. It begins with the same listing of all of the many kinds of trees and exotic flora, followed by a similarly sorrowful account of the plight of the noble Native Americans, including examples of Indian elocution and bravery. It also details hunts and other such gentlemanly sports. Though Drayton has clearly read *Notes on the State of Virginia*, and like Jefferson he asserts the world's natural order and harmony, his text differs from Jefferson's by discussing at length South Carolina cash crops: rice, indigo, cotton, and others, including tobacco. Unlike Jefferson, Drayton proudly asserts that Carolina's success was entirely due to the introduction of rice and slaves in 1695.[35] He argues that slaves are an essential part of the plantation, as without their labor Carolina would "revert to a state of nature" (144). Unlike Ogilvie, he includes some details about the task labor system of assigning rice plots "proportioned to the strength of the negroes who work them" (116). But he does not explain how the rice is harvested, and he also sidesteps discussion of the incredibly grueling labor of milling the rice by hand. Instead, just as Ogilvie shifts from a description of the plantation's architecture to images of nymphs and dryads, Drayton's discussion of rice farming focuses on the successful invention of the new water-powered milling machine in 1691 (the same year Ogilvie's poem was published), including a diagram and picture.

Absent from both Ogilvie's and Drayton's texts is an intimate knowledge of the rice agriculture about which they were writing. Judith Carney sees these production and harvesting methods as part of a "knowledge system."[36] Carney demonstrates that the same technology of the banks, trenches, drains, and floodgates used in South Carolina had been used for centuries in western Africa. When the Caribbean planters began their colony in South Carolina and were searching for a crop, it was the slaves in Carolina that developed the colony's principal cash crop. Carney's transatlantic geography, comparing West African and North American rice cultivation, provides an account of the origin and dissemination of rice technologies that McCusker and Menard call for in *The Economy of British America*.[37] The history of the slave's knowledge system has been repressed in the literature by individuals such as Ogilvie and Drayton, even though Carolina planters seemed conscious of the fact, as they were deliberate about purchasing slaves from the regions of Africa that grew rice in order to benefit from their knowledge.[38]

Although Drayton says African labor was essential for the building of Carolina, he locates rice's origins and history elsewhere in a manner that is contradictory and confused. Early in the text, he claims it comes from the East Indies, but later he explains that the same kind of rice and method of cultivation was practiced on the Nile River in Egypt (115, 228–31). He includes an ostentatiously learned chart of how and where rice is cultivated around the world that significantly excludes Africa, but on the very next page he describes a variety of rice called "Guinea rice" that is "principally cultivated by negroes" (124). As Peter Wood has explained, the subject of Carolina rice's origins was a mystery often mused over, one Swiss correspondent stating that "it was by a woman that Rice was transplanted into Carolina" from seeds brought over in a slave ship.[39] Carney shows that the Carolina method of rice production is exactly like that practiced in western Africa and not at all like that practiced in Asia. Although other scholars are skeptical of Wood's and Carney's claims about the extent of the role such an African knowledge system played in the development of Lowcountry agriculture, all agree that the slaves typically farmed their own plots, milled the rice, and worked the complex system of rice architecture by themselves without much supervision using the system of labor called tasking.[40] The planter's demand for high rates of productivity meant grueling labor, but in contrast to slaves in the Tidewater region, the slaves in the Lowcountry worked on their own. This practice is understandable if, as Carney argues, they could tap into their own knowledge system, which probably explains why in the Lowcountry, unlike most other regions of the Americas, the famous Gullah communities were able to retain a dialect of their African language and its culture well into the twentieth century and even today.

Although Ogilvie says that the Carolina planters paternalistically tutored the slave in the ways of agriculture, it is more likely that the slaves tutored the planters. Even South Carolina's famous Palmetto furniture comes from West Africa.[41] In both Ogilvie's poem and Drayton's history, a displacement occurs at precisely the moment in the text when what would logically follow is a description of the planting, harvesting, and milling of the rice. Ogilvie's symbolic displacements happen through nymphs, romantic love, gallant deer hunts, filial sentiment, and gentlemanly estates with beautiful gardens and big libraries. Drayton's displacement is his demonstration of a mastery of knowledge about world history, classical texts, and modern science. Through his scientific and historical descriptions, Drayton performs the character of "The Planter" that Ogilvie celebrates in his poem. Both anxiously repress the slave's knowledge system and the planter's somewhat superfluous existence.

CARIBBEAN SUGAR

Like their North American counterparts, Caribbean authors also located themselves in the republic of letters that linked the Atlantic world; by engaging in such scientific and belletristic discourses, the Creole elite grew anxiously self-conscious of their relationship to their compatriots in London.[42] But in addition to such commonalities between the Creole elite in the Tidewater, Lowcountry, and Caribbean regions, there were also some important differences. Caribbean literature is far more explicit and detailed about how the cane is grown, how the sugar is processed, and how the slaves are managed, including the ethical dilemmas for planters about the morality of slavery. Compared to the Tidewater and Lowcountry literature, the Caribbean literature is exhaustively detailed and more impressively encyclopedic. Caribbean literature is also far more comfortable representing relationships between whites and blacks. In contrast to Cooke's representation of the virtuous maiden in *Sotweed Redivivus* and Ogilvie's representation of the tragic yet gallant white romance and noble families in *Carolina*, Caribbean literature appears almost obsessed with—at the same time titillated by and afraid of—sex between the races, including lengthy accounts of interracial romance, elaborate policy recommendations for managing sex between the races and their offspring, and even a pornographic poem about the allures of black women titled "Sable Venus."[43]

Edward Long's enormous three-volume tome *The History of Jamaica* (1774) is famous for its vicious racism and unequivocal proslavery position that denied the humanity of slaves, but at the same time it is the only available source for the first known poem composed in Latin by a free black, Francis Williams. Bryan Edwards's equally large two-volume *The History, Civil and Commercial, of the British Colonies in the West Indies* (1793) includes lengthy explanations of the gang labor system, the daily regimen of slaves from sunup to sundown, and the various divisions of labor and assignments depending on the stage in the process.[44] His description is not simply that of a natural historian but a manager, noting exactly when they wake up, what they do, when they eat, when they are more productive, as he is clearly attempting to maximize efficiency. This includes rotating shifts at night.

Maximizing efficiency was important for the sugar colonies since the competition was fierce, driving prices down, yet the basic technology remained the same throughout the century, and useful land on the islands was finite. Edwards is more ambivalent than Long about the humanity and character of Africans and their role as slaves. Both Long and Edwards, however, include copious demographic data on slaves, free blacks, maroons, and whites. Long estimates the ratio of blacks to whites in Jamaica at about eight to one, and Edwards estimated the average ratio throughout the Caribbean at about seven to one.[45] In fact, Long's data is remarkable for vaguely estimating the white population to the nearest hundred "for want of an exact account" but knowing the exact number of slaves. This peculiar fact is less remarkable if one notes that slaves were considered by law to be property, like cows, whose calculus must be exact because they were taxed.[46]

Similar to the impressive scope, thorough detail, and directness in describing plantation management that we find in Long's and Edwards's histories, James Grainger's lengthy georgic poem *The Sugar Cane* (1764) is four books of more than six hundred lines each and more closely follows Virgil's pattern than most other English georgics. Typical of georgic poetry, it oscillates between excessive pastoral descriptions of lush, copious fertility and the threats to that fertility, such as hurricanes and bugs. Like the histories of his fellow Caribbeans, but very unlike the literature of the Tidewater and Lowcountry regions, Grainger details the use of fertilizers and the organization of labor: "As art transforms the savage face of things . . . Let not thy Blacks irregularly hoe: But, aided by the line."[47] Throughout there is the paternalistic attitude toward slaves that you would expect, as Grainger figures himself as their tutor and protector, and they are figured as willing, "cheerful" workers naturally suited to hard labor. Somewhat less confident about the goodness of slavery than the Lowcountry planters but more confident than those from the Tidewater, James Grainger in his poem *The Sugar Cane* is remarkably detailed and multifaceted, juxtaposing a plea for slaves' freedom with advice on how to purchase and take care of them. Like Cooke, Grainger seems to hope for a free labor force, but unlike Cooke, Grainger expects the labor force in the Caribbean to remain black and has no ideas for how to transition from slave to free labor.

The literary criticism of North American and Caribbean literature differs in the same way that the literature itself does. The critical attention to Tidewater literature emphasizes the scientific and philosophical background of individuals such as William Byrd II and Thomas Jefferson, because that is what those authors emphasize about themselves. Likewise, most recent scholarly attention to Caribbean literature inevitably focuses on the nature of its labor, because that is what its literature talks about.[48] Moreover, as my own essay on Grainger's poem demonstrates, recent scholarly attention repeats the critical reception these works received when they were published, as the reviews in eighteenth-century periodicals also focused on the question of slavery and the production of sugar.[49]

Thus, if my critical method is to locate the oddly missing thing in the literary work and extrapolate from that the ideological repression unique to the region, the Caribbean authors seem to present more of a challenge—their encyclopedic style appears to leave nothing out. Perhaps their thoroughness and interest in the efficient management of every aspect of life on the island is itself a symptom of the uniqueness of sugar, which more than any other cash crop prefigured the revolution of industrial-scale agriculture. Unlike the North American colonies, many Caribbean planters were absentee landlords, living in the British Isles, often acting as lobbyists for the sugar trade, and therefore required the kind of comprehensive accounts of labor management that we see in Long, Edwards, and Grainger, but not in Jefferson and Drayton.

In addition to the absence of the landlord, and also of the writer, of the Caribbean region, there is also an absence within the literature. What is missing is the problem of infertility. Both Long's and Edwards's natural histories and Grainger's poems emphasize the natural fertility of the islands, and the lush flora and fauna is gushed about in florid detail. Similarly, their obsession with women of color also led them to assert the fertility of African women and to worry about procreation. Of course, nothing is more important to the management of a labor force than its procreation, which is why, etymologically, the word "proletariat" comes from the Latin word for breeder. Grainger's poem celebrates the slaves' natural increase (1:610–15), as if this population growth was due to their own fertility—a fertility analogous to the botanical plenitude—even though these authors knew that this was not the case. As many scholars have described, conditions on eighteenth-century sugar plantations were so harsh that the mortality rate was higher than the fertility rate, requiring the sugar plantations to constantly purchase new slaves from Africa.[50] Grainger would have known this intimately because he published the first medical treatise about caring for dying slaves in the Caribbean. His poem documents various threats to the health of the island residents, including hurricanes, earthquakes, and diseases caused by insects and worms, but his medical treatise also insists on the problems of nutrition and overwork.[51] As abolitionists repeatedly argued, the management of sugar and slaves was a calculated management of death—not only of people (both blacks and whites) but also sustainable ecology. Historians have noted that European colonizers transformed a lush, diverse ecosystem into a sugar factory completely dependent on imports of rice, wheat, and wood from North America.

In Grainger's poem, this basic contradiction between fertility and infertility is metaphorically sublimated through a romantic digression. This episode of passionate love is in some ways similar to Ogilvie's but differs in significant ways. The lover named Junio is sent from the Caribbean to England for his education and there meets Theana, also from the Caribbean, whose "charms still triumph'd o'er Britannia's fair" (2:444). The plot resembles *Romeo and Juliet* as his father opposes their union, but when the patriarch dies, Junio travels back across the Atlantic in order to reunite with his "Indian bride" (2:512). Alas, she has been struck by lightning, and when he finally arrives, she is close to death. Her final words are, "Welcome, my Junio, to thy native shore! . . . Live and live happily . . . my little, all I give." Her symbolic meaning is the Creole planter's relationship to the Caribbean, his identity, and all that it gives him. The difference between Grainger's romantic digression and Ogilvie's is the context for the story and its meaning. Ogilvie's story about death from sexual shame reflects the social importance of genteel family loyalty, and it clearly displaces the economic question of plantation management. The context and meaning for Grainger's story about death and unrequited love is the character's *Creole* identity, and rather than displace plantation management (which Grainger covered thoroughly in earlier parts of the poem, though this is the only moment in the poem that suggests the pervasive absenteeism of Caribbean plantation ownership), it adds a lengthy discussion of various forms of death from natural disasters (lightning, hurricanes, and disease).

Hence, the interlude is part of an extended and intense dialectic of hyperbolic death and fertility—a dialectic addressed most intently at precisely the moment when it is in fact displaced from the question of plantation management onto the questions of disease and natural disaster (i.e., onto tragic, rather than systemic death) that interrupt true love.

REGIONS AND REGIONALISMS REVISITED

Belletristic literature from the Tidewater, Lowcountry, and Caribbean regions were part of the same circum-Atlantic culture, but a comparative trans-Atlantic analysis reveals regional differences symptomatic of the varying forms of labor management, the deep ideological conflicts inherent within those forms, and how authors sublimated that conflict in their literature. Writers of Tidewater tobacco literature avoided the workings of the plantation altogether, seemingly embarrassed by their own economy, leading them to sublimate their embarrassment through the mythic image of the virtuous yeoman farmer. In contrast, Lowcountry rice literature uniquely expressed unabashed gratitude to the slave system, but this gratitude repressed the knowledge system that the slaves brought with them along with their labor. Caribbean sugar literature was more modern than any other literature in its proto-industrialist treatment of slavery (and arguably also more sophisticated, rigorous, and poetically adept) but could not bring itself to confront the systemic death that this nascent form of capitalism produced. To be clear, my comparative regional analysis focuses not on states (Virginia versus South Carolina) but on regions marked by their ecology, economy, and form of labor management. Within South Carolina and Georgia, for instance, the coastal Lowcountry region was significantly different from the states' more elevated interiors, whose economy was eventually dominated by cotton. Likewise, the northwestern part of Maryland was more similar to Pennsylvania than to the rest of the state around the Tidewater Chesapeake.

Situating my essay about the literature of agrarian capitalism within the long conversation about the history of regionalism, transnationalism, and alternative mappings of literary history that is surveyed in the introduction to this volume, I suggest a critique of an often-cited opposition between the roots and the routes of culture—roots being a core concept for the regionalist aesthetics of the Agrarian movement in the 1930s and routes being a core concept for the transnationalist and transatlantic work of James Clifford, Paul Gilroy, and many others. In his 1949 essay on culture, T. S. Eliot argued that regionalism was necessary "to grow a contemporary culture from the old roots."[52] Eliot echoes the manifesto-like collection of essays *I'll Take My Stand: The South and the Agrarian Tradition* (1930) by John Crowe Ransom, Donald Davidson, and others who championed a "culture of the soil" and a literature in harmony with its "economic foundations" of land and labor.[53] At this moment in history, regionalism was not just a name assigned by scholars of esoteric literary history but a question of national policy debated in the mainstream media. The stakes for such debate about the relationship of North and South were high: the Southeast was the poorest region with a per capita income less than half that of the Northeast; it had more debt and less public infrastructure, and politically it felt underrepresented in the national dialogue. The responses to such conditions in the midst of the Great Depression were diverse. Arguing explicitly against the Agrarians, Howard Odum and Harry Estill Moore's *American Regionalism: A Cultural-Historical Approach to National Integration* attempted a "new science of the region" by synthesizing political, literary, historical, anthropological, and sociological data to assert that a regional approach could best resolve national conflicts by focusing national policy on viable development strategies.[54]

Nevertheless, the exact definition of the region remains troubled, and almost humorously, Odum and Moore begin their book like Herman Melville's *Moby Dick*, with a long list of quotes collected by a sub-sub-librarian, posing widely differing definitions of their own leviathan. On the one hand, in their more negative moments, they often find themselves left with nothing else to unify the region of the "Old South" except for the politically expedient and culturally traumatic "sectionalism" of the Civil War, Reconstruction, and Jim Crow. On the other hand, in their more positive moments, they defer somewhat mystically to the region as an "organic" unit "basic to evolution of all culture."[55]

In opposition to both the Agrarian's quest for roots and the mystified organicism of Odum and Moore that underpins their problematic mapping of the nation-state, scholars such as Paul Gilroy emphasize the routes (homophone intended) of culture, arguing that cultural identities emerge out of what he calls, borrowing the concepts of Deleuze and Guattari, "rhizomatic transfigurations"—the upshot of his theory being that national, regional, and/or local identities are grounded not so much in place as they are through movement and complex transatlantic relations.[56] A contemporary of the Agrarians, Walter Prescott Webb, in his book *Divided We Stand: The Crisis in a Frontierless Democracy* (1937), responded to Frederick Jackson Turner's famous frontier thesis by arguing that the modern corporation was the single most important factor shaping American society and suggested something he called a "new feudalism" in which the North exercised hegemonic control over the South through a complex network of capitalist relations. Such relations are visible in what he called "zones of contact" such as railroads, military bases, banks, universities, magazines, and so on (a terminology that might seem strikingly similar to the conceptualization of "contact zones" theorized by more recent scholars such as Paul Gilroy and Mary Louise Pratt, drawing on the work of Mikhail Bakhtin).[57]

I pose this dichotomy between roots and routes to work toward a theory of the region—a theory that is dialectical in its consideration of opposing political agendas, historical in its consideration of cultural continuities and discontinuities across the centuries, and comparative in its analysis of the literature from different regions. My essay is a partial answer to how to think through this dichotomy about the ways cultural symbols and literary style are connected to particular locations in light of the historical complexity of such ideological roots and their rhizomatic routes. What both Paul Gilroy and the Agrarians have in common is an appreciation for the relationship between art and economics, an oppositional stance toward a hegemonic nation-state, and a sense of the eighteenth century as a foundational moment for their contemporary cultural identity. How they differ is in their cultural memory of the slave trade, their attitude toward cosmopolitanism, and their understanding of local differences and global relationships.

More fundamentally, the Agrarian image of the South is nostalgic and ideologically represses its real economy (i.e., transatlantic commerce and slave labor), and John Crowe Ransom would eventually in 1945 repudiate his earlier views and his Agrarian friends by arguing that the regionalist attempt to recover an "original innocence" leads to a literary form that expresses its relationship to the economy "vicariously or symbolically, not really."[58] In contrast to the Agrarians, the artwork created by Kara Walker out of what Gilroy calls the "lived crisis of global capitalism" foregrounds transnational hybridity and movement, but arguably both Walker and Gilroy neglect many of the social and economic details of the eighteenth-century Atlantic world that made each location historically unique—in particular what might make the experience of slaves and slave owners in South Carolina different from that of Virginia, Haiti, or Texas. In other words, Gilroy's emphasis on the routes of culture (including the movement of slave bodies and commodities such as rice, tobacco, and sugar) over its roots may need to be qualified by a thicker description of local economies and the labor of different regions—labor that did not move about easily but instead produced something, day in, day out.

Admittedly, there is a tension in my essay. On the one hand, as critics of regionalism such as Roberto Dainotto and others have argued, the region is a metaphorical fantasy that mediates complex conflicts both at the global and local levels. The discursive defining of a region certainly involves a lot of fantasy and mythmaking. On the other hand, I also argue that the region is materially and economically produced. Am I risking a geographic determinism, of the kind actually favored by the Agrarian movement, which suggested that the soil gave definition to their cultural heritage? I would answer no, since rather than privileging an ahistorical landscape, I am focusing on the labor that shaped that land and the historical dialectic that produced the region. The tension between place and movement, between region and world, is both imaginary and real. As Kara Walker's art exhibition in the closing Domino refinery reminds us, the region is produced within a transatlantic context by the labor of the bodies that inhabit that region; the significance of that labor and the uniqueness of the culture it created are very much a part of today's world culture, even if most of us now experience that uniqueness through a vicarious and figurative identification, if not also through the globally marketed commercial products of cheap cigarettes, instant rice, and flavored rum that nostalgically recollect historical economies.

NOTES

1. Hilton Als, "The Sugar Sphinx," *New Yorker*, May 8, 2014, http://www.newyorker.com/online/blogs/culture/2014/05/kara-walker-domino-sugar-factory-sphinx-sculpture.html (accessed July 4, 2014); Paul Carter Harrison, Carol Diehl, Brenda Marie Osbey, Clyde Taylor, Dennis Kardon, and Barbara Lewis, "Symposium on the Recent 'Mammy' Sculpture of Kara Walker," *Black Renaissance / Renaissance Noire* 14, no. 2 (2014): 92–103.

2. For instance, see Robert Jackson, *Seeking the Region*, 7–9. For a thorough analysis of the position of the South, as defined by *Plessy v. Ferguson*, in relation to the nation, see Duck, *Nation's Region*. On the global South, see McKee and Trefzer, "Preface," 678.

3. Armitage, "Three Concepts of Atlantic History," 11–27.

4. Zuck, "Cultivation, Commerce, and Cupidity," 59–60.
5. Philip D. Morgan, *Slave Counterpoint*, 187–94.
6. Drayton, *A View of South-Carolina*, 162.
7. Kenneth Morgan, "Colonial American Rice Trade," 439, 449.
8. Dunn, "English Sugar Islands," 50.
9. Chaplin, *Anxious Pursuit*, 6.
10. Edwards, *History*, 2:128–31, 227–37; Roughley, *Jamaica Planter's Guide*, 221–31.
11. Dunn, *Sugar and Slaves*, 189–90.
12. Ibid., 200.
13. Brathwaite, *Development of Creole Society*, 100–101.
14. Goudie, *Creole America*, 9–10.
15. Sheridan, *Doctors and Slaves*, 195.
16. Dainotto, *Place in Literature*.
17. Sweet, *American Georgics*.
18. Steven W. Thomas, "Taxing Tobacco," 73–96.
19. Jefferson, *Writings*, 164.
20. Ibid., 293.
21. Charles Miller, *Jefferson and Nature*, 209.
22. Jefferson, *Writings*, 109–10; Philip Gould, *Barbaric Traffic*, 13.
23. Cooke, *Sotweed Redivivus*, 21. Subsequent references will be given parenthetically.
24. Jefferson, *Writings*, 293.
25. Jefferson, *Papers*, 1:363.
26. Weaks-Baxter, *Reclaiming the American Farmer*, 7.
27. McCusker and Menard, *Economy of British America*, 10.
28. Breen, *Tobacco Culture*, 60.
29. Landon Carter's Diary, June 14, 1756, quoted in Sobel, *World They Made Together*, 32.
30. Sobel, *World They Made Together*, 54–63.
31. Baker, *Securing the Commonwealth*, 51.
32. Shields, *Oracles of Empire*, 88.
33. Kenneth Morgan describes this network in "Colonial American Rice Trade." For a more general discussion of the importance of family networks for the integration of the Atlantic world, see Hancock, *Citizens of the World*.
34. Ogilvie, *Carolina*, 24, line 327. Subsequent line references will be given parenthetically.
35. Drayton, *View of South-Carolina*, 160. Subsequent line references will be given parenthetically.
36. Carney, *Black Rice*, 81.
37. McCusker and Menard, *Economy of British America*, 178.
38. Wood, *Black Majority*, 60.
39. Wood, *Black Majority*, 36.
40. Philip Morgan, *Slave Counterpoint*, 182.
41. Wood, *Black Majority*, 122.
42. Mulford, "New Science," 88.
43. Edwards, *History*, 2:27.

44. Ibid., 2:128–31, 227–39; Roughley, *Jamaica Planter's Guide*, 221–77.
45. Edwards, *History*, 2:2; Long, *History of Jamaica*, 2:377–88.
46. Long, *History of Jamaica*, 2:377, 380.
47. Grainger, *Sugar Cane*, book 1, line 266–69. Subsequent references will be given parenthetically.
48. Gilmore, *Poetics of Empire*; Sandiford, *Cultural Politics of Sugar*; Irlam, "'Wish You Were Here'"; Egan, "'Long'd-for Aera.'"
49. Steven W. Thomas, "Doctoring Ideology," 96–98.
50. Sheridan, *Doctors and Slaves*, 239.
51. Ibid., 31.
52. Eliot, *Notes*, 53.
53. Rubin, *I'll Take My Stand*, xxix, 53; Ransom, "Aesthetic of Regionalism," in *Selected Essays*, 47.
54. Odum and Moore, *American Regionalism*, vii, 4, 18, 524–32.
55. Ibid., 43.
56. Gilroy, *Black Atlantic*, 4.
57. Webb, *Divided We Stand*, 131, 160; Bakhtin, *Dialogic Imagination*, 15, 45; Pratt, *Imperial Eyes*, 4; Gilroy, *Black Atlantic*, 6.
58. Ransom, "Art and the Human Economy," in *Selected Essays*, 189.

CHAPTER SIX

Captive in Mexico
Zebulon Pike and the New American Regionalism

Andy Doolen

SINCE THE INSPIRING geographical revisionism of the 1990s, spatially minded scholars have been remapping the study of U.S. history, culture, people, and institutions within distinctive networks of "transnational connectivities," which bypass the nation's political borders and resist state power and practices.[1] Spatial models such as the hemispheric, transatlantic, and black Atlantic, among others, reflect a growing awareness that nation-states are, and always have been, leaky containers. In the progressive models common in cultural studies, the national border stands as a subversive site, at once literal and metaphorical, where the flows of transnational individuals and groups expose and deconstruct the hegemonic practices of the nation-state. By tracing the circulation of histories, cultures, peoples, and institutions through "contact zones," scholars uncover intricate local patterns of difference, subaltern agency, hybridization, and territorialization.[2]

Yet even this progressive variation of transnationalism does not necessarily require a wholesale rejection of state practices and national institutions, ideas, and identities. Broad in its theoretical conception, transnationalism takes many forms, and its objectives and priorities vary radically depending on both field and discipline.[3] My transnational model rests on a basic premise: the process of territorialization in the early United States—relentlessly acquiring territory, making and unmaking boundaries, expelling Native Americans and importing slaves, and constantly mapping and remapping the coordinates of (white) personhood—cannot be easily divorced from the nation-state. Thus, this essay, which examines the exploratory writing of Zebulon Pike, is grounded in specific historical linkages between the western borderlands and the United States in the aftermath of the Louisiana Purchase. In their cogent introduction to *Continental Crossroads: Remapping U.S.-Mexico Borderlands History*, Samuel Truett and Elliot Young argue that "national borders are where territorialization becomes real, where physical markers and barriers are erected, and agents of the state regulate the movement of people, goods, and information."[4] The new American regionalism invoked in this essay's title proposes a transnational model that fixes attention simultaneously on the constitutive linkages between the nation-state and its changing western border.

A key precept in this essay is that empire-building in the early United States was never *exclusively* the top-down product of the state, its prominent actors, and their strategic planning. The federal state certainly was a major force and steadily growing in power: it purchased territories, surveyed and sold the land, possessed the exclusive right of negotiation with Indian tribes, organized territorial governments, conducted foreign diplomacy, and increased or decreased border security, depending on the situation. However, it was the hazy, ever-shifting boundary between state and nonstate actions that made the dynamic so effective in acquiring and organizing territory. Joint ventures involved in mapping the continent, distributing land, financing cotton production, building infrastructure, developing steam power, and organizing cross-border raids spurred the process of territorialization. In this light, the commonplace notions in historical scholarship of a weak undersized state and the natural limits of a restrained Jeffersonian republic miss a fundamental point. It is precisely the fact that the federal state could never dominate territorialization through sheer military and political muscle that distinguished U.S. empire-building at this stage.[5]

The invention of a continental imaginary was an essential element in the process of territorialization. Travelers, novelists, politicians, newspapermen, explorers, poets, merchants, and many others—state and nonstate actors alike—collectively authored the spatial logic of an enlarged republic.[6] They made it possible to imagine the future extension of U.S. sovereignty beyond the Mississippi River. Their discourse blurred the lines between political materials (legislation, diplomacy, directives, and correspondence) and cultural materials (newspapers, novels, travel writing, poetry, and popular rituals). Only in retrospect does the separation between these two discourses seem neat. These "cartographic texts," as Thomas Hallock defines them, were embedded in the process of territorialization, explicitly addressing issues of possession and ownership and attempting to legitimate U.S. occupancy of contested territories.[7] Cartographic texts are integral to the practices of territorial conquest, creating what Neil Brenner and Stuart Elden call the "territory effect" of state power. The territory effect—the idealistic stories told about the land itself—depicted a God-given national territory and strengthened the Anglo-American conviction that their modern republic was not repeating the violent history of colonialism in North America.[8] My analysis of this ideological formation lends credence to David Gutiérrez's observation that the "power to *explain*" the conquest of Mexican territory, ultimately, was the "critical aspect" of empire-building in the early United States.[9]

Between 1804 and 1806, five U.S. government expeditions explored the largely unknown and virtually unmapped western territory known as the Louisiana Purchase.[10] The stunning acquisition had inspired a wide-ranging discourse in the United States about its terrain, climate, Native and European inhabitants, and trade routes. These writings—mainly composed of accounts of exploration and travel—informed the distinctive process of U.S. territorialization in the decades following the Louisiana Purchase. The published accounts of the exploring expeditions were, as Peter Kastor has observed, "the first concerted effort within the United States to describe the Far West."[11] Indeed, exploratory writing, by expanding the national imaginary to encompass the immense western borderlands, had a specific function in creating the territory effect of an acquisitive nation-state.[12] Veiling the United States' spatial interventions and conquests behind a range of empirical metrics and catalogues of eternal natural features, exploratory writing rationalized the extension of state power into contested border zones.

In U.S. frontier lore, the remarkable journey of Meriwether Lewis and William Clark and their Corps of Discovery stands as the epitome of the enlightened aims of republican expansion. Their contemporary, the explorer Zebulon Pike, remains an awkward fit in this patriotic tradition, since his 1806 expedition into the southwestern borderlands ended disastrously after he became lost and led his men into Spanish territory. Spanish troops captured the wayward expedition near Santa Fe and transported the men to Chihuahua for questioning. Spanish officials had good reason to believe that the expedition was part of Aaron Burr's rumored plot to invade Mexico with a filibustering army. Not only had Burr's associate, General James Wilkinson, planned the Pike expedition; its movement into the southwest also coincided with the alarming news that Burr's private army was traveling down the Mississippi River. Pike was eventually released after Spanish officials determined that his expedition was not part of the conspiracy to invade the colony. Unfortunately for him, he returned home at the height of the Burr conspiracy trial, and the winding trail of rumor and suspicion led directly to Pike and his errant expedition. He promptly began composing an account of his explorations that he hoped would clear his name and promote his expedition's achievements. This essay argues that Pike's *An Account of Expeditions to the Sources of the Mississippi and through the Western Parts of Louisiana*, while rarely read today, remains an important resource for understanding the relationship between territory and empire, and specifically the emergence of a new American regionalism at a crucial juncture in U.S. history.

CAPTIVES IN MEXICO

The surviving members of the Pike expedition who returned to the United States in 1807 had endured a frightening ordeal of hunger, fatigue, and imprisonment.

Nothing went right after the men caught sight of the "Grand Peak" in the distance that years later was named in honor of Pike. Guided by a poor, secondhand tracing of Alexander von Humboldt's map of the region, Pike took his men up the Arkansas River, but soon they were lost in a frigid mountainous maze. Eventually, they crossed a river that they mistakenly believed was the Red—it actually was the Rio Grande, putting them in foreign territory. Royalist troops pursued the tattered expedition to their rough stockade, where a U.S. flag flapped overhead on a makeshift pole, and took Pike's ragged men prisoners.[13] They were transported to Chihuahua for questioning—an obvious warning that Spain was frustrated by repeated violations of its territorial sovereignty—and eventually escorted back to the Texas-Louisiana border in June 1807.[14]

Pike could not have chosen a worse time to return home. The Burr treason trial was in full swing, and Pike's superior, General Wilkinson, who had authorized Pike's mission, was testifying against Burr. Swept up in the scandal, Pike was rumored to be either a commander in Burr's army or a pawn oblivious to the plot. With a cloud of suspicion shadowing his expedition, Pike collected his logs, journals, and sketches and wrote a history of his expedition that he hoped would remove the stigma of complicity and celebrate the success of his enterprise.[15] Exploratory writing normally refrained from drawing attention to humiliating experiences of being lost, because they called into question the strength of the explorer's command and his knowledge of the territory. Of course, Pike's expedition does not fit neatly into this context, since he was writing also to restore his reputation. He had been accused of deliberately crossing the border into Spanish territory so that royalist forces would arrest him and carry him deeper into Mexico, a ruse that supposedly would allow him to spy for Burr and Wilkinson. If Pike was to allay any doubts about his association with the Burr conspiracy, he had little choice but to claim that it was his incompetence that had stranded his party in foreign territory.

It is remarkable, considering these obstacles, how Pike converted his failure into a national narrative about the ascendancy of republican principles in Mexico. Transnational stories of captives in Africa, Latin America, and Native America were a staple of U.S. popular culture during the early 1800s. As Paul Baepler observes about the wildly popular Barbary captivity narratives, more than a hundred editions were published in the United States between 1798 and 1817.[16] Anglo-American sailors deprived of their liberties in North Africa offered Pike a familiar rhetorical model that could explain his humiliating ordeal to readers while also recouping his sense of national purpose. He could also draw on the recent experiences of Anglo-American filibusters captured during Francisco Miranda's failed 1806 invasion of Venezuela. Ten unfortunate citizens had been sentenced to death and at least twenty-six others to a life of slavery; a Spanish tribunal rejected outright their pleas that Miranda had duped them by not disclosing his true intentions. In 1808 Congress, after receiving a petition from the thirty-six prisoners in Cartagena, had urged President Jefferson to liberate the men from their cruel incarceration.[17] That same year, Commander James Biggs, who had served under Miranda, recounted his experiences in a thrilling tale about Miranda's foolhardy scheme to spark a revolution in South America.[18] Like Pike, Biggs also hoped that his story might clear his name and counter the "fictions of rumour and the exaggerations of ignorance" that had tarnished the reputations of the brave men who had joined Miranda's filibustering expedition and suffered such hardships.[19] In short, the popular captivity genre might aid Pike in rehabilitating his own tattered reputation.

The experience of captivity gave Pike a rare inside look at Mexico, and he took advantage of it, when composing his account, to defend himself and his errant expedition into Spanish territory. The captivity scenario, when embedded in a personal narrative, is a useful device for reporting on encounters with a foreign culture. On the road from Santa Fe to Chihuahua, he notes road conditions, commits geographical features to memory, and covertly attempts to acquire Spanish maps. Unable to rein in his national pride, he teaches the people about the free republic to the north, until his loose talk finally compels his Spanish captors to try to silence him.[20] Yet the garrulous commander has already learned that the Mexican people are unhappy and ready to revolt. In every destitute village the royal procession passes through with its prized prisoner, Pike, who speaks no Spanish but claims to hear people grumbling about royal authority and whispering about a revolution. Here he turns his disgrace into an opportunity to reassert his patriotism and national loyalty. While he may have been stripped of his most valuable masculine virtues, his liberty and authority, he refuses to surrender his original mission to survey the geopolitical terrain. His covert view of Mexico shows how republican principles were beginning to revolutionize the colony.

The presence of other U.S. citizens in Mexico, however, undermines Pike's attempt to embody an expansive U.S. sovereignty. One standard element of the captivity narrative is its depiction of how foreign blood, customs, and rituals threaten the prisoner's identity. Following suit, Pike identifies the Other—the Spaniards as well as their impoverished Mexican subjects—but this binary collapses when he encounters other U.S. citizens, some captives like himself and others living there by choice. These exiles appear intermittently in the Pike narrative: prisoners who survived Philip Nolan's raid on Texas in 1801; a former federal official who is now a foreign mercenary in charge of a military academy and munitions factory in Chihuahua; smugglers lurking near the international boundary line at the Sabine River, ready "to embrace an opportunity of carrying some illicit commerce with the Spaniards"; and a fugitive whom Pike suspects first of being an "agent of Burr's" but discovers later is wanted for the murder of a U.S. military officer.[21] Their presence poses a challenge to Pike the author. Suspected of conspiring with Burr and Wilkinson, Pike needs to distance himself from his criminal countrymen—the filibusters, the mercenary, the freebooters, and the murderer—as much as he did his Spanish captors.

The Nolan filibusters presented a delicate problem for Pike, since he could not easily depict them as outlaws. Philip Nolan had preceded Pike as a trusted aide to James Wilkinson. An Irish immigrant from Belfast, Nolan actually grew up in Wilkinson's Kentucky household after the Revolutionary War and eventually became Wilkinson's trusted commercial agent. Among his many responsibilities, Nolan piloted the general's keelboats down the Ohio and Mississippi Rivers to New Orleans. Nolan was well known for daring raids into the borderlands. He lived with the Comanche and learned their language, customs, and politics, and he studied Comanche techniques for capturing wild mustangs.[22] He earned some degree of fame when on one occasion, in 1799, he entered New Orleans with twelve hundred horses, which, as Pekka Hämäläinen writes, caused a "trading fever that sent large numbers of American merchants to the plains."[23] Few U.S. citizens at the time, if any, possessed more knowledge than Nolan did about the region's geographical and political complexities.[24] Jefferson knew about him and even sent a personal request that Nolan deliver one of his finest mustangs to Monticello, but he never made the journey.

On several occasions, Spain complained to the U.S. State Department about Nolan, but no effort was made to halt the illegal raids of Wilkinson's protégé. By 1800 Spanish officials thought Nolan's ambitions had outgrown the horse trade—he could be spying for Wilkinson, organizing a filibustering raid, or joining forces with the Comanche for attacks on settlements in Texas and New Mexico. When Spain denied Nolan and his men passports and licenses, he brazenly led his force into Texas anyway. Soon afterward, royalist troops intercepted his expedition on the Texas plains, shot him dead, and routed his thirty-man party. The survivors were imprisoned for years in Chihuahua and surrounding villages and anxiously awaited an execution order to arrive from Madrid.[25] They desperately hoped that Jefferson might come to their rescue, but unfortunately for them, Nolan's raids had aggravated Spanish officials.[26] Reluctant to antagonize them any further, Jefferson declined repeatedly to negotiate the prisoners' release.

Even though they enjoy some status in Texas historiography, Nolan and his filibusters have largely been excluded from U.S. historiography and are little more than a footnote in Pike criticism. However, their captivity and terrible fate, I believe, constitute a key symbolic event in the Pike narrative. Implicated in an unlawful conspiracy, Pike responds to the presence of the Nolan men by dividing legitimate from illegitimate forms of territorialization. He aims to maintain the picturesque view of a future republican empire in the midcontinental interior that he had experienced in his northern expedition, but he cannot maintain this view if he endorses illegal cross-border raids, so for him to include the Nolan men is a gamble. The explorer suspected of espionage had to be careful not to identify himself too closely with an unlawful nonstate action led by Wilkinson's other protégé; such an association would run the risk of merging the two parties in the public mind and undermining the explorer's attempt to define his mission as a worthy national achievement. But the imprisoned Nolan men are essential to the primary objective of Pike's cartographic narrative: the plight of these nonstate actors provides a parallel narrative to that of the government explorer, which assists him in drawing a crucial distinction between legitimate and illegitimate modes of expansion.

Their presence assists Pike the author in articulating a compelling explanation for his own failure in Spanish territory. In travel writing about early North America, failure is not an unusual experience. Franklin contends that stories of failure—of the defeated, the lost, and the dead—are central to a narrative tradition in which the traveler survives tragedy if only to memorialize "all those people who cannot come back in word or deed."[27] Failure was an additional burden for the traveler to handle after returning home and facing the daunting challenge of finding meaning in an unsuccessful journey. The traveler, after surviving a crossing marked by suffering and blown expectations, attempts to soothe the thousand cuts of defeat during the narrative process. These stories span historical periods and cross generic lines—from Christopher Columbus's epistolary confession of disillusionment and Mary Rowlandson's tragic tale of captivity to Hector John de Crèvecoeur's account of a farmer's flight from revolutionary violence and Herman Melville's seafaring narrators who carry home their haunting memories of the disappeared. In short, travel writing produced in the New World constitutes a record of suffering travelers and explorers who are compelled to tell their stories. Like Ishmael being drawn into a mournful funeral procession in *Moby Dick*, the impulse to enter the narrative process is the way the survivor begins to salvage a sense of hope from the ruins of a journey.

As soon as Pike returned to the United States, he cleared up the mystery of the Nolan expedition by publishing a letter about his encounter with the marooned survivors. In Pike's *Account of Expeditions to the Sources of the Mississippi and through the Western Parts of Louisiana*, an expanded memorial about the Nolan men had a dual function: establishing a narrative of parallel captivities and distinguishing the two different types. Pike finds traces of the Nolan men on the journey to Chihuahua and realizes that he has been following in their footsteps. A Spanish official shows off Nolan's rifle, a prized possession, and Pike meets Caesar, Nolan's former slave.[28] In Chihuahua, Solomon Colly, a Nolan man and fellow prisoner, serves as one of Pike's translators. Two episodes, in particular, provide some clues about Pike's decision to include the tragedy of the Nolan expedition. Prior to Pike's departure from Chihuahua, Colly approaches him with "tears in his eyes and hoped I would not forget him when I arrived in the United States." Later, Pike encounters a second prisoner, the Nolan man David Fero, who by coincidence once served under Pike's father in the U.S. Army; Fero has escaped his imprisonment in order to enlist the aid of his former commander's son.

This reunion of white brothers constitutes what Nelson refers to as a "fraternal performance" in the masculinist and racial construction of U.S. national identity.[29] While the scene seems to suggest that the two parallel narratives have merged precisely at this moment of sympathetic expression, the reunion actually signals the key difference between their experiences. Embracing these lost men, the sympathetic Pike aims to recover the full measure of the white masculinity he has surrendered on being captured in foreign territory. He once again embodies his command, reminding readers of his republican mission, displaying the manly virtues that Pike employed to bring peace to warring Native nations. His embrace, alas, also distances him from the Nolan men, who have violated the law and encroached on Spanish territory in the pursuit of private gain. Pike makes this important, if subtle, distinction.

Nevertheless, he cannot turn Fero away when he shows up and begs for help. Their bond—national, fraternal, and racial—proves overwhelming. Faced with a man who was "formerly a brother soldier," he asks, "could I deny him the interview from any motives of delicacy?" Of course, Pike cannot:

> No; forbid it, humanity! Forbid it every sentiment of my soul! Our meeting was affecting, tears standing in his eyes. He informed me the particulars of their being taken, and many other circumstances since their being in the country. I promised to do all I could for him consistent with my character and honor, and their having entered the country without the authority of the United States. . . . I bade him adieu and gave him what my purse afforded, not what my heart dictated.[30]

The reunion between Pike and Fero is the most sentimental scene in Pike's narrative, and for good reason. By 1807 the Nolan men had been imprisoned for six years and could entertain little hope of being freed. Their fate was unknown back home; they had been abandoned by the United States, doomed to die in Mexican captivity. It is no coincidence that the only tears shed in Pike's account are those of two former U.S. soldiers facing either a life sentence or capital punishment for crossing illegally into Spanish territory. Not merely returning home with news of the condemned prisoners, Pike makes an impassioned plea that their lives be spared from Spanish cruelty. Pike casts himself as the embodiment of honorable republican manhood, inevitably splitting apart the two parallel captivity narratives. He reminds the reader that he was temporarily detained on an official mission; unlike the disgraced Nolan men, he never permanently surrendered his liberty.[31]

In expressing sympathy for the Nolan men, Pike must be careful not to appear to endorse the treasonous class of nonstate violence associated with Burr. In the foregoing passage, Pike acknowledges that the Nolan men had broken the law and undermined U.S. foreign policy. Yet filibusters were not always perceived as criminals or freebooters in the blind pursuit of riches, and Pike's embrace of the Nolan men shows that he is also aware of their popular appeal in not only the U.S. West but also eastern ports, such as New York and Baltimore, where filibustering and privateering expeditions were organized and financed. When these private militias were seen as fortifying border security or challenging Spanish prohibitions on trade, they could persuasively lay claim to republican traditions of protecting the public welfare and nurturing the expansion of free trade.[32] Of course, Spanish officials, seeing a real threat to the security of their northern provinces, worried constantly about the activities of privateering and filibustering enterprises.[33] Nolan's activity, in particular, occupied the attention of José Vidal, a Spanish commandant at Concordia, across the river from Natchez. The astute Vidal believed that this "enterprising American," hardly remembered today, was in the vanguard of redefining the Anglo-American conception of natural rights. Echoing Wilkinson's analysis, Vidal describes how these border-crossing Anglo-Americans were driving the process of territorialization two years prior to the Louisiana Purchase extending U.S. jurisdiction beyond the Mississippi River: "the greatest thing on which they base their liberty is saying that they are free to go wherever they please."[34] His insight reveals the sometimes indecipherable boundary between state and nonstate power. Forecasting how the process of territorialization will unfold in the coming decades, Vidal concludes that the United States "will always affect ignorance of such expeditions" since they advance the primary objective of territorial expansion. In the end, as Vidal had learned from his years on the border, "Americans will commence, little by little, to mine those precious possessions of His Majesty."[35] Indeed, Pike weeps for David Fero precisely because Fero is not Aaron Burr. Some U.S. citizens in Mexico might have acted rashly without state sanction, but they are not agents of treason or devoid of civic virtue.

On the contrary, they are a new breed of republican individual, forging a new amalgamation of territory and politics in borderlands far removed from the guiding hand of their Washington fathers. Nevertheless, these individuals seem fully aware of their obligations to a larger transnational political community. Or so Pike suggests in the final pages of his *Account*. His captivity has opened his eyes to a surprising development not yet seen by his remote fellow citizens on the Atlantic seaboard: a broad spectrum of the Mexican nation—malnourished miners and peasants, disaffected priests and officers, and two enlightened governors in the northern provinces, Don Antonio Cordero and Don Simon de Herrara—ready to fight for republican principles. These governors were blessed with "super-excellent qualities," Pike notes, sharing an intense "hatred to tyranny of every kind."[36] Rather than discussing his capture or justifying his mistakes, he sends the clear message that even if his expedition went off course, the transnational diffusion of

U.S. sovereignty into Mexico is preparing the ground for revolution. It was the essential territory effect of an expanding U.S. republican empire.

TRANSNATIONAL PASSAGES

In *Empire*, Michael Hardt and Antonio Negri refer to the ancient dream that inspired political theorists as dissimilar as Locke, Jefferson, Tocqueville, and Marx: an unbounded territory free of political obstacles, open to pure human desire, and ready to be transformed into a space of liberty. They envisioned North America as the space for this dream to become reality.[37] This ancient dream was inherent in the U.S. experiment in federalism. It was distinguished by the expansion of sovereignty across space, continually resisting the forces of control and always opening and renewing itself in a territory where typical European forms of centralization and hierarchy were absent. For Hardt and Negri, "this new sovereignty does not annex or destroy the other powers it faces but on the contrary opens itself to them, including them in the network." In this consensus model, political power circulates continually through the bodies of mobile citizens and their protective grid of federal, state, and local governments. In contrast to the European model of a transcendent sovereign and bounded territory, the Anglo-American network promised to lessen the concentration of political and economic power by distributing it across a larger territory.

The ancient dream of the "utopia of open spaces" also inspired the political desires of Zebulon Pike, even though he has never been counted among the esteemed intellectuals or political thinkers of his era.[38] His prose often echoes the "rising glory" poetry and oratory of literary nationalism, which traced the westward course of empire from Greece and Rome to the North American continent. At these moments, Pike seems like a true believer in the fantastical territorial effect that Hardt and Negri locate at the core of the U.S. political system; however, his bitter ordeal taught him a humiliating lesson about continental spaces theoretically open to republican desire. The presence of Spain, powerful Native nations, and an inhospitable landscape made further expansion very dangerous. While his rhetoric celebrated the transnational diffusion of U.S.-style liberty into northern Mexico, his captivity revealed a hazardous process of territorialization. Pike's patriotic tone mixed awkwardly with his somber ambivalence about a suddenly overextended republic: the Louisiana Purchase had precipitated this crisis by fusing the United States and Mexico together in a violent, undefined, and unstable borderland. His southwestern expedition had carried him into contested territories circumscribed by the same imperial borders and bureaucratic obstacles that held back social and political progress in Europe. The North American continent seemed to be no better space than Europe for realizing the ancient dream of democracy.

This irony, I believe, constitutes the Pike narrative's unique contribution to our understanding of U.S. empire-building in the early 1800s. This irony is also the defining characteristic of the new American regionalism that Pike helps readers decipher in his *Account*. His arduous journey through an immense geography running from present-day Minnesota to northern Mexico inspired a crucial insight about the future domain of U.S. sovereignty. Political domination of such a massive, contested territory was futile. In one representative episode, prior to being captured, Pike's failure to convince the Pawnee governing council to reject Spain and accept the United States as the dominant power in the region left an indelible impression on him. For centuries, powerful nations such as the Pawnee, Comanche, Sioux, Osage, and Apache had determined the balance of power in the midcontinental interior. As the Pawnee had demonstrated to Pike in their refusal to fly only the U.S. flag, they were skilled diplomats and very aware of their power. Discouraged, Pike confessed that the Pawnee, still flying the Spanish flag, would never yield to declarations of sovereignty from one U.S. officer and his twenty haggard troops. It was not simply Spain and its barrier of Native allies that ruined Pike's dream of an open space for republican empire. Traveling through the present-day Great Plains, Pike believed that he had discovered a vast inland desert unsuitable for agrarian settlement. This fictional barrier, later named the Great American Desert, is clearly distinct from the physical constructions of border fences and walls by contemporary states. However, the desert barrier served a similar function in delimiting both the actual and imaginary geography of the United States. During the 1810s and 1820s, as Stephanie LeMenager observes, the agrarian argument for U.S. Manifest Destiny on the continent had not yet achieved hegemony, so the perception of an inland desert convinced many Anglo-Americans that agrarian expansion and settlement was impossible and foolhardy.[39] LeMenager's perceptive analysis juxtaposes the desert barrier with the riverine flow of western empire. In stark contrast to the extensive network of waterways, the desert barrier forced a reassessment of the process of territorialization. Thus, for LeMenager, the inland desert, whether real or imaginary, operated as a heterotopia, a space "interrupting accepted national histories and forcing a reevaluation of what kind of future might develop from the nation's past."[40] She expertly traces the way nineteenth-century literary narratives continually revised Pike's 1810 fiction of a local, oppositional landscape. For instance, the fear that the growing republican empire would wither away in the Great American Desert inspired Cooper's ominously titled novel *The Prairie* (1827). The novel delivers a plea for a return home, LeMenager writes, "for a restorative reflux of U.S. settlers from the Far West."[41] By the 1820s the westward agrarian surge appeared to have confronted its geographical limits.

While the import of their expeditions varies widely, the explorers have long enjoyed an honored position in U.S. history. The contrast between Pike and his rivals Lewis and Clark tends to be plain and unforgiving. The triumphant, resourceful, and heroic Lewis and Clark reached the Pacific Ocean and established the U.S. claim on Oregon; a disoriented and unqualified Zebulon Pike was taken captive and paraded from Santa Fe to Chihuahua as an example of Anglo-American weakness and ineptitude.[42] Unfortunately, for Pike, his mistaken belief in the Great American Desert came to define his canonical value in U.S. history. The geography of the national narrative runs longitudinally, never more so than when the subject is continental expansion, so the grim significance of Pike's inland desert, as the graveyard of the westward-advancing agrarian empire, is patently obvious. The flawed explorer figuratively stands in for the early struggles of the United States to comprehend the mysterious territory and inhabitants it aimed to subdue and civilize. Even in this light, though, Pike's wayward journey has a silver lining, since it causes him to stumble on the hidden problems and dangers that will challenge U.S. hegemony on the continent.

The new American regionalism heralded in Pike's *Account* required a transnational perspective that can shift our understanding of the longitudinal axis of U.S. exploratory writing. Previously unseen aspects of this writing flicker and emerge, since the expeditions, and the very writings we are trying to translate, transport us beyond national boundaries and into the contexts of other regional, national, and hemispheric contexts.[43] Viewed in the setting of the remote borderlands, Pike does not seem as blind and untutored as the old regional and national narratives have made him out to be. Even if the inland desert impeded agrarian expansion, Pike predicted that the arid interior would soon achieve prominence as a hub for inter-American free trade. He envisioned a commercial passage that would connect the United States to Mexico and the Pacific Ocean, open up new markets in the hemisphere and Pacific Rim, and facilitate the free flow of people and goods. An inter-American commercial network, influenced and controlled by republican laws and values, would loosen the oppressive grip of mercantilism on the world. In short, his errant, humiliating journey honed his spatial awareness. Inspired to look beyond an agrarian world, he discovered a different future for the United States, an untapped geography of liberal imperialism.

I do not wish to suggest that Pike's transnational perspective was disconnected from events in Washington and the Atlantic metropolises. In fact, he seems to be responding directly to an economic crisis that had inspired some gloomy predictions about an impending national disaster. England and France, at war with each other, were attacking neutral U.S. vessels, seizing them and their cargos, and impressing sailors. Jefferson and the heavily Republican Congress, pressuring the two countries to halt their attacks, implemented a highly controversial embargo on European exports. The embargo, conceived as an Anglo-American alternative to the European system of war, failed to prevent the attacks. Even worse, the embargo caused economic hardship at home and sowed grave doubts about the viability of republican government.[44] If nonviolent commercial coercion was the alternative to war, then the long-term security of the nation was at risk. The end result, McCoy explains, was that the Jeffersonians reluctantly "[accepted] war as the dangerous but necessary means of furthering the Revolutionary vision of free trade."[45] The embargo had exposed a fatal flaw in the republican experiment.

While the embargo fixed the Anglo-American gaze on transatlantic trade with Europe, Pike encouraged readers to look toward the U.S.-Mexico borderlands and a southwestern passage that held enormous economic and political potential for the United States. In Washington, Republicans and Federalists were fighting over whether domestic industry or foreign trade was the best catalyst for healthy economic growth. From the borderlands he explored and interpreted in his account of his expeditions, Pike grasped how the Louisiana Purchase was already changing the direction of the economy. Industrious settlers were producing an agricultural surplus that only the expansion of export markets could absorb, and in the decades that followed, the process of territorialization aimed for the seamless integration of domestic industry and foreign trade. The Washington schism seemed irrelevant in a vast western territory where the borders between domestic and foreign spaces were as porous and interconnected as the western rivers.[46]

For Pike, the southwestern passage could restore and strengthen the experiment in republican-imperial expansion. By following his trail into the southwest, Anglo-Americans could still achieve an alternative to European systems of war and political domination, while reinforcing their commitment to the public welfare over self-interest. In light of the conflict in Washington, Pike's sense of emerging inter-American commerce offered a radical resolution to the economic and political crisis.

Finally, Pike predicts that U.S. principles are already loosening the Spanish stranglehold on Mexico. An oppressed people are beginning to wake up to the possibility of freedom. Indeed, he is writing on the cusp of a momentous shift in inter-American commerce between the United States, Mexico, and other breakaway Spanish colonies. In this light, Pike's major achievement may be that the territory effect depicted in his *Account* helped make liberal imperialism an acceptable and patriotic endeavor in the early 1800s. His foresight explains why, for at least twenty years following the publication of his journal, after his untimely death in 1813 at the Battle of York, Pike was "easily the most commanding figure of this early period of exploration."[47] The awesome commercial potential of the border corridor, William Goetzmann writes, was the "the lodestone that drew Americans into the Southwest."[48] Policy makers and military officers studied Pike's journal, and traders, filibusters, and explorers carried it with them into the southwestern portions of the Louisiana Purchase, using it as a travel guide and studying its pages and maps for clues of trade routes to Santa Fe.[49] Of course, as I have argued here, Pike's *Account of Expeditions to the Sources of the Mississippi and through the Western Parts of Louisiana* was much more than a travel guide through largely unknown lands. In its pages, readers discovered a model of U.S. sovereignty defined by the transnational circulation of people, commodities, and information. Pike's travels had given him, and his readers—past and present—a more nuanced understanding of the changing boundaries of a continental nation.

NOTES

Some material in this essay also appears, in very different form, in my book *Territories of Empire: U.S. Writing from the Louisiana Purchase to Mexican Independence* (Oxford University Press, 2014).

1. Grewal, *Transnational America*, 3.
2. I am referring to Pratt's spatial concept. See Pratt, *Imperial Eyes*. The intellectual roots of contemporary transnationalist scholarship are found in the work of three noteworthy critics. In his 1916 formulation of a "Trans-National America," Randolph Bourne looked beyond a narrow view of national racial origins to the positive value to be found in a multicultural America. See Bourne, "Trans-National America." In his study of Reconstruction, W. E. B. DuBois rejected a nation-centered historiography that paid little attention to the African American experience, and his studies of the international slave trade and pan-African networks would guide later theoretical conceptions of the black Atlantic. Finally, in his classic *The Spanish-American Borderland*, Herbert Bolton, Frederick Jackson Turner's former protégé, envisioned the West not as a space synonymous with American civilization but as a geography of accommodation and contestation.
3. For a helpful overview of the different variations of transnationalism in academic discourse, see Vertovec, "Conceiving and Researching Transnationalism."
4. Truett and Young, *Continental Crossroads*, 2.
5. Classical theories of imperialism and the historiography of U.S. expansionism overlap in this key area: both underline the power of a central state, the decisions of its policy makers and military leaders, and the projection of political, military, and economic power toward the periphery. On the theories of imperialism across history, see Thornton, *Doctrines of Imperialism*; Reynolds, *Modes of Imperialism*.
6. While he may be discussing the state/nonstate dynamic in a contemporary context, Weizman's central point is that a diffuse collection of authors ultimately defines the process of territorialization. See Weizman, *Hollow Land*.
7. Hallock, *From the Fallen Tree*, 202.
8. See Brenner and Elden, "Henri," 354.
9. Gutiérrez, "Significant to Whom?" 69.
10. Lewis and Clark explored the Missouri and Columbia Rivers to the Pacific Coast (1804–6); Mississippi scientist William Dunbar, aided by George Hunter, led a group up the Ouachita River to the Hot Springs of present-day Arkansas (1804); Zebulon Pike headed two expeditions, exploring the upper Mississippi River and the southwestern purchase, which took his party into present-day Kansas, Missouri, Colorado, Arkansas, and New Mexico (1805–7); and Thomas Freeman and Peter Custis ascended the Red River more than six hundred miles before Spanish troops forced them to return home (1806).
11. Kastor, "'What Are the Advantages of the Acquisition?'" 1019.
12. Brenner and Elden, "Henri," 373.

13. Donald Dean Jackson, *Jefferson and the Stony Mountains*, 253.
14. Several others remained imprisoned until 1809. See ibid., 262.
15. Contemporary scholars still repeat this myth about Aaron Burr organizing the Pike expedition as part of the conspiracy to invade Mexico. For example, Fresonke's reading of Pike is based on the erroneous assumption of a critical consensus on the Burr conspiracy. Judging by the notes, a 1947 article constitutes the major source of Fresonke's depiction of the episode. See Fresonke, *West of Emerson*, 44.
16. Baepler, *White Slaves, African Masters*, 24.
17. *Report of the Committee*.
18. Biggs, *History of Don Francisco*. Two more editions of this popular narrative were released in 1809 and 1811.
19. Ibid., x.
20. Pike, *Journals*, 1:419.
21. Ibid., 1:422, 447, 434. Before switching his allegiance to Spain, the Anglo-American mercenary Peter Walker had a short but promising career in U.S. government service. Having worked under Andrew Ellicot in 1798 during the federal survey of the U.S.–Spanish Florida boundary, Walker was named assistant, in 1800, to the territorial secretary, John Steele. Walker made no secret of his desire to lead an expedition up the Red River in search of a passage to Santa Fe, and Ellicot and William Dunbar recommended him to Jefferson for such a mission. During 1804–5, Walker's career took a mystifying turn after he led a private expedition up the Red River in search of a route to Santa Fe. He renounced the United States and accepted the commission of lieutenant in the Spanish service. He was well known for his surveying and mapmaking work; his two maps of the southwestern portions of the Louisiana Purchase, delivered to Governor Salcedo, eventually found their way into the hands of U.S. officials. Walker met Zebulon Pike in Chihuahua, boarding the prisoner and serving as one of his translators. As Flores notes, most of what is known about Walker's Spanish career comes from Pike's recollection of their discussions. Cox, "The Louisiana-Texas Frontier, II"; Flores, *Jefferson and Southwestern Exploration*, 39–40.
22. This turning point in Nolan's career occurred in the early 1790s on the midcontinental plains, when a Comanche party stripped him of his possessions, probably because he had trespassed on Comanche land. Stranded without horses or weapons, Nolan opted to live with the Comanche, the dominant power in the region. The two years he spent with them aided his rapid rise to prominence in the borderlands. See Chipman, *Spanish Texas*, 213–14.
23. Pekka Hämäläinen, *Comanche Empire*, 146.
24. Flores has concluded that "Nolan possessed more information about Texas than almost anyone on the frontier, and both Americans and Spaniards were coming to realize it." Flores, *Journal of an Indian Trader*, 11.
25. For a recent account, see Haley, *Passionate Nation*.
26. For years the Nolan men lived in this state of legal limbo, awaiting their imminent executions, until an official decree arrived from Spain and stated their punishment. According to Ellis Bean, the remaining eight prisoners were to throw dice; whoever rolled the low number would be the one executed for their crime, and after throwing a four, Ephraim Blackburn was the unlucky man. Bean certainly thought the excessive punishment did not fit the crime. Unlike Pike, Bean did not return home with his patriotism intact. Writing in

1816, a disillusioned Bean condemned Jefferson for vigorously defending the U.S. prisoners taken during the Algerine crisis while callously allowing the Nolan men to waste away in a country more vicious to captives than Algiers. In Bean's 1816 account, the ruined men are victims of Spanish cruelty, but they also symbolize the hypocrisy of republican foreign policy and a feckless president who have failed to free them from their terrible fate. Bean's memoir was not published in his lifetime. It first appeared in Yoakum's 1855 *History of Texas*. On Bean's fascinating career, see Jackson, *Indian Agent*; and Lay, *The Lives of Ellis P. Bean*.

27. Wayne Franklin, *Discoverers, Explorers, Settlers*, 135.

28. Pike, *Journals*, 1:416. Caesar apparently had passed into the possession of Peter Walker, the mercenary who supervised the military academy in Chihuahua. Caesar also went by the Spanish name Juan Bautista. Another of Nolan's slaves escaped during the skirmish on the Texas plains. See Loomis, "Philip Nolan's Entry into Texas in 1800."

29. Nelson, *National Manhood*.

30. Pike, *Journals*, 1:416.

31. Fero was eventually released from prison to fight for Spain during the Mexican revolution. After switching sides and joining the insurgent forces, Fero was charged with disloyalty and beheaded. Jackson includes this information in a note in Pike, *Journals*, 1:416. For other brief mentions of Fero, see also Hubert Howe Bancroft, *History of Mexico*, 306; Rodriguez and Guedea, "How Relations between Mexico and the U.S. Began."

32. U.S. officials found it nearly impossible to prosecute the men who filibustered in Spanish lands because local juries, especially in the border regions, refused to convict parties of men admired widely for their patriotic zeal. See Warren, *The Sword Was Their Passport*; Owsley and Smith, *Filibusters and Expansionists*.

33. Weber, *Spanish Frontier in North America*, 296.

34. Houck, *Spanish Régime in Missouri*, 2:290. Jose Vidal should not be confused with Pedro Vial, who spent more than twenty years in the region mapping trading routes to Santa Fe. Pedro Vial, also known as Pierre Vial, was a native of France. See Loomis and Nasatir, *Pedro Vial*.

35. Houck, *Spanish Régime in Missouri*, 2:290.

36. Pike, *Journals*, 1:441.

37. Hardt and Negri, *Empire*, 168.

38. Ibid., 169.

39. LeMenager, *Manifest and Other Destinies*, 74.

40. Ibid., 7.

41. Ibid., 69.

42. Of course, Pike was at a disadvantage when it came to Lewis and Clark. Nicholas Biddle deserves some portion of the credit for the legacy of Lewis and Clark, since he skillfully transformed the journals of Lewis and Clark into a triumphant narrative about Anglo-American destiny on the continent. There are many studies of Biddle's authorship but none more incisive than Nelson's brilliant analysis of Biddle's transformation of the journals into a narrative of heroic national achievement. See Nelson, *National Manhood*, 61–101.

43. Transnational frameworks, while occasionally caricatured for transcending sociopolitical landscapes, actually occupy multiple territories at once. My sense of how exploratory writing, by definition, enters/exits different "contexts" draws on Claudia Sadowski-Smith's

reflections on border studies. See Sadowski-Smith, "Introduction: Comparative Border Studies," 284.

44. McCoy, *Elusive Republic*, 223. On the embargo, see also Perkins, *Prologue to War*; Malone, *Jefferson the President*; Rothman, *Slave Country*; Smelser, *Democratic Republic*; James E. Lewis, *American Union and the Problem of Neighborhood*; Steven Watts, *Republic Reborn*.

45. McCoy, *Elusive Republic*, 210.

46. I am drawing on McCoy's analysis of the Louisiana Purchase; see ibid., 205. Even though there is much to admire in Steven Watts's *Republic Reborn*, I do not share his overarching, bifurcated view of "a massive, multifaceted transformation away from republican traditions and toward modern liberal capitalism in America" in 1790–1820 (xvii). Certainly, the rise of entrepreneurial capitalism transformed some segments of the United States, which became increasingly defined by self-controlled bourgeois individualism. However, this did not necessarily entail the abandonment of outdated republican ideological controls such as virtue and the public good, which other segments of society, such as U.S. slaveholders, adapted to changing economic and political circumstances. Nevertheless, one does not have to accept his thesis about the shift from republicanism to liberalism to benefit from his excellent book.

47. Cox, *Early Exploration of Louisiana*, 151.

48. Goetzmann, *Exploration and Empire*, 52.

49. On the development of trade routes to Santa Fe, see Loomis and Nasatir, *Pedro Vial*, 235–61. One of the most important early enterprises to reach Santa Fe from Saint Louis was the McKnight-Baird party. Using Pike's journal as a map, they arrived in Santa Fe in 1812, and their goods were confiscated. Charged with being involved in the Hidalgo revolt, the men were imprisoned in Chihuahua. In 1821 William Becknell, hearing of Mexican independence, arrived in Santa Fe with pack mules loaded with goods. He made a profit, returned to Saint Louis to purchase more wagons, and left again for New Mexico. The Santa Fe Trail had become a viable trade route. Discussing the impact of Pike's journal, Leo Oliva offers this summary: "it is safe to declare that everyone who ventured forth from the United States to establish contact with northern Mexico after 1811 benefited either directly or indirectly from Pike's expedition and journal." Oliva, "Enemies and Friends," 36.

CHAPTER SEVEN

On the Hudson River Line

Postrevolutionary Regionalism, Neo-Tory Sympathy, and "A Lady of the State of New-York"

Duncan Faherty

THE BRITISH POSSESSED Manhattan for as long as they could. The city served as a major egress point after the revolution, and the logistics of withdrawing thousands of troops, emancipated slaves, and refugee Loyalists proved daunting. Finally, on November 25, 1783, nine months after declaring a ceasefire and eleven weeks after signing the Treaty of Paris, George Washington paraded the vestiges of the Continental army down Broadway to celebrate the city's liberation.[1] Forced to abandon Manhattan seven years earlier, Washington likely found it unrecognizable on his return. During the occupation, the British remodeled the cityscape by seizing property, securing fortifications, and forcing scores of patriots into shantytown encampments. Suspicious fires, still smoldering as Washington marched in, were likely the last parting gifts of disgruntled Loyalists. Perhaps, most hauntingly, the British had dumped the bodies of more than eighteen thousand prisoners of war—victims of starvation, disease, and abusive mistreatment—either directly in the harbor or in shallow shoreline graves.[2] The city was battered, scorched, and embittered; its docks and waterways, formerly crowded symbols of New York's prominence, were choked with the bones of the dead.[3] Despite all this devastation, or rather because of it, Washington's return was embraced as a harbinger of better days.

For decades after the British retreat, Evacuation Day (as the anniversary became known) was raucously observed in the New York area. Enthusiasm for the holiday began to wane in the mid-nineteenth century, especially after Abraham Lincoln legislated the annual recognition of a national day of Thanksgiving in 1863.[4] The promotion of a federal holiday to foster collective unity effectively subsumed local traditions within the overarching framework of the nation. Prior to this erasure of regional sentiments by executive decision, New Yorkers annually commemorated Washington's reentry as an instantiation of local pride. Indeed, even as city officials struggled to rebuild, they sought to cultivate Washington's favor by granting him "the freedom of the City" in a 1785 ceremonial declaration. Touched by this tribute, Washington conveyed his public thanks in a widely circulated letter expressing his hope that the "devastations of War" might "soon be without a trace." Prophesizing that New York would crucially shape the emerging republic, Washington forecast that "your State (at present the Seat of the Empire) may set such examples of wisdom and liberality, as shall have a tendency to strengthen and give permanency to the Union at home, and credit and respectability to it abroad." After christening it the Empire State, Washington closed his letter by noting that "the primary object of all my desires" was for New York to anchor national growth. If the United States was destined to emerge on the world stage, Washington proposed, New York was to serve as its city on a hill.[5]

On the surface, Washington's optimism concerning the futurity of the nascent republic—and New York's centrality in that unfolding—might retrospectively read as emblematic of postwar buoyancy. Flattered by a symbolic gift from a still-recovering city, Washington may have intended to nurture local morale during a protracted rebuilding period. Considered in another light, Washington's optimistic figurations also project his vision of a federated expansion as a means of countering the allure of parochial interests. Indeed, whatever motivated Washington's public intent has to be considered alongside his simultaneous, more private expression of reservations over New York's potential damaging influence. These affective reservations percolate within a personal letter Washington wrote on the same day he recorded his gratitude to local officials. Within this second letter, inscribed to James Duane, the region functions not as a harbinger of an unfolding empire but rather as a locus of destabilization that undermined the cohesiveness of the fragile national confederation. This more candid expression of Washington's cynicism about the prospects for confederated unity details his reaction to a lawsuit recently adjudicated under New York's Trespass Act. A contrapuntal archive to his publicly sanguine predictions, this second letter registers paranoia over regional influence on the development of the republic.

Passed by the state legislature in 1783, New York's Trespass Act authorized citizens to claim compensation for any damaged, destroyed, or occupied property that they had been forced to abandon during the revolution. One of the most publicly monitored of these suits involved a patriotic widow whose alehouse had been commandeered and operated by the British during the occupation. This case, *Rutgers v. Waddington*, sparked a great deal of interest, in part because Washington's former chief of staff, Alexander Hamilton, conducted the defense.[6] Fearing that a series of blatantly anti-Loyalist legislative acts passed by the state (essentially depriving Loyalists of civil and financial protections) would threaten the hard-won peace accord with England, Hamilton orchestrated the defense to preserve the embryonic international standing of the United States. Hamilton argued that if Waddington was found guilty under the Trespass Act, such a judgment would "violate a solemn Treaty of peace & revive the state of hostility," and in so doing it would "infringe the Confederation of the United States" and "endanger the peace of the Whole."[7] In his concluding statement before the court, Hamilton urged that the legislation be declared invalid based on the doctrine of judicial review. Despite the absence of a federal judiciary under the Articles of Confederation, Hamilton prevailed by essentially arguing to a state court that a state lacked the authority to pass legislation that contradicted or undermined federal treaties and regulations.

Sent copies of the trial transcripts, Washington reviewed them with great interest. His private letter to Duane records his "hearty assent" to the judgment of the court, as well as his concerns about the damaging potential of local partisanship: "It is painful, to hear that a State which used to be foremost in Acts of liberality, and its exertion to establish our federal system upon a broad bottom and solid ground is contracting her ideas, and pointing them to local and independent measures; which, if persevered in, must Sap the Constitution of these States (already too weak), destroy our National character, and render us as contemptible in the eyes of Europe as we have it in our power to be respectable."[8] This vision of New York counters Washington's proclamations about its potential imperial centrality; in its place emerges consternation over how local antipathy might undermine a presumptive national unity. While the defeat of a patriotic widow is an odd cause for Washington to champion, like Hamilton, his concerns about the international reputation of the United States overdetermined his response. Within this elite vision of national futurity, sovereignty resided not with individual citizens but in the federal legislature that was elected to represent their concerns.

The juxtaposition of sentiments concerning national futurity contained within these two missives—the public hopes versus the private fears—are even stranger when we consider that they are essentially addressed to the same recipient: James Duane. The adopted ward of Robert Livingston, Duane represented New York at the Continental Congress, was appointed the first U.S. mayor of New York, and served as the presiding judge in *Rutgers v. Waddington*. Moreover, he was a confidant of Washington and Hamilton, and he shared their belief that the republic had little to gain from lingering tensions with England.[9] Incestuous nodes in the same communication network, the letters accentuate variations in public and private discourses concerning the realities of postrevolutionary politics. In his performative role as symbolic head of state, Washington emanated a deep faith in the viability of a national empire and in permanency. More private correspondence evinces his anxieties over how local interests might undermine the health of the embryonic confederation. But much more than this dichotomy of stability or chaos, a familiar way of thinking about this period, Washington's correspondence also stresses the crucial role of regional interests in forging the emerging sociopolitical landscape. For Washington, there was no question about New York's importance: if it labored in the service of union it would function as the seat of empire; if infected by the disease of partisanship it would cripple any potential for federated collectivity.

Washington's letters of April 10, 1785, considered conjointly, evince how many postrevolutionary elites labored to curtail sectionalism by promoting a vision for national expansion that subsumed local dissent within a larger geographical frame. Or again, the defeat of the patriotic widow's claims demonstrates just whose rights counted in pursuit of the shibboleth of a national imaginary. The decision sublimated the individual and the state in favor of a still abeyant federal common good. The episode serves as an encapsulation of how the local and, perhaps, parochial concerns of some New Yorkers misaligned with an elite vision for the postrevolutionary landscape; moreover, the judgment enacted a presumptive corrective to others who sought to assert agency via the Trespass Act. Following the insightful work of Ed White, I maintain that this episode makes vivid how the project of the republican megasynthesis (i.e., the project of many critics of the early republic but also the work of the Founders themselves) was really "the battle to control, fuse, and systematize not only discourse but, more importantly, practical ensembles, to manage, direct, and structure the division of the time."[10] The ardent patriots who supported the Trespass Act were one such ensemble, an assemblage judged at odds with the parasitic project of national consolidation. The case of *Rutgers v. Waddington* serves as but one instantiation of a widespread elite interest in quelling dissent as a means of fostering a national, as opposed to regional, sense of collectivity.

Following the often unacknowledged logic of Washington's letters, I want to speculate about how local partisan tensions in New York were a hallmark of cultural production from the region. In other words, these letters reveal a largely unacknowledged archive in which divergent registers of the prospects for notational synthesis reside. As a corollary to that claim, this essay explores how the scale of region might complicate our sense of the development of American literature and to think about how this narrower scale might differently inflect our understanding of "the distribution of the sensible" in the early republic.[11] In the habitual move to synthesize early postrevolutionary literary production within a national framework (even an expanded frame that maps the imperial dimensions of the early republic), the dissensus of regional interests have habitually been condemned by a kind of critical eminent domain. The implications of Washington's first letter—his hopes for New York to be the throne of a national empire—are familiar to us; yet we remain ill equipped to grapple with the challenges posed by his second letter, which anxiously fears the local trumping the nascently national. The multivalent partisanship coursing through New York like revolutionary aftershocks remains largely unplotted in typical narratives about U.S. cultural development. Such neglect springs from the constraining import of a synthesizing federal narrative of development, a rubric that dampers affiliations counter to that hegemony. Indeed, the idea of a postrevolutionary New York state of mind remains an anathema to early Americanists because *regionalism* does not comfortably align with either the desire to trace the growth of a national culture or the more expansive spatial turn of Atlantic studies.[12]

Early Americanists have seldom deployed the local as a measure of the tensions of expansion and consolidation, for, like Washington, we have publicly overinvested in national collectivity and the international dimensions of the early republic. By offering a different trajectory, one not oriented by synthesis, this essay is grounded in a consideration of the work of a neglected early U.S. pseudonymous writer who only identified herself as "A Lady of the State of New-York." In two texts published at the turn of the nineteenth century, *The Fortunate Discovery; or, the History of Henry Villars* (1798) and *Moreland Vale; or the Fair Fugitive* (1801), A Lady explores the parameters of how the lingering tensions arising from Loyalist legacies and neo-Tory sentiments shaped cultural order in the New York area after the revolution. In both novels she underscores how the event disrupted normative and (from her point of view) essential patterns of inheritance, even as she suggests how the populations of her imagined New York can only achieve stability by recognizing their connections to the authority of a prerevolutionary English order.

Following Amy Kaplan's groundbreaking reconfiguration of the relation of the domestic to the foreign, we have grown too accustomed to reading interiors as microcosms of larger national discourses.[13] While much fruitful work has deployed this paradigm, the collapse of the domestic with the national has obfuscated our interpretations of the multivalent legends on the postrevolutionary map. Habituated to a critical tradition shaped by Whiggish notions of development, we routinely deploy a classificatory praxis that excommunicates any object that cannot easily enfold within this synthesizing model. We forget all too frequently that Lincoln legislated a national holiday to enact an accumulating cohesiveness, and we ignore how the proclamation subtly erased regional identities such as those indexed by Evacuation Day celebrations. The work of A Lady of the State of New-York challenges this paradigm and these erasures, and her texts cannot easily be taxonomized within a traditional definition of the narrative concerns of the early U.S. canon. Like Washington's second letter, A Lady's vision of postrevolutionary New York does not comfortably align with our dominant configurations of the period. A reconsideration of how the work of A Lady provides a particular index for thinking about New York as an early American region also underwrites an unpacking of how the project of canon formation privileged nation over region. Such a distorted sense of the geographical diversity of early U.S. literature has obscured the lingering presence of Loyalist sentiments and naturalized the synthesizing resistance to dissent in the early republic.[14]

MAPPING THE EMPIRE STATE

Following the foundational work of Cathy Davidson's *Revolution and the Word* (1986), the early canon of the U.S. novel has coalesced around texts that can be interpreted as foregrounding issues of nation formation.[15] This critical orientation has distorted our understanding of the aims, ambitions, and geographies of postrevolutionary fiction and redacted the operant sense of what texts are objects worthy of study. A renewed attention to the scale of region, and its impact on literary production, would liberate us from habitual attempts to construct a canon of early U.S. novels via the tenets of the republic synthesis schematic. For the majority of contemporary readers of early postrevolutionary U.S. fiction, New York remains unmapped and invisible. While Manhattan bears witness to the ruinous seduction of the titular protagonist of Susannah Rowson's *Charlotte Temple* (1791/94), and even as the city's harbor provides a watery grave for the mysterious Clithero in Charles Brockden Brown's *Edgar Huntly* (1799), the presence of New York in the canon of early U.S. literature remains muted. The fact that Rowson's and Brown's limited representations serve as the two most familiar renditions of eighteenth-century Manhattan arises more from their ubiquity as the two most prominent early U.S. writers, rather than from any sustained attempt to register the importance of New York for the early republic. Compared to this relative absence, Philadelphia, Boston, Pennsylvania, and New England serve as familiar touchstones. Such a literary cartography belies the growing political importance of New York for the United States, especially in the late eighteenth century, during which time it did emerge as the Empire State despite the persistent partisan divisions that impacted its growth.

In the two decades following the revolution, no state in the republic underwent a more dramatic reconfiguration than New York. The state's population almost doubled between 1790 and 1800 (rising from 340,120 to 589,051) and increased yet again to almost one million (959,049) by 1810. In the words of Alan Taylor, while New York was "slow to develop as a colony," it would soon become "the most dynamic state in the newly independent American Republic."[16] Manhattan not only served as the first capital of the new nation but increasingly became an influential force in the Electoral College (New York, for example, was the determining factor in the pivotal and divisive election of 1800). The state was home to regular complements on the presidential slate, from Aaron Burr in 1800 to George Clinton in 1804 to Daniel Tompkins in 1816 to Martin Van Buren in 1832. This consistent vice-presidential presence at the very least complicates typical narratives about Virginia and Massachusetts as the only seats of power and influence. The prominence of New York in the domestic political arena coincided with its importance as an essential pivot in the economic development of the nation.[17] The city's colonial harbor had long served as a central hub for international commerce, and its status as a site of economic and strategic importance only increased after the war. Far from a terra incognita, New York State was a nexus for the development of the early republic.

New York's unprecedented growth, unmatched by any other region, was spurred not only by an influx of immigrants from neighboring states but also by the economic conditions of the postwar period, which saw a variegated redistribution of Loyalist wealth and property. Compared to the other twelve colonies, New York had an almost feudal land allocation system with nearly two million acres of land along the Hudson concentrated in the hands of five families (the Schuylers, Renssalaers, Clintons, Livingstons, and DeLancys). Arguably, on a certain level, all early nineteenth-century questions about New York property are an exploration of the ramifications of this consolidated wealth. Unlike other areas such as Massachusetts, where even the wealthiest merchants (figures such as Paul Revere and Sam Adams) very early on aligned with the revolutionary cause, patriot mobilization in New York was especially plebian. In New York much larger percentages of middling and elites were divided over the revolution, including figures such as Joshua Waddington, who continued to prosper in Manhattan even after the war.[18] These long-standing divisions only hastened the kinds of acrimonious strife that characterized the city in the postrevolutionary period.

To better understand how dissention was serially quarantined and excised, more direct attention needs to be afforded to how the postrevolutionary Federalist project aimed at consolidating power in the service of a centralized government. Moreover, we will cultivate a more nuanced and fluid sense of literary history if we, following Ed White's work, confront how many critics have adopted a similar model in terms of articulating such federated consolidation as inevitable and progressive. Despite the important postrevolutionary growth of New York, it largely remains unmarked on the canonical timeline of early U.S. literature until the publication of Washington Irving's popular *The Sketch Book of Geoffrey Crayon* (1819) or James Fenimore Cooper's *The Spy* (1821). Critics routinely neglect the early Irving, texts such as *Letters of Jonathan Oldstyle* (1802), or *Salmagundi* (1807), or *A History of New York* (1809), in favor of lavishing critical attention on his 1819 tales.[19] Similarly, the regional dimensions of Cooper's earliest works are often sublimated in favor of interpreting his novels as national allegories. Seizing on their international reputations as paradigmatically *American* writers, critics project Irving and Cooper as emblematic of a post–War of 1812 turn toward national consolidation.[20] In this classificatory configuration, Cooperstown and Sleepy Hollow model the problems of all postrevolutionary towns faced with the challenges of "goaheadism," while Natty Bumpo and Rip Van Winkle represent a nostalgic imagination quaintly out of joint with dominant notions of futurity.[21] The recurrent figuration of Irving and Cooper as the progenitors of the American Renaissance reflects how the field diagnoses the early part of the nineteenth century as a fallow time in literary production. The tradition of quarantining off the first two decades of the nineteenth century as an ungenerative period remains central to our praxis for many reasons, not the least of which is that textual production in this era reflected more local and regional cultural identities than it did protonational ones.[22]

In countering the pejorative equation of regionalism as synonymous only with local color writing, Douglas Reichert Powell offers the term "critical regionalism" as a means of thinking about how "places and their cultural artifacts [function] as dense palimpsests of broader forces."[23] In reaffirming the importance of region despite and against its assumptive conflation with provincialism, Powell contests its reduction to a generic signifier in opposition to the expansive possibilities of the national or the cosmopolitan. By upholding the rhetorical and social dimensions of location, Powell registers the significance of the regional scale to illuminate the local conditions that shape cultural production and reception. As such, Powell echoes Raymond Williams's framing of regionalism as defined (starting in the late nineteenth century) in the wake of "cultural centralization" as "a modern form of the 'city-country' divide." For Williams, the social and rhetorical assumptions typically encoded in the term "regionalism" disavow an object from a canonical standard. The counterclassification of nonregional texts renders objects and subjects from particular spaces as "essentially general, even perhaps normal, while the life and people of certain other regions, however interestingly and affectionately presented, are well, regional."[24] By unveiling the critical processes that solidify cultural norms, Williams reveals how canonization excommunicates other kinds of texts because of their perceived deviating standards.

While Williams and Powell focus on later critical paradigms, their cautions about the marginalization of certain regional authors registers the often unacknowledged coercive aims of canonical construction. In particular, the classificatory patterns of British literary criticism that Williams critiques mirror the erasures enacted by our long-standing neglect of New York as an important site of cultural production in the early republic. Much in the same way that early Americanists consistently frame Boston and Philadelphia as the influential hubs for cultural production, British literary criticism that invested in a nationalist project, as Williams's work underscores, privileged cultural production from specific regions as sites of national importance. Whether the classificatory patterns were formed at Oxbridge or New Cambridge hardly matters: in both cases a discernible pattern of canonical recognition predicated on privileging what really were coteries of regional authors as representative of a national culture emerges. In the habitual move to synthesize early postrevolutionary literary production within a national framework (even an expanded national framework that maps the imperial dimensions of the early republic), the dissensus of regional interests have been deaccessed from our canonical taxonomies. Scholars have downplayed New York's importance in the cultural and literary development of the United States not because of an absence of textual artifacts but because of the formation of what is imagined as a national canon around regional artifacts from other spaces.

Early scholars of U.S. literature invested in the idea of national culture in part to underwrite the legitimacy of their work (and, perhaps, their own positions within a profession dominated by *English* literary studies), yet recent interventions in the field demonstrate how literary production was more directly influenced by the circulation and trade of bodies, goods, and ideologies (slaves, commercial goods, sentiments, and sensibilities) across presumptively static borders than it was by any nascent nationalism.[25] Following the contributions of this work on spatiality, a reinterrogation of domestic locatedness need not repress the possibilities of the circum-Atlantic turn but rather deepen its geographic complexity. Instead of figuring the nation as *the* site of contact within larger webs of association, turning to region potentially scales our horizons of inquiry more intimately, even as we remain aware of larger patterns of influence. The locatedness of cultural production—the contextual differences resulting from state and regional affiliations—have a particular resonance even if they also catalog the flow of information and goods on a global scale. In this regard, Washington's Janus-faced figurations of New York's influence as both wellspring of national unfolding and contaminating source of local dissensus suggest how we might register both local conditions and a participation in circum-Atlantic flows simultaneously. Such a bilateral approach to cultural production would provide a more accurate mapping of the fluidity with which different localities functioned as nodes of contact within a larger global matrix.

In unseating the pervasive influence of Benedict Anderson's figuration of imagined communities, Trish Loughran complicates our understanding of the simultaneity of a U.S. national identity by evincing how print culture refracted the relationships of part to whole that the new republic called into being by virtue of locatedness. Loughran argues that the "Revolution sought (however imperfectly) to redistribute the social, political, and economic power of the imperial center back through the diverse sites that comprised North America's colonial periphery."[26] In the aftermath of the revolution, the importance of the state or regional identity became even more enhanced—and thus more pronounced—for charting the social and political dimensions of cultural production. In other words, without foreclosing the possibility that some forms of nascent nationalism did exist as early as the 1790s, it remains important to recognize (as Washington's optimistic public letter suggests) that such an ideology was still a highly speculative imaginary rather than an actually experienced reality. As Stephen Shapiro observes, "not only were state (lowercase) and provincial affiliations still prevalent" during this period, but also that "differentiating regional determinations were crucial to the novelistic representations of social experience in the 1790s."[27] Thinking alongside Loughran and Shapiro allows us to understand that one of the reasons that U.S. literary production remains understood as suffering a period of declension after the burst of publication in the 1790s stems from an attachment to conceptions of national imagined communities. The fragmentary influence of regional networks remains harder to inscribe within synthesizing narratives; yet, by taking regional affiliation more seriously, a more complex portrait of the early nineteenth century will emerge. Moreover, such a critical turn toward the importance of regionalism will also move us beyond the residual shopworn myths about the New England mind (or any other exceptionalist mind) as synonymous with a national identity.

Instead of trying to pigeonhole regional political affiliations and revolutionary legacies into some preexisting national schema, we might more profitably attend to the complexity of regional differences as expressions of local tensions and ideologies. Central to late eighteenth- and early nineteenth-century textual production emanating from New York was a consistent questioning of sympathetic attachments to Loyalist losses. Ruma Chopra has recently argued that Loyalists in New York were more attached to "the symbols of the British Empire—legal protection of property and liberty, civil government, and constitutional process—more deeply" than they were devoted to any tangible sense of British identity.[28] These symbolic affections may well have fallen along class lines, and they certainly infuse any number of lawsuits (either for reparations or reintegration) argued before the New York courts. On either side of the ideological divide, the question of legal protections concerning property remained a vexed and recurrent issue in New York, even as it seldom arose with the same kind of venom or frequency in other states and regions. For postrevolutionary New Yorkers, the question of whether the break from colonial control had actually strengthened or undermined these legal principles festered, and responses to the issue can be seen in a number of literary texts authored in the region (we might for example read Isaac Mitchel's *The Asylum* [1804/11], the most popular U.S. gothic novel of the nineteenth century, as an interrogation of this issue). One strain of this thinking, sympathetic to the rights of Loyalists, which championed a suppression of the uncertainties of revolutionary energies inflects Hamilton's decision to defend Waddington, Washington's relief at the outcome of the case, as well as the novels of A Lady of the State of New-York.

COURTING NEO-TORY SYMPATHIES

A palpable attachment to Loyalists permeates the work of the pseudonymous author who identified herself as "A Lady of the State of New-York." The affective concerns of A Lady gesture toward the difficulties facing postrevolutionary Loyalists in the New York region; and in many ways her work traces the acute sentiments of dislocation and dispossession held by many Loyalists as they struggled to retain the possibility for self-determination in the wake of political change. These neo-Tory sentimental attachments infuse her first novel, *The Fortunate Discovery; or, the History of Henry Villars* (1798).[29] Like many other postwar novels, including *Charlotte Temple* (1791/94) and *Amelia; or, The Faithless Briton* (1798) (both also texts set in New York), *The Fortunate Discovery* revolves around wartime romance. In contradistinction to other popular manifestations of this trope, *Discovery* does not climax in the unmasking of a British officer as a reprobate deceiver. The steadfastness of the British suitors depicted in *Discovery* never wavers, and they legally marry young American women without any clandestine intrigues. Such a union reverses the kinds of ruinous connections between military figures and young women that we have habitually imagined as a central canonical trope of the early U.S. novel and exhibits the greater bandwidth of the period's textual spectrum.

In many ways, the plot of *Discovery* anticipates what will become a recursive trope of many of Cooper's revolutionary-era novels (exemplified in, say, *Lionel Lincoln* [1825] and *Wyandotte* [1843]), wherein British officers openly court American women and return to England largely untroubled by political divides. In each of these texts, the revolution exists as an occasion for melancholic reflection on how the event ruptured and destabilized kinship networks, rather than as a cause for a retrospective nationalist celebration. Less concerned than Cooper with the sociopolitical roots of the event or even in diagramming the limitations of partisanship, the work of A Lady nonetheless validates the hereditary transmission of capital. Her first novel, in other words, underwrites a kind of neo-Tory position that halfheartedly endorses a desire for more political representation for the colonists while more overtly decrying how dogmatic thinking disrupts properly configured hierarchies. In short, A Lady's first novel privileges class stratification, property rights, and ancestral connections, over and above all other contending forms of social organization. In so doing, the narrative moves to synthesize instabilities within an overarching sense of a progressive futurity by reaffirming how properly managed households can suitably order domestic landscapes. As such *Discovery* provides an antidote to the popular tropes of the seduction genre, evincing the ways in which revelations about fractured familial connections need not result in near incestuous tragedy or the ruination of women. Rather, the novel depicts military personnel (and, shockingly, British military personnel) as honorable individuals intent not on hedonistic pleasure but on creating stability through properly aligned marital relationships.

Perhaps the most striking feature of A Lady of the State of New-York's first novel is its steadfast refusal to affirm the glory of republican citizenship that categorizes what we might call early Federalist novels. These other texts, for example, such as Royall Tyler's *The Algerine Captive* (1797) or Martha Meredith Read's *Margaretta; or the Intricacies of the Heart* (1807), share a similar conservative orientation but carefully harmonize hierarchical order with a democratic ethos. Despite her temporal proximity to the revolution itself, A Lady does not undertake such careful ideological navigation in her novels. These other texts move to avoid charges of antirepublicanism by judiciously divorcing their privileging of station and rank from European traditions, recasting it as emanating from a more nuanced conception of a naturally elite subject position. The work of A Lady has no such trepidations about disguising her neo-Tory sympathies; indeed, her first novel affectively disarticulates the revolution (and its complex politics) from the social nexus it examines, notwithstanding its continual gesture toward the later stages of the war in New York as its narrative setting.

Set in the waning months of the revolution, the narrative actions of *The Fortunate Discovery* primarily unfold in two locations: the estate of the Villars family in the Hudson River valley and in Manhattan during the British occupation. The novel opens with a British officer, Henry Hargrave, imploring the Villars to nurse his wounded comrade back to health after he has been wounded in a skirmish on the outskirts of their property. In a series of elaborate revelations, Hargrave discovers that he is the long-lost (and long-feared-dead) son of the Villars. The narrative registers the family's backstory to explain the oddity of this revelation by describing how Mrs. Villars had been cast off by her father, Lord Beauclair, because she had disobeyed his wishes and married for love instead of in service of the family's class allegiances. After they elope, Lord Beauclair imprisons the couple until they eventually escape and venture to New York to seek their independence. During this transatlantic crossing their young son falls overboard and is believed to have drowned. In fact, Hargrave was unknowingly rescued by the beloved family nurse (who also falls overboard), who brings him back to his grandparents' estate. With the help of his actual grandmother, the nurse convinces Lord Beauclair to adopt the "orphaned" boy, now renamed Hargrave in order to disguise his real identity, as his ward. During the final winter of the war, Lord Beauclair dies brokenhearted and bequeaths all his property to Hargrave since he has no hope of rediscovering his daughter. When news reaches Manhattan concerning his inheritance, Hargrave accepts his birthright and adopts his grandfather's aristocratic mantle. He marries a close friend of the Villars, while his formerly convalescent comrade marries his sister. The entire social network departs New York during the war's concluding turn and returns to England to enjoy a life of peaceful remove.

The title of *The Fortunate Discovery* implicitly asks a rhetorical question, and the answer is embedded in how Hargrave discovers who his biological parents are and learns that he has in fact legitimately inherited his "adoptive" grandfather's aristocratic title. Scholars have long examined the representation of the discord between parents and children as a prime means of interpreting the trauma of the revolution.[30] The plot of *Fortunate Discovery* replicates some of these canonical motifs, but it veers away from this recognizable pattern by having Hargrave's assumption of an aristocratic title serve as the impetus for social reformation. The novel ends with a mass migration, of virtually every decent character in the novel, back to England as a reconstituted extended family unit (one that encompasses in-laws and multiple newly married couples); such a reunited family structure is discordant with the fractured endings typical of most canonical early U.S. novels. Cursory readings might misunderstand this as simply enacting a seemingly retrograde longing for aristocratic order, but the novel offers a more nuanced vision of sociality by moving to redefine the principles of titled authority. The point remains clear: aristocratic power in and of itself is not bad, but an abuse of that privilege decidedly hampers social development. The problems of the past do not arise because a Lord Beauclair exists; rather, they spring from how the previous holder of the title misunderstood his role in the social compact. An indelible sentimental affirmation of the symbolic importance of the title resonates throughout the text; even as it recursively suggests that the damage caused by its attendant authority directly results from a misalignment of moral sense. The new Lord Beauclair brings an innate clarity and compassion to his position, one that ostensibly immures him from the petty vindictiveness of his grandfather.

The revolution only serves as a backdrop for the plot of *The Fortunate Discovery*; indeed, the external crisis barely disrupts the lives of its characters. Since the realities of the war never encroach into the foreground, A Lady navigates around the need for any sustained exposition. Her Loyalist sympathies emerge in her framing of the war as absent, in how it hovers on the edges of the plot not so much as a political context but as a ghostly reminder of how orthodoxy always functions to disrupt the social order. The initial description of Mr. Villars underscores that he has "retired" to a "sequestered spot" in a "remote village in the northern parts of the State of New-York" in an effort to "shun the din of war" (1–2). Locating the novel during the revolution, the novel registers Villars' politics by noting that he was "a Briton," who was "prepossessed in favor of America" (2). The narrative delicately positions Villars as a quasi-neutral figure—a "Briton" who prefers independence, but only if it can be achieved peacefully through diplomatic means: in many ways this figuration mirrors the sentiments of many New York Loyalists and patriots alike prior to the outbreak of hostilities.[31] The "tranquility" that defines the retired life of the family during the first several years of the war fractures (in the middle of the opening paragraph) when reports reach them that "the enemy [was] fast approaching" (3). The ambiguity of the syntax renders it almost impossible to determine which side constitutes the advancing enemy. The blurry composition does not necessarily signify an antipatriotic sentiment; rather, it stresses that the proximity of the crisis itself imperils the family. In other words, the "frequent skirmishes" fast approaching unsettle the region no matter which side prevails (3). During one of these skirmishes, Hargrave brings his wounded comrade to the Villars household, enters into their domestic sphere, and begins the unfolding of the plot's machinations.

In many ways, the present-but-absent war serves to reconstitute the family. Villars's own flight from an English aristocratic denial of self-determination fails to enflame him with any radical pretensions; rather, the more gentle solution of replacing the sovereign figure in charge of the purse strings makes his flight for freedom, and on some level the fight for independence itself, less of a struggle against oppression and more of a cautionary tale about dogmatism and the protections against it provided by an authoritative benevolence. More overtly concerned with restoration than revolutionary possibilities, the tale endorses the reclamation of an appropriately configured titled authority to arrange the social order in lasting and generative ways. The narrative records no anxieties about the instabilities of a postrevolutionary society, in large part because all of its characters absent themselves from North America. Indeed, the novel presents New York, and in particular Manhattan, as a space comfortable with both politely boarding British soldiers and having its virtuous republican daughters marry officers charged with assisting in the occupation. Failing to ever divulge a patriotic countersensibility to juxtapose with her Loyalist sentiments, A Lady sublimates the justness, or even the ambitions, of the revolutionary cause within her novel.

Even as Mr. Villars represents the most patriotic sentiments encoded in the novel, his stronger preference for no bloodshed always encloses his slight partiality for the American cause. The Loyalist impulses of the characters establish their investment in networks of affiliated households above other political concerns, suggesting that patriarchs matter more than heads of state for guaranteeing stability. This might seem akin to a kind of nascent Federalism, but the insistence on the proper authority of an aristocratic title betrays that this neo-Loyalism outstrips any Federalist feelings. The disarticulated vision of the revolution offered by A Lady of the State of New-York offers a "novanglophilia" which differs from that of other Federalist writers, and this divergence may point toward why her texts have been so largely ignored.[32] Her response to crisis takes the form of a vision of social formation founded on the idea that a properly ordered household—regulated by a particular kind of transmissible hierarchy—remains the only method by which to establish a sustainable futurity.

The Fortunate Discovery whitewashes the discord of the revolution in favor of reaffirming the idea that the hereditary conduction of title and of property safeguards kinship networks, and that the din of other systems of organization endangers that surety. While it offers a corrective to the kinds of dictatorial authority of the elder Lord Beauclair, the novel stands apart from other early American novels by forecasting a sustainable future cemented in the English countryside. Like Hamilton, Duane, and Washington's sense of relief over the defeat of the widowed alehouse owner in favor of transatlantic accord, A Lady of the State of New-York overwrites the presence of local tensions by projecting a future-oriented amity. She synthesizes cacophony in favor of a kind of prerevolutionary social landscape, one that, while no longer viable in North America, is still offered by a writer who willfully identifies herself (as Joshua Waddington continued to do as well) as "of New York" and, presumably, expected that designation to identify her to both the marketplace and readers. By promoting stasis and restoration over fracture and redesign, *The Fortunate Discovery* endorses lineage over politics and home as a shelter from crisis.

Her own, presumably self-authored regional nomination functions as the primary means of categorizing the text, the vehicle by which she identifies herself for her audience. So what, finally, are we to make of the connections between "of

New-York" and the sentimental marriage plot yoked to a Loyalist politics that ends with the postrevolutionary flight of American women to estates in England? Arguably, when A Lady identifies herself as "of New-York" she enacts a self-professed regional signifier. Raymond Williams's sense that regionalism provides a means of differentiating texts or voices that reside outside the process of "cultural centralization" offers one way to locate the neo-Tory politics of a *Fortunate Discovery*; but, in so doing, it is important to underscore that there was no such cultural centralization in place during this period. The formation of the early American canon around certain sentimental tropes does not mean that other variations on these themes did not exist. A certain blindness results from reducing the complexity of these variegated texts, from following Leonard Tennenhouse's argument that "one cannot overstate the redundancy of these narratives," or the almost "limitless tolerance for repetition" on the part of early American readers.[33] Such accountings obscure how a text such as *Fortunate Discovery* essentially pushes against the confining move toward normalization that follows from the kind of critical streamlining that results in an anachronistic centralization of culture production. To label all sentimental or seduction narratives as redundant essentially blurs the trees in an effort to oversimplify a motley landscape as a forest. In the variations between and amid texts one might begin to chart not an undifferentiated map of the development of the United States but a way to think about how variations might produce regional or local topographies of note. Given the lasting and visible presence of Loyalist figures in New York during the revolution, in many ways the figures of *Fortunate Discovery* would be right at home within that ethnoscape (if they could be guaranteed immunity from persecution and prosecution). The return to England at the conclusion of the war reflects the experience of a host of refugee Loyalists; so again, while the text fails to replicate a canonical vision of the postrevolutionary experience, it does in many ways reflect the realities of many postrevolutionary New Yorkers.

LINGERING LOYALIST LEGACIES

In a footnote concerning the "frequency" with which early American narratives feature questions about the transmission of wealth, Karen Weyler submerges a reference to A Lady by noting that the plots of both *The Fortunate Discovery* and *Moreland Vale* "hinge upon a denouement of newly-discovered British patrimonies with inherited wealth."[34] Weyler's insightful volume charts the relationship between, as its subtitle encodes, "sexual and economic desire in American fiction," and, as such, she does not focus on regional inflections of these issues but rather moves to chart national ones across time. Still, even without remarking on the specific geographical identity of the author of these novels, Weyler figures them as a distinct pair apart from other novels that feature industrious labor as the means by which to achieve independence. My aim is not to quibble with Weyler's characterization of these two texts as having an anonymous publication history rather than a pseudonymous one but rather to note how sensitivity to region as a signifier might open up the conditions of possibility for examining how authorial location shaped the presentation of sexual and economic desire in the early republic. If we took the lingering Loyalist legacies percolating in postrevolutionary New York seriously, we might better understand that while these texts do have denouements about inherited wealth, their engagement with British patrimony does not spring out of nowhere in either novel's final turns—indeed, such an interest was present from each text's opening pages. These regional neo-Tory fictions of the early republic suggest how the issue of economic independence, for a particular audience at least, was always already tied to prerevolutionary land ownership that the rebellion had complicated but not completely overwritten.

Like *The Fortunate Discovery*, A Lady of the State of New-York's second novel, *Moreland Vale; or the Fair Fugitive* (1801), seeks to forge solidarity around the issue of Loyalist dispossession to galvanize support for traditional forms of hereditary transmission. Both novels revolve around resuturing the social fabric, which has been rent by the disruptions of the revolution. As is the case with her first novel, A Lady's neo-Loyalist sentiments serve as a means of charting the import of the regional inflections of revolutionary history. Narrowing our scope away from the larger index of the nation, and resurrecting the outlining plots of these novels from their sublimation in a critical footnote, would allow us to unpack the parameters of Ed White's charge about "our limited understanding of the variegated conservative front" encoded in the literature of the early republic.[35] Thinking about regional differences across the complex terrain of what we always rush to aggregate as "Federalism" would allow us to more accurately map the topographies of these conservative strands of cultural production.[36]

On the surface the plot of *Moreland Vale* offers little tangible connection to the revolution.[37] Yet, like *The Fortunate Discovery*, this second novel considers the ways in which the crisis of a loss of patriarchal authority affects social formations. The plot of *Moreland Vale* revolves around the tumultuous courtship of Eliza Vernon and Henry Walgrove, but much of its narrative action spurs from how Eliza's stepmother defrauds her after the death of her father. By forging a new will that denies Eliza her rightful birthright, the novel circulates around questions of inheritance and the hereditary transmission of property according to prerevolutionary dictates.[38] A nearly averted rape, a kidnapping, the physical abuse of an elderly woman, a shipwreck, and an attempted murder later, Eliza legally establishes the validity of her father's legitimate will when several figures who have been missing return to New York and testify to her father's real intentions. After establishing the forged will as fraudulent, Eliza returns to Moreland Vale to the delight of her father's old servants and the neighboring farmers. The entire spiral of dispossession and repossession is referred to as "the revolution which had taken place at Moreland Vale," as the novel redefines revolution as the process by which the law recognizes proper notions of authority (140). In this regard, the central concern of the novel functions as a means of asserting legitimate and ancestral rights of property ownership.

Relocated in her ancestral estate and finally married to Walgrove, Eliza finds sustained solace in the larger communal network that forms around her in upstate New York. Several couples—whose marriages seem to flow from that of Eliza's own union like dominos in a carefully articulated chain—purchase the land adjoining the Vale. These adjacent estates insulate the property from further disruption by creating a sheltering ring of associated households. The figures that have played either a large or a minor role in her restoration effectively remake the region in their own image. In this regard, A Lady's conclusion mirrors the kind of vision of social stability through careful matchmaking that Elizabeth Temple undertakes at the end of *The Pioneers* (1823). As I have argued elsewhere, Temple takes on this work in an effort to populate upstate New York with a sufficient number of anchoring households to underwrite social stability.[39] The reconstituted landscape figured at the end of *Moreland Vale* optimistically suggests that a network of mutually reinforcing households can immure a central one from the dangerous uncertainties that had caused instability among its key constituents in the past.

In essence, A Lady allegorizes how the revolution disrupted Loyalist land claims in New York to demonstrate the necessity of recognizing the validity of these hereditary claims by virtue of Eliza's struggle. Her father's legacy, his literal and figurative will, is compromised by usurpation and manipulation, even as his attraction to the possibilities of a new social arrangement (exemplified by his second marriage) reveals itself as a turbulent seduction. Eliza's stepmother has an insatiable nongenerative sexual appetite, embodied in her rampant attempt at an extramarital affair and her quick remarriage. These traits position her as an unstable source of community formation; she exists, irreducibly, as all desire without the possibility of social reproduction. While she does not represent any overt political position, the form of her disingenuous pilfering of Eliza's property echoes how many postrevolutionary Americans sought to profit from the seizure of Loyalist landholdings. Symbolically, she represents a kind of unhinged revolutionary spirit, one that has no sense of legality, social justice, or civil decorum. That the novel seeks to redress this embodied disruption through the legal system underscores how A Lady conceives of the issues of landownership and regimes of order as constitutive of the cultural landscape of the postrevolutionary era. While there is no overt acknowledgment of the Trespass Act or reintegration lawsuits in the novel, the legal machinations that suffuse the plot of *Moreland Vale* are, without question, reflections of the legal struggles for property rights unfolding in the courtrooms of New York on a daily basis during this period.

While there is a pressing need for a more complex topography in general in U.S. literary studies, the issue is particularly acute for the first two decades of the nineteenth century—a territory still largely ignored. There is an unfortunate quasi-disciplinary schism that often short-circuits any sustained conversation between the increasingly separate fields of early Americanists and U.S.-Americanists, one that might be solved by a richer sense of the interstitial period between these areas of inquiry. Neglecting the importance of region, and ignoring a period when region was a routinely deployed authorial signifier, means that we continue to frame cultural production from the 1820s onward as if it largely had no connection to earlier traditions. By continuing to make this canonical jump over a period of intense cultural production, we have anachronistically continued to embrace an illusory conception of a national culture born from faulty notions about the simultaneity and transregional dissemination of print production. As Jared Gardner has insightfully argued, cultural production in the early nineteenth century flourished in pages of magazines (texts with regional circulations and identities), which often aimed at using "print not to eradicate the spaces between the voices, but to make them productive, communicative."[40] Even as the editors of these magazines fostered a dialog across and amid regional affiliations and local conditions, they had to do so by first acknowledging that these differences shaped their contemporary moment. We need to recapture the same kind of nuanced sense of commonality and difference if we really want to come to terms with the complexities of early U.S. cultural production. Building bridges, in other words, depends on an accurate understanding of the local conditions in order to properly ground the abutments.

In altering the scale of our analysis, the complexities of the development of U.S. literary production become more refined and better articulated. To focus on the local is not to ignore the national or global, and to think of New York in the aftermath of the revolution does not invalidate other dimensions of that crisis; rather, such a reorientation might afford a more nuanced sense of the interplay between individual and nation, between the different dimensions of the domestic, between dissent and synthesis, and the multivalent ways in which they all intersect with the projects of political and canonical consolidation. Diverse ensembles, deviating histories, and divergent canons await fortunate discovery; in order to bring them into focus, we simply need to complicate our operant sense of the geographies of literary production beyond the confining and overdetermining frame of the always already inevitable nation.

NOTES

1. A royal decree suspended further hostilities in February 1783, and later that September the Treaty of Paris brought a final end to the Revolutionary War. While accurate numbers

are difficult to reassemble, Burrows and Wallace estimate that in addition to all the military personnel who disembarked from Manhattan during the withdrawal, approximately thirty thousand Loyalist civilians and several thousand former slaves joined the British exodus. See Burrows and Wallace, *Gotham*, 256–59.

2. Patriot prisoners were largely incarcerated in retrofitted British ships or in a hastily reconfigured factory, the Old Sugar House in Lower Manhattan, and conditions in both spaces were notoriously horrid. Indeed, more patriot soldiers and seamen perished from incarceration than from all the battles of the war combined (more than double, according to Burroughs's calculations). For more information, see Burrows, *Forgotten Patriots*.

3. Various early nineteenth-century reports, some no doubt apocryphal, describe how bones from the prisoners would periodically wash ashore for years after the war. These stories coalesced during the first decade of the nineteenth century when various civic and political organizations lobbied to memorialize the deceased prisoners. Some of the remains were gathered and interred in 1808, then later reinterred at Fort Green in 1873.

4. Lincoln's creation of an annual Thanksgiving holiday for the last Thursday in November meant that the two holidays were inevitably too close in proximity to coexist. A *New York Times* story concerning a 1924 attempt by the Sons of the Revolution to revive the holiday also suggests that while there were attempts to cast the event as "a grand national holiday," it had never held more than a regional significance because it was really "only New York's" day of remembrance. See *New York Times*, October 19, 1924, 12.

5. George Washington to the Mayor, Recorder, Alderman, etc of the City of New York, April 10, 1785. While I have not yet located any public reprintings of Washington's letter in New York, it was clearly written for public consumption, and his letter was reprinted in newspapers outside of the New York area, including, for example, the *Essex Journal* (Newburyport, Mass.) on May 25, 1785, and the *Pennsylvania Packet, and Daily Advertiser* (Philadelphia, Pa.) on May 23, 1785. For published versions of all letters cited here, see Washington, *Writings*.

6. In the aftermath of the war, acrimonious lawsuits filed by patriots attempting to recoup damages from Loyalists were commonplace in New York. When the widowed patriot Elizabeth Rutgers sued Joshua Waddington (*Rutgers v. Waddington*) for having occupied and damaged her property, the case drew particular public interest. Waddington, who remained in New York after the war, had operated the alehouse under the direction of the British military shortly after the occupation and remained in charge of the brewery until the city's liberation. Rutgers received a split verdict, with the court awarding her a tenth of what she requested as recompense. In rendering the court's judgment, the presiding judge (James Duane) argued that "no state in this union can alter or abridge, in a single point, the federal articles," effectively agreeing with Hamilton that even in the absence of a federal judiciary, no state could alter congressional decrees. For a more detailed examination of *Rutgers v. Waddington*, see Julius Goebel Jr., *History of the Supreme Court*, 113–37. Hamilton went on to defend at least forty-four other Loyalists who were prosecuted under the Trespass Act over the next several years.

7. This language comes from Hamilton's brief number six for the *Rutgers v. Waddington* case as transcribed and reprinted in *The Law Practice of Alexander Hamilton*, 382.

8. George Washington to James Duane, April 10, 1785.

9. Duane's desire to promote international accord with England can be traced to his initial support of the Galloway Plan (which advocated for the creation of a colonial parliament to work in conjunction with the crown) and his early opposition to the Declaration of Independence. While Duane altered his views when war proved inevitable, his commitments to international reconciliation resurfaced after the war. For more information on Duane, see Alexander, *Revolutionary Conservative*.

10. White, *Backcountry and the City*, 9.

11. The theorist Jacques Rancière uses the phrase "the distribution of the sensible" to define the process by which aesthetics function to create a shared sense of meaning for a community, one that contains an embedded sense of political meaning. See Rancière, *Politics of Aesthetics*.

12. The renewed attention to mobility by scholars thinking about the revolutionary Atlantic world has fruitfully expanded our horizons of inquiry, but the embrace of mobility has not yet effectively dislodged the centrality of the nation-state. All too often figuring the development of a national culture still remains an inevitable end point of our critical trajectories.

13. See Kaplan, *Anarchy of Empire*.

14. Indeed, New York State remained a hotbed of reintegration lawsuits well into the first decade of the nineteenth century, as dispossessed Loyalists became emboldened by the court's undoing of the Trespass Act and actively pursued litigation in order to reclaim property that had been confiscated by patriots. In *Libertie's* Exiles, Maya Jasanoff argues that by 1784 overt retaliations against Loyalists had waned in many of the formerly British-occupied cities of the emerging republic but notes this was not the case in New York (318). New York serves as a central touchstone for Jasanoff, both before and after the war, in part since so many wealthy Loyalists continued to reside in the region in its aftermath.

15. Davidson, *Revolution and the Word*. This redacted reading of Davidson's groundbreaking intervention, a long-standing neglect of the more nuanced layers of her argument, has obscured the ways in which she examines a wider range of texts and contexts than we normatively reimagine.

16. Alan Taylor, *William Cooper's Town*, 4.

17. In the immediate aftermath of the revolution, as Daniel J. Hulsebosch argues, "New York remained a strategic port and became a headquarters for continental expansion." See Hulsebosch, *Constituting Empire*, 12.

18. Joshua Waddington remained a successful businessman in Manhattan after he prevailed against Rutgers's struggle for reparations. In 1787, for example, he was named the director of the Bank of New York (the first U.S. bank whose charter was written by Hamilton in 1784).

19. Jerome McGann makes a similar argument in a recent essay, which examines the changes Irving undertakes in subsequent editions of his *History of New York*. See McGann, "Washington Irving."

20. Typecast as harbingers of the impending rebirth of U.S. literary production—after its imagined dormancy during the early nineteenth century—Irving and Cooper are routinely plotted as cornerstones of a bourgeoning national culture because critics customarily read them as precursors of later developments. This tendency exemplifies the problematic

schism between scholars working on postrevolutionary literature and scholars more focused on cultural production from the last two-thirds of the nineteenth century. For an in-depth articulation of this issue see Gustafson, "Histories of Democracy and Empire."

21. Cooper coins the phrase "goaheadism" to describe what he sees as a restless push forward in American society, with no regard for precedent or tradition. He first uses the phrase in his novel *Home as Found* (1838).

22. It has been a long-standing assumption of dominant literary histories of the United States that after the explosion of textual production in the 1790s, there was a decline in both the number of novels and the numbers of initiate authors published in the United States. Such accounting is flawed and overly reliant on Lillie Deming Loshe's foundational bibliographic work *The Early American Novel* (1907). That Loshe's incomplete statistics have long held sway, I want to suggest, underscores the potency of the desire to read the early U.S. novel as principally and inherently about nation formation. Lyle Wright's informative *American Fiction, 1774–1850: A Contribution toward a Bibliography* (1969), a text whose very subtitle underscores its incompleteness, registers the publication of thirty-four novels between 1801 and 1811, compared to Loshe's tally of twenty-one for the same period. Loshe proposes the last decade of the eighteenth century as the zenith of novel production, when according to her count thirty novels were first published. Wright's more complete accounting clarifies that, in fact, more new novels appeared between 1801 and 1811 than during the period of 1790–99 (34 to 30 and not 22 to 30, as Loshe's previous cataloging would suggest).

23. Power, *Critical Regionalism*, 19.

24. Raymond Williams, *Writing in Society*, 230.

25. See, for example, Armstrong and Tennenhouse, "Problem of Population."

26. Loughran, *Republic in Print*, 238.

27. Shapiro, *Culture and Commerce*, 13–14.

28. Chopra, *Unnatural Rebellion*, 223.

29. A Lady of the State of New-York, *The Fortunate Discovery; or, The History of Henry Villars*. Hereafter all references to this text will be cited parenthetically.

30. See, for example, Fliegelman, *Prodigals and Pilgrims*.

31. Considered in this light figures such as the patriotic James Duane (whose earlier support for the Galloway plan only wavered when the British sent troops to the United States) and the Loyalist Joshua Waddington who labored (and profited) as a businessman in New York before, during, and after the revolution, have much in common with Mr. Villars.

32. The phrase is from Gura, "Study of Colonial American Literature," 310.

33. Tennenhouse, *Importance of Feeling English*, 45.

34. Weyler, *Intricate Relations*, 221 n. 7.

35. Ed White, "Divided We Stand," 6.

36. My use of "topography" here borrows from Cindi Katz's insightful definition in "Vagabond Capitalism and the Necessity of Social Reproduction." Katz writes: "'Topography' offers a political logic that both recognizes the materiality of cultural and social difference and can help mobilize transnational and internationalist solidarities" (709).

37. A Lady of the State of New-York, *Moreland Vale; or, The Fair Fugitive*. Hereafter all references to this text will be cited parenthetically.

38. The legitimate will in the novel seemingly dates to before the revolution (or at least

signals that it is representative of that legal regime), as Eliza's father remarries after the war and her stepmother's avaricious nature is continually marked as reflective of an emergent social order that the novel's heroine has to overcome in order to restore order to the social landscape. Eliza's efforts are finally aided by an aged military acquaintance of her father's, General Preston, who honorably served in the war (although the novel never marks for which side).

39. See Faherty, *Remodeling the Nation*, 133–42.
40. Jared Gardner, *Early American Magazine Culture*, 101.

CHAPTER EIGHT

"*I Was Now Living in a New World*"
Frederick Douglass, Herman Melville, and New Bedford's Cosmopolitan Locality

Jennifer Schell

IN HIS SECOND AUTOBIOGRAPHY, *My Bondage and My Freedom* (1855), Frederick Douglass describes the roughly four years he spent living and working in New Bedford, Massachusetts, using figurative language reminiscent of a colonial-era explorer: "I was now living in a new world." To this revelation, he adds a sleep metaphor: "[I] was wide awake to its advantages." Both here and elsewhere in the memoir, Douglass represents New Bedford as a special city, a cosmopolitan land of opportunity where a formerly enslaved black man could begin a remarkable career as a world-famous abolitionist. Although he mentions the racial intolerance of some members of the white working classes—the ship caulkers who refused to work with him—Douglass stresses that, of all the places he visited after leaving Maryland, it was New Bedford, New England's preeminent whaling city, where he was able to find work, support his family, further his education, and, most importantly, participate in community life.[1] When contrasted with the plantations and cities of the South, this "new world" was remarkable, indeed.

Frederick Douglass was not the only nineteenth-century American writer to describe New Bedford as a singular and wondrous place. So did Herman Melville. In December 1840 Melville visited this city—and the neighboring village of Fairhaven, located just across the Acushnet River—where he signed the papers for a whaling voyage. All told, he spent roughly nine days wandering the streets of the small metropolis before his vessel departed for the South Pacific in search of whales.[2] Ten years later, Melville fictionalized his impressions of the city in the opening pages of *Moby-Dick* (1851), which describe Ishmael's stay at the Spouter Inn and his friendship with Queequeg. These chapters also highlight New Bedford's economic productivity, its commercial importance, and its cosmopolitan characteristics. As *Moby-Dick* demonstrates, all of these features made this small New England port very different from others of its kind.[3]

In addition to Douglass and Melville, numerous other nineteenth-century authors—Thomas W. Smith, Reuben Delano, and William Whitecar Jr.—wrote and published sketches of New Bedford. Anonymously written pieces addressing the city appeared in *Flag of Our Union, Ballou's Dollar Monthly Magazine, The Liberator,* and *The National Anti-Slavery Standard*.[4] Many of these texts also mark New Bedford's whaling affiliations and cosmopolitan features. For some reason, though, none of this creative and journalistic output—not even that produced by Douglass and Melville—has attracted much scholarly attention. Of all the essays in Robert S. Levine and Samuel Otter's *Frederick Douglass and Herman Melville: Essays in Relation* (2008) none address the authors' representations of New Bedford. The introduction notes that "in late 1840 and early 1841, when they were young men still unsure of vocation, Douglass and Melville both walked the streets of New Bedford, Massachusetts," but it stops short of discussing their written impressions of the city.[5] Robert K. Wallace's *Douglass and Melville: Anchored Together in Neighborly Style* (2005) also focuses on biographical details. After juxtaposing Douglass's and Melville's descriptions of New Bedford and marking their superficial similarities, Wallace enumerates all the places where the two men may have encountered one another. He admits that no credible, tangible evidence of such an encounter exists, but he asserts, "still, the thought of these two young men meeting in New Bedford is sufficiently tantalizing that biographers and poets will continue to speculate as to what might have happened if they had."[6] Though intriguing, Wallace's biographical speculation belies the complexity of Douglass's and Melville's evocations of New Bedford and neglects to take into account the numerous other representations of the city produced by less familiar antebellum writers.

Even though many of these authors and their works have fallen into obscurity, the archive of texts they produced is important because it indicates that portraits of New Bedford were fairly common in nineteenth-century American print culture. This raises at least two important questions: Why were so many authors prompted to write about this particular New England city? And why did so many of these writers focus on cosmopolitanism? Part of the fascination lay in the fact that, by the midpoint of the nineteenth century, the American whale fishery was a globally dominant economic endeavor, and New Bedford was the single largest and wealthiest whaling port on the entire Eastern Seaboard. According to Charles Melville Scammon's *The Marine Mammals of the Northwestern Coast of North America* (1874), the whaling industry's most profitable year was 1853, during which the value of its imports was $10,730,637.94.[7] Significantly, this wealth had a decided impact on the size of New Bedford's populace. Because of the fishery's renown, men from all over the world flocked to New Bedford seeking employment in the nautical, artisanal, or mercantile trades. As a result, the city's citizenry grew rapidly, increasing from 3,947 to 22,300 individuals between the years 1820 and 1860.[8]

The whale fishery also diversified the city, transforming it from a provincial seaside village into a cosmopolitan maritime port. According to Eric Jay Dolin, author of *Leviathan: The History of Whaling in America* (2007), the industry's labor force consisted of "a polyglot mixture of white and black Americans, Pacific islanders, Portuguese, Azoreans, Creoles, Cape Verdeans, Peruvians, New Zealanders, West Indians, Columbians, and a smattering of Europeans."[9] Of note, this list should be expanded to include the Native American and Asian mariners who worked in the trade.[10] Most of these itinerant sailors did not make permanent homes in New Bedford, but they did stay in the city for days, sometimes weeks, at a time, thereby temporarily adding to the diversity of the population. In addition to mariners, the whaling industry also provided employment for many other men and women, including dockworkers, day laborers, prostitutes, coopers, blacksmiths, chandlers, sailmakers, shipbuilders, merchants, ministers, innkeepers, shipping agents, and customs officials. This population was also quite varied with respect to nationality, race, and ethnicity.[11]

Another factor that contributed to the diversity of New Bedford's population was the fact that many of the businessmen occupying positions in the upper echelons of the whaling industry were Quakers. Members of this religious group first became involved in the fishery when it was located on Nantucket, and many of them followed the trade when it removed to New Bedford.[12] As committed abolitionists, New Bedford's Quaker residents often welcomed fugitive slaves into their midst and protected them from southern slave catchers. Prior to the enactment of the Fugitive Slave Act of 1850, many of these free blacks stayed in New Bedford, working on the wharves and whaling vessels.[13] Ultimately, these men, together with their wives and children, helped create the "spirited" and "educated" African American community that Douglass describes in *My Bondage and My Freedom* (212).

As all of this historical evidence indicates, nineteenth-century New Bedford was a very diverse, cosmopolitan place. Significantly, the men and women who made up the city's citizenry formed distinct communities, organized according to various factors, such as race, ethnicity, class, gender, and religion. When antebellum authors wrote about New Bedford, they tended to have different personal, political, and/or literary goals for their writing, so they tended to focus their attention on one or another of these different communities. Thus, they produced dramatically different accounts of place. My contention is that in order to understand the particularities of New Bedford's regional identity—what I would call its cosmopolitan locality—it is necessary to assemble these various accounts and examine them together. This approach makes it possible to see that, despite their differences, New Bedford's diverse inhabitants were united by a sense of purpose and pride because almost all of them were employed by the whale fishery.[14] What my analysis of antebellum representations of this city reveals, then, is that, in the antebellum years, an urban locality could be defined by both its cosmopolitan characteristics and its industrial affiliations.

My use of "cosmopolitan locality" has been influenced by the scholarship of David Harvey and Jeremy Waldron, both of whom discuss the operation of cosmopolitan identities in conjunction with urban and regional identities. In his book *Cosmopolitanism and the Geographies of Freedom* (2009), Harvey notes that "The meaning of 'place' as a generic concept in relation to cosmopolitanism has . . . lain largely unexamined." After making this claim, Harvey goes on to pose the question: "So what might be the role of local loyalties, of the affective social life that circulates in particular places, in relation to cosmopolitan projects?"[15] While this is an intriguing question, I am more interested in another query: what happens to regional identity when the population of that locality is cosmopolitan? Here, Jeremy Waldron offers some insight. In his essay "What Is Cosmopolitan?" he notes that "Cities like New York, Paris, London, and Bombay are the urban centers of world culture; they are great centers of trade, tourism and migration, where peoples and their traditions mingle and interact." To put it another way, these places are cosmopolitan. Using New York City as his case in point, Waldron argues,

> A person who grows up in Manhattan, for example, cannot but be aware of a diversity of cultures, a diversity of human practices and experiences, indeed a diversity of languages clamoring for his attention. . . . It is another matter whether we call this a single culture—"New York culture"—a culture of diversity, or whether we say (as I think) that it is just *many fragments* that happen to be available at a given place and time and that that does not amount to the existence of a *single* culture in any socially or philosophically interesting sense of "singularity."[16]

Importantly, in the above quotation, Waldron employs an either/or approach to his conceptualization of New York City. For Waldron, the metropolis can be seen as either a "single culture" or as "many fragments." Even though this claim has some merit, I would argue that a both/and approach would be a more productive—and accurate—mode of analysis, because it does not preclude the idea that cosmopolitan cities can possess some kind of cohesive local identity, that disparate peoples living in different communities in the same metropolis can share common bonds. What is especially compelling about viewing urban identity in this way is that it makes it possible to understand better the complex sense of regional identity and mutual connection that the residents of antebellum New Bedford possessed. In so doing, this approach helps account for the numerous and varied representations of city produced by these different individuals across the nineteenth century.

In the 1850s and 1860s, two of Boston's mammoth story papers—*Flag of Our Union* and *Ballou's Dollar Monthly Magazine*—published anonymously authored articles about New Bedford. The first piece, titled "New Bedford," appeared in the former in August 1858, and the second, titled "Sketches of New Bedford," appeared in the latter in March 1861. Although one is more explicit about its political goals than the other, both of these pieces attempt to endow the city with symbolic status, by positioning it as a synecdoche for the nation.[17] In this way, these articles use New Bedford's prosperity as evidence that the American political project, and the capitalist climate it fosters, is a smashing success. Opening with grandiose descriptive flourishes, the author of the first piece asserts:

> Among the most attractive cities of Massachusetts is New Bedford, famed for its large participations in the whale fisheries. This city is beautifully located on the western bank of the Acushnet River, near to Buzzard's Bay. The land rises from the water with a gentle slope to the western limit of the city, displaying the buildings and gardens to great advantage to an observer on the water, or upon the opposite side of the river. It is a place of great prosperity, and much individual wealth, and a liberal and refined taste is exhibited in the public edifices. There are also many private residences that are built and furnished, without and within, with a solidity and magnificence quite unusual in American cities. These give an appearance of substantial prosperity to New Bedford, which is well borne out by the generally comfortable and tidy aspect of the city in all its details.

The most important aspect of this passage is the hyperbolic praise it lavishes on New England's "famed" whaling city. Throughout this quotation, the author employs the words "prosperity," "wealth," and "magnificence," all of which testify to the affluence of New Bedford's diverse populace. To create an implicit synecdochic connection between the local and the national, the author goes on to discuss various aspects of New Bedford's historical development, noting that, during the American Revolution, many of the city's "hardy mariners . . . turned their attention to privateering the enemy's vessels," an activity he calls "a gallant and hazardous pursuit." Then he concludes with a tribute to the prosperity of New Bedford's contemporary residents, whom he characterizes as "intelligent, public-spirited, and hospitable."[18]

Much like its predecessor, "Sketches of New Bedford" also begins by bestowing extravagant plaudits on the city. The initial paragraphs spend a great deal of time describing the "attractive aspect[s]" of various buildings and commending the "tree-loving propensities" of the inhabitants. With a complimentary comparison to another famous northeastern city, one that once happened to be the national capital, the article maintains that "the streets are laid out on the rectangular plan of Philadelphia. The upper part of the city is the best built. The houses on County Street are noted for their beauty, and this thoroughfare is closely planted with shade trees." From here, the piece segues into a discussion of New Bedford's theological diversity—a direct result of its cosmopolitan qualities—commenting that "the churches . . . are about eighteen in number, among which the Methodists have four; the Baptists, two; the Presbyterians, two; Congregationalists, one; Episcopalians, one; Unitarians, one; Roman Catholic, one; Seamen, one; and colored persons, three." Although these passages do not mention wealth or the whaling industry, others certainly do. According to the piece, "The whale-fishery and the manufacture of the product of that fishery are the principal branches of business in which the inhabitants are engaged, and the prolific sources of their wealth."[19] Importantly, this statement also stresses the cohesiveness of New Bedford's religiously diverse and cosmopolitan populace.

To make its national synecdoche explicit, the closing paragraph of the piece proclaims, "Their [the whalemen's] enterprise and daring added enormously to the wealth of the country, and the beautiful city we have delineated is a tangible proof of the importance of the business. The rapid growth in extent and wealth of our American cities is directly attributable to the character of our political institutions." After juxtaposing local matters with national concerns, the article concludes with a grand theory: "Had this country remained a colonial dependency, its progress might indeed have been rapid as compared with Europe, but not at all comparable with mighty strides it has taken as an independent nation, in every art and science which serves to advance mankind."[20] As it draws to a close, then, this piece encourages Americans to take pride, not just in New Bedford and its economic successes but in the United States and its various other enterprises.

Not all periodicals highlighted New Bedford's national importance or its representative qualities, though. As an abolitionist stronghold, the city attracted the attention of authors who wrote for both anti- and proslavery newspapers. Although their descriptions of the city vary according to their political beliefs, these writers shared an interest in New Bedford's whaling industry and its cosmopolitan black community. On October 29, 1846, the *National Anti-Slavery Standard* published an anonymous article titled "Communications. Coloured Seamen—Their Character and Condition," which noted that the New Bedford whale fishery afforded black sailors opportunities unavailable to them in the other maritime trades: "Now this is the case with a large majority of coloured men in the whaling service, that when having acquired a thorough knowledge of the art and skill in capturing whales, together with navigation and seamanship, it qualifies them to fill the offices of boatsteerers, third, second, and first mates, and sometimes captains of whaling vessels."[21] Well aware that many of New Bedford's residents harbored fugitive slaves aboard their whaling vessels and in their homes, southerners registered their displeasure in newspaper articles such as "Insult and Outrage upon the Rights of the South," which dubbed New Bedford, a "den of negro thieves and protectors," a "sink of iniquity and lawlessness," and a "rank stew of fanatics and outlaws."[22] Preoccupied with abolitionist issues, these periodical articles attempt to put their descriptions of New Bedford's whaling industry and cosmopolitan populace to use to accomplish various sectarian political goals, not inspire national pride.

Of course, periodicals were not the only nineteenth-century texts that included portraits of New Bedford. As noted above, many antebellum whalemen-authors published memoirs, some of which addressed the city and its famous fishery. Perhaps not surprisingly, these depictions of New Bedford vary dramatically depending on the author and his aspirations for his writing. In *A Narrative of the Life* (1844), Thomas W. Smith criticizes the corrupt business practices of New Bedford's whaling captains and ship owners. An Englishman by birth and a common foremast hand by trade, Smith mentions that, on arriving in New Bedford, "I was lame, destitute, and a stranger in a strange land, and no one seemed willing to be burdened with me or my afflictions, seeing no prospect of reward, as I was unable to labor." After characterizing himself in this pitiable manner, he explains, "I met the captain of the ship, who informed me that the owners were not willing to pay me any thing for my share of the oil, and that they had compelled him to go to the custom house and sign some papers, to testify that I was a passenger on board, and had worked my passage in the ship. On being thus informed, I was surprised that a man of his standing in society . . . should debase himself so low as to comply with the request of the owners . . . for the purpose of defrauding a poor, destitute sailor."[23] Together with Smith's description of his physical aliments, this passage effectively serves to generate sympathy for his lamentable plight. In his descriptions of New Bedford and its storied whaling industry, then, Smith advances a compelling critique of the unscrupulous business practices of those ship captains and owners who tried to cheat common sailors of their wages.

Much like Smith, Reuben Delano seeks to elicit the emotions of his readers by portraying himself as an object of pity. His political agenda has far less to do with labor protest and much more to do with temperance reform, however. In his *Wanderings and Adventures* (1846), he describes New Bedford as a den of inequity, which corrupts innocent mariners and turns them into chronic inebriates. Throughout the memoir, Delano depicts himself as utterly unable to resist the alluring temptations of the city's various barrooms and boardinghouses. In one fairly typical instance, he decides to travel to New Bedford to collect his earnings from his last whaling expedition. Before he departs on his excursion, he vows to maintain a regimen of "total abstinence." All of his efforts fail miserably, because as Delano explains, "In New Bedford I fell in with some of my old shipmates and asked them if they had settled their voyage, and some of them informed me that they had. I informed them that I was bound along to settle mine, and they offered to bear me company, but it was not long before I found myself in a tavern with a glass in my hand." For Delano, this event launches a daylong drinking binge, which ends late in the afternoon when he finally returns home. Characterizing alcohol as both a slave-driving "tyrant" and a mechanism of "Satan," he describes numerous similar episodes, which occur in quick succession.[24] All this is to say that, for Delano, New Bedford has special symbolic significance. Although he is not openly critical of the city, the metropolis represents a realm of temptation, where otherwise capable, globe-trotting seamen like himself are transformed into helpless drunkards.

In his memoir, *Four Years Aboard the Whaleship* (1860), common sailor William Whitecar Jr. offers readers a thoroughly ambivalent portrait of New Bedford. Over the course of the book, he oscillates between applause and criticism, thereby combining some of the approaches employed by his predecessors and contemporaries. Whitecar begins by describing New Bedford's waterfront districts. According to him, "bustle and activity was everywhere apparent; ships loading, discharging, repairing, &c., in every direction." While he admires the determination and skill with which the laborers perform their various tasks, Whitecar perceives the wharves as a noisome and "Babel-like confusion," from which "a stranger is glad to escape." Clearly, he does not appreciate the more cosmopolitan aspects of this labor force. With respect to the fishery and its impact on the city, though, Whitecar adopts a somewhat more objective tone: "Whichever way we cast an eye we see oil casks or whalebone, harpoons or lances, or some one or other of the various et ceteras belonging to the whaleman's pursuit; in fact, the yield of the whale supports New Bedford, and is the nucleus around which clusters all the manufactures of the city; and its vitality as a community must ever depend upon the number of vessels it sends out in pursuit of the whale."[25] Emphasizing the importance of the industry to the city's identity, Whitecar characterizes New Bedford as a whaling center whose prosperity and "vitality" are entirely dependent on the fishery. To do so, he underscores the peculiar implements—the harpoons and lances—of whale hunting and the special products—the oil casks and whalebone—of the trade.

Because he spends several days in New Bedford before his vessel departs, Whitecar furnishes his readers with descriptions of other parts of the city. With some admiration, he notes, "In my perambulations through this city of whalemen I found that it was laid out with something like care—the streets, like those of Philadelphia, at right angles; many of the houses neat and well-built, and, with the exception of a part of one street near the river, wear a quiet and respectable aspect." Calling attention to the prominence of the whale fishery and the plan of the city, Whitecar, like the anonymous author of "Sketches of New Bedford," synecdochically connects the local and the national by favorably comparing New Bedford to Philadelphia. Curiously, Whitecar tempers his praise with a description of one of the city's more iniquitous districts: "One street is an exception to the rule, it being occupied by houses of ill-fame, where many a dollar, earned by exposure to the storm on a long voyage, has been filched from the hardy mariner by the harpies who occupy its tenements."[26] Adopting a more reproachful tone, Whitecar laments the fact that the citizens of New Bedford allow these "harpies" to "filch" from the brave whalemen who work in the city's famous and prosperous whale fishery. Through all of this confusing imagery and commentary, Whitecar manages to advance a complex and multifaceted portrait of New Bedford, which demonstrates that the city's identity—its cosmopolitan locality and its whaling affiliations—was available to be appropriated by authors interested in both national synecdoche and urban reform.

Over the course of his lifetime, Frederick Douglass often discussed the time he spent living and working in America's largest and most cosmopolitan whaling port. Thus, representations of New Bedford appear in his autobiographies, his journalism, and his speeches.[27] Importantly, I am not the only scholar to notice Douglass's fascination with and interest in this particular city. In her book *Black Cosmopolitanism: Racial Consciousness and Transnational Identity in the Nineteenth-Century Americas*, Ifeoma Kiddoe Nwankwo contends that "the New Bedford sections [of *My Bondage and My Freedom* and *Life and Times*] . . . reveal Douglass' embrace of a racially based notion of community, one that includes free Blacks as well as slaves."[28] Although this observation is an astute one, I do not think it fully addresses the symbolic complexity of Douglass's New Bedford writings. Certainly, Douglass describes the city as the place where he first began to embrace the black community, but he also depicts it as the place where he began his journey toward self-made manhood. Thus, he positions New Bedford as a symbolic example of what the United States could become if it abolishes slavery. Much like some of the authors writing for *Flag of Our Union* and *Ballou's Dollar Monthly Magazine*, then, Douglass appropriates New Bedford and its cosmopolitan locality for the purposes of synecdochic nationalism.

As Daniel Walker Howe observes in *Making the American Self: Jonathan Edwards to Abraham Lincoln* (1997), "the nineteenth-century ideal of the self-made character was concerned as much with social utility and personal fulfillment as with social mobility. To be self-made was to have made, not money, but a self."[29] Most, if not all, of Douglass's descriptions of New Bedford testify to his commitment to these ideals. The transcriber of an antislavery speech that Douglass gave in Glasgow, Scotland, in 1846 reports him as saying that

> When he got his freedom, he went to work on the wharves in New Bedford, and he worked in a manner which he had never done when he was a slave. . . . He had a wife and a little one to take care of and provide for, and this was the main-spring of his actions. Before he had been moved to action by the lash; now he was operated upon by the hope of reward, and of benefiting those he loved, his wife and child. . . . In these circumstances there was no work too low, too dirty, too menial for him. He was ready to clean the chimney or sweep the cellar—he was ready for anything—he had a wife and child to take care of. *Slavery is not working hard.* He did it with delight, and the happiest moments he had ever spent in his life was working on the wharves of New Bedford for his wife and child.[30]

In this lengthy passage, freighted with nostalgia, Douglass describes New Bedford as a utopian place that affords former slaves the opportunity to work for themselves and their families. In so doing, the city gives these men the chance to earn money and develop a sense of themselves as autonomous, socially mobile men. As the refrain "wife and child" indicates, Douglass was especially appreciative of the opportunity to serve his family as its provider and patriarch.

By 1849 Douglass began to speak about the advantages New Bedford offered to all its black inhabitants. In an article for the *Liberator* titled "Can't Take Care of Themselves," he emphasizes the hardships experienced by these various men and women: "They came to New Bedford poor, friendless, without money, education." Although he admits that "they came to face a bitter prejudice of the community, and to bear up under a climate too cold for Southern constitutions," he stresses that, because they were allowed to work for themselves, they managed to persevere through all of this adversity. Thus, he concludes "a people freer from crime, more upright in their dealings, more industrious in their habits, and more neat in their persons than are the colored people of New Bedford, cannot be found among the working-classes of any town or city in the American Union."[31] Though moderated a bit by his concessions about racial prejudice and cold weather, this article contains much the same utopian impulse—and commitment to self-made manhood—as Douglass's earlier speech.

Although it is longer and more detailed, the portrait of New Bedford that appears in *My Bondage and My Freedom* is very similar to its predecessors, especially insofar as it represents an extended treatise in support of self-made manhood and wage labor. Douglass begins his description of the city with a comparison of the affluence produced by the whaling industry and cotton plantations: "Judge, then, of my amazement and joy when I found—as I did find—the very laboring population of New Bedford living in better houses, more elegantly furnished—surrounded by more comfort and refinement—than a majority of the slaveholders on the Eastern Shore of Maryland." (210). This consideration of regional economic issues continues into the next paragraph, which posits a theory about the nature of southern slavery and northern wage labor. Simply put, Douglass suggests that the working classes of the North possess a "superiority of mind," whereas the physical laborers of the South prefer to use "simple brute force" (210). As proof of these claims, Douglass describes New Bedford's waterfront activities according to an industrial metaphor: "everything went on as smoothly as the works of a well adjusted machine. How different was all this from the noisily fierce and clumsily absurd manner of labor-life in Baltimore and St. Michael's!" (210). Next, he provides several specific examples of how Northerners economize their labor by using their intellect to devise efficient ways of accomplishing their goals. As he emphasizes, "everything was done here with a scrupulous regard to economy, both in regard to men and things, time and strength" (211). Thus, in Douglass's eyes, Yankee frugality and ingenuity generate wealth and prosperity, while southern stubbornness and obtuseness yield inefficiency and waste.

What Douglass emphasizes throughout these sections of the book is that the North's modes of labor organization improve the standard of living for both working-class whites and African Americans. As an example, he describes the following self-made man: "Mr. Johnson, himself a colored man, (who at the south would have been regarded as a marketable commodity,) who lived in a better house—dined at a richer board—was the owner of more books—the reader of more newspapers—was more conversant with the political and social conditions of the nation and the world—than nine-tenths of all the slaveholders of Talbot county, Maryland" (210). Lest his readers mistake his cosmopolitan friend for a member of the upper classes, Douglass notes, with some amazement, that "Mr. Johnson was a working man, and his hands were hardened by honest toil" (210). With respect to its abolitionist argument, this portion of the book is fairly effective, for it completely dismantles the idea that the productivity and affluence of the South are dependent on slave labor. As Douglass demonstrates, wage labor—when managed properly as it is in New Bedford—can yield just as much prosperity.

As Nwankwo observes, this part of *My Bondage and My Freedom* serves another important function, insofar as it explains the formation of the city's insular African American community. Above, Douglass highlights several of the advantages that New Bedford's capitalist infrastructure affords its black citizenry. His point is that, in New Bedford, a physical laborer, such as the aforementioned Mr. Johnson, can become a self-made man and enjoy a fairly comfortable existence, which, in turn, makes it possible for him to learn about and participate in local, national, and global affairs. A little later in the narrative, Douglass explains that several of the laws enacted by the city of New Bedford and the state of Massachusetts also work to the benefit of African Americans. Thus, he notes that "there was nothing in the constitution of Massachusetts to prevent a colored man from holding any office in the state" (211). He also observes that "in New Bedford, the black man's children—although anti-slavery was then far from popular—went to school side by side with the white children, and apparently without objection from any quarter" (211). Because they are prosperous and literate and because they benefit from antisegregationist policies, New Bedford's free blacks and fugitive slaves form a cohesive group that works to promote and protect their common interests.

Throughout the remainder of *My Bondage and My Freedom*, Douglass delineates some of the characteristics of New Bedford's African American community. To demonstrate the strength of the group's loyalties as well as their commitment to maintaining their freedom, Douglass tells a "story" about a "would-be Judas," a free man who threatened to betray a fugitive with whom he had an argument (212). According to Douglass, the community members scheduled a meeting at which they confronted the "betrayer" and threatened to kill him. Fleeing from the premises before his punishment could be enacted, the individual in question "availed himself of an open sash, and made good his escape" (212). To conclude the anecdote, Douglass notes that, "This little incident is perfectly characteristic of the spirit of the colored people in New Bedford," and he stresses that the African Americans living in the city are "educated up to the point of fighting for their freedom, as well as speaking for it" (212). To put it another way, these individuals are all autonomous, powerful self-made men.

As Douglass initially describes it, New Bedford's African American community seems to consist of a seamlessly unified group of like-minded individuals, who work together to accomplish their goals. Later in the text, though, Douglass seemingly undermines this idea by noting some of the fissures inherent in the group. What he indicates is that this community has an internal hierarchy all its own: "Up to that time, a colored man was deemed a fool who confessed himself a runaway slave, not only because of the danger to which he exposed himself of being retaken, but because it was a confession of a very *low* origin! Some of my colored friends in New Bedford thought very badly of my wisdom for thus exposing and degrading myself" (220). This statement clearly demonstrates that, insofar as the city's African American community was concerned, free blacks enjoyed more respect and occupied positions of higher status than former slaves. It is worth noting, though, that in revealing his humble origins, Douglass did not necessarily endanger his special status as a self-made man or his privileged position with white abolitionists. Knowing that he began his ascent to self-made manhood from the position of a slave, not a free black, likely made these individuals that much more impressed by his determination and accomplishments.

In addition to marking some of the biases of New Bedford's African American residents, Douglass also comments on the racial prejudices of the city's white citizenry. These observations threaten to subvert some of his claims about the opportunities the city affords to black men, especially insofar as self-made manhood is concerned. On arriving in the whaling port, he seeks employment as a ship caulker, a trade he learned in Baltimore: "I applied to that noble-hearted man [Rodney French] for employment, and he promptly told me to go to work; but going on the float-stage for the purpose, I was informed that every white man would leave the ship if I struck a blow upon her" (213). Thus, all of Douglass's efforts to ply his trade are thwarted by the white men who resent his presence in their workplace. Importantly, in the following sentences, Douglass does not express any frustration or resentment about his situation. Although he admits "this is a hardship," he contends that it is "not a very serious one." According to his logic,

> The difference between the wages of a calker and that of a common day laborer, was an hundred per cent, in favor of the former; but then I was free, and free to work, though not at my trade. I now prepared to do anything which came to hand in the way of turning an honest penny; sawed wood—dug cellars—shoveled coal—swept chimneys with Uncle Lucas Debuty—rolled oil casks on the wharves—helped to load and unload vessels—worked in Ricketson's candle works—in Richmond's brass foundry, and elsewhere; and thus supported myself and family for three years (213).

What Douglass stresses here is that the prejudice he endured in New Bedford was a small price to pay for the freedom he enjoyed. Tellingly, he describes this freedom as the freedom to work, and he highlights all of the various laborious tasks he performed in the service of providing for his family. By underscoring his personal humility and his modest origins, this passage ultimately serves to reinforce, not undermine, Douglass's status as a self-made man.

In the end, Douglass's descriptions of his life in New Bedford in *My Bondage and My Freedom*—and elsewhere in his speeches and journalism—reveal a great deal about the character of the city and its cosmopolitan locality. While he does not necessarily highlight the beauty of its mansions, admire the organization of its streets, criticize the business practices of its whaling merchants, or condemn its brothels, he demonstrates that this port possessed a prosperous population of black and white wage laborers. Douglass also indicates that New Bedford supported a cosmopolitan community of free blacks and former slaves, dedicated to supporting their families and improving themselves. In so doing, he advances a compelling endorsement of self-made manhood and presents the city as a potential synecdoche for the nation.

With good reason, most scholars who address Herman Melville's urban writing discuss his relationship with and his representations of New York City. In his book *Tolerable Entertainment: Herman Melville and Professionalism in Antebellum New York* (2006), John Evelev seeks to situate "Melville's work within a new class landscape in antebellum New York City." Wyn Kelley has similar goals. In her monograph *Melville's City: Literary and Urban Form in Nineteenth-Century New York* (1996), she "intend[s] to recover Melville's dialogue with New York—the town, the city, and the culture of letters and arts that celebrated it." At one point, Kelley notes that *Moby-Dick* begins with descriptions of both New York and New Bedford, but her subsequent discussion focuses much more on the former than the latter. More recent scholarship, such as Christopher Sten's "City of Hope and Fear: Douglass and Melville in the Nation's Capital" (2008), broadens the scope and examines Melville's depictions of Washington, D.C.[32] My goal here is to further expand the critical purview and provide an analysis of Melville's representations of New Bedford in the opening chapters of *Moby-Dick*. As I would suggest, Ishmael's depictions of the city must be read in the context of his evolving friendship with Queequeg and his discussion of the development—and devolution—of the American whale fishery.

Not insignificantly, Ishmael's observations about the whaling city vary from chapter to chapter as his mood shifts. When he first arrives in New Bedford on a cold night in late December, Ishmael is still suffering from the "hypos" that originally prompted him to seek a berth on a seagoing vessel. Thus, he observes that "it was a very dubious-looking, nay, a very dark and dismal night, bitingly

"I Was Now Living in a New World"

cold and cheerless. I knew no one in the place." Ishmael's subsequent comments also stress the city's dismal atmosphere. He pauses "in the middle of a dreary street shouldering my bag, and comparing the gloom towards the north with the darkness towards the south." Because of his self-indulgent melancholy mood, Ishmael meanders through the streets of New Bedford consciously rejecting one cheerful-looking inn after another: "With halting steps I paced the streets, and passed the sign of 'The Crossed Harpoons'—but it looked too expensive and jolly there. Further on, from the bright red windows of the 'Sword-Fish Inn,' there came such fervent rays, that it seemed to have melted the packed snow and ice from before the house.... Too expensive and jolly, again thought I, pausing one moment to watch the broad glare in the street, and hear the sounds of the tinkling glasses within." Heading for the waterfront, Ishmael continues his fruitless search for a more suitable inn. Again, he emphasizes the gloom: "Such dreary streets! blocks of blackness, not houses, on either hand, and here and there a candle, like a candle moving about in a tomb" (3, 9). All about him, he sees graves rather than homes and hearths.

With his mind filled with thoughts of death and darkness, Ishmael comes to a rather unimposing building, whose door has been left open. Pressing onward, he enters the edifice and finds himself confronted by a sight that baffles his senses: "It seemed the great Black Parliament sitting in Tophet. A hundred black faces turned round in their rows to peer; and beyond, a black Angel of Doom was beating a book in a pulpit. It was a negro church; and the preacher's text was about the blackness of darkness, and the weeping and wailing and teeth-gnashing there. 'Ha, Ishmael, muttered I, backing out, Wretched entertainment at the sign of 'The Trap!'" (9–10). Ishmael's impressions of the scene—which very well could take place in Frederick Douglass's African Methodist Episcopal Zion church—are rather curious.[33] Later in the text, he commends New Bedford for its racial and ethnic diversity, and he forms an especially intimate transnational and transracial bond with Queequeg. At this point in time, though, Ishmael is not acquainted with New Bedford's cosmopolitan-ness or his bosom companion. What's more, he is still suffering from a severe bout of melancholy. Thus, he is not ready to embrace this sector of New Bedford's populace. Frightened by what he sees, Ishmael flees from the church for the relative safety of the Spouter Inn, which despite its "dilapidated" appearance seems to be "the very spot for cheap lodgings, and the best of pea coffee" (10).

The next day, after a restful and transformative night with Queequeg as his bunkmate, Ishmael embarks on a "daylight stroll" through the streets of New Bedford in order to see the sights. Like other nineteenth-century sailor-authors, he describes the city by assessing its cosmopolitan features. He goes so far as to characterize this metropolis as being more diverse than several other famous ports: "Even in Broadway and Chestnut streets, Mediterranean mariners will sometimes jostle the affrighted ladies. Regent Street is not unknown to Lascars and Malays; and at Bombay, in the Apollo Green, live Yankees have often scared the natives. But New Bedford beats all Water street and Wapping. In these last-mentioned haunts you see only sailors; but in New Bedford, actual cannibals stand chatting at street corners; savages outright; many of whom yet carry on their bones unholy flesh. It makes a stranger stare." He goes on to list the various different peoples present in the streets of New Bedford: "But besides the Feegeeans, Tongatabooans, Erromanggoans, Pannangians, and Brighggians, and, besides the wild specimens of the whaling-craft which unheeded reel about the streets, you will see other sights still more curious, certainly more comical. There weekly arrive in this town scores of green Vermonters and New Hampshire men, all athirst for gain and glory in the fishery" (31). What is important to mark about both of these extracts is Ishmael's generous, playful tone. In the first passage, he pokes fun at the ways in which globe-trotting sailors frighten the citizens of the world's various ports. Meanwhile, in the second quotation, he laughs at the expense of the bumbling greenhorns, who come to New Bedford from the rural reaches of New England in order to work on the city's famous whaling ships. Because Ishmael has befriended Queequeg, he is no longer a victim of his "hypos," and he is able to appreciate some of the more ridiculous aspects of the encounters between peoples from vastly different corners of the earth.

At this point, Ishmael turns his attention to New Bedford's wealth. Describing the city as "a queer place," he declares, "The town itself is perhaps the dearest place to live in, in all New England. It is a land of oil, true enough: but not like Canaan; a land, also, of corn and wine. The streets do not run with milk; nor in the spring-time do they pave them with fresh eggs. Yet, in spite of this, nowhere in all America will you find more patrician-like houses; parks and gardens more opulent, than in New Bedford." Comparing the city to Canaan, Ishmael highlights its illustrious streets and mansions. He goes on to explain that all of this wealth comes from the proceeds of the whaling industry: "Yes; all these brave houses and flowery gardens came from the Atlantic, Pacific, and Indian oceans. One and all, they were harpooned and dragged up hither from the bottom of the sea." With respect to the people of the city, Ishmael contends that "In New Bedford, fathers, they say, give whales for dowers to their daughters, and portion off their nieces with a few porpoises a-piece. You must go to New Bedford to see a brilliant wedding; for, they say, they have reservoirs of oil in every house, and every night recklessly burn their lengths in spermaceti" (32). Taken altogether, these descriptions of New Bedford might appear to be fairly complimentary. I would suggest, though, that they are far more critical than not. In the first passage cited above, Ishmael notes that New Bedford's wealth is derived from one resource, namely whales. While his attitude toward this detail is somewhat difficult to discern, his Canaan metaphor would suggest that he sees this single-minded focus as problematic. Of course, later on,

Ishmael characterizes the city's residents as wasteful for the way in which they "recklessly" squander the products of their trade.

Like other visitors to New Bedford, Ishmael highlights the beauty of the city. He poetically explains, "In summer time, the town is sweet to see; full of fine maples—long avenues of green and gold. And in August, high in air, the beautiful and bountiful horse-chestnuts, candelabra-wise, proffer the passer-by their tapering upright cones of congregated blossoms. So omnipotent is art; which in many a district of New Bedford has super-induced bright terraces of flowers upon the barren refuse rocks thrown aside at creation's final day." On a surface level, this passage is markedly uncritical. Above, Ishmael applauds the residents of New Bedford for the way in which they have managed to create a beautiful metropolis on "barren refuse rocks." Just like some of his counterparts who wrote for nineteenth-century periodicals, he admires the trees that line the city streets and the flowers that bloom in its gardens. With much fanfare, Ishmael concludes his discussion of New Bedford with a romantic paean to the beauty of the women of the city: "And the women of New Bedford, they bloom like their own red roses. But roses only bloom in summer; whereas the fine carnation of their cheeks is perennial as sunlight in the seventh heavens" (32–33). However praiseful they may be, these passages must be read in light of the fact that, over the course of the book, Ishmael travels from New Bedford to Nantucket, tracing the evolution of the whale fishery back to its almost defunct origins. By moving from a place of prosperity to a place of poverty and marking the industry's excesses as he does in these passages, Ishmael foregrounds the eventual demise of the whaling industry. The fact that he describes New Bedford in late summer and early autumn—not in the wintertime of his actual visit—further reinforces this idea.

The following Monday morning, Ishmael and Queequeg leave the Spouter Inn and head toward the waterfront to board the schooner that will take them to Nantucket. As they depart from New Bedford, Ishmael furnishes readers with his last description of the city:

> On one side, New Bedford rose in terraces of streets, their ice-covered trees all glittering in the clear, cold air. Huge hills and mountains of casks on casks were piled upon her wharves, and side by side the world-wandering whale ships lay silent and safely moored at last; while from others came a sound of carpenters and coopers, with blended noises of fires and forges to melt the pitch and betokening that new cruises were on the start; that one most perilous and long voyage ended, only begins a second; and a second ended, only begins a third, and so on, for ever and for aye. Such is the endlessness, yea, the intolerableness of all earthly effort. (59–60)

Other antebellum American writers, including William Whitecar Jr. and Frederick Douglass, employ such descriptions in order to praise the modes of labor organization employed by the whaling fishery. Ishmael, however, has a different purpose in mind. He turns his depiction of New Bedford's wharves into a philosophical and religious meditation on the futility of man's "earthly effort" in the face of his inevitable mortality. With this rather foreboding statement, he and Queequeg leave New Bedford for Nantucket, never to return.

As all of this evidence from various arenas of nineteenth-century American print culture indicates, New Bedford was a rather small, but very famous, metropolis. Taken individually, none of the periodical articles, memoirs, or novels discussed above presents a complete picture of the city and what I have called its cosmopolitan locality. Nineteenth-century New Bedford was a very diverse place in which many different groups of people—from various races, classes, and ethnicities—formed their own distinct communities, each of which had its own cultural particularities and political goals. Thus, New England's most prominent whaling metropolis possessed, among others, an activist African American community, a prosperous working-class community, a devout Quaker community, and a globe-trotting sailor community. When the various members of these communities wrote about New Bedford, they often put their descriptions to use on behalf of their various political interests, which included abolition, urban reform, synecdochic nationalism, and/or self-made manhood. As separate texts, then, these pieces certainly display antebellum New Bedford's tremendous diversity. As a collective, however, they reveal even more, for they demonstrate the remarkable degree to which the whaling industry bound together the city's cosmopolitan residents, giving them all a sense of unity, pride, and common purpose.

NOTES

1. Douglass, *My Bondage and My Freedom*, 213. Subsequent references will be given parenthetically. Before arriving in New Bedford, Douglass also spent some time in New York City and Newport, Rhode Island.

2. Heflin, *Herman Melville's Whaling Years*, 14; Wallace, *Douglass and Melville*, 15–21.

3. Melville, *Moby-Dick*, 9–60. Subsequent references will be given parenthetically.

4. Thomas W. Smith, *A Narrative of the Life*; Delano, *Wanderings and Adventures*; Whitecar, *Four Years Aboard the Whaleship*; "New Bedford," 252; "Sketches of New Bedford," 205–9.

5. Levine and Otter, introduction, 3.

6. Wallace, *Douglass and Melville*, 21.

7. Scammon, *Marine Mammals*, 243. For more on the whaling industry and its global dominance, see Schell, "A Bold and Hardy Race of Men," 14; Dolin, *Leviathan*, 205–52.

8. Mulderink, *New Bedford's Civil War*, 35.

9. Dolin, *Leviathan*, 223.

10. See Grover, *Fugitive's Gibraltar*, 8; Manjiro, *Drifting*, 88–99; Shoemaker, *Living with Whales*, 1–10.

11. Lytle, *Harpoons*, 184; Bernard, *Life and Times of John Manjiro*, 59–60.

12. For more on Nantucket and its Quaker residents, see Macy, *History of Nantucket*, 56–63; Schell, "A Bold and Hardy Race of Men," 59–66. For more on New Bedford and its Quaker residents, see Grover, *Fugitive's Gibraltar*, 10–11, 16–18.

13. Some of these individuals include Lewis Temple, John Jacobs, and John Thompson. A blacksmith by trade, Temple established his own shop where, in 1848, he invented a harpoon that completely revolutionized the industry. Lytle, *Harpoons*, 184. Almost as soon as they arrived in New Bedford, Thompson and Jacobs embarked on whaling voyages. Both published memoirs, but neither has much to say about New Bedford. Thompson, *Life of John Thompson*, 107–8; Jacobs, "A True Tale of Slavery," 126.

14. In this respect, New Bedford represents a precursor to twentieth-century cities such as Detroit, Michigan, and Pittsburgh, Pennsylvania, whose respective associations with the automobile and steel industries helped unite their residents and create local affiliations.

15. Harvey, *Cosmopolitanism*, 169.

16. Waldron, "What Is Cosmopolitan?" 232, 231.

17. As scholars have noted, early American authors often embraced national synecdoche. Miller, *Empire of the Eye*, 17; Motley, *American Abraham*, 2. Crèvecoeur was one of the first authors to see synecdochic potential in the American whaling industry. See *Letters from an American Farmer*, 108–65; Schell, "A Bold and Hardy Race of Men," 34–35.

18. "New Bedford," 252.

19. "Sketches of New Bedford," 206.

20. Ibid., 209.

21. "Communications. Coloured Seamen," *National Anti-Slavery Standard*, October 29, 1846. Boatsteerer is another name for harpooner.

22. Originally published in the *Transcript* of Portsmouth, Virginia, this article was reprinted in "Trouble among the Tyrants," *Liberator*, February 3, 1854.

23. Thomas W. Smith, *Narrative of the Life*, 226, 227.

24. Delano, *Wanderings and Adventures*, 84–87.

25. Whitecar, *Four Years Aboard the Whaleship*, 16, 17.

26. Ibid., 17.

27. "Great Anti-Slavery Meeting in Glasgow," *Liberator*, May 15, 1846; "Can't Take Care of Themselves," *Liberator*, December 21, 1849; "Stop My Paper," *Frederick Douglass' Paper*, July 24, 1851; "A Review of Anti-Slavery Relations," *Liberator*, December 16, 1853.

28. Nwankwo, *Black Cosmopolitanism*, 126.

29. Howe, *Making the American Self*, 137.

30. This speech was reprinted in *Liberator*, May 15, 1846. Similar descriptions of New Bedford appear in "Stop My Paper"; "A Review of Anti-Slavery Relations."

31. "Can't Take Care of Themselves."

32. Evelev, *Tolerable Entertainment*, viii; Kelley, *Melville's City*, 2, 168; Sten, "City of Hope and Fear," 23–36.

33. Wallace, 20–21.

SECTION 3

Countermappings
New Spaces in Old Places

CHAPTER NINE

Tribal Christianity

The Second Great Awakening and William Apess's Backwoods Methodism

Harry Brown

THE MORAVIAN CEMETERY in Bethlehem, Pennsylvania, used between 1742 and 1910, lacks the strange allure and palpable antiquity of Boston's Copp's Hill or Salem's Charter Street burial grounds. We find here no broken, blackened gravestones etched with a winged death's head, a weeping willow, or a melancholy rhyme. The Moravians left only plain slabs, neatly aligned and austerely inscribed with names and dates. The beauty of the place resides not in its artifice but in the idea manifested in its seemingly unimaginative regularity. Looking more closely at the inscriptions, we find Joseph and Mary Indian, Lenape converts, resting beside Count Nicholas Ludwig von Zinzendorf and Bishop David Nitschmann, fathers of the Moravian community. Their uniform, unadorned memorials signify their equality as God's children, all races and nations leveled in death before the Creator. Here is reform Christianity preached in stone.

In Britain in the mid-eighteenth century, the Moravian conviction in spiritual equality inspired John Wesley and early Methodist leaders, who gathered outdoors in contempt of Anglican authority and ministered vigorously to the sick, the poor, and the criminal. In the United States, Methodist circuit riders roamed the cities and the backwoods proclaiming the brotherhood of the races and urging social reforms according to gospel principles. A Methodist hymn popular in the period, composed in 1747 by Wesley's brother, Charles, calls believers from the highways and hedges:

> Come, sinners, to the Gospel feast,
> let every soul be Jesus' guest.
> Ye need not one be left behind,
> for God hath bid all humankind.[1]

The Methodists' embrace of "all humankind" fostered astonishing growth during the Second Great Awakening. Between 1780 and 1850 the number of Methodists grew from fourteen thousand to more than two million, and the number of Methodist preachers grew from fewer than fifty to almost eight thousand. By the mid-nineteenth century Methodism was the largest religious denomination in the United States. Through its energetic outreach to rural communities neglected by other denominations, Methodism approached universality.[2]

Swept up in what he called the "overwhelming flood" of revival, the Pequot William Apess converted in 1813 at the age of fifteen, while indentured to the uncompromising Presbyterian master William Williams. Forbidden by Williams to attend Methodist meetings, Apess ran away and joined the fight against the British and French Canadians at the Battles of Plattsburgh and Chateauguay. When the war ended, he wandered among the Iroquois communities in Canada and eventually returned to Connecticut. He married the Pequot Mary Woods in 1821 and began preaching to scattered Methodist congregations, although the Methodist Episcopal Church refused him a license to do so. Frustrated by the pretense of church leaders and convinced that he had been called by God, he turned to the group calling themselves the "Protestant Methodists," a more egalitarian congregation, who ordained him in 1829.

Apess's ordination marked the beginning of a notable career as a writer and reformer. Within a few years he produced *A Son of the Forest* (1829), the first autobiography written by an Indian without the aid of an amanuensis, as well as a series of exemplars for Indian converts, collected in *The Experiences of Five Christian Indians of the Pequod Tribe* (1833). In 1834 he effected unprecedented legislation, successfully lobbying the Commonwealth of Massachusetts for the autonomy of the Mashpee tribe, a legal struggle he documented in *Indian Nullification of the Unconstitutional Laws of Massachusetts* (1835). In 1836 he delivered a lecture on the history of Indian oppression in New England, recorded in his final and most eloquent work, *Eulogy on King Philip* (1836). Later in 1836, Apess fell into debt and vanished from public life. He died in New York City on April 10, 1839, succumbing to "apoplexy" at the age of forty-one.[3]

Apess's public life coincided with the height of the Second Great Awakening, a time, according to Nathan O. Hatch, when "the most distinctive feature of American religion was . . . a remarkable set of popular leaders who proclaimed compelling visions of individual self-respect and collective self-confidence." Hatch explains that the revival was led by "a whole range of rootless and visionary preachers" who were "bold, self-educated, self-confident, and inventive," hopelessly divided in doctrine but united in "a passion for expansion, a hostility to orthodox belief and style, a zeal for religious reconstruction, and a systematic plan to labor on behalf of that ideal." For Hatch, the Second Great Awakening represents not only a revival of faith but also a popular agitation for social equality. The singular story of the period, Hatch claims, is "the demand of religious insurgents to be recognized as the latest advance of Christ's kingdom."[4]

We encounter a void of research, however, on the extraordinary rise of Methodism in the United States and the central role of "visionary preachers" and "religious insurgents" such as Apess, particularly in the backwoods communities where they won so many converts and redefined rural belief. Hatch is unsatisfied with our current understanding of early Methodism, which remains bound to the assimilationist vision that early missionaries were "bearers of civilization to the uncouth, unrestrained society of the frontier."[5] Mark A. Noll concludes more broadly that "much remains unknown about how Methodist thinkers related to the broader social, political, and intellectual contours of the United States."[6]

More particularly, we find no sustained exploration of the connection between religious revival and region, a significant gap considering that American Christianity, to a large extent, took a new shape on the rural margin of the early republic. With its intermixed cultures, the frontier changed Christianity as much as Christianity changed the frontier, particularly through the work of Indian missionaries to Indians, such as Apess. While these missionaries felt compelled to bring the Gospel to their unconverted brethren, they also felt deeply alienated from white Christians and established religious institutions. As a result, they sought to adapt the Gospel more deliberately to Indian experience and to the particular circumstances of the tribal communities they met in their circuits. Consistently frustrated by bigotry, political compromise, and hierarchical control within the Methodist Episcopal Church, Apess recognized that the greatest potential for reforming Christianity existed outside established congregations in rural areas, beyond the reach of religious authorities. His accounts of Pequot conversions in his autobiography and in *Experiences* describe private, vernacular, multicultural worship, held in a forest grove rather than a church, attended by both whites and Indians, and spoken in a blend of English and Native languages. For Apess, these local communities could achieve among themselves the egalitarianism impossible within larger congregations, which became fractured by debates over Indian removal and the ordination of Indian ministers.

Apess's work establishes the foundation for tribal Christianity, an idea that Indian writers and Methodist leaders would not clearly articulate until the second half of the twentieth century. While Indian missionaries such as Apess tend to share the assimilationist view that agriculture, commerce, and Christianity are Indians' only paths to survival, they also search for ways to synthesize tribal experience with the new religion. In this adaptation of the Christian message to Native consciousness in rural New England, Apess saw the potential not only to save Indian souls but also to promote real social reform, to protect Native cultural vitality, and to sustain a more tolerant democracy.

In this sense, Apess's writing constitutes a form of "mapping," in Denis Cosgrove's sense of the term, in which "spiritual, political, or moral" transformation becomes entangled with spatial or "mathematical" orientation.[7] At this pivotal moment in the history of American belief, the backwoods exists in two dimensions. On the one hand, it encompasses a physical locale, maybe a muddy field outside town or a forest clearing on a local Indian reservation, beyond the reach of the religious establishment, where roaming preachers could inflame raucous and diverse crowds with freestyle and deeply personal modes of evangelizing. On the other, it encompasses an imaginary territory, a metaregion not specific to the Northeast, the West, or the South, where Apess and others like him could reconceive both race and faith in opposition to hierarchical and oppressive orders.

ITINERANCY, THE CAMP MEETING, AND RELIGIOUS POPULISM

American Methodism expanded with the nation itself. New wilderness settlements created a need for more preachers, and Methodist preachers, more than others, rushed to meet this need. In Hatch's words, these backwoods missionaries pursued a "greater preaching destiny" to minister to those "beyond the reach of any church organization."[8] Francis Asbury, a founding bishop of the Methodist Episcopal Church in the United States, recognized the importance of itinerant preachers in spreading Methodism in newly settled lands. Asbury intended to form an episcopacy that was "genuinely apostolic," represented by the energetic and deeply committed circuit rider with a "firm resolve to travel permanently on behalf of his flock and to share the deprivation of the itinerant preachers—and thus to partake of genuine apostolic suffering."[9] In their *Doctrines and Discipline of the Methodist Episcopal Church in America* (1798), Asbury and fellow Methodist bishop Thomas Coke define their "travelling plan": "Our grand plan, in all its parts, leads to an itinerant ministry. Our bishops are travelling bishops. All the different orders which compose our conference are employed in the traveling line; and our local preachers are, in some degree, travelling preachers. Everything is kept moving as far as possible; and we will be bold to say, that, next to the grace of God, there is nothing like this for keeping the whole body alive from the centre to the circumference, and for the continual extension of that circumference on every hand."[10] In Asbury's formulation of the "travelling plan," itinerancy partakes of the experience of early Christian apostles, but it also represents a dynamic, new evangelical paradigm for a diverse and rapidly expanding society. Every local congregation, moreover, becomes a "centre" within the larger "circumference" of Methodist belief. From the beginning, American Methodism recognized the multidimensionality of the backwoods, the correlation between geographical "extension" and spritual rebirth.

Staged by itinerant preachers on the fringes of this expanding society, the camp meetings reached out to Native communities in all quarters of the nation, far beyond Apess's northeastern orbit, and transformed them *en masse*. The missionary

John McFerrin describes a Cherokee camp meeting in North Carolina in 1829: "Just as the sun was setting, I reached the camp ground. . . . I saw the Cherokees coming from every direction, and many already present. Every thing seemed to declare that God was at work with the people. . . . There was supposed to be a larger collection of Cherokees at this meeting than was ever assembled for religious purposes in this nation before. I have attended many camp meetings among the whites, but I never witnessed more order or deeper solemnity in all my life than I witnessed on this occasion."[11] Another Methodist missionary, James Finley, describes a similar experience among the Wyandottes in Ohio:

> By the time of the evening meeting, our company had increased to several hundreds. This was a solemn and impressive scene. . . . The candles fixed on sticks stuck in the ground; the light reflecting from the green boughs that hung over us; the soft and mellow voices of three or four hundred Indians, rising and seemingly filling the blue vault with heavenly echoes; and the grove made vocal with the praises of the Great Spirit, formed a scene delightfully interesting and sublime. . . . Here I fully realized the saying of the prophet Isaiah, xxxv, 1, 2, "The wilderness and the solitary place shall be glad for them; and the desert shall rejoice and blossom as the rose."[12]

In *Experiences*, Apess, like McFerrin and Finley, remembers the emotional outpouring of the meetings, where "the preachers poured the thunders of the law upon them, as if God himself had spoken to them."[13] Mary Woods Apess memorably describes the fervor of the meetings as "electric fire [going] through every part of me, cleansing me throughout soul, flesh, and spirit" (83).

These transformative gatherings manifested a larger trend that Hatch calls "religious populism," a mode of preaching that "pursued converts wherever they could be found, opened leadership to all, and allowed popular idioms to color worship and preaching."[14] In other words, these camp meetings localized the more universal inclusiveness of the larger Methodist mission. Hatch views this synthesis of democratic and evangelical ideals as a peculiarly American phenomenon. "Deep and powerful undercurrents of democratic Christianity distinguish the United States from other modern industrial democracies," Hatch writes. "Religious leaders have pursued people wherever they could be found; embraced them without regard for social standing; and challenged them to think, to interpret Scripture, and to organize the church for themselves."[15] Drawn to the camp meetings by this promise of inclusiveness, servants, slaves, and dispossessed Indians embraced Methodism as a path to both spiritual and temporal deliverance. Here, Indians such as Apess and Woods, or McFerrin's Cherokees and Finley's Wyandottes, need not feel alienated from the Gospel. They may even feel a new responsibility for their own moral being and a control of their spiritual destiny. David Walker Howe observes that the Second Great Awakening "was remarkable for embracing . . . 'all sorts and conditions of men.'" The revivals and camp meetings, he claims, "taught self-respect and demanded that individuals function as moral agents." In this way, Howe concludes, "the Awakening empowered multitudes."[16]

Like other accounts of the Second Great Awakening, however, Hatch's and Howe's do not specifically consider the relation between region and the powerful wave of populist revival, mostly overlooking the significant fact that the wave crested spectacularly on the rural margins of American society. This failure to link revival with region suggests that revival itself resists charting and geographical containment. As the parallel accounts of Apess in Connecticut, McFerrin in North Carolina, and Finley in Ohio attest, backwoods revivalism was a metaregional phenomenon, occuring not in a specific place but in a specific *kind* of place, bounded less by geography than the social and spiritual conditions flourishing there. Inevitably, the populist appeal of the Methodist revival "terrified other more established denominations," who saw in the empowerment of unknown rural "multitudes" the danger of upsetting the social order.[17] William Williams forbids the adolescent Apess to attend the meetings and considers his servant's affiliation with the Methodists an act of insubordination. Apess recalls, "it was openly said that the character of a respectable man would receive a stain, and a deep one too, by attending one of their meetings. Indeed the stories circulated about them were bad enough to deter people of 'character!' from attending the Methodist ministry" (18). In this emblematic conflict between Williams and Apess, the Presbyterian sanction against Methodism takes the form of a prohibition to go outside of town to join the camp meeting.

Apess's perception of the Methodists as faithful outcasts is what draws him, a disaffected Pequot, into the woods and into their ranks. He confesses that public attacks on the "character" of the Methodists "had no effect on me." After all, he says, "I thought I had no character to lose in the estimation of those who were accounted great." He finds the Methodists a "clever company," respectable enough in appearance and conduct, and "more kind and gentlemanly," in fact, than most people he knows. More important, their language "was not fashioned after the wisdom of men" but rather contained "the power of God." They preached with a plainness that conveyed both divine authority and democratic inclusiveness. They are, he concludes, "the true people of God." He watches with concern as the "storm of persecution" rises against the ascendant Methodists, but he relates that the oppressive "Pharisees" and "worldlings" succeeded only in "cementing the brethren more closely together." Apess records his own awakening to moral agency at his first Methodist meeting, when he was only eight years old. "I listened to the word of God with the greatest degree of attention," he recalls. "It was not long before I resolved to mend my ways and become a better boy" (18, 19, 12).

Later, when he begins his own itinerant ministry, he spurns those who attack his race, his poverty, and his lack of education and social grace, as instruments of "the evil one," and he rejects any self-doubt as an infernal temptation to give up his mission. "Many a severe combat have I had with the enemy respecting my competency," he writes, "and I come to the conclusion that if I could not give *'refined!'* instruction, and neglected to discharge my duty to God and my fellow men on that account, I could not enjoy his smiles." Bigotry, public ridicule, and Apess's suspicion of his own incompetence only serve to validate his work, and, just as the besieged Methodist communities are "cemented" by persecution, Apess receives any challenge to his mission as further confirmation of its justice and necessity. He concludes, "I now felt it more strongly my duty, and an inward satisfaction in preaching the 'word.' . . . My mind was now exercised about entering the work as a missionary" (48). As he weathers persecution and overcomes his doubt, Apess becomes one of the many empowered by the peculiarly democratic religious revival of the Second Great Awakening, particularly as it takes shape in rural areas, beyond the reach of "worldlings" such as Williams.

APESS'S DISPUTE WITH THE METHODIST EPISCOPAL CHURCH

Besides provoking fear of anarchy in more established denominations, the populist revival also created tension within the Methodist establishment, particularly as newly energized rural congregations, ruled more by local idioms and practices than by Methodist orthodoxy, shifted the base of Methodist belief to the backwoods, a movement embodied by the trajectory of Apess's own preaching career. The British Methodist Conference denounced American camp meetings as "highly improper" and "productive of considerable mischief," seeming to echo the scolding of William Williams and Methodism's own harshest enemies.[18] Although Asbury affirmed the power of camp meetings to assemble large segments of a mostly rural and dispersed population and to inflame the frontier with the love of Christ, Methodist leaders remained concerned about unsanctioned preachers who might unleash unpredictable torrents of popular feeling and thus undermine the integrity and progress of the church, especially as these potential rogues roamed the backwoods circuits beyond their sanction. In this sense, the tensions within the expanding Methodist congregations arose as a result of the growing influence of dispersed communities of believers and the localized style of preaching done there.

Apess's dispute with the Methodist Episcopal Church regarding his ordination originates in his initiation to the faith, when the plain and powerful language of the rural meetings teaches him contempt for empty words and rituals. While indentured to Judge William Hillhouse in 1809, Apess mocked the rote prayers of his Presbyterian master, who subjects his family to his recitations and commands them, in turn, to repeat his words. He confesses, "I soon could pray as well as he; and of course I did not care for his prayers any longer." This contempt for rote language defines Apess's own ministry. He draws a distinction "between those who preach and those who read." Those who preach, he writes, do so "with divine power, which made the language of the speaker eloquent and sublime, and withal called the attention of those who heard it to seek the salvation of their souls." Those who read merely compile "a selection of fine sentences, and read off in an elegant style, which only seemed to please the ear and lull the people to sleep" (64, 65).

Throughout his ministry, Apess refuses to be coerced by such words without sincerity or divine authority, even when spoken by Methodist leaders. Like the corps of itinerant preachers marshaled under Asbury's "travelling plan," Apess identifies with the apostles, whose authority was confirmed at Pentecost, not by an arbitrary board of elders but, rather, by tongues of divine flame. He writes, "We read in the Bible that in former days, holy men spoke as they were moved by the Holy Ghost. I think this is right, and believe more in the validity of such a call than in all the calls that ever issued from any body of men united" (43).

Here we find the central dilemma of Apess's ministry and the origin of his rift with Methodist authorities. What originally attracts Apess to the Methodists—their inclusiveness and steadfastness against the "Pharisees"—is precisely what makes it impossible for him to accept their censure. In empowering Apess, the Methodists empowered him to challenge their authority. Weary with the church's refusal to ordain him, he finally declares, "I could not sheath my sword," continuing to hold meetings and to preach in spite of the elders' refusal to sanction his ministry. Apess responds by asserting his own apostolic purity: "I could not see how I was in error in preaching *Christ Jesus, and Him crucified* and of course could not conscientiously confess as erroneous that which I believed to be right." He furiously rejects the elders' perceived view that "no person is called of God to preach his word unless ordained of man," and he concludes in disgust, "No comment is necessary on this fact" (46).

Apess ultimately indicts the Methodist Episcopal Church for the same hypocrisy and empty formalism that the Methodists saw among the hierarchical Anglicans and Presbyterians. O'Connell suggests that Apess's conviction in the "validity" of his "call" illustrates the acute "tensions within the evangelical community under the influence of revivalism" between the authority of individual "inspiration" and that of the "institutionalized church." O'Connell claims that "Apess positions himself with those who stress the limitations of the ways of men and the greater reliability of God's." For Apess, feeling the call to preach from within had greater authority than any examination or licensing procedure. O'Connell concludes that "Apess had simply ignored the rules, and it was, I suspect, for this reason that the Conference refused his request."[19] In short, he recognized that authority to preach derived not from the "pharisaical" bishops but from the local congregations inflamed by the Gospel. Just as Williams's stance against Methodism took the form of a prohibition to go to the woods, Apess's assertion of spiritual self-determination ultimately takes the form of a flight to the woods, a radical rural itinerancy beginning with his identification with disaffected Indian believers.

Apess hints that racism motivated the elders' decision to deny him a license. As an itinerant, he realizes painfully that some of his brethren see him not as an authority but as a curiosity—an Indian aping a preacher. On one occasion, he recalls "a great concourse of people who had come out to hear the Indian preach, and as soon as I had commenced, the sons of the devil began to show their front—and I was treated not with the greatest loving kindness, as one of them threw an old hat in my face, and this example was followed by others, who threw sticks at me." Later he finds his wife, who had been staying at a boardinghouse, "quite unwell." Her hosts had denied her a light for her room and proper medicine when she fell ill. "I pretty soon learned," he writes, "that the treatment she received was very unkind, if not cruel—not fit for a dog, and what surprised me was that the woman of the house where my poor wife was boarded, and who treated her so bad, *professed to be a Methodist*" (44, 52–53).

Robert Warrior finds Apess's suspicions compelling, considering that the ordination of Indians and blacks would have "severely limited the allure of the Methodist message to the broadest base of whites," including many, like those in Apess's more hostile audiences, who refused to accept the equality, let alone the moral instruction, of an Indian. Apess's dispute with the Methodist Episcopal Church indicates a greater conflict within Methodism itself, as it expanded into the backwoods during the Second Great Awakening. While their universal embrace and egalitarian ideals fostered initial growth, they also stunted growth among certain groups of whites. As Warrior argues, the Methodists had to appeal not only to slaves, Indians, and poor whites, but also to those "who owned slaves, indentured servants, and tenements."[20] In this sense, limiting the ordination of Indians seems a political compromise necessary for spreading Methodism to a broader white constituency.

Frustrated with these institutional compromises, Apess turned from the Methodist Episcopal Church to the more radical Protestant Methodists, a collection of various disaffected congregations united in opposition to the Methodist Episcopal hierarchy. Following his defection, Apess writes, "I felt a great deal happier in the *new* church than I did in the *old* church—the government of the first is founded on *republican*, while the latter is founded on *monarchical* principles—and surely in this land where the tree of liberty has been nourished by the blood of thousands, we have good cause to contend for *mutual rights*, more especially as the Lord himself *died to make us free!*" (55). The Protestant Methodists offered Apess not only ordination and legitimacy but also a realization of his vision for a purely egalitarian Christian society based in rural communities. Even the terms he uses to describe the structures of authority within the two congregations—"republican" and "monarchical"—echo political debates that sought the proper orientation of power to geography, the opposition of a republic of autonomous rural communties against a centralized monarchical or federal government. Apess's religious revolt not only maps to the republican assertion of local authority but also establishes a theological ground for his Indian conversion narratives, invariably described as localized rural epiphanies.

APESS'S MISSION TO THE MISSIONARIES: A SON OF THE FOREST

In its final edition, *A Son of the Forest*, published in the same year Apess was ordained, is divided into two parts: a conversion narrative detailing Apess's youthful misadventures, spiritual struggles, and eventual ordination; and a long appendix arguing for the Semitic origin of the Indians and affirming their place among God's children. Drawing from a range of ethnographic studies, including Elias Boudinot's *A Star in the West; or, A Humble Attempt to Discover the Long Lost Ten Tribes of Israel* (1816), Apess observes numerous parallels between the language, ritual, and art of the Hebrews and those of his own people. He concludes that the Indians are "none other than the descendents of Jacob and the long lost tribes of Israel" (74).

This belief in the origin of Christians and Indians within a common faith tradition figures significantly in Apess's ministry, which stands on the egalitarian theology that "Christ died for all mankind—that age, sect, color, country, or situation made no difference" (19) and that heaven is a kingdom of pure equality, unlike earthly kingdoms, purged of slavery and oppression. Apess's "republican" theology reflects the widespread urge during the Second Great Awakening to eradicate class distinction and social privilege within reformed congregations on the frontier, where these distinctions were less relevant or altogether absent. Hatch explains that "obscure Christians without social grace and literary education went beyond merely denying the right of the clergy to ascribe authority to themselves. They began to piece together a popular theology that inverted the traditional assumption that truth was more likely to be found at the upper rather than at the lower reaches of society. . . . These popular theologies appropriated Christ's teaching that the power in the church should emanate from below, that the first should be last, and that the chief should not lord it over others but become a servant of all."[21] Apess himself draws no distinction between civil and religious liberty—both, he believes, work "'hand in hand' accomplishing the designs of God, in promoting the welfare of mankind."[22]

Apess's dual concern for the "designs of God" and the "welfare of mankind" manifest themselves as a curious ambivalence in *A Son of the Forest*. On the one hand, the autobiography relates a formulaic sequence of youthful ignorance and dissipation, initial conversion and backsliding, and final repentance and rebirth in God's grace. Apess begs no forgiveness, however, but instead lays the blame for his disobedience, petty crimes, and drunkenness on the whites who have cruelly mistreated him and his Indian brethren.

In his new, more radical stance against the Pharisees within the ranks of the Methodists themselves, Apess embraces Christianity not to reform the Indians but to reform Christians. He sees himself as a missionary to the missionaries, who too often point to the mote in their Indian brother's eye while missing the beam in their own. He writes, "If a good [white] missionary goes among them [the Indians], and preaches the pure doctrine of the gospel, he must necessarily tell them that they must 'love God and their neighbor as themselves—to love men, deal justly, and walk humbly.' They would naturally reply, your doctrine is very good, but the whole course of your conduct is decidedly at variance with your profession—we think the whites need fully as much religious instruction as we do" (33). In this spirit of instructing the instructors, he vehemently condemns whites' introduction of "ardent spirits" to the Indians as a primary reason for their decline, and he attributes the "cruel and unnatural conduct" of his Indian grandparents, who nearly beat him to death, to whiskey, "that curse to individuals, to families, to communities, to the nation" (7, 47). While historians trace the parallel courses of the Second Great Awakening and the temperance movement, temperance was not only a plank in the Christian social platform for Apess but also a more radical indictment of white depredation.[23] Apess blames the "cursed stuff" for the disintegration of Indian families such as his own and concludes, "How much better would it be if the whites would act like a civilized people, and instead of giving my brethren of the woods 'rum!' in exchange for their furs, give them food and clothing for themselves and children. If this course were pursued, I believe that God would bless both the whites and natives threefold" (33).

Apess cites racial violence by whites as another reason for Indians' apparent delinquency. He leaves school because he is beaten and derided by his teachers and flees his lawful master William Williams because he is brutally beaten by a chambermaid.[24] After he has taken part in the American victory at the Battle of Plattsburgh, his patriotic elation is diminished by the slurs and threats of his fellow militiamen, as well as a deeper awareness that he cannot share the rights he has defended. This awareness sharpens when he witnesses the passage of the Removal Act in 1830, which he recognizes in *Eulogy on King Philip* as an imperialistic appropriation of natural resources in order to enrich the government.[25]

Cheryl Walker suggests that Apess's conversion narrative is fundamentally different from traditional exemplars, such as Jonathan Edwards's "Personal Narrative" (1740), which explain sin as an innately human condition. Instead, Apess attributes his own wretchedness to "family genealogy and [social] context," representing sin in a way that "seems far more temporal and earthbound" compared to Edwards's understanding.[26] Irene Vernon likewise characterizes Apess's "use of Christianity to seek and question issues of justice" for Indians as "very creative" in a period when Christianization was mostly synonymous with forced cultural assimilation.[27] Like other "visionary" and "insurgent" preachers during the Second Great Awakening, Apess saw democratic reform as the natural partner of religious revival. Combating these moral and political injustices justifies the conversion of the Indians; failing to do so renders any Christian mission empty and pharisaical.

In this way, Apess represents the religious populism and democratic empowerment that Hatch and Howe describe as central phenomena of the Second Great Awakening. In another way, however, he remains excluded from what these historians generally perceive as a broadly inclusive movement. His experiences of personal bigotry and national depredations against Indians reflect the insoluble conflict between Apess's belief in the transformative power of Christian love and his endless frustration with supposed Christians who too often wield false doctrine as a tool of exclusion and oppression. From this frustration, Apess becomes aware that true reform could not take place within an institutional context, even among the relatively progressive Methodists, as he moves doctrinally toward a more definite break from church hierarchy and geographically toward his own tribal base. Apess's uniqueness and "creativity" as a convert and reformer depends on his gradual orientation toward a unique and creative form of rural belief.

TRIBAL CHRISTIANITY:
THE EXPERIENCE OF FIVE CHRISTIAN INDIANS

Apess experiences an epiphany when he visits the Iroquois reservations in Ontario following the Battle of Chateauguay. Comparatively isolated from white influence, these idyllic communities demonstrate to Apess "the utmost order and regularity." The months he spends here are the happiest of his youth and inspire him to admire the "wisdom of God in the order" and the "beauty of creation," particularly in contrast to the socially disordered and morally ruined reservations of New England (33). Although the Iroquois lack Christianity, they are free from the injustice, poverty, and alcoholism that plague the converted Indians in the United States. He finds here all the social reforms sought by the Methodists—yet, somewhat vexingly, without Methodism.

This crucial moment in Apess's search for the egalitarian core of Christianity, one more regionally oriented, represents a second conversion experience, in which he gains a new consciousness of the way Christianity might be practiced in the wilderness, transcending empty words and political compromises and synthesized with the tribal life otherwise destroyed by American Christianity. Although he never disavows Christianity in favor of paganism, he comes to recognize that the greatest potential for reforming Christianity exists outside any established church, among a local community with a shared experience of isolation. "Having been excluded from the pales of the church," he writes, "I viewed myself as an *outcast from society*." He turns then to his *"first love*," to the Indians of his "native tribe" (46).

Earlier, when he returns to Connecticut after his service in the militia, he joins a small religious community led by his aunt, Sally George, whose conversion he documents in *Experiences*. He describes their gatherings as a Christian fulfillment of the peaceful but pagan Iroquois communities he visits in Canada. These gatherings are private, multicultural, and vernacular, held in a woodland grove rather than a church, attended by both whites and Indians, and spoken in a blend of English and Pequot. Apess writes, "These seasons were glorious. . . . We knew nothing of dead languages, except that the knowledge thereof was not necessary to serve God. We had no house of divine worship, and believing 'that the groves were God's first temples,' thither we would repair when the weather permitted. The Lord often met with us, and we were happy in spite of the devil. Whenever we separated it was in perfect love and friendship" (40). Methodist missionaries to Indian settlements relate similar spiritual awakenings at the wilderness camp meetings. John McFerrin and James Finley find among the Cherokee and Wyandottes a more vital faith that transcends language and tradition and seems to speak interchangeably of God and the Great Spirit. For McFerrin and Finley, however, bigger is better. The more Indians flock to the meeting and make noise, the more they see God's presence in the wilderness. Aunt Sally's meetings are more intimate—the fewer present, the stronger their bonds of "love and friendship." McFerrin and Finley, moreover, preside over the Indians with ministerial authority. Although Aunt Sally holds no such power, she is a minister in her own right, who derives her apostolic authority not from a board of elders but from natural grace and humility, as well as the respect given to her by local people. In his idyllic recollection of Aunt Sally's meetings, Apess seems to recognize that these local communities of believers could achieve among themselves the harmony and egalitarianism untenable within larger Methodist congregations.

Like Apess's description of Aunt Sally's gatherings in *A Son of the Forest*, the short conversion narratives collected in *Experiences* model tribal Methodism, autonomous and isolated from church authority. Apess emphasizes the significance of the backwoods settings where these conversions take place. Tormented by thoughts of suicide during their wilderness sojourns, Hannah Caleb, his own Aunt Sally, and Anne Wampy enact symbolic deaths before they can be reborn in grace. Caleb relates her story to Apess, who records it in her words: "I used to roam whole days in my native forest, weeping and wailing on account of my sins. . . . As I was walking by the side of a large pond, the enemy whispered to me to throw myself in and there end my days of sorrow and affliction. I was quick to obey. I got up on a log for that purpose; but a voice seemed to say to me, 'Hannah, my mercy is as free for thee as this water, and boundless as the ocean.' The tempter fled; my mind was calm, and I returned home" (146).

When she wavers, and thoughts of death return, she turns not to the camp meetings but back to the lonely wilderness, where she finally experiences her spiritual awakening: "Christians could not help me. I then turned from the world and the prayers of the saints and went into the wilderness and sat myself down, and I had the impression that I must sing.... My whole soul was lost in wonder, love, and praise to God. I was enabled to join the heavenly company, and sing the wonders of redeeming grace" (146–47). Apess transcribes George's parallel experience of retreat, solitude, and salvation:

> I had become now a wanderer alone, as it were, in my native woods; and one day as I was passing by a large, deep brook, the enemy of my soul tempted me to destroy myself in that place, by casting myself in.... I fell to earth as one dead.... And while in this situation, I saw the pit of destruction opened for poor sinners.... I lay in this situation for some time as helpless as an infant, begging for the mercy of God.... The Lord heard my prayer and sent down his melting grace into my soul; and before I rose from the ground I was translated into the kingdom of God's son.... There was a change in everything around me, the glory of the Lord shone around, all creation praised God, [and] my burden and my fears were gone. (149)

Wampy relates a similar experience in broken English, transcribed by Apess:

> When Christian come talk with me, me no like 'em; me no want to see 'em; me love nobody; I want no religion.... By me, by me very much troubled; me get sick, me afraid I die—me go pray, go off all alone in the woods—me afraid I go to hell; me pray. By me, by Jesus, come take me by the hand lead me a great way off—show me one place look like hell; me come close to it so me feel it—me afraid I fall in; me cry to Jesus to have mercy on poor me. He take me by the hand again and lead me back ... then me feel light, like one feather; me want to die, me want to fly— me want to go home; me love every body, me want to drink no more *rum*. I want this good religion all the time. (152)

These parallel accounts of temptations to suicide, prostration before God, and final redemption model the Methodist experience of spiritual rebirth, but they are unorthodox in their backwoods setting and their removal from a general congregational context to a more local or solitary one. Their turning away from the Christian community toward wilderness solitude also signals the crucial divergence between Apess's model of Indian conversion and institutional Methodist practice represented by the much larger communal camp meetings. Although Caleb and George return to the meetings after their private awakenings, Apess remarks that they were "always diligent to seek Jesus in ... the groves, the forest." George was "left in general to wander to and fro, up and down the forest with [her] native kin" and "without any education as to understanding the letter in any way whatever" (150, 148).

These conversion narratives suggest that many Indian converts, like Apess himself, found it difficult to meet whites on common ground, both geographically and spiritually, even within the tolerant Methodist congregations, so they had to withdraw to their own local communities. Caleb, George, and Wampy convert by way of not a camp meeting but a private awakening in the woods that obviates any church authority. In the woods, Caleb becomes childlike and Christlike in her simple expression of unconditional love for her enemies: "I could say there was no more enmity in my heart, that I loved white people as well as my own. I wonder if all white Christians love poor Indians. If they did, they would never hurt them anymore" (147). In relating her story, Apess models an unmediated communion between the believer and God, an adherence to the letter of the Gospel, and a true leveling of all people before God. This elemental form of Protestantism seemed to appeal to Indians who felt more comfortable in a forest grove than a teeming meetinghouse and, as such, represents a metaregional phenomenon uniquely compatible with tribal experience.

CHRISTIAN AND INDIAN

We find a different and perhaps more common model of Indian conversion in Peter Marksman, an Ojibwe who became a missionary to his own tribe and adopted white cultural prerogatives. In his own conversion narrative (1844), Marksman describes his zealous ministry among his wayward kin: "Poor 'prodigal son!' As soon as I had done preaching I asked them, who 'will arise and go to his father?' And they all, men, women, and children, rose up, saying, 'We will arise up and embrace Christianity!' And, Monday morning, they all brought their images and bad medicines to me. I took them all, and piling up those images and bad medicines, I did burn and destroy them before their eyes."[28]

This account raises the persistent question voiced by later generations of Native writers. How can one be a "Christian" and an "Indian" at the same time? Significantly, Apess's model of conversion resolves this dilemma in a time when the difference between these two identities seemed irreconcilable, and his writing maps this resolution both geographically and spiritually. Caleb, George, and Wampy stand apart from Marksman because the women do not reject their former lives as a prodigious error, nor do they purge their Pequot words and tokens. In short, they do not sacrifice being Indian in order to become Christian.

In *A Son of the Forest*, Apess describes his own experience of backwoods solitude, despair, and salvation. Returning to his family, Apess takes a wrong turn and becomes lost in a swamp. With every step, he writes, "I became more and more entangled—the thickness of the branches above me shut out the little light afforded by the stars, and to my horror I found that the further I went, the deeper the mire." He finds himself in a "labyrinth of darkness . . . shut out from the light of heaven—surrounded by appalling darkness—standing on uncertain ground." Finally, in the depth of despair, he humbles himself and begs God for mercy. And "behold," Apess writes, "he stretched forth his hand and delivered me from this place of danger. . . . I found a small piece of solid earth, and then another, so that after much difficulty I succeeded once more placing my feet upon dried ground." Like Caleb, George, and Wampy, he is left exhausted and elated by the love of God: "I then fell upon my knees and thanked my blessed master for this singular interposition of his providence and mercy" (42).

Ron Welburn argues that this experience has a double meaning. On the one hand, Apess's swamp is John Bunyan's Slough of Despond, a place of trial, doubt, and spiritual renewal.[29] Christian tradition, Welburn reminds us, has long envisioned the wilderness as a place of trial and purification. In the first chapter of the Gospel of John, the prophet John the Baptist says, "I am the voice of one crying in the wilderness! Make straight the way of the Lord!"[30] After receiving baptism from John, Jesus also retreats to the desert, where he endures fasting and temptation in solitude before returning to Galilee, spiritually fortified, to begin his mission.

At the same time, Welburn argues, Apess's swamp is also a place of "vision quest" that prepares Apess for his mission: "The initiation ritual Apess undergoes is not simply a passage into a new and white religion, but into a state of mind preparing his commitment first to 'saving' the souls of his 'brethren,' and, more importantly, to his learning to negotiate the images of Christianity in order to attack white hypocrisy."[31] Welburn reads Apess's experience in the swamp as, simultaneously, Christian allegory and Native ceremony. Like the Pequots whose conversion he documents in *Experiences*, Apess finds a way to be both Christian and Indian, although he must sever himself from the larger Methodist congregation and retreat into a tribal enclave to do so.

As a missionary Indian, Apess embodies both the conflicts and the hopes of assimilation and emerges during the Second Great Awakening as a paradoxical symbol of both cultural survival and cultural extinction. On the one hand, the Christian notion that all races are God's children allows Apess to claim more applied forms of social and political equality, like many other "visionary" and "insurgent" preachers of this volatile period. On the other hand, conversion compels him to abandon beliefs and practices integral to their identity. Apess and other Indian converts such as Caleb, George, and Wampy mediate this conflict by conceiving a model of wilderness conversion and Christian worship that is compatible with tribal identity rather than inimical to it. While these missionaries tend to share the assimilationist view that agriculture, commerce, and Christianity are Indians' only paths to survival, they also search for ways to synthesize tribal ways with the new religion. In this way, Apess is one of the extraordinary figures of the Second Great Awakening who, in Hatch's words, "used democratic persuasions to reconstruct the foundations of religious authority."[32] Even more specifically, however, Apess's writing allows us to map this reconstruction to a specific kind of place conceived, like Cosgrove's imaginary maps, both spatially and spiritually.

In 1988 the Native American International Caucus of the United Methodist Church, descendants of those first Indians drawn to the Methodist camp meetings, issued *The Sacred Circle of Life*, a document that proposes to reconcile Christian evangelism with the preservation of tribal identity. It asserts that "cultural conversion as an imperative of Christian evangelism must be eliminated," that the Church might bring the Gospel to the Indians without demanding that they cease to be Indians. The document concludes, "the integration of Christian and Native American traditional spiritual teachings can bring excitement, healing and renewed efforts for self-determination to a people frustrated by the lack of sensitivity to them as people and to their culture."[33]

In the context of this recent recognition of the value of cultural and religious "integration," we might see Apess not as a disgruntled agitator, defeated by drink, nor even as one of many energetic republican revivalists but, more uniquely, as a prophet of greater tolerance and cultural coexistence. His disenchantment with the Methodist Episcopal Church and his developing awareness that reform could take place only in the backwoods, among small independent tribal congregations, signals the beginning of a search for a more authentic faith: consistent with the egalitarian ideal embodied by the Moravian grave slabs, continuous with tribal traditions rather than in conflict with them, and celebrated in a forest grove where one might commune equally with God and the Great Spirit. Many old Indians such as Anne Wampy, tongue-tied by new languages and bent low by new laws, must have cared little for the difference.

NOTES

1. Charles Wesley, "Come, Sinners, to the Gospel Feast." *Hymnary.org*, accessed May 29, 2009, http://www.hymnary.org/hymn/UMH/339.
2. Hatch, *Democratization of American Christianity*, 220; Daniel Walker Howe, *What God Hath Wrought*, 177, 178.
3. O'Connell, introduction to *On Our Own Ground*, xxi.
4. Hatch, *Democratization of American Christianity*, 55–56.
5. Ibid., 223.
6. Noll, *America's God*, 331.
7. Cosgrove, *Mappings*, 14.
8. Hatch, *Democratization of American Christianity*, 4.
9. Ibid., 83.
10. Asbury and Coke, *Doctrines and Discipline*, 42.
11. McFerrin, "Cherokee Mission," 216–17.
12. Finley, *Life among the Indians*, 310.
13. Apess, *On Our Own Ground*, 66. Subsequent references will be given parenthetically.
14. Hatch, *Democratization of American Christianity*, 85.
15. Ibid., 5.

16. Howe, *What God Hath Wrought*, 188.
17. Hatch, *Democratization of American Christianity*, 3.
18. Ibid., 50.
19. O'Connell, introduction to Apess, *On Our Own Ground*, 43, 56.
20. Warrior, *People and the Word*, 25.
21. Hatch, *Democratization of American Christianity*, 44–45.
22. Apess, *On Our Own Ground*, 55.
23. Howe, *What God Hath Wrought*, 167.
24. Apess, *On Our Own Ground*, 11–12, 22.
25. Ibid., 155.
26. Walker, *Indian Nation*, 42–43.
27. Vernon, "Claiming of Christ," 77.
28. Marksman, "Indian Convert," 255.
29. Welburn, *Roanoke and Wampum*, 88.
30. John 1:23 (King James Version).
31. Welburn, *Roanoke and Wampum*, 88.
32. Hatch, *Democratization of American Christianity*, 11.
33. Native American International Caucus, *Sacred Circle of Life*, 659.

CHAPTER TEN

"We, Too, the People"

Rewriting Resistance in the Cherokee Nation

Keri Holt

CHEROKEE LITERARY WRITING has its origins in defining locality. Like all Native American communities, the Cherokee have a complex literary history that involves multiple forms of expression, including oral traditions and unwritten, nonalphabetic practices.[1] In the early 1820s, however, a Cherokee silversmith named Sequoyah developed a syllabic alphabet for writing the Cherokee language. The Cherokee syllabary, which was officially adopted by the Cherokee Nation in 1825, resulted in the rapid growth of Cherokee literacy and print culture during the early nineteenth century. The Cherokee Nation established their own printing press in 1828 and, in addition to religious, political, legal, and educational texts, published the *Cherokee Phoenix*, a newspaper written in both English and Cherokee that circulated throughout the Cherokee Nation and the United States between 1828 and 1834.[2]

The establishment of the Cherokee press coincided with U.S. efforts to remove the Cherokee from their land, and early Cherokee writing focused extensively on the removal crisis as Cherokee writers used their newly established press to assert their national sovereignty and challenge U.S. removal policies. As part of this effort, the *Cherokee Phoenix* became a primary forum for mapping the Cherokee land as a sovereign, independent nation for readers living within and outside of its boundaries. More specifically, the *Cherokee Phoenix* provided Cherokee writers with a means of countering U.S. efforts to determine the significance of their homeland. "Our views, as a people, on this subject have been sadly misrepresented," stated Elias Boudinot, the first editor of the *Cherokee Phoenix*. "These views we do not wish to conceal, but are willing that the public should know what we think of this policy which, in our opinion, if carried into effect, will prove pernicious to us."[3] Here Boudinot privileges the *Cherokee Phoenix*, for its ability to not only present the Cherokees' opposition to removal but also represent those views accurately due to its close proximity to the Cherokees' local concerns and conditions.

At stake in the removal debates were two different ways of mapping the lands occupied by the Cherokee people, which were located within the states of Georgia, Alabama, Tennessee, and North Carolina. The Cherokee argued that this land represented a sovereign, independent nation, defined by fixed and formal boundaries that clearly separated it from the United States. Meanwhile, proponents of removal (led by the state of Georgia and the Jackson administration) argued that the lands occupied by the Cherokee belonged to the United States. From their perspective, the Cherokee lands represented a "permissive and temporary" locality whose boundaries were provisional and whose residents were "tenants at will," subject to the laws of the states and U.S. federal government.

Examining these two efforts to map the Cherokee land provides a compelling opportunity to explore the close relationship between definitions of locality and nationhood. For the United States, mapping the Cherokee locality had immediate implications for determining the size of the nation, as well as the legitimacy and scope of its authority. For the Cherokee, mapping this locality was a means of defining and differentiating their own national boundaries and power. In other words, the Cherokee's efforts to map their locality shows how local communities, rather than being subject to national power, serve to define an independent national space.

The maps set forward in the *Cherokee Phoenix* during the removal crisis also provide a useful lens for exploring the role that language and literary expression play in defining local and national spaces and determining their relationship to one another. In opposing the removal policies, the Cherokee relied on two different languages and rhetorical strategies to define their national sovereignty. In some cases, they relied on their native language and writings to map the Cherokee lands as a distinct and independent nation. The *Cherokee Phoenix*, for instance, printed government proceedings and official political documents written by the Cherokee national council and principal chief that defined the boundaries of the nation and attested to its governing authority. Meanwhile, the existence of the *Cherokee Phoenix* itself helped define Cherokee national sovereignty. By printing a newspaper that described the local conditions and views of the Cherokee Nation in the Cherokee language, the Cherokee were able to define themselves as a literate community that valued reading and writing, while also demonstrating the active and efficient use of their native language—characteristics needed to represent the Cherokee community as a "civilized" nation for a white U.S. audience.

At the same time, the *Cherokee Phoenix* also relied heavily on the language of the United States to map their land as a sovereign nation, citing U.S. laws and political documents, as well as U.S. presidential speeches and the nationalist rhetoric of the American Revolution to assert their national claims. Furthermore, the Cherokees' strategic use of native language and literacy to define their nation was a tactic borrowed directly from the United States, a nation that relied extensively on written documents and the establishment of an active print culture to define itself as an independent "republic of letters." In this regard, the *Cherokee Phoenix* sought to define the Cherokee Nation, in part, by borrowing the language and discursive practices of the very nation from which they were trying to assert their separation and independence.[4]

Focusing specifically on the Cherokee writings published in the *Cherokee Phoenix*, this essay explores the complex bilingual literary strategies that the Cherokee used to map their locality as a nation both distinct from yet also closely aligned with the United States. By using two different languages and rhetorical strategies to define the Cherokee Nation—the "native" language and local writings of the Cherokee people and the nationalist language of the United States—the *Cherokee Phoenix* illustrates the process of countermapping local and national communities. While countermapping involves strategies of spatial and rhetorical resistance, however, the Cherokee had to walk a fine line between resisting U.S. efforts to map their land and promoting acceptance for the alternative national map they sought to instill. By drawing on the local or "native" language and rhetorical practices of the Cherokee people, the *Cherokee Phoenix* was able to map the Cherokee Nation in terms that were clearly separate, sovereign, and distinct from the map of the Cherokee lands set forward by U.S. print culture. At the same time, though, these methods of countermapping caused the Cherokee Nation to be perceived, problematically, as a threatening and destabilizing opponent of the United States. Ironically, the Cherokee efforts to countermap their locality threatened to undermine the alternative map they sought to put in place. As a result, the *Cherokee Phoenix* was ultimately engaged in two different processes of countermapping that involved first, defining their land as an independent nation, and second, encouraging readers to recognize that nation as a space that could be compatible with and complementary to the United States.

This second process of countermapping is evident in the way that the *Cherokee Phoenix* used the language and rhetoric of the United States to map the Cherokee lands. Although such a process might seem to run counter to the Cherokees' efforts to define their nation in sovereign, independent terms, the Cherokees' use of the language and rhetoric of U.S. nationalism allowed them to counter the negative perceptions associated with their efforts to define their nation in native terms. Finding the right balance between these local ("Cherokee") and nonlocal ("U.S.") strategies of countermapping was a constant struggle in the pages of the *Cherokee Phoenix*, and by studying the interplay between these two methods of national definition, the newspaper illuminates not only the complex dynamics of countermapping but also the close relationships between defining national and local spaces. On the one hand, the Cherokees' decision to rely on the language of the United States to assert their national authority, rather than on their own local forms of language and literary expression, seems to illustrate the extent to which nations exert superior control and authority in defining local spaces, whether they have a valid claim over those localities or not. By defining their nation through the language of the United States, the Cherokee undermined their own authority and autonomy, relying exclusively on the United States to define their nation in legitimate and acceptable terms. On the other hand, using the language and rhetoric of the United States also enabled the Cherokee to control and manipulate public perceptions of the United States, to the point where they were able to rewrite the United States as a dishonorable, hypocritical nation, while the Cherokee Nation emerges as the superior model of "American" nationalism that the United States should imitate. By examining these literary techniques—whereby the Cherokee transform their apparent submission into a critical position of control—this essay draws attention to the ways that localities can define, transform, and even undermine national boundaries and authority. Although we often assume that nations define and control localities, the *Cherokee Phoenix* illustrates how nations are irrevocably subject to the critical perspectives and literary representations of local communities.

THE CHEROKEE PHOENIX: MAPPING A NATION IN TWO LANGUAGES

The *Cherokee Phoenix* was a primary medium for defining and defending the Cherokee Nation. The newspaper was established in the Cherokee capital of New Echota in 1827 by the Cherokee general council, which allocated funds to cover the production costs and salaries for the paper's printer and editor. The newspaper remained "the property of the Nation," subject to "the direction of the Cherokee Legislature" for the duration of its run.[5] In practice, though, the Cherokee government remained relatively uninvolved in the day-to-day management of the newspaper, relegating these responsibilities to the editor, who was trusted "to form such regulations . . . as will appear to us the most conducive to the interests of the people for whose benefit the paper has been established."[6]

The first editor of the *Cherokee Phoenix* was Elias Boudinot. Educated at the Foreign Mission School in Cornwall, Connecticut, Boudinot readily embraced the assimilation program promoted by the school, changing his name from Gallegina or "Buck" Watie to "Elias Boudinot" after the current president of the American Bible Society, who had also served as president of the second Continental Congress. While at the Mission School, Boudinot learned to read and write in English, converted to Christianity, and adopted the manners and lifestyle of his white neighbors. In 1826, however, Boudinot sparked controversy when he married Harriet Gold, a local white woman whose family had been strong supporters of the Mission School. Believing that his cultural assimilation had earned him the respect and esteem of his Connecticut neighbors, Boudinot was stung by the vocal opposition to the marriage. Residents held public protests and burned the couple in effigy, and the local Congregational church issued a formal statement of opposition, prompting the eventual closure of the Mission School. In light of this reaction, Boudinot and his wife left Connecticut and returned to the Cherokee territory, where he became a vocal advocate for Cherokee national sovereignty.[7] In promoting Cherokee nationalism, however, Boudinot continued to encourage the Cherokee to adopt the political, economic, and cultural practices of the white residents of the United States, believing that acculturation was necessary to ensure the success and survival of the Cherokee Nation.[8]

As editor of the *Cherokee Phoenix*, Boudinot used the newspaper to promote this dual agenda of encouraging cultural assimilation while promoting Cherokee nationalism. This joint focus is evident in the prospectus for the newspaper, which was presented to the Cherokee government in 1827 and reprinted in the paper on February 28, 1828.

> As the great object of the *Phoenix* will be the benefit of the Cherokees, the following subjects will occupy its columns:
> 1. The laws and public documents of the Nation.
> 2. Account of the manners and customs of the Cherokees and their progress in Education, Religion, and the arts of civilized life, with such notices of other Indian tribes as our limited means of information will allow.
> 3. The principal interesting news of the day.
> 4. Miscellaneous articles, calculated to promote Literature, Civilization, and Religion among the Cherokees.[9]

This description reveals two distinct emphases. On the one hand, the *Cherokee Phoenix* was meant to represent the immediate conditions, views, and practices of the Cherokee people, providing a place for the Cherokee to document local activities and perspectives in their own terms, which would, in turn, provide evidence for defining their land and community as a sovereign and independent nation. On the other hand, the *Cherokee Phoenix* was also meant to illustrate the extent to which the Cherokee people had modified their local beliefs and practices to imitate the political and cultural practices of the United States. By documenting the Cherokees' "progress in Education, Religion, and the arts of civilized life," the *Cherokee Phoenix* sought to define Cherokee nationalism using the terms and standards set by the United States. To this end, the *Cherokee Phoenix* relied on a complex combination of local and nonlocal forms of expression to assert their national status, defining their locality as a sovereign nation by representing their own native interests and conditions while simultaneously borrowing and imitating the national terms of the United States.[10]

The bilingual dimensions of the newspaper illuminate this dual approach. The *Cherokee Phoenix* was printed in both English and Cherokee. Although the newspaper did not provide complete translations of its entire content in both languages, Boudinot made an effort to ensure that "all matter which is of common interest will be given in both languages, in parallel columns."[11] By printing material in the Cherokee language, Boudinot highlighted his commitment to defining the Cherokee Nation in local, native terms. According to Boudinot, the Cherokee language was best suited for representing "the sentiments . . . of the Cherokees." Representing the Cherokee as a people able to read and write effectively in their own native language was also an important means of illustrating that they were capable of establishing and supporting an independent nation by perpetuating "the diffusion of intelligence in their mother tongue."[12]

At the same time, the newspaper's use of the Cherokee language was also a means of illustrating how the Cherokee people had adopted the national practices of the United States. By showing that the Cherokee could read and write effectively in their native language, the *Cherokee Phoenix* was able to characterize the Cherokee Nation as a "civilized" nation that, like the United States, could operate as a literate and successful "republic of letters." The fact that some of the Cherokee content of the newspaper was also translated into English enabled U.S. readers to evaluate the quality and use of their literary endeavors, while also implying that the Cherokee language could operate as an equivalent and effective mode of literary and political expression. For example, the publication of Cherokee laws, which were printed alongside one another in English and Cherokee, allowed U.S. readers to see how the Cherokee were using their native language to produce laws that were comparable and equivalent to U.S. laws. The fact that the newspaper was published in both English and Cherokee further supported the literacy and literary strengths of the Cherokee Nation since its editor and contributors were clearly able to express themselves in both languages. In this regard, the use of both English and Cherokee allowed the *Cherokee Phoenix* to define the Cherokee Nation in terms that were both similar to the United States and different from it.

The *Cherokee Phoenix* relied on this bilingual strategy more broadly, drawing not only on these two different languages but also on different sets of texts and rhetorical strategies to define their locality in national terms. In some cases, the *Cherokee Phoenix* defined the nation using works written by Cherokee citizens. In other cases, the newspaper relied on documents issued by the United States. This bilingual approach was dictated, in part, by their audience, which was composed of both Cherokee and non-Cherokee readers. Boudinot referred to these audiences directly, which he identified as the newspaper's "home" and "distant" readers, and the bilingual dimensions of the newspaper were intended to define the Cherokee Nation in terms that would be acceptable to both groups. By representing the Cherokee Nation through native and nonnative discursive practices, the *Cherokee Phoenix* sought to present a particular image of "civilized" nationhood that was rooted in the local conditions of the Cherokee community yet could also be recognized and accepted by the citizens of the United States.[13]

For the first few months of its existence, the *Cherokee Phoenix* privileged the local voice and language of the Cherokee people to assert Cherokee national sovereignty. Boudinot printed more content in the Cherokee language in these earlier issues than he did in later editions, and the newspaper drew specifically on political documents written and authorized by the Cherokee government to define the boundaries of the Cherokee Nation and affirm its national authority. The first issues of the newspaper published a complete copy of the Cherokee Constitution, which was printed in three installments between February 21 and March 6, 1828.

The Cherokee Constitution, which had been written at a convention held in New Echota between July 4 and July 26, 1827, was an important document in mapping the Cherokee Nation. Although the Cherokee Nation had been successfully governed by a tribal council and judicial system without the existence of a formal, written constitution for more than fifty years, members of Cherokee government argued that a formal constitution was needed to protect their land as the United States became increasingly interested in acquiring it. In drafting a national constitution, the Cherokee council did not create a completely new system of government or alter the existing political structure and governance of the Cherokee Nation.[14] What the Cherokee Constitution did accomplish, however, was defining the Cherokee Nation in a written document whose form and terms could be recognized and respected by the United States.

Delegates to the New Echota convention intentionally modeled the Cherokee Constitution after the U.S. Constitution, at times even borrowing specific words and phrases from the U.S. Constitution to describe the structure, powers, and purpose of the Cherokee government. Consider, for instance, the preamble to Cherokee Constitution:

> We, the representatives of the people of the Cherokee Nation, in Convention assembled, in order to establish justice, ensure tranquility, promote our common welfare, and secure to ourselves and our posterity the blessings of liberty; acknowledging with humility and gratitude the goodness of the sovereign Ruler of the Universe, in offering us an opportunity so favorable to the design, and imploring His aid and direction in its accomplishment, do ordain and establish this Constitution for the Government of the Cherokee Nation.

The phrasing of the Cherokee preamble mimics the preamble of the U.S. Constitution almost exactly, and by defining the Cherokee Nation using the same constitutional language that defined the United States, the Cherokee sought to ensure that their nation would be viewed as equally legitimate and acceptable. Furthermore, the repetition of this constitutional language maps the Cherokee Nation as a space committed to the same rights, values, and principles as the United States, another ground for promoting their national legitimacy and acceptability.[15]

As much as this preamble attempts to define the Cherokee Nation in terms that were identical to the United States, however, it also highlights some important differences between these nations, most notably concerning the Cherokees' acknowledgment of "the goodness of the sovereign Ruler of the Universe." In contrast to the U.S. Constitution, which asserts a clear separation between religion and government, the Cherokee Constitution defines a nation where religion and government were more closely intertwined. Such differences, situated in a document that otherwise closely imitates the structure and language of the U.S. Constitution, allowed the Cherokee to define their nation in terms that were still distinct from the United States.

The Cherokee Constitution continues to strike this balance between imitating the language and structure of the U.S. Constitution and asserting its difference throughout the document. Like the U.S. Constitution, the Cherokee Constitution outlines a representative government, composed of "three distinct departments, the Legislative, the Executive, and the Judicial," and each branch is described in terms that are similar to the United States, including a bicameral legislature, an executive branch made up of a principal chief and assistant principal chief, and a judicial system composed of a supreme court and network of circuit courts. The powers accorded to each of these branches are described in terms nearly identical to the U.S. Constitution, as evident in declaration that "No person, except a natural born citizen, shall be eligible to the office of Principal Chief; neither shall any person be eligible to that office, who shall not have attained the age of thirty-five years," and the existence of a "necessary and proper" clause which states that "the General Council shall have power to make all laws and regulations which they shall deem necessary and proper for the good of the Nation." The Cherokee Constitution also features a "Bill of Rights" which carefully follows the language and policies expressed in the U.S. Constitution, noting that Cherokee citizens will be guaranteed "the free exercise of religious worship" and the "right of a trial by jury," and ensuring that "no person shall for the same offence be twice put in jeopardy, nor shall any person's property be taken or applied to public use without his consent."[16]

The Cherokee Constitution also contains many features that set it apart from the U.S. Constitution, particularly regarding the close relationship between politics and religion, as indicated by Article VI, which states that "no person who denies the being of a God or a future state of rewards and punishment shall hold any office in the civil department of this Nation." Other differences emerge in Article I, which opens with a detailed description of the boundaries of the Cherokee Nation. In contrast to the U.S. Constitution, which does not delineate national boundaries, the entire first section of the Cherokee Constitution is devoted to identifying "the boundaries of this nation embracing the lands solemnly guaranteed and reserved forever to the Cherokee Nation." Beginning with the northern boundaries "on the North Bank of Tennessee River at the upper part of the Chickasaw old fields," the Cherokee Constitution describes the southern, eastern, and western boundaries in exhaustive detail, unlike the U.S. Constitution, whose first article focuses on the powers granted to Congress.

This difference draws attention to the Cherokees' reason for writing their own constitution in the first place. Rather than simply establishing a national government, the Cherokee Constitution was meant to define and protect this specific locality from interference by the United States. By carefully identifying the boundaries of the nation and asserting their title to it in the first section of their constitution, the Cherokee wanted to assert not just their national authority but the particular location where their national authority needed to be recognized and respected. Article I also identifies another key difference between the Cherokee Nation and the United States by asserting that "the lands therein are, and shall remain, the common property of the Nation." In contrast to the United States, where lands were held in private ownership, the Cherokee Nation is clearly defined as the collective property of its citizens. By asserting this collective ownership so early in their constitution, the Cherokee insisted that their land be recognized as a different kind of national space than the United States—a national space that could not legally be sold or transferred without the approval of the Cherokee Nation.

By modeling the Cherokee Constitution so closely on the U.S. Constitution, the Cherokee granted the United States significant influence in defining their nation.[17] Nevertheless, the differences between these documents also allowed the Cherokee to assert that their nation was not wholly defined or determined by the United States. For as much as the Cherokee Constitution was modeled on the language and political structure set forth in the U.S. Constitution, the Cherokee were careful to emphasize that this document—and the nation it defined—were composed by the Cherokee people and adapted to reflect their local conditions and interests.[18]

Boudinot's decision to publish the Cherokee Constitution as the leading feature in the first issues of the *Cherokee Phoenix* further enhanced its status as a "native" assertion of national sovereignty. The newspaper printed the full text of the Cherokee Constitution in English and Cherokee, and, in contrast to other bilingual portions of the newspaper, which placed the Cherokee text immediately following the English language text, Boudinot printed the Cherokee Constitution in parallel columns, so that each portion of the text was positioned next to its corresponding translation (fig. 2). This format enabled English-speaking readers to identify the similarities between the U.S. and Cherokee Constitutions while simultaneously emphasizing that the Cherokee Constitution was a native document that had been composed in the Cherokee language for local use.

Publishing the Cherokee Constitution in the *Cherokee Phoenix* allowed Boudinot to further emphasize the "native" character of the document as he responded to readers' comments about it. The close similarities between the U.S. and Cherokee constitutions led many readers to believe that the Cherokee people had assistance in drafting their constitution, and Boudinot responded to such criticism

Figure 2. The Cherokee Constitution, published in the *Cherokee Phoenix*, February 28, 1828. Courtesy of the Digital Library of Georgia.

directly, noting in an editorial dated March 20, 1828, "We were not a little diverted, in noticing lately . . . a motion made in the House of Representatives . . . to ascertain, what white persons have assisted the Cherokees in forming the late constitution."[19] Boudinot used this opportunity to emphasize that the Cherokee people were solely responsible for writing their constitution. "Our object, when we commenced to pen this article, was to correct the mistake, under which some may labor, and to declare once for all, that no white man has had anything to do in framing our constitution, and all the public acts of the Nation. The Cherokees only are accountable for them," concluded Boudinot, "and . . . we hope this practice of imputing the acts of Indians to white men will be done away."[20] Here, Boudinot clearly identifies the Cherokee Constitution as a locally produced and locally authorized document, produced by the independent actions of the Cherokee government, rather than through U.S. involvement or assistance.

The *Cherokee Phoenix* published other government documents that were intended to define the Cherokee Nation in local or native terms, particularly in its early issues. Following the publication of the Cherokee Constitution, the *Cherokee Phoenix* published a series of laws recently passed by the Cherokee national council, once again printing these laws in parallel, bilingual columns. Boudinot emphasized that these laws had already been put into effect, noting that the Cherokee language version of them "[has] already been circulated in this Nation in a pamphlet form." By publishing these laws in the *Cherokee Phoenix*, Boudinot directed them toward a white, non-Cherokee audience. "Our readers at a distance will perhaps be gratified to see the first commencement of written laws among the Cherokees," stated Boudinot, and by providing these readers with evidence of the Cherokees' local laws, he hoped to demonstrate to these distant readers that the Cherokee were capable of governing their nation independently and effectively.[21]

The laws published in the *Cherokee Phoenix* provided detailed information about practices of the Cherokee government and its ability to retain order within the nation.[22] Covering a range of criminal and civil issues, these laws featured prohibitions on theft, public violence, and murder; restrictions on the sale of liquor and the practice of gambling; and regulations for law enforcement. On a civic level, the *Cherokee Phoenix* reprinted laws for acquiring business licenses, collecting taxes, and maintaining roads and infrastructure. At the international level, it printed laws that specifically focused on protecting Cherokee national boundaries by setting clear regulations on non-Cherokee residents conducting business in the Cherokee Nation, levying special taxes on commerce occurring between the Cherokee Nation and the United States, and prohibiting non-Cherokees from using or developing Cherokee lands without paying established fees. The national council also prohibited selling Cherokee land to people outside of the nation, noting that such attempts to buy or sell land without approval by the national council would be met with heavy fines. By publishing these laws, the *Cherokee Phoenix* characterized the Cherokee Nation as a space that was carefully managed and controlled by the Cherokee government, as well as a space whose boundaries were clearly defined and maintained.

Much like the Cherokee Constitution, the Cherokee laws emphasized similarities between the Cherokee Nation and the United States. The Cherokee laws concerning criminal activity, taxation, and the regulation of businesses would have looked familiar to U.S. readers, and by publicizing these parallels, the *Cherokee Phoenix* meant to convince U.S. readers that the Cherokee Nation was governed in a manner similar to their own. At the same time, the *Cherokee Phoenix* worked hard to ensure that these laws were perceived as the product of the Cherokee Nation. Each law that appeared in the paper was signed by the Cherokee principal chief or the members of the general council who had proposed it, and, once again, the presence of the Cherokee language version of these laws, printed alongside the English translation, allowed the newspaper to emphasize that these laws had originally been composed in the Cherokees' native language for local use. To further emphasize the native composition of these laws, Boudinot included reports of meetings held by the Cherokee national council, where delegates proposed and debated national laws and policies. By including these reports, the *Cherokee Phoenix* reinforced the perception that the Cherokee people were capable of independently composing and enforcing their own national laws. Though their laws and government clearly imitated the example set by the United States, the documents published in the early issues of the *Cherokee Phoenix* insisted that the Cherokee Nation was a locality successfully managed by its own national government, which was operating in its own distinctive and locally oriented terms.

As much as these rhetorical tactics were intended to assert Cherokee nationalism in terms that were acceptable to white U.S. readers, reaction to this approach was not favorable. The publication and circulation of the Cherokee Constitution and the Cherokee laws and government proceedings were largely viewed as an aggressive challenge by readers in the United States. The state of Georgia was particularly vocal in denouncing the Cherokee Constitution as a disruptive political document that threatened to alter the boundaries and undermine the authority of the United States. "Here within our own territory, upon the land forming a part of our sovereign property, is a Government exercising authority independent of ours and denationalizing our citizens in order to strengthen itself in opposition to our will," wrote John Forsyth, the governor of Georgia, in November 1828.[23] Others similarly described the Cherokee Constitution as a document of "defiance" that sought to take land away from the United States and define a new and unauthorized nation. According to this view, the documents published in the *Cherokee Phoenix* represented more than acts of independent self-definition. The Cherokee Constitution and Cherokee laws represented an attempt to transform

U.S. boundaries in "defiance of the authority of the States of Georgia, Tennessee, Alabama, and North Carolina."[24]

Georgia and other proponents of removal worked hard to discredit the Cherokees' local or native assertions of nationalism by characterizing them as destabilizing documents that threatened the sovereignty of the United States. "An Indian tribe in the heart of the Union has assumed an attitude of independence by forming a constitution and ought to be opposed," stated the Georgia legislature in 1828, which, together with Governor Forsyth, petitioned President Adams to formally denounce the Cherokee Constitution as a hostile and illegal attempt to claim U.S. territory.[25] As the *Cherokee Phoenix* drew added attention to the Cherokee Constitution and the laws and activities of the Cherokee government, other proponents of removal questioned not just the content but also the quality of these local documents. Lewis Cass, the U.S. superintendent of Indian affairs, dismissed the Cherokee laws as inferior and ineffective, characterizing them as "too ignorant and barbarous to establish and maintain a government, which shall protect its own citizens and preserve the necessary relations and intercourse with its neighbors."[26] The state of Georgia similarly dismissed the Cherokees' documents as insubstantial statements of sovereignty. "We are aware that the Cherokee Indians talk extravagantly of their devotion to the land of their fathers, and of their attachment to their homes, and that they have gone very far toward convincing the General Government . . . of [their] title to the Georgia lands."[27] In response to these "fragile" and "extravagant" claims of nationalism, the Georgia legislature passed a series of resolutions that offered different interpretations of the Cherokee locality. In place of the "guaranteed" boundaries and title set forth by the Cherokee laws and constitution, the Georgia legislature rewrote this same space as a "permissive and temporary" location whose residents were subject to the authority of the state. The legislature also redefined the authority of the Cherokee people, denying their independence and placing them under the jurisdiction of the state. "Georgia has the right to extend her authority and laws over the whole territory, and to coerce obedience to them from all descriptions of people, be them white, red or black, who may reside within their limits." Under this language, the Cherokee people no longer represented independent citizens but rather "tenants at will, and . . . [Georgia] may, at any time she pleases, determine that tenancy by taking possession of the premises."[28]

As Georgia and the administration of the newly elected president, Andrew Jackson, intensified their efforts to claim the Cherokee lands, the *Cherokee Phoenix* changed its rhetorical strategy for asserting national sovereignty. Since the publication of their own national documents had been interpreted as a disruptive act of defiance, the Cherokee needed to find a way to countermap their nation in less incendiary terms. Instead of relying on Cherokee documents and the use of the Cherokee language to assert the boundaries, title, and authority of the Cherokee

Nation, Boudinot turned to other forms of expression—namely, the language of U.S. nationalism—by publishing articles that focused on the documents and rhetoric of the United States. In doing so, the *Cherokee Phoenix* deemphasized, to the point of nearly erasing, the Cherokees' own role in defining their land as an independent nation, rewriting the Cherokee Nation as a space that had been wholly defined and determined by the United States.

REORIENTING THE COUNTERMAP:
THE TERRITORIAL POLITICS OF LANGUAGE

In addition to reprinting the Cherokee Constitution and national laws, the *Cherokee Phoenix* published a range of other articles that argued for Cherokee national sovereignty, including formal editorial essays, correspondence between the Cherokee national council and the U.S. government, letters from subscribers, and copies of the Cherokee memorials, which were formal petitions that the Cherokee national council submitted to the U.S. government to express their opposition to the proposed removal policies.[29] The majority of these articles were written by Cherokee authors. Nevertheless, although they were "native" documents, these writings increasingly relied on the language and rhetoric of U.S. policy and nationalism to present their arguments for Cherokee sovereignty. Many of these writers acknowledged this strategy directly. "In the archives of the United States are to be found public documents that afford abundant evidence to convince the world that this land is the soil of the Cherokees," stated Principal Chief John Ross in a statement issued to the national council, which was published in the *Cherokee Phoenix* on October 21, 1829. References to these "public documents," which included formal treaty agreements, presidential speeches, and invocations of the U.S. Constitution and other U.S. laws, soon became the primary means for defining the Cherokee Nation within the *Cherokee Phoenix*. A memorial printed on October 12, 1829, explains the logic of this strategy. "As we seek truth rather than victory, and to inform the public so that its opinion may have its proper and legitimate effect, we shall present a concise statement of these relations from official sources." By using these "official sources," Cherokee writers wanted to reframe their national claims as statements of "fact" rather than subjective statements of opinion. Motivated by a desire to reveal "truth" rather than attain "victory," the Cherokee presented their national claims as an attempt to illuminate existing policies, as opposed to promoting radical and self-interested change. In doing so, the *Cherokee Phoenix* attempted to reorient public perceptions of the Cherokee Nation, by defining it as a space that was not opposed to U.S. interests but fundamentally aligned with them.

Of course, in making this argument, the Cherokee also granted the United States primary authority in defining this "truth," placing the Cherokee Nation in a subordinate position by suggesting that the "official" writings of the United States carried more authority and legitimacy than their own documents. Here, it's worth noting that Cherokee writers had previously drawn on the public documents of the United States by modeling their own laws and constitution after those of the United States. Their tactics here are different, though. Rather than adopting and adapting the language of the United States to express national sovereignty in their own words, the writers published in the *Cherokee Phoenix* made a conscious effort to sideline native voices and let the documents of the United States speak for them directly.

U.S. treaty agreements were the primary documents that Cherokee writers used to define their national sovereignty. Numerous articles cited these treaties, and they were particularly prominent in the Cherokee memorials, which were reprinted as leading features in the *Cherokee Phoenix* from late 1828 onward. Adopting the style and tone of a report, these memorials reviewed the history of treaties that had been negotiated between the United States and the Cherokee, identifying the dates and locations where they signed and summarizing the terms of each agreement. The memorials also included quotations from specific treaties. A memorial published in the August 12, 1829, issue of the *Cherokee Phoenix* exemplifies this strategy:

> In 1791, a treaty was concluded at Holston between the United States and the Cherokee by which the boundary line was established, and the Cherokee claim to the land, east and south of the line extinguished. The 7th article of that treaty is as follows: "The United States solemnly guarantee to the Cherokee Nation, all their land not hereby ceded." It was further stipulated, that . . . any citizen of the United States, committing any offence within the Cherokee territory, should be punished as if the same had been committed "within the jurisdiction of the State or District to which he may belong, against a citizen thereof. . . . In 1798, a further cession of their territory was made by the Treaty of Tellico and the United States, in the 6th article, agreed to "continue the guarantee of the remainder of their country FOREVER."[30]

This memorial makes the same claims presented in Article I of the Cherokee Constitution—identifying the specific boundaries of the Cherokee Nation and asserting their "guaranteed" title—but it uses a different set of documents to do so. By citing the 1791 Treaty of Holston and the 1789 Treaty of Tellico, the Cherokee memorials defined the Cherokee Nation exclusively through the language and authority of the United States. As a result, the Cherokee Nation emerges as a creation of the U.S. government, rather than a nation authored by the Cherokee people.[31]

In citing these documents, Cherokee authors emphasized not only the specific language of the treaties but also the fact that this language had been repeated in multiple treaties over time. The memorials and articles published in the *Cherokee Phoenix* cited different treaties, but Cherokee writers noted that the United States consistently referred to the Cherokee as the "Cherokee Nation" and defined their land as a "guaranteed" possession in nearly all the treaty documents. By citing these repeated statements, Cherokee writers argued that these documents did not represent a limited or one-time recognition of Cherokee sovereignty. Instead, the treaties illustrated a long-standing precedent of recognizing this locality as a distinct and independent nation. A memorial published in the December 18, 1829, issue of the *Cherokee Phoenix* sums up the effects of citing this well-documented treaty history.

> We have the faith and pledge of the United States, repeated over and over again, in treaties made at various times. By these treaties, our rights as a separate people are distinctly acknowledged, and guaranties given that they shall be secured and protected. So we have always understood the treaties. The conduct of the Government towards us from its organization until very lately, the talks given to our beloved men by the Presidents of the United States, and the speeches of the Agents and Commissioners, all concur to show that we are not mistaken in our interpretation.[32]

By showing how the Cherokees' rights and title had been repeatedly stated in multiple treaties, Cherokee writers used this language to bolster the legitimacy of their national claims. In doing so, they distanced themselves from playing any role in asserting their status "as a separate people." Although they acknowledge that this sovereign independence represents their own "understanding" of the treaties, they take care to emphasize that the United States has interpreted these documents the same way, citing the "conduct" of the government, the "talks" given by U.S. presidents, and the "speeches" of U.S. Indian agents and commissioners by way of support. In this regard, they attempt to circumvent any accusations that their claims represent a biased, self-interested interpretation of the treaty documents. More importantly, this strategy allows them to portray the United States as the original author and supporter of the Cherokee Nation. Rather than relying on the views of their own people to validate their claims, these Cherokee authors defer to the interpretive authority of the United States. Their claims of sovereign independence are not based on their own interpretations but are made credible by the views and actions of the United States.[33] Under this model, mapping the Cherokee land as an independent nation emerges not as an act of Cherokee resistance but as an action produced and sanctioned by the United States.

Articles published in the *Cherokee Phoenix* also redefined the origins of the Cherokee Nation by drawing on the U.S. Constitution. Although the U.S. Constitution does not make specific reference to the Cherokee lands, the Cherokee memorials and other antiremoval articles regularly cited the U.S. Constitution's descriptions of treaties and treaty-making powers to affirm their national status. "The constitution of the United States (article 6) contains these words," states an 1829 memorial. "'All treaties made under the authority of the United States shall be the supreme law of the land, and the judges in every State shall be bound thereby, any thing in the laws or constitution of any State to the contrary notwithstanding.' The sacredness of treaties, made under the authority of the United States, is paramount and supreme, stronger than the laws and constitution of any State."[34] Though these words do not define the Cherokee Nation directly, they support Cherokee sovereignty by defining the conditions set by U.S. treaties as "supreme law." In addition, the language of the U.S. Constitution allows the Cherokee to defend themselves against Georgia's efforts to claim their land, since the constitution expressly forbids any state from interfering with treaty conditions.

At this point, it is worth recalling that the Cherokee already had their own "official" documents to make these national claims. The Cherokee Constitution asserted the "supreme sovereignty" of the Cherokee Nation, and the *Cherokee Phoenix* had published several laws prohibiting the residents of Georgia or any other U.S. state from claiming the Cherokee lands. As the removal debates intensified, however, the *Cherokee Phoenix* increasingly replaced these local or native documents with documents written by the United States in order to relocate the origins of their national government within the founding documents of the United States. "The jurisdiction, then, of our nation over its soil is settled by the laws, treaties, and constitution of the United States, and has been exercised from time out of memory," stated an 1829 memorial, defining the Cherokee Nation in relation to a longer and more recognizable political history.[35] Other editorials likewise invoked the U.S. Constitution to assert and legitimize their national claims. "I invoke the genius of the Constitution of the United States, for protection," stated an 1829 letter to the editor, which credits this document for defining the Cherokee as "the rightful and original owners" of their land.[36] Through this method of argument, the *Cherokee Phoenix* maps the Cherokee Nation as a nation sanctioned and protected by the U.S. Constitution, sharing the same political origins as the United States.

Even though this use of the U.S. Constitution and treaty documents allowed the *Cherokee Phoenix* to project a certain equivalence between the Cherokee Nation and the United States, the newspaper was careful to emphasize that the United States was solely responsible for defining the Cherokees' national status, specifically due to its command of language. "It ought to be remembered too, in the conclusions of the treaties to which we have referred, and most of the treaties subsisting between the United States and this nation, that the phraseology, composition, etc. was always written by the Commissioners, on the part of the United States, for obvious reasons: as the Cherokees were unacquainted with letters."[37] Emphasizing their lack of knowledge and experience with written language, the Cherokee deny that they had any involvement in defining the Cherokee Nation. Through this rhetorical strategy, the national status of the Cherokee land once again emerges as something composed and authorized entirely by the United States, without any assistance or provocation from the Cherokee people.

The *Cherokee Phoenix* further represented the Cherokee Nation as a nation authored by the United States by citing presidential speeches. George Washington was regularly cited as the "Great Father" of the Cherokee Nation, and the newspaper identified his policies promoting education, agriculture, and republican government as a central foundation for the Cherokee Nation. "Gen. Geo. Washington, that truly great and illustrious man, deserves a particular notice," commented one editorial. "Under his administration, originated this liberal and kind policy which the United States have exercised towards the Indians, and under which the Cherokees have made laudable improvement, in agriculture and civilization; . . . the happy effects of it are now to be seen in almost every house."[38] Other articles similarly credited Washington with "bring[ing] the Cherokees into the pale of civilization by establishing friendly relations with them, by treaties, and introducing the mechanic arts among them."[39] To illustrate this influence, the *Cherokee Phoenix* reprinted many of Washington's letters and speeches. An 1828 article titled "Washington and the Cherokees," for instance, includes a speech Washington delivered to "his beloved men of the Cherokee Nation" that outlines the "path I wish all the Indian nations to walk."[40] Specifically, he encourages the Cherokee to "exert themselves in tilling the ground and raising . . . useful animals" and to adopt a representative system of government similar to that of the United States. "Beloved Cherokees—The wise men of the United States meet together once a year, to consider what will be for the good of all their people. . . . [and] I have thought that a meeting of your wise men once or twice a year would be alike useful to you."[41] In citing this speech, the *Cherokee Phoenix* suggests that the definitive characteristics of Cherokee nationalism—namely its republican government and "civilized" agricultural practices—have their origins in the words of President Washington. "The advice I here give you is important as it regards your nation," concludes Washington. By "walking in the path which I have described," the Cherokee will not fail to establish an "industrious and respectable" nation. On the basis of such encouragement, noted another editorial, "he was indeed a 'father' to them."[42]

The *Cherokee Phoenix* cited the speeches and letters of other U.S. presidents to reinforce the perception that the Cherokee Nation was "fathered" by the United States. An editorial published on August 12, 1829, includes a speech delivered by President Madison that sets forth clear guidelines for establishing an independent Cherokee Nation, guidelines that, again, involve imitating the practices of the United States. "I have a further advice of my Red children. You see how the country of the eighteen fires is filled with people. They increase like the corn they put into the ground. . . . The reason, my Red children, is plain. The white people breed cattle and sheep. They spin and weave. Their heads and their hands make all the elements and productions of nature useful to them. It is in your power to be like them."[43] Like Washington, Madison outlines specific activities in which the Cherokee must engage to be recognized as an independent nation, activities that include farming, cultivating livestock, establishing permanent settlements, and engaging in domestic practices such as spinning and weaving, with the goal of sustaining their own homes and engaging in local trade. By encouraging the Cherokee to "be like" the citizens of the United States, however, Madison goes a bit farther as his advice implies that these practices will enable the Cherokee to establish a nation equal to the United States. "The Great Spirit has given you, like your white brethren, good heads to contrive, and strong arms, and active bodies. Use them like your white brethren of the eighteen fires, and like them, your little sparks will grow into great fires."[44] Here, Madison not only argues that the Cherokee people are physically and intellectually equal to the citizens of the United States; he also insists that the Cherokee have the ability to establish a self-sufficient nation that is separate from yet also equal to their "brethren of the eighteen fires." Once again, the origins for this independent nation lie in the plan set forward by President Madison. His words are the source for the Cherokees' equal and independent national future. Rather than identifying their own native "founders," the Cherokee present themselves as a nation founded by the leaders of the United States, who carefully constructed the Cherokee Nation in their own national image.

In conjunction with these presidential speeches, the *Cherokee Phoenix* provided readers with evidence that the Cherokee people had followed this presidential model. "The beneficent policy which is here so simply, but beautifully recommended, has partially succeeded with many tribes, [but] in the Cherokee Nation, it has produced the most triumphant results," observed one article, which had cited one of Washington's speeches in extensive detail.[45] The *Cherokee Phoenix* published numerous articles illustrating the success of Cherokee farming practices, including data from an 1824 census, which documents the number of Cherokee residents who operate stable and successful farms and other businesses.[46] The newspaper also provided information about the spread of Christianity, the progress of literacy, and the establishment of a successful education system, all of which had been encouraged by Presidents Washington, Jefferson, and Madison. By covering these local activities, the *Cherokee Phoenix* made a rare departure from its efforts to define the Cherokee Nation through the language and actions of the United States. While the newspaper acknowledged that these aspects of "civilized" nationhood were produced by the Cherokee people, Boudinot was careful to credit the United States with establishing these local conditions. Reports of the literary, agricultural, and political development of the Cherokee Nation were continually framed in relation to the guidance offered by the United States. Within the *Cherokee Phoenix*, the Cherokees' "triumphant" development of an independent nation had its origins in the words of U.S. leaders and citizens. "The history of the prosperous and improving condition of our people in the arts of civilized life and christianization, is before the world," stated an editorial written in June 1829, which goes on to emphasize that "the cause which have produced this great change and state of things, are to be traced from the virtue, honor, and wisdom in the policy of the Administration of the Great Washington—the Congress of the United States and the American People."[47] By continually citing the advice and policies set by former U.S. presidents and other governmental leaders, the *Cherokee Phoenix* established a new frame for reading all forms of native Cherokee action and expression. Although the Cherokee were currently taking an active role in defining and shaping their land as a nation, the newspaper emphasized that these efforts were originally imagined, composed, and promoted by the United States.

From a persuasive standpoint, the Cherokee had much to gain by deferring to the authority of the United States. Characterizing the United States as the author of the Cherokee Nation allowed the newspaper to reinforce the assumption (held by a majority of its "distant" readers) that the United States represented a superior governing authority. Given that the *Cherokee Phoenix* needed to convince its U.S. readers to accept the validity of their national claims, it makes sense that the newspaper would adopt this deferential attitude, which was more likely to attract the support of a U.S. audience.

Nevertheless, there is something problematic about these tactics, particularly considering the nationalist goals of the *Cherokee Phoenix*. "As the *Phoenix* is a national newspaper, we shall feel ourselves bound to devote it to national purposes," stated Boudinot, who consistently presented the newspaper as the representative "voice" of the Cherokee people, "justly contain[ing] the views of the nation."[48] By relying so heavily on the language of the United States and deemphasizing the Cherokees' role in defining that nation, however, the *Cherokee Phoenix* seemed to contradict its stated intentions to "faithfully publish" the local views, experiences, and conditions of the Cherokee people.[49] Paradoxically, the content of the *Cherokee Phoenix* undermined and displaced the authority of the Cherokee people at the same time that the paper claimed to represent a strong, independent, and native national voice.

Scholars have commented on the contradictory dimensions of this national rhetoric, noting how the *Cherokee Phoenix* simultaneously asserts and denies the literary and literate authority of the Cherokee people. As Philip Round describes it, the *Cherokee Phoenix* "self-consciously manipulated print," alternating "between humble and defiant rhetorical postures" in an effort to demand national sovereignty, while also garnering sympathy and support.[50] To this end, even though the Cherokee seem to take a passive and submissive role in defining their nation by deferring to the language and authority of the United States, these same tactics allow the *Cherokee Phoenix* to reposition the Cherokee Nation to aggressively counter and critique U.S. removal policies. Boudinot and his fellow contributors to the *Cherokee Phoenix* were well aware that their initial efforts to define the Cherokee

Nation by publicizing their own documents and local activities had been viewed as a hostile attack on the boundaries and authority of the United States. By redefining the Cherokee Nation as a national locality composed and authorized by the United States, however, the *Cherokee Phoenix* was able to counter this perception and recast its arguments for sovereignty as consistent and complicit with existing U.S. policies. Rather than promoting radical change or introducing disruptive action, the *Cherokee Phoenix* reoriented its nationalist claims as an attempt to preserve the boundaries and principles of the United States. An editorial published on October 21, 1829, exemplifies how the language of the United States enabled the Cherokee to reposition themselves as U.S. allies. "Our treaties of relationship are based upon the principles of the federal constitution. . . . Much, therefore, depends on our unity of sentiment and firmness of action, in maintaining those sacred rights, which we have ever enjoyed."[51] As nations jointly authorized by the U.S. Constitution, the United States and the Cherokee Nation should no longer be viewed as antagonists. "United" by the same national principles and committed to the same "sacred rights," the Cherokee Nation and the United States emerged as nations whose interests were compatible and mutually supportive. In contrast, then, to the prevailing perception that the Cherokee Nation represented a defiant, self-interested, and threatening locality, the *Cherokee Phoenix* rewrote its national demands in terms that portrayed the Cherokee as an "innocent nation of people, who are in perfect peace with the United States."[52] These rhetorical tactics, in effect, allowed the *Cherokee Phoenix* to map the Cherokee locality as an independent nation without disrupting or transforming the map of the United States. In this regard, although defining the Cherokee Nation through the language of the United States may seem like a passive act of subordination, these rhetorical tactics enabled the *Cherokee Phoenix* to aggressively reposition the Cherokee Nation so that this locality no longer posed a challenge to the United States.

More than simply redefining the Cherokees' critical position, this rhetorical strategy allowed the *Cherokee Phoenix* to take an even bolder step by recasting the United States as its own opposition. By defining the Cherokee Nation as the creation of the U.S. government, the *Cherokee Phoenix* was able to characterize any attempt to challenge its boundaries and sovereignty as an attack on the authority and founding principles of the United States. Although this tactic denies the Cherokee people the authority to define their own nation, deferring to the language of the United States allows the *Cherokee Phoenix* to rewrite the United States' own efforts to claim the Cherokee lands. Rather than protecting and retaining U.S. property, the removal policies proposed by Georgia and the Jackson administration were recast as a destructive threat to the authority and integrity of the United States. "If such proceedings [e.g., the removal policies] are sanctioned by the majority of the people of the United States, the Union is but a tottering fabric, which will soon fall and crumble into atoms," asserted Elias Boudinot in an editorial published

January 8, 1831.[53] Significantly, the precarious state of the United States is not due to Cherokees' demands for sovereignty. Instead, the stability and integrity of the United States were threatened by the actions of its own citizens, who have the power to "sanction" the removal policies that run counter to their own national laws and rhetoric. "The integrity of the Union is at stake," concludes another editorial, which specifically exempts the Cherokees' claims of national sovereignty from representing any threat to the United States: "As respects the Cherokees, their duty is plain—they cannot err. . . . They are surrounded with guarantees which this Republic has voluntarily made for their protection and which once formed a sufficient security against oppression. If those guarantees must now be violated with impunity for purposes altogether selfish, the sin will not be at our door, but at the door of our *oppressor* and our faithless *Guardian*."[54] Here, the *Cherokee Phoenix* clearly identifies the United States as the dangerous and destructive party. "Surrounded" by these U.S. "guarantees," the Cherokee Nation posed no risk to the current status of the United States, and from this position, the Cherokee transform their passive submission to the language of the United States into an assertion of power. As a nation defined by the United States, the Cherokee retain a rightful and legitimate status—they "cannot err." Instead, Georgia and other U.S. proponents of removal emerge as the "oppressors" and "faithless guardians" in this situation, not only because their actions fail to protect the Cherokee Nation, but also because they "violate" the United States' own sovereign authority. By relying on the language of the United States, the Cherokee ultimately occupy a superior position because they show a greater respect for U.S. law than the citizens and government of the United States do.

This language of failed guardianship provides another example of how Cherokee writers used the rhetoric of U.S. nationalism to assert their national sovereignty. The *Cherokee Phoenix* regularly used the metaphors of "parent and child" or "guardian and ward" to describe their relationship to the United States, deliberately invoking the rhetoric that the United States used to justify their separation from Great Britain during the Revolutionary War. "The *guardian* has deprived his *wards* of their rights," wrote Boudinot in a November 12, 1831, editorial. "The sacred obligations of treaties and laws have been disregarded, [and] the promises of Washington and Jefferson have not been fulfilled."[55] By using this language, Boudinot placed the Cherokee Nation in the same position as the early United States, a position intended to prompt sympathy and respect from a U.S. audience. Such rhetoric would have been particularly influential in the late 1820s, given that the United States had recently celebrated the fiftieth anniversary of the Declaration of Independence, ushering in an extended period of commemorative celebrations that John Quincy Adams declared the "American Jubilee."[56] The jubilee prompted an enthusiastic return to the rhetoric of liberty, independence, and republican nationalism that marked the revolutionary and early national period, and by repeating this language, the Cherokee hoped to capitalize on this commemorative enthusiasm by likening their situation to that of the early American colonists. If the residents of the United States were justified in declaring national independence from their own "faithless guardian" in 1776, this rhetoric suggested that the United States should support the Cherokees' efforts to do the same.

The repetition of this language also enabled the Cherokee to present an aggressive critique of the United States. As Andrew Burstein has noted, the anniversary of U.S. independence prompted citizens to compare their current circumstances with the nation's patriotic past, encouraging them to ask, "The Jubilee has come and found us how?"[57] By characterizing the United States as an "oppressor" and "faithless guardian," the *Cherokee Phoenix* portrayed the United States as a nation that had betrayed its founding principles. Aligned with Great Britain, the United States no longer represents the values or interests on which it was established. Instead, the Cherokee Nation emerges as the superior example the United States needs to follow in order to reclaim its national heritage. In doing so, the *Cherokee Phoenix* reverses the power dynamic between these two nations, such that the United States becomes a dangerous and disruptive threat to its own authority and integrity, while the Cherokee Nation emerges as an exemplary model and ally of American nationalism. For as much, then, as the Cherokee seem to surrender their own agency and submit to the United States by defining their nation through U.S. language and documents, this rhetorical choice ends up empowering the Cherokee. By defining their nation through the language of the United States, the Cherokee are able to transform this apparent passivity into an aggressive position of control—a position that allows them to attack and discredit the United States while simultaneously recognizing and supporting U.S. authority. In this way the newspaper presents an unusual form of resistance, where the Cherokee sought to criticize and counteract the authority of the United States by expressing their admiration and allegiance to its boundaries, government, and founding principles. In short, within the pages of the *Cherokee Phoenix*, Cherokee writers presented their resistance to the U.S. government by performing and promoting their complicity with it.

REWRITING AMERICAN NATIONALISM

The Cherokees' rhetorical strategy of "resistant complicity" highlights the close relationship between national and local designations. On the one hand, the *Cherokee Phoenix* illustrates the extent to which localities are defined and determined by national authority. The significance of the Cherokee land—whether it was to be read as an independent nation or as part of the United States—depended on the way the United States viewed and defined it. Though the Cherokee could define their nation using their own local terms and activities, they were aware that these local assertions carried little weight compared to the language of the United States. By citing U.S. laws, treaties, and presidents to define the Cherokee Nation, the *Cherokee Phoenix* acknowledged this authority. The United States was ultimately responsible for establishing and expressing the sovereignty of the Cherokee locality in recognizable and acceptable terms.

On the other hand, the Cherokees' rhetorical strategies also illustrate the extent to which nations are determined by localities. The boundaries, authority, and national significance of the United States depended on the way that the Cherokee locality was defined. When the Cherokee lands were defined as a "permissive and temporary" locality, the United States could define itself as a powerful and expanding federal nation, whose constituent states held a great deal of autonomy and authority. In contrast, when the Cherokee used the language of the United States to define their locality as an independent nation, the United States emerged as a corrupt and hypocritical nation in decline. Aware that their locality could significantly influence the way people perceived the United States, Cherokee writers strategically altered their rhetorical tactics so that the stakes of their arguments involved, not just the national future of the Cherokee people, but the future of the United States as well.

The rhetorical tactics on display in the *Cherokee Phoenix* thus exemplify how localities can control and manipulate the significance of a nation, while simultaneously being bound and determined by national authority. While the power that nations exercise over localities is usually readily apparent, the *Cherokee Phoenix* illuminates the other side of this relationship by showing how localities can transform public perceptions of the nations that define them—an aspect of local literary discourse that is often overlooked. Of course, in addressing the rhetorical power and control that the *Cherokee Phoenix* exercises over the United States, it is important to remember that these efforts failed to achieve the national recognition and legitimacy that the Cherokee sought. Although their use of U.S. nationalist language and rhetoric allowed the Cherokee to present a strategically sophisticated case for their own sovereignty, the United States refused to accept these arguments, a refusal that marked the emergence of a new model for defining U.S. nationalism that was based on race rather than letters and literacy.

By continually invoking U.S. treaties, laws, presidential speeches, and the U.S. Constitution to define their nation, the Cherokee sought to portray themselves as a nation that had been created by the same terms and practices that had created the United States. Just as the United States had defined itself through its written documents, which were drafted and supported by its own literate citizens, the Cherokee believed that defining their nation through similar and, in some cases, the same national documents would be enough to earn the respect and support of the United States. The United States, however, was unwilling to accept the Cherokee Nation on these equal terms. Confronted with their own national rhetoric and practices, the only way the United States could take possession of the Cherokee locality without contradicting their own national principles and commitments was to find some other grounds of difference between the two communities. By characterizing the Cherokee "a peculiar people, a race set apart," the United States introduced a new condition for defining national space that allowed them to circumvent the assertions of equality set forth by the Cherokees' nationalist arguments.[58] Rather than representing a republic of letters, the United States in the early nineteenth century was increasingly defined as a republic of white citizens—a model of nationhood that the Cherokee could not borrow or imitate.

Critics have often commented on how the Cherokee removal debates mark the emergence of a more racialized model of nationalism in the early nineteenth century. As James Ronda has described it, the debates surrounding Cherokee removal led to a "fundamental reordering of the national landscape," such that nations became defined by "racial borders." Rather than marking a space defined by specific governing practices and political principles, nations were redefined as spaces that were "set apart" for occupation by distinct and homogeneous racial communities.[59] Although the Cherokees' rhetorical strategies failed to define a sovereign and independent Cherokee Nation, their literary history nevertheless helps identify an important shift in U.S. nationalist ideology, once again revealing how localities are deeply implicated in defining and transforming public understandings of nationhood.

NOTES

1. Daniel Justice addresses the complexities of defining and studying Cherokee literature in *Our Fire Survives the Storm*, part 1.

2. Theda Perdue provides a history of the Cherokee press and the *Cherokee Phoenix* in *Cherokee Editor*.

3. Boudinot, "To the Public," *Cherokee Phoenix*, February 21, 1828.

4. This process of "borrowing" U.S. language and rhetoric can be likened to the discursive practice of mimicry, which Homi K. Bhabha examines in relation to colonized communities, though it is important to account for key differences between the somewhat independent status of the Cherokee Nation and other colonized groups when examining this method of critique and resistance. See Bhabha, *Location of Culture*.

5. Boudinot, "To the Public."

6. Ibid.

7. For more on the controversy surrounding the Boudinot/Gold marriage, see Gaul, *To Marry an Indian*.

8. Boudinot, "To the Public."

9. Ibid.

10. Although the *Cherokee Phoenix* presented itself as a representative voice of the Cherokee Nation, it is important to emphasize that the newspaper represented the views of a small

part of the Cherokee Nation, namely, educated, upper-class residents who supported cultural assimilation. For examinations of the limited perspective of the *Cherokee Phoenix*, see Konkle, *Writing Indian Nations*; McLoughlin, *Cherokee Renascence*.

11. "Prospectus," *Cherokee Phoenix*, February 28, 1828.

12. Boudinot, "To Cherokee Correspondents," *Cherokee Phoenix*, May 6, 1828.

13. For more on the bilingual dimensions of the newspaper, see Round, *Removable Type*, 123–49.

14. McLoughlin, *Cherokee Renascence*, 400–405.

15. For more on the parallels between the language of the Cherokee and U.S. constitutions, see Angela Hudson, "'Forked Justice."

16. Restrictions on the office of the principal chief can be found in article IV, section 2. The "necessary and proper" clause appears in article III, section 16, and the Cherokee "Bill of Rights" appears in article VI.

17. Hudson, "'Forked Justice,'" 64.

18. McLoughlin, *Cherokee Renascence*, 396.

19. Boudinot, "To Correspondents," *Cherokee Phoenix*, March 20, 1828.

20. Ibid.

21. Boudinot, "Cherokee Laws," *Cherokee Phoenix*, March 13, 1828.

22. Copies of the Cherokee laws appeared as the leading article in the *Cherokee Phoenix* between March 6, 1828, and July 9, 1828.

23. These statements are taken from a report delivered to the Georgia legislature by Governor Forsyth that was published under the title "Georgia and the Cherokees," *Cherokee Phoenix*, November 26, 1828.

24. "Report of a Joint Committee in the Legislature of Georgia on the Cherokee Lands," *Cherokee Phoenix*, March 6, 1828.

25. See Duckett, *John Forsyth*; Andrew, *From Revivals to Removal*.

26. Cass, "Documents and Proceedings."

27. "Report of a Joint Committee."

28. Ibid.

29. Round, *Removable Type*, 123–49.

30. "The Cherokee Indians, Concluded," *Cherokee Phoenix*, August 12, 1829.

31. The *Cherokee Phoenix* also published articles written by non-Cherokee writers that used the same rhetorical strategies to define and defend the Cherokee Nation, most notably the work of Jeremiah Evarts. Evarts's essays were published in the *Cherokee Phoenix* between September 16, 1829, and February 17, 1830, under the heading "The Present Crisis."

32. "To the Honorable the Senate," *Cherokee Phoenix*, January 20, 1830.

33. An 1830 memorial published in the *Cherokee Phoenix* includes an appendix of additional documents written by a range of U.S. officials to further attest to the way that the United States had interpreted the status of the Cherokee lands. See "Indians Memorial of the Cherokee Legislature" (1829), *Cherokee Phoenix*, April 14, 1830.

34. Ibid.

35. Ibid.

36. "Communicated," *Cherokee Phoenix*, March 11, 1829.

37. "Washington and the Cherokees," *Cherokee Phoenix*, March 20, 1828.

38. Ibid.
39. Boudinot, "To the Public," *Cherokee Phoenix*, November 12, 1831.
40. "Washington and the Cherokees," *Cherokee Phoenix*, March 20, 1828.
41. Ibid.
42. Boudinot, "To the Public," *Cherokee Phoenix*, November 12, 1831.
43. "The Cherokee Indians," *Cherokee Phoenix*, August 12, 1829.
44. Ibid.
45. Ibid.
46. "Indian Emigration," *Cherokee Phoenix*, May 21, 1828.
47. "Indians Memorial," *Cherokee Phoenix*, June 17, 1829.
48. Boudinot, "To the Public," *Cherokee Phoenix*, February 21, 1828.
49. Ibid. McLoughlin discusses how the *Cherokee Phoenix* was presented as the authentic "voice" of the Cherokee Nation. See *Cherokee Renascence*, 403–6.
50. Round, *Removable Type*, 140. For further examination of the paradoxical dimensions of Cherokee writings, see Denson, *Demanding the Cherokee Nation*; Gaul, "Editing as Indian Performance"; Konkle, *Writing Indian Nations*; Sweet, *American Georgics*.
51. "General Council Message," *Cherokee Phoenix*, October 21, 1829.
52. "Indians Memorial," *Cherokee Phoenix*, June 17, 1829.
53. Boudinot, "From the Editor," *Cherokee Phoenix*, January 8, 1831.
54. Boudinot, "To the Public," *Cherokee Phoenix*, November 12, 1831.
55. Ibid.
56. Adams first referred to "America's Jubilee" in his inaugural address in March 1825. See also Burstein, *America's Jubilee*.
57. Ibid., 242. See also 228–54 for the critical undercurrents of jubilee rhetoric.
58. *The Speech of Mr. Forsyth of Georgia, on the Bill Providing for the Removal of the Indians*, 7.
59. Ronda, "'We Have a Country,'" 742–43. For other discussions of the emergence of a racialized model of nationhood during Cherokee removal, see Hudson, "'Forked Justice'"; Konkle, *Writing Indian Nations*; McLoughlin, *Cherokee Renascence*; Perdue, *Cherokee Editor*.

CHAPTER ELEVEN

African American Literature of the Gold Rush
Janet Neary and Hollis Robbins

IN 1902, SAN FRANCISCO news digest *The Pandex of the Press* published the first installment of Mary Ellen Pleasant's "Memoirs and Autobiography."[1] One of the most successful African American entrepreneurs of the nineteenth century, Pleasant dictated her story to famed newspaperman Sam Davis, also known as "Nevada" Sam, giving an account of her life in the East in Philadelphia and New Bedford before arriving in San Francisco at the height of the Gold Rush.[2] Her elegant opening sentences distance her narrative from other African American autobiographies of the period and suggest the importance of place within African American memoir. "I was born on the nineteenth day of August, 1814. Some people have reported that I was born in slavery, but as a matter of fact I was born in Philadelphia, at number 9 Barley St."[3] Pleasant's formulation exploits the complicated relationship between geography and African American identity in the antebellum context: the parallelism of "slavery" and "Philadelphia" operates as both a straightforward refusal of slavery—Pleasant claims birth in a free state to free parents—and a knowing commentary on U.S. slavery itself, which turns on the grammatical interchangeability of slavery and Philadelphia.[4] The opening reads as a corrective: not only was Pleasant not a slave, but also she casts the idea of being born "in slavery" as absurd.

Regional identity has been a primary mode of self-expression within African American memoir in the form of the slave narrative, partly because slavery often denied identity based on parentage and family structure. Consider the region mapped in the first line of Frederick Douglass's 1845 narrative: "I was born in Tuckahoe, near Hillsborough, and about twelve miles from Easton, in Talbot county, Maryland."[5] Lindon Barrett argues that "geography, a local physical space, even more than the year of birth, becomes . . . the most ineradicable marker of self and identity."[6] Pleasant's playful engagement with this convention of slave narration, using an *exact* articulation of place ("number 9 Barley St."), works to distinguish her memoir from the slave narrative genre, even while she acknowledges it as a point of departure. Her gestures toward and engagement with the conventions of slave narratives speak specifically to her recognition of her public image, which was bound up with the tropes and stereotypes of slaves and enslavement—she was most often referred to in the papers as "Mammy Pleasant," a name she hated—as much as it was bound up with the scene of the southern plantation.[7] Writing from San Francisco, which Eric Gardner calls an "unexpected place," Pleasant invokes geography to unsettle narrative expectations and offer her own countermapping, responding to readers' assumptions that a black woman's narrative is always in some ways a slave narrative, involving the move from property to freedom.[8] Yet Pleasant's opening also confirms that slavery *was* a place, a place she could and did want to distance herself from. In fact, as the most complete historical accounting of Pleasant attests, "Her insistence that on August 19th, 1814, she was born to free parents, like much of her past, remains a source of controversy."[9]

Her first biographer, Helen Holdredge, writing in 1953, contended that she was born a slave of a white father, on a plantation near Augusta, Georgia, in 1815.[10] After extensive research, historian Lynn Hudson leaves the question unresolved, noting that Pleasant's opening may have been a deliberate act of self-construction designed to distance herself from the assumptions that went with a slave past.[11] What has been determined is that Pleasant's move west sometime in 1850 was part of a broader migration of African Americans who wished to escape the increased surveillance in the East entailed by the Fugitive Slave Act and to pursue greater opportunities for wealth and property ownership in the West.

Among the immigrants to California were James Williams, author of the 1873 narrative *The Life and Adventures of James Williams*, republished in 2002 under the title *Fugitive Slave in the Gold Rush*, and William H. Newby, political activist and San Francisco correspondent for *Frederick Douglass' Paper*, who wrote under the penname "Nubia" throughout the early 1850s. The writings of Williams and Newby elaborate the complicated and often vexed relationship African Americans had to westward expansion, which has been overlooked in dominant historical accounts of the Gold Rush opportunity myth.[12]

Although California was admitted to the Union in 1850, the new state was characterized by its lax enforcement of federal laws—including the fugitive slave law—and gaps in the enforcement of property rights resulting from the sudden transition from Mexican to U.S. governance. In January 1848, when gold was discovered in Sutter's Mill, near what was to be Sacramento, the United States was still formally at war with Mexico. The Treaty of Guadalupe Hidalgo on February 2, 1848, ended the war, and California became a U.S. holding. Land claims granted under Mexican rule were contested. President Zachary Taylor, a Whig from the slaveholding South, was elected in November 1848 and urged California to apply for statehood. Political events moved rapidly. The constitutional convention opened in September 1849, and a state constitution prohibiting slavery was approved in October. On November 13, 1849, the new constitution was adopted, and, almost a year later, California was admitted to the Union on September 9 as part of the Compromise of 1850.

Gold Rush California—a new space and a new place—thus represented new possibilities for black citizens, as well as an important testing ground for African American rights. Although Pleasant's narrative remains unfinished—we never learn her reasons for moving to California or her experiences there—her move west in conjunction with her emphasis on place in the opening of her narrative call for us to rethink the relationship between African American literature and geography. The narrative arc of travelers to California—the factual, first-person accounts of the perilous journeys, close calls, self-assertive staking of claims, of seeking economic opportunity—shares certain stylistic elements with the slave narrative genre; moreover, blacks writing from California often explicitly referenced slave narratives either to attract readers or distinguish the narratives (as Pleasant does) from the genre. Pleasant's self-conscious use of place to frustrate stereotypical readings of her life operates as a model for how we might rethink the role of geography within African American literature more broadly and how we might theorize regionalism in African American studies.

By looking at accounts of the West in the black press in the East, letters from black immigrants to California, and narratives produced in the West and centered on African American experiences of the Gold Rush, this essay contributes to a reassessment of the American West in the landscape of nineteenth-century African American studies, particularly by moving away from the primarily southern notion of African Americans as property toward the more active role of African Americans seeking property rights in the West. In focusing on Williams's and Newby's California writings, this essay adds to the scholarship reorienting antebellum African American literary study westward, but perhaps more importantly, it contributes toward the more complex understanding of locality engaged by many of the essays in *Mapping Region in Early American Writing*, shifting African American studies away from an unacknowledged regionalism, in which a relatively small number of primary texts produced in urban centers in the Northeast have dominated the critical conversation and become emblematic of black experience.[13] Though Williams's narrative opens with his birth into slavery in Maryland and subsequent escape north, *Life and Adventures*, published by San Francisco Women's Union Print in 1873, takes as its primary subject Williams's immigration to and experiences in the West between 1851 and 1873. Newby (writing as Nubia) was largely silent on his life before he arrived in San Francisco, eschewing the narrative of immigration or escape to create himself as the voice of black California on the political, cultural, social, and racial questions of the day. Both men's writings reflect the way that regionalism provides both limits on and possibilities for reframing the received view of the African American experience in the mid-nineteenth century.

Building on archival work by historian Quintard Taylor and literary scholars Eric Gardner, Edie Wong, and Stephen Knadler, we contend that African American literature of the Gold Rush is a critical site for mapping and reevaluating the interplay between social and aesthetic formations within nineteenth-century African American literature more generally.[14] In investigating the persistent mythical status of Gold Rush California as a site of racial and class equality, individual opportunity, and legal protection, we suggest that recent scholarship of the era needs to heed the writings of African Americans of the period that opposed these myths from the beginning.[15] The uneven applications of law and justice after statehood recorded in Williams's narrative and Nubia's letters in *Frederick Douglass' Paper* provide a starting counternarrative to the myth of spontaneous or "natural" brotherhood that prevailed in white journalists' and prospectors' writings about the Gold Rush. In sum, this paper seeks to insert the West and its attendant mythologies more deeply into African American studies (both as a regional and aesthetic concern), as well as to reassert the importance of African American writings into the reconsideration of regional myths.

"THE WEST WAS ANOTHER NAME FOR OPPORTUNITY": EARLY REPORTS FROM THE GOLD RUSH AND THE MYTH OF EGALITARIANISM

Alongside fortune hunters from around the globe, newspaper reporters from across the country raced to California after gold was discovered in Sutter's Mill in January 1848. Writers found a region wide open for depiction, description, and designation. While San Francisco and a few other Bay Area towns were settled and named, the vast expanse of territory east of the Bay near what is now Sacramento was unsurveyed, unnamed, and unclaimed. Unlike Mary Ellen Pleasant's Philadelphia, San Francisco in 1848 had no settled street names and numbers and wouldn't for another decade.[16] Contemporary writers described a landscape of people, emphasizing the demographic as well as the geographic characteristics of the region. Standard reports of life in the camps and in the mines listed the various "types" who thronged to the region to look for gold: New Englanders, southerners, Germans, Chinese, Mexicans, fugitive slaves and free blacks, Native Americans, Hawaiians (or Kanakas), Russians, and motley others.[17]

Bayard Taylor's *El Dorado* (1850), a collection of his *New York Tribune* pieces from 1848 and 1849, emphasized the "marvelous" diversity of men in the camps: "Nothing less than a marvel like that of California could have brought into juxtaposition so many opposite types of human nature. We had an officer of the Navy, blunt, warm-hearted and jovial, a captain in the merchant service, intelligent and sturdily-tempered, Down-Easters, with sharp-set faces—men of the genuine stamp, who would be sure to fall on their feet wherever they might be thrown; quiet and sedate Spaniards, hilarious Germans, and some others whose precise character was more difficult to determine." Taylor itemizes the "ignorant adventurers" from countries "nearest the golden coast—Mexico, Peru, Chili, China, and the Sandwich Islands."[18] He maps a place peopled by immigrants from other places: a gathering place, a landscape of faces. Although his description relies on hierarchical categories of race and nation, Taylor celebrates the dream of striking it rich as a great equalizer. Leonard Kip's lesser-known *California Sketches with Recollections of the Gold Mines* (1850) echoes Taylor's account:

> Launches were constantly arriving from the various ships; well filled teams were every moment dropping their freight beside the several stores; a continual stream of active population was winding among the casks and barrels which blocked up the place where the sidewalks ought to have been; and in front, an auctioneer was knocking down goods to a crowd, which every nation helped to compose; principally Americans, but liberally sprinkled with Chinese, Chilians, Negroes, Indians, and Kanakas; while the comical conjunction of red shirts, gold epaulettes, Spanish ponchoes, long queues and coonskin caps gave it an almost carnival aspect.[19]

Kip understands California's distinguishing characteristics to be the "carnivalesque" mixing of people from different locales and backgrounds; the variety of national costumes on display is emblematic of the new social freedoms enabled by this mixing. "Negroes" and "Indians," excluded from the designation "Americans," are part of the "active population" come to California for wealth. The tone of these early narratives, which begin with a description of the international throng and move quickly to accounts of life in the gold camps, is representative of Gold Rush coverage in the white press: a broad-strokes anthropological gaze listing the variety of "types" brought together by the equalizing force of the Gold Rush.

Rudolph Lapp's indispensable *Blacks in Gold Rush California* notes that early coverage of the discovery of gold in California in the black and abolitionist press was largely identical to coverage in the white press and often took the form of simply reprinting articles from other papers.[20] The October 5, 1848, *North Star*, for example, republished an account of "Gold Mania" from the *New York Journal of Commerce*, noting the variety of individuals at work panning for gold by "washing sand" in northern California rivers: "Two thousand whites and as many Indians are now engaged in washing the sand. All labor of every other kind has stopped except a little farming. Mechanics, doctors, lawyers, merchants, sailors and soldiers, have all gone in mass to the gold region. . . . Steady working men average $10 per day, though many times a hundred dollars has been collected in a day by one man."[21] Reports such as these emphasize the metallic fertility of the land itself. The political stakes of the region's soil had been made explicit in the name of the

Free-Soil Party, established in upstate New York in the summer of 1848 to oppose the expansion of slavery in the western territories. Gold Rush writers promoted the idea of California soil as not only filled with gold but also free.

African American gold seekers responded to these reports in numbers. They traveled west primarily via shipping routes from the Eastern Seaboard, around South America and up the West Coast to California, or via the Chargres River across the Isthmus of Panama; more rarely, they made the trip overland.[22] In some cases, these pioneers wrote home about their success, adding firsthand testimony to early accounts reprinted from white papers. In an 1851 letter to his wife, for example, Peter Brown paints a picture of independence, financial success, and an absence of racial discrimination in the gold fields of California: "I am now mining about 25 miles from Sacramento City and doing well.... I have been working for myself for the past two months ... and have cleared three hundred dollars. California is the best place in the world to make money. It is also the best place for black folks on the globe. All a man has to do, is work, and he will make money."[23] On January 4, 1849, the Free-Soil newspaper *National Era* (soon to begin serializing Harriet Beecher Stowe's *Uncle Tom's Cabin*), citing letters from recent immigrants, lauded the hold that the French motto *Liberté, égalité, fraternité* had taken in the region: "Liberty, equality, fraternity has been beautifully exemplified in the recent discoveries of the gold mines in California."[24] According to the accounts of letter writers, all the inhabitants forsook their callings and went to dig gold, each for his own benefit. Lawyers and doctors and merchants stood side by side with sailors and soldiers and laborers, up to their knees in water; and each had himself the fruits of his own labor—even the Indians were allowed to have the gold they collected. Again, the land itself, rich with gold, seemed to be productive of human accord in these reports. California was a region of wholesome abundance. Even Frederick Douglass, writing in the *North Star*, observed that "the wealth of California is, as it should be, shared by colored as well as white men."[25]

However, despite the early promise of a free-soil California, optimistic early reports soon gave way to a more skeptical and finally cautionary rhetoric that reveals the egalitarianism of the early Gold Rush was riven with racial tensions that were reflected in the uneven distribution of justice and law in the region. The *North Star* and *Frederick Douglass' Paper* (and occasionally the *National Era*) expressed increasing skepticism about the opportunities for black prospectors in the western territories, warning former slaves and free blacks not to be fooled by myths of unity and innate fellow-feeling in the camps. On March 29, 1849, for example, the *National Era* warned, "We are desirous of seeing the Territories peopled by citizens from all sections of our country, as the product of such a fusion of various elements is apt to be a good one. But we cannot hear without indignation of the removal of slaves to that Territory.... The Yankees who have gone to California care for nothing but gold; and when they see how easy it is to get along with gold-digging by having slaves to do all the menial work, they will soon grow acquiescent, and become slaveholders themselves."[26] As a matter of fact, on the ground, anxieties about slavery's threat to free labor began to eclipse larger political considerations of how California fit into the nation's balance of power. The feeling in the mining camps was that slavery gave slaveholders an unfair advantage that violated the independent, entrepreneurial spirit of the mines. Slavery was a threat, therefore, not only to nonslaveholding laborers but also to the vision of an idyllic international throng working in easy accord. Locals' concern about the extension of slavery into California actually made them distrustful of slaveholders *and* black immigrants. Historian Leonard Pitts writes about the complex relationship between xenophobia and antiblack feeling at the mines, "The treatment of immigrant Spanish Americans in the mines hinged also on the slavery question. They came into California precisely when the Yankees felt most irritated on this score and could see most clearly the parallels between Negroes and their masters, on the one hand, and peons and patrons, on the other. Yankee prospectors ejected from the mines with equal vigor any combination of bondsmen and masters.... The prospectors put into effect a local code prohibiting the mining operations of all master-servant teams, whatever their relationship."[27] Furthermore, California's treatment of slavery was not the only political consideration for black immigrants. Although California was admitted to the Union as a free state, a vocal and politicized section of the population was as opposed to admitting black people into the state as it was to slavery, an opinion expressed in this March 15 article in *The Californian*: "Not a single instance of precedence exists in the shape of physical bondage of our fellow men.... We desire only a white population in California; even the Indians among us, as far as we have seen, are more of a nuisance than a benefit to the country; we would like to get rid of them.... In conclusion we dearly love the Union, but declare our positive preference for an independent condition of California to the establishment of any degree of slavery, or even the importation of free blacks."[28] As this editorial shows, the myth of egalitarian culture in the mines was undercut by antiblack discourse that emerged in the debates over California's statehood, as well as by racial tensions occasioned by labor competition at the mines. Moreover, the expanded economic opportunities and increased social freedom that characterized the Gold Rush actually diminished as California instituted a variety of mercantilist legislation that aimed to consolidate capital for the United States but also consolidated an ideal national subject that excluded both foreigners and African Americans, whose citizenship—as our reading of Williams's narrative will show—was tenuous and often contested in the courts.[29]

For black readers of *Frederick Douglass' Paper*, by 1851, skepticism of tolerance, let alone egalitarianism, was more common. "The colored people in this State are made the beasts of burden, by which 'political demagogues' ride into power," Nubia warned repeatedly.[30] For all Americans looking for investment, California was a risky proposition, writes Nubia, noting that "universal distrust has operated seriously against the prosperity of the State. No one can invest money in real estate, as the title to almost every foot of ground is disputed, and the banks have ceased to be safe depositories."[31] California promised little but villainy, Nubia argued, especially for the nonwhite population. Even so, the national narrative of equality and opportunity prevailed.

NARRATIVES OF CITIZENSHIP, LAW, AND OWNERSHIP: TWO AFRICAN AMERICAN ACCOUNTS

As the early accounts show, the Gold Rush had a dramatic effect on California demographics: before 1849, some 300,000 Native Americans were estimated as living in California. Between 1848 and 1854, nearly 300,000 people emigrated to California from the eastern states, as well as from China, Mexico, Hawaii, Chile, and Europe. By the end of 1850, 3,000 Chinese (mostly Cantonese) had arrived in San Francisco; by the end of 1852, some 30,000 more had arrived. By 1852, there were about 2,000 black men and women living in California. By 1870, there were fewer than 30,000 Native Americans left in California.

In response to the arrival of large numbers of foreign, nonwhite miners, on April 13, 1850, California's legislature passed the Foreign Miners Tax of 1850, applied to Chinese and Mexican miners, which levied a monthly $20 fee/license for the right to mine. The tax was repealed on March 14, 1851, as being too onerous, but it was reinstated in 1852 at a rate of $4 per month. The Indenture Act of 1850 allowed whites to declare Indians vagrants and auction off their labor for four months. All mining operated in a legal gray area. Property obtained from the Mexican government was not legally valid until the passage of land laws in 1851. Local custom dictated claims valid if the miner worked a claim measuring 150 square feet; as long as there were ongoing signs of active digging, the claim was his without dispute. Claims were often designated by the first person or group of people to work them. For example, the first places James Williams encounters when he arrives in Sacramento in search of mines are Negro Hills and Kelsey's Diggings. Negro Hills was a mining camp on the lower American River located near Mormon Island. It developed into a bustling town founded by an African American from Massachusetts named Kelsey.[32] These sorts of local agreements were widely hailed as representing the capacity of rustic frontiersmen to achieve productive self-government in a lawless society. Recent scholarship into the culture of the early gold fields (before 1850) has argued that indeed there existed an articulated culture of "fairness," equality, and self-government in the camps, particularly when the camps were composed primarily of a homogeneous group of literate, East Coast Americans of European descent. Richard Zerbe and C. Leigh Anderson recently claimed that "the prediction that the mines would be the scene of chaotic violence was wrong. Rather than anarchy or violent gang rule, what quickly emerged in the California goldfields were social institutions and rules for gold mining that relied upon a system of norms without unusual violence. Each mining district drew up an explicit contract, usually in writing. As one observer wrote in 1848, 'it is curious how soon a set of crude regulations sprung into existence, which everybody seemed to abide by.'"[33]

Zerbe and Anderson's article is an attempt to explain the widespread existence of law-abiding "civil society" based on "norms of fairness" that "helped to facilitate collective action and produce order among the California gold miners."[34] The relative absence of violence in these societies, they claim, was a function of a shared culture and similar principles among the miners. However, the evidence that Zerbe and Anderson provide are accounts from newspapers and diaries written by educated white men.[35] Several dozen pages into their study, Zerbe and Anderson acknowledge that "violence and the failure of cooperation in the gold fields were primarily among racial or ethnic groups, such as between Whites and Hispanics, Whites and Chinese. . . . The American miners especially harassed the Chilean, Mexican, Chinese, Native American, and French miners," but this fact does not seem to influence the authors' conclusion that "a period of 'almost Arcadian honesty' lasted well into 1849."[36]

By contrast, although James Williams describes the functionality of the system of ad hoc self-governance that characterized life in the mines, noting, "We had no law in the country at that time and we miners constituted a law for ourselves," his narrative captures a much more delicate balance between risk and reward for a fugitive slave in the Gold Rush. Williams experiences a greater degree of freedom in the West, arguing that "a man who has made his escape from the blood-hounds . . . could be free and safe from all danger of being apprehended" in California, but the status of black citizens is still uncertain.[37] Yet, as the readings below will show, Williams's account of an ad hoc miners' trial, his role in a number of freedom suits, and the vigilante justice to which he is subjected as a black man in California all challenge the predominant myth of the communal egalitarianism of the Gold Rush. Reflecting on his early years in California, after his arrival in May 1851, Williams writes that "Any man that made up his mind to go to the mines at that time, he must be a man that feared no noise, or else he had better stay at home, for the miners feared no noise at that time, it being a newly-settled country, with wild beasts but also wild people" (23). Nevertheless, ironically, it is the "wildness" of the region that enables the increased freedom Williams experiences. Although the narrative was published after the passage of all three Reconstruction amendments, *Life and Adventures* captures a moment of economic and democratic potential in the West before all these formal structures were in place.[38] As Williams's narrative shows, the promise of national legal enfranchisement encapsulated by Reconstruction was often less inclusive in practice than Williams's experience of the "wild" antebellum West.

Writing in real time rather than in hindsight, William H. Newby, writing as Nubia in *Frederick Douglass' Paper*, shared Williams's concern with the status of black citizenship in the newly organized state and offered his own account of his relationship of the treatment of foreign nonwhite miners to the status of black Americans in the region. Relatively little is known about Newby's life before California. He was most likely born in 1828 of a slave father and free mother in Virginia, then moved to Philadelphia with his mother after his father died. He was presumably self-educated and became widely read.[39] Newby traveled to San Francisco in 1851 and almost immediately emerges as a political figure, signing his name to petitions protesting an 1850 law denying the rights of "Negroes, mulattoes, and Indians" to testify in court.[40] Newby was a vocal and active member of the black community, becoming a Mason and, in 1853, helping establish the San Francisco Athenaeum, a literary and debating society. After 1854, his regular column for *Frederick Douglass' Paper* (signed "Nubia") became required reading for eastern blacks who continued to debate emigration to the western territories. His letters, rarely about his own experience, engage the issue of being a new immigrant to a region almost wholly populated by immigrants. At a time and place where nearly everyone was identified by a geographic marker (a Swede, a rangy Kentuckian, a southerner), Nubia, in his first published letter, speaks emphatically in first-person plural as a representative of San Francisco:

> Your not being in the receipt of any regular correspondence from California, and knowing your great interest in all that concerns the welfare of "our people," has induced me to pen this epistle. You can form no idea of the progress made by the colored people in this city within the short space of two years. We have three churches, one Baptist and two Methodist. . . . We have one Literary Association the "San Francisco Athenaeum." . . . We are steadily progressing in all that pertains to our welfare. . . . We have a large number of respectable ladies here, and their influence is felt and acknowledged. San Francisco presents many features that no city in the Union presents. Its population is composed of almost every nation under heaven.[41]

Nubia sees himself as "of San Francisco," "a Californian" tied to "our people" and to the greater project of ending slavery. "The First of August [Emancipation Day] was celebrated here very spiritedly," he writes, marked by speeches by prominent antislavery activists from England and the eastern United States. In San Francisco a person of color could make a home and a living within a supportive community. But the status of nonwhites in California was legally precarious, Nubia insisted, particularly regarding the laws limiting testimony by nonwhites in legal cases, but in regard to land ownership, too. "The native Californians of Spanish extraction are rapidly being dispossessed of their immense property by the shrewd Americans. This has been effected by purchase, by marriage, and by the looseness of the law," he wrote in February 1855.[42] Nubia also offered jarring accounts of the plight of

Chinese laborers in mid-1850s San Francisco, as these new immigrants to foreign soil faced increasing legal and institutional discrimination:[43] "The Legislature is in session. Mr. Flint (one of the members) asked leave to introduce a bill to prevent Chinese and *all others* not eligible to citizenship, from holding mining claims," Nubia reported in 1855. "If this bill should pass, it will strike a terrible blow at the colored miners, some of whom are in possession of the best claims in the State."[44] Nubia's letters make plain that the carnivalesque image of social freedom was a myth.

To contextualize the uniqueness of Nubia's intervention, two years before Nubia arrived in San Francisco, newspapers in New York and New England articulated concern but not alarm about the possible extension of slavery to California; three months later, in the June 27, 1849, issue of the *New York Tribune*, the West Coast correspondent wrote that in California one could see "the Southern slaveholder beside the swarthy African, now his equal."[45] Lapp himself calls the exodus to California following the "American Dream" and notes that many of the blacks who traveled to California were seeking gold to purchase freedom for their families.[46] A letter from California published in the August 22, 1849, *New Bedford Mercury*, read by many blacks (perhaps even by Mary Ellen Pleasant or her family)—in what Jennifer Schell describes as "cosmopolitan" New Bedford—proclaims, "There are no gentlemen here. Labor rules Capital. A darkey is just as good as a polished gentleman and can make more money."[47] The article is designed to promote emigration to California and, in so doing, champions an idea of the region that seems to have taken hold in the early American and African American imagination.

The *North Star*'s coverage of the Gold Rush through most of 1849 was ambivalent, as Douglass lamented the probable dangers to black emigrants to California, while acknowledging that "it was unreasonable to expect that black Americans would reject any possible economic springboard in order to measure up to the standards of the more financially secure, idealist white abolitionists."[48] Even the great abolitionist John Greenleaf Whittier, reviewing Bayard Taylor's *El Dorado* in the *National Era* on July 4, 1850, promulgated the standard narrative that the existence of gold to be had easily in California would be good for blacks and white alike:

> Much of what [Taylor] describes has already become familiar to us from the notes of a thousand gold-seekers, who have sent home such records as they could of their experiences in a strange land: "It will appear natural," says our author, "that should be the most democratic country in the world. The practical equality of all the members of the community, whatever might be the wealth, intelligence, or profession of each, was never before so thoroughly demonstrated. . . . A man who would consider his fellow beneath him, on account of his appearance or occupation, would have had some difficulty in living peaceably in California."[49]

By contrast, Nubia's letters made clear that mines were not seized equally; only certain individuals were exalted. While coverage of the Gold Rush, the California constitutional debates, and Chinese labor issues in the *New York Daily Times*, Littell's *Living Age*, *Harper's Monthly*, and a selection of other widely read publications in the 1850s continued to disseminate a Gold Rush opportunity myth, Nubia and other writers for *Frederick Douglass' Paper* saw Chinese labor disputes as well as broader concerns about the legal standing of nonwhites in California courts as directly undermining the egalitarian Gold Rush myth still operating in the American cultural consciousness.[50]

Nubia maps his identity as a Californian, speaking also for the native inhabitants of the region as he surveyed the transformations wrought by immigrations:

> Everything is changing in California. The whole face of the country is changed. Everywhere is to be seen the fruit of Yankee industry and enterprise. In five years from a desolate wilderness, where roamed the grizzly bear, and the uncouth digger, Indian cities, towns, villages, well stocked and beautifully laid out farms, have sprung up as if by magic. The poor natives can hardly realize the change, so recently the lordly possessors of thousands of acres, and so suddenly wrested from their grasp, and this so quietly, so legally, so easily effected. . . . Truly, these Americans are a strange people; they as effectually destroy nations by their crushing civilization, as their fixed bayonets.[51]

"These Americans" included, without irony, Newby's own community. "The colored people of this city and, I believe, throughout the State are not surpassed anywhere for energy and enterprise. Quite a number are engaged in mercantile pursuits."[52] There is some equality, he suggests, in enterprise and initiative.

Like Newby, James Williams, though he experiences some success in the mines and is treated with more respect than he often was in the East, offers in his narrative a litany of the legal and extralegal challenges he faces in the West, which demonstrates the precariousness of his citizenship. The overwhelming concern of Williams's narrative is the distinction between law and justice, complicated by the distinction between law and local custom, exacerbated by the unsettled nature of Gold Rush California. The initial absence of institutional law, on the one hand, enabled economic and civic opportunities for blacks in California, yet, on the other hand, left them vulnerable to the often racist caprices of local custom.

Informed by his experience as a former slave, Williams's insistence on the law is intimately tied to his theory of economic justice—that a man is paid for the work he does, that each man party to a contract acts in good faith, and that, in the event of a breach of contract, the law will enforce economic redress. As the informal trial that takes place at one of the mines to address a theft between two miners shows, Williams's initial experience of "justice" reflects his new social standing as an equal—a miner among miners—even while it suggests the dangers that exist for an independent black man in the West.

> I was one of the miners that was present on an occasion to try another miner for the crime of stealing $50 from another. We put a rope around his neck and intended to frighten him, and he said if we let him down he would tell. So we let him down and he went and got the money. Had he not got the money, what the result would have been I am unable to tell the reader. One thing I am about to affirm, I would never have consented to have let them take the man's life. I was the only colored man in the crowd, and it was left for me to pass my opinion, and I said, "If he gives up the money, let him go," for I felt greatly opposed to taking the man's life; yet in a body of men there are always different opinions, and I do not think the poor fellow would have had lenity shown to him, it being thought a very dastardly trick for one miner to steal from another. (23)

Here, the absence of formal law allows for equality among the miners, who enforce a form of ad hoc justice. As the first event Williams describes in the West, the scene establishes the new social recognition available to him. Despite being "the only colored man in the crowd," Williams's opinion is valued as an economic peer, and, as such, his opinion holds as much weight as that of the other miners. Yet the actual implications of the scene are difficult to ignore. Williams is subject to this type of ad hoc justice as a black man in a way that the other miners are not. After relating the facts of the case, he takes the opportunity to reflect on their significance and his feelings about them. It is at the moment the threat of capital punishment is raised that he invokes his race: "I would never have consented to have taken the man's life. I was the only colored man in the crowd." As a former slave writing in 1873, Williams perceives the stakes of the potential lynching differently than the other miners.[53] The solidarity of the miners is interrupted in that moment by the violent potential of a near lynching and the implications such rogue justice carries for a black man.

Williams maps his sense of justice, linked to economic protection, onto the unfamiliar landscape. Ironically, the equality granted to Williams as a miner in this scene erodes as institutional forms of law and justice become formalized in the region. Reflecting on the change from these early days, in which the miners in California had to be "a law to themselves," Williams argues that an increase in institutional law will improve the condition for blacks, noting that "the state of things is much better now in California than was the case on my arrival there. Many adventures have been made by persons from the States, colored and white. There are now instances on record where both classes have gathered considerable of this world's goods" (23). However, Williams contradicts his own assertion that an increase in law protects black economic gains later in the narrative, declaring, "I have seen more law in California than any other part of the world which I have traveled in, but, according to my belief, *little justice*" (51). California occupies a liminal space within the national structure, such that law has expanded to protect economic "adventures" or speculation; yet the very unpredictability that makes it possible for "colored" people to participate in this accumulation of wealth makes all speculators and adventurers vulnerable to exploitation and crime.

In Williams's narrative, the law either works to disenfranchise blacks or fails to guarantee the protections it sets forth; in each case, the rights of white property owners are ultimately prioritized over the rights of black citizens. For example, after fighting for—and winning—the right for black men to work on the levee in Sacramento in 1855, Williams reports that he took a job working for a mine owner who uses the racism of the region to cheat Williams out of his pay: "I . . . went to work in the Southern mines for a man, at $100 per month, and, after working for him some six months, he either raised a false report or caused one to be raised, in order to get a certain class of men to pursue me, to make me leave the place, to elude paying me my money, and he accomplished his design. Meeting him sometime after, and asking him for my money, he told me that were he me, he would not want any money—that I should be glad I got off with my life, much less receiving any money" (27). Williams seems to suggest here that the mine owner does not himself have a problem with black laborers but is an opportunist who exploits the racism of "a certain class of men" to default on his contract with Williams. Again, the specter of racial lynching haunts the scene of economic injustice.

As institutional law begins to formalize and replace the ad hoc forms of justice practiced in the mining camps, Williams—and other blacks in California—fare only marginally better. Williams includes the story of Susan Neal in his narrative to illustrate that the shift from being treated as property to being considered a property owner is perhaps not as stark as one might imagine. Neal is a slave who "came from Alabama to California with her owners, and gained her freedom by coming to California." After gaining her freedom, Susan marries Charles Neal, who dies and leaves her in debt. Williams relates that immediately,

> there was a suit brought against her for his debts. . . . Sometime after paying that debt, a certain lawyer and a judge said that if she could pay one debt, she could pay them for fees due them. So they commenced suits against her for their fees. The day the trial was to come off, I met her in the street, crying. I said to her, "What is the matter, Aunt Susan?" She answered, "What has always been the matter with me?—the same thing that has always been the matter with me is the matter with me now. The people down South have got all my labor, and I have come to California, and got free, and made a little money, and now the white folks are trying to rob me of that." (55)

Despite obtaining her freedom in California, Neal understands her experience there to be a continuation of the exploitation she has received at the hands of whites, but, notably, their exploitation in California comes in the form of the legal system itself.

Williams includes this incident because it is also an example of an instance in which he, too, is defrauded by schemers who use legal channels and official contracts to carry out their economic fraud. After meeting Neal, crying in the street, Williams steps in to help her, making a deal that he will pay her debts in exchange for taking ownership of her property on her death. However, while Williams is out of town, opportunists, whom he describes as his "enemies" and people "that had never done anything for [Neal]," step in and convince the elderly, now infirm, woman to change her will and leave the property to them. When he discovers this, Williams decides that "they all wanted the property more than I did" and so writes, "I offered to compromise with them by their paying me the moneys that I had paid out, with interest. They did so, and set a trap to rob me out of half the money, and succeeded in it" (56). The schemers enter into a bad-faith contract with Williams, demonstrating that, although he is recognized as an independent actor, it is a hollow recognition that does not stave off the economic abuse to which he has been subject all his life.

Even when the law purports to protect the rights of black citizens, it is often overturned by acts of vigilante justice. Another instance of Williams aiding a slave brought to California ends with a favorable court decision overturned by a violent mob. Further, the incident, worth reproducing in full here, shows that social tensions in the West at this time are not reducible to black/white race relations; the black solidarity on which Williams depended during his work on the Underground Railroad in the East was less predictable in the West, despite the extension of North-South conflicts into California:

> Be it known that about that time there was a number of slaves brought into California by their masters, one of which was a woman, brought there by her master, who would not allow one man or men to go to his house. But I went there, taking a white man with me at the time, and took her away. In a few days her master comes to my establishment, bringing with him an officer, who presented a pistol at me, saying at the same time "Williams, you must go and get that woman you stole from Mr. Wholeman or I will blow your brains out." "Very good, sir," says I, "come on," leading the way. Taking him direct into lawyer Zabriskie's office I alleged my complaint against him for pointing a six-shooter at me, and he was held for trial, which was given in my favor. Of course I retained her, and in one week after this woman left and went back to her master, telling him that I threatened to shoot him. His party getting after me caused me to leave there, and on the boat plying between Sacramento and San Francisco I was attacked by a party of Missourians and beaten very badly, and had to be rescued by the captain, after having run into the ladies' saloon. (24)

Though Williams is threatened at gunpoint by an officer of the law, his first recourse is legal, "taking him direct into lawyer Zabriskie's office," where he prevails.[54] But his initial triumph over the master is undercut by both the former slave's betrayal and the vigilante attacks by southern sympathizers that drive him from the region. As he makes his escape, he is attacked again by proslavery Missourians on the ship. Despite the development in laws to protect black citizens, California was an unpredictable locale in which neither the court's decision nor the social terrain of the East could be depended on.

Williams's experience of racial slavery fundamentally informs his understanding of the social checks on the economic and civic possibilities of California as new laws are passed to protect speculators:

> Some are now enjoying the benefits of their labor, whilst others, who worked hard in the mines and have gathered a large portion of this world's goods and have had no advantage, neither will they ever reap any advantage hereafter from their privations, although they have borne the burden in the heat of the day—collected the spoils; but, ah, they have sown sparingly—they have sowed the good seed sparingly, I mean; but ill-gotten means never stay long with the receiver. Some have plundered and robbed, perhaps I may say truthfully, murdered; anyway, just so that I get—no matter about the remaining—just so I get my booty, I have never thought of wronging any one out of their dues. That is what made me so bitter against the slaveholders. By reading this book, ere this you are convinced that I have been bitter against such men. But for the Emancipation Proclamation I should be the same this day, although, like many others, I have been accused through life falsely. (23–24)

After stating that both "colored and white" people have been successful in California, Williams raises the specter of exploitation in this passage, which returns him to the topic of racial slavery. The reason, he claims, he has such strong feelings about theft and exploitation is because of his experience of slavery. His analogy of the exploitation in the West with racial slavery attempts to state the case in purely economic terms, suggesting that slavery's biggest affront is that it "wronged men of their due"—violating an implicit labor contract in which men are paid for the work they do; however, the analogy also cuts the other way, implying a specifically racial component to the exploitation in the West, such that the laws protecting black and white speculators are revealed to be unable to fully protect black laborers. It is at this moment that Williams references his own position as a racial subject by suggesting that the reader must be "convinced that [he has] been bitter against [the slaveholders]" for "wronging him of his due." He declares that he would be bitter still were it not for the Emancipation Proclamation, but now that he is paid for his work, he harbors no bitterness toward former slaveholders. Yet the fact that he anticipates (and exploits) his readership's expectation of his bitterness signals a set of race relations not fully set aside by the legal end of slavery.

This moment of direct address discloses Williams's relationship with his readers, who he imagines are interested in reading about his exploitation as a slave. Instead, he supplies a narrative that primarily addresses his exploitation as a free economic actor in the West. The fact that Williams is judged—by the reader and "many others"—before they know his story points to his subject position as a black man as well as his self-conscious use of slave narrative conventions, which offer the exploitation of the black slave for the edification of the white reader.[55] By declaring he is no longer bitter against slaveholders because slaveholding is no longer legal, Williams affirms his philosophy of economic justice—"just so I get my booty"—while suggesting the precariousness of the legal structures protecting black workers in the region.

Williams's recollected account is validated by Nubia's immediate assessment of legal rights for nonwhites in California. In his first letter for *Frederick Douglass' Paper*, Nubia begins by acknowledging the deprivations suffered by blacks in California, including the lack of the vote or the inability to testify in court against a white citizen, but he addresses as well the conditions of the Chinese: "we have no oath against any white man or Chinaman," he writes, but he characterizes the Chinese as alien in the course of arguing for black legal equality.[56] Whites would support black witness testimony but not Chinese.[57] Such legal recognition would be an important step on the road to citizenship. Nubia's lack of solidarity with the Chinese is not surprising. Wong purports that "the Chinese exclusion movement further exposed the tenuous status of black citizenship in the era leading to *Plessy v. Ferguson* (1896)," while Helen Jun argues that black Americans were grappling with the "heathenism" of the Chinese at a time when black "claims to citizenship had been largely predicated on negotiating discourses of Christian morality."[58] Jun suggests that Nubia's letter "expresses clear empathy toward the 'persecuted' Chinese, even as it simultaneously objectifies Chinese immigrants through an anthropological gaze that methodically recounts their foreign signs of bodily and cultural difference."[59]

While Nubia's first letter to Douglass is perhaps ambiguous on the question of empathy, his second transforms ambiguity into wit: "it is my impression there never was such a thing as prejudice against color. In the United States, color indicates inferiority of condition, simply because the lowest and most degraded condition is found among persons of color. If the prejudice is against color, why is there no prejudice against a black horse, or a black dog, or any other black quadruped?"[60] Nubia cannot seem to make up his mind whether kinship with the Chinese in San Francisco helps or hurts the cause of black Americans, noting that other groups, such as the Chinese and Native Americans, were complicating the question of how to fight oppression in the courts and the legislature.

In the closing remarks of a letter on local politics published in the April 6, 1855, issue, Nubia muses sardonically on the relationship of African Americans to other nonwhites: "The papers from the interior are filled with accounts of horrible murders, lynchings, starvation among Indians, &c. Alas! the poor Indian, unable to adapt himself to the circumstances of civilization, he soon becomes the object of charity. But at this moment I am reminded of the Negro-hating Cherokees, and my milk of human kindness is suddenly turned to gall. NUBIA."[61] Clearly historical obstacles to accord among the oppressed remained potent. No social or educational structures existed to work toward expanding the franchise around which disparate disenfranchised groups (blacks, Chinese, Native Americans, Mexicans) could coalesce.

Notably, the successive editions of Williams's own narrative published between 1873 and 1893—which include sections on the "Chinese in California" and "The Modocs"—resist both the formation of cross-racial hostilities and the false equivalences of the egalitarian myth of the times. It is this aspect of the text that makes it a critical early example of comparative racialization for Wong, who argues that Williams's narrative "'point[s] the way' . . . to a reading practice that makes difference and heterogeneity of historical experience the basis for cross-racial connection and political critique."[62] Building on Wong's claim, we argue that Williams's nuanced understanding of regional conflicts and western expansion form the basis of his critique of the variable power of the law to guarantee the rights of citizenship. Just as he understands his economic exploitation in the West in terms of his experience as a former slave, he understands western expansion and Indian removal as of a piece with the economic exploitation of African Americans. A signal example of this is Williams's chapter on the Modoc War. Williams condemns the U.S. treatment of the Modoc Indians and paints the leader of the uprising, Captain Jack, as an American hero and martyr for the cause of justice in the United States. Strikingly, Williams compares the episode with the failure of Reconstruction to redress the wrongs of slavery, noting that, although there was a legal basis for hanging Jefferson Davis, he was allowed to live, while Captain Jack, accused of treason, was put to death. The difference in the two cases, Williams asserts, is race. If Davis "had been a poor Indian," Williams claims that he would have been hanged; he exhorts his reader to remember that "God created the Indian, the same as any American" (100).[63] The economic failure of Reconstruction is further represented as a consequence of the United States' failure to mete out justice fairly because of its inability to address the racism of the nation. The promise of federal unification and equality for freedmen and women is belied by regional corruption:

> Reader, I believe that [in hanging him] they were trying to deal with Captain Jack like they deal with the freedmen down South, but Jack didn't see the point; they used to send out agents to collect money for the freedmen and distressed soldiers during the war, and they would stick the money in their pockets; they would also bring great donation of clothing and provisions to them from different parts of the Northern States, and what did they do with them? They could not pocket that, but they made an auction, and sold [the donations] to the highest bidder, and those poor freedmen, who could not buy at auction, had to take a spin around the block and go without. (99)

Despite the empathetic condemnation of the legal system, Williams valorizes Captain Jack's investment in the law. In his final speech, Captain Jack acquiesces to his fate, declaring, "You are the law-giving party. You say I must die. I am satisfied if the law is correct" (101). With the inclusion of these final words, Williams represents Captain Jack—and therefore freemen and women who turn to the law for redress for their economic exploitation—as more American than the white Americans who put him to death or the Americans who default on the promises of Reconstruction.

While Williams's narrative has been addressed by scholars such as Wong and Knadler in the larger context of African American literature, William Newby is still a relatively unknown figure outside research on race, abolition, and California.[64] Newby is partly to blame; while he played a leading role as a political leader and activist in black California politics, he downplayed his role in his newspaper correspondence, using his pen for witty commentary rather than trumpeting success:

> We are holding a series of meetings in this city, of a political character, but no practical good can result from them. The time is consumed in idle and unprofitable discussion, and were it otherwise, the result would be the same. Remonstrances and prayers are futile. We cannot arouse their fears (the whites) by the one, and they have no fears or consciences to be affected by the other. The cold word "interest," is the "*lever*" that will move the world. All the colored people in the State have not as much political influence as one "naturalized Irishman." What, then, is to be done? We must acquire an influence that will purchase the removal of our disabilities.[65]

Nubia's letters both reveal and equivocate his efforts to negotiate a complicated and unpredictable political environment in which alliances and allegiances to other oppressed populations, particularly the Chinese, were contemplated but remained unforged.

The letters of Nubia and the narrative of Williams provide a stark contrast to the writings of Frederick Jackson Turner, who spent little time on the California gold fields and subsumed the events following the discovery of gold in 1848 to his broader, romantic narrative of the frontier West, a vision that would come to define the great myth of the Frontier: "Western democracy included individual liberty, as well as equality. The frontiersman was impatient of restraints. He knew how to preserve order, even in the absence of legal authority. . . . It followed from the lack of organized political life, from the atomic conditions of the backwoods society, that the individual was exalted and given free play. The West was another name for opportunity. Here were mines to be seized, fertile valley to be preempted, all the natural resources open to the shrewdest and the boldest."[66] For Williams, Newby, and thousands of other African Americans, Gold Rush California was an opportunity to renegotiate citizenship and seek economic and civic participation. The West served as both a geographical location and a conceptual space that might offer political freedom but clearly required new forms of engagement with settlers from across the globe, with equally pressing concerns about citizenship and labor. For Williams, Wong argues, "African enslavement, Chinese exclusion, and Indian removal are tragic expressions of the constitutive violence of Americanization and western incorporation."[67] The African American perspective on the still-prevalent myth that "the individual was exalted and given free play" needs further attention, as does the pessimism of Frederick Douglass and others that California would offer few opportunities to fugitive slaves and free blacks seeking fortune. The literature of African Americans in Gold Rush California speaks to a richer and more complicated narrative of the era.

NOTES

A portion of this essay previously appeared in Janet Neary's "Mining the African Literary Tradition: James Williams's *Fugitive Slave in the Gold Rush* and the Contours of a Black Pacific" in *ESQ: A Journal of the American Renaissance* 59, no. 2 (2013): 329–74. Copyright 2014 by the Board of Regents of Washington State University.

1. Pleasant, "Memoirs and Autobiography," 1–6.

2. Pleasant was both literate and self-conscious in the crafting of her personal narrative, yet her text shares many of the thorny issues of authenticity and literary authority that slave narratives faced. Her autobiography was to be published in several installments, but she only completed one before falling out with Davis, which describes her life until age thirteen, before she reaches San Francisco.

3. Pleasant, "Memoirs and Autobiography," 4.

4. For historical context on African Americans in the North in this period, see Litwack, *North of Slavery*.

5. Douglass, *Narrative*, 13.

6. Barrett, "African-American Slave Narratives," 422.

7. See Lynn M. Hudson, "Making of 'Mammy Pleasant.'"

8. See Eric Gardner, *Unexpected Places*.

9. Lynn M. Hudson, "Making of 'Mammy Pleasant,'" 11.

10. Holdredge, *Mammy Pleasant*, 8.

11. Lynn M. Hudson, "Making of 'Mammy Pleasant,'" 11–12.

12. Williams circulated a version of his autobiography in pamphlet form beginning in 1853. First editions of *Life and Adventures* were published between 1873 and 1893, with Williams adding material at each printing. The quotations in this essay are drawn from the 2002 edition, reprinted from the 1893 Sickler edition and retitled *Fugitive Slave in the Gold Rush*.

13. In addition to Gardner, on African American literature of the West, see Knadler, *Remapping Citizenship*; Wong, "Comparative Racialization"; Worden, *Masculine Style*, esp. chapter 2, "Between Anarchy and Hierarchy."

14. See Eric Gardner, *Unexpected Places* and "Early African American Print Culture"; Knadler, *Remapping Citizenship*; Wong, "Comparative Racialization"; Quintard Taylor, *In Search of the Racial Frontier*; De Graaf et al., *Seeking El Dorado*.

15. On Williams's engagement with contemporary debates about Chinese and American Indian political identity, see Wong, "Comparative Racialization."

16. *Bay of San Francisco*, 2:144.

17. See Stillman, *Spreading the Word*, for analysis of newspapers and guidebooks, adver-

tisements, and pamphlets that provided information to gold seekers in the early days of the Gold Rush.

18. Bayard Taylor, *El Dorado*, 3, 77.

19. Kip, *California Sketches*, 7. The same mode of description operates in Kip's pessimistic fictional treatment of his experiences in *Volcano Diggings*.

20. Lapp, *Blacks in Gold Rush California*, 12.

21. *North Star*, October 5, 1848.

22. On black routes to California, see Pilton, Newsletter.

23. De Graaf et al., *Seeking El Dorado*, 8–9.

24. *National Era*, January 4, 1849.

25. *North Star*, November 30, 1849.

26. *National Era*, March 29, 1849.

27. Pitts, *Decline of the Californios*, 58.

28. Qtd. in Eaves, *History of California Labor Legislation*, 82.

29. On the relationship between mercantilist legislation and Williams's narrative, see Neary, "Mining"; Wong, "Comparative Racialization."

30. *Frederick Douglass' Paper*, May 4, 1855.

31. *Frederick Douglass' Paper*, August 24, 1855.

32. Supported by gold discovered in the nearby mines, Negro Hills was vital through 1855 when it was plagued with racial tensions, including "physical confrontations between Caucasian and African American miners, which resulted in injuries, deaths, and arrests." See Clarence Caesar, "The Negro Hill Area," California Historical and Cultural Endowment, California State Library, http://www.cde.ca.gov/ci/hs/im/negrohill.asp.

33. Zerbe and Anderson, "Culture and Fairness," 115.

34. Ibid., 115–16.

35. The previous quotation, for example, is taken from J. T. Brooks's *Four Months among the Gold-Finders*. Brooks's narrative is a hoax, although apparently many of the facts contained in it are accurate. See Watson, "Spurious California." In fact, all of the source material for this economic study comes from the pen of white diarists and historians. Neither Nubia nor Douglass appears in the index.

36. Zerbe and Anderson, "Culture and Fairness," 135–36.

37. Williams, *Fugitive Slave in the Gold Rush*, 22. Subsequent citations will be given parenthetically.

38. On the geography of postbellum slave narratives, see Andrews, introduction to *Slave Narratives after Slavery*.

39. Newby advocated for the 1855 California Convention of African Americans in Sacramento and chaired the Committee on Resolutions. Newby also had a hand in establishing California's first black newspaper, the *Mirror of the Times*. After 1857, Newby left California to serve as private secretary to the French consul general to Haiti, but he soon returned to the United States. He died in 1858. See Lapp, *Blacks in Gold Rush California*, 223–35, 263.

40. Fisher, "Struggle for Negro Testimony," 314.

41. Nubia, "Progress of the Colored People of San Francisco," *Frederick Douglass' Paper*, September 22, 1854.

42. Nubia, "From Our California Correspondent," *Frederick Douglass' Paper*, March 6, 1855.

43. On the treatment of Chinese immigration to the West in the black press and the relationship of the Chinese exclusion movement to debates over black citizenship in a slightly later period—California's economic depression in the 1870s—see Wong, "Comparative Racialization."

44. Nubia, "From Our San Francisco Correspondent," *Frederick Douglass' Paper*, June 15, 1855.

45. *New York Tribune*, June 27, 1849.

46. Lapp, *Blacks in the Gold Rush*, 18.

47. *New Bedford Mercury*, August 22, 1849; Schell, "Bold and Hardy Race of Men."

48. Lapp, *Blacks in the Gold Rush*, 17.

49. Whittier closes by quoting Taylor's allusions to France: "The security of the country is owing in no small degree to this plain, practical development of what the French reverence as an abstraction, under the name of *Fraternité*. To sum up all three words, Labor is respectable. May it never be otherwise while a grain of gold is left to glitter in California soil!" "Review of *El Dorado*," *National Era*, July 4, 1850.

50. A letter by "J. T." in *Frederick Douglass' Paper* on June 17, 1852, hints at the struggle by the writer to find common ground with the Chinese.

51. Nubia, "From Our San Francisco Correspondent," June 15, 1855.

52. Ibid.

53. For historical context, see Gonzalez-Day, *Lynching in the West*.

54. Joseph C. Zabriskie was a white abolitionist and prominent attorney at the time. See Quintard Taylor, *In Search of the Racial Frontier*, 78.

55. This reading of Williams's narrative departs from Wong, who asserts that "it begins as a conventional slave narrative. . . . The testimonial form falls away as Williams moves westward" ("Comparative Racialization," 801). We argue that Williams self-consciously highlights his narrative's connection to the slave narrative genre to suggest a continuation of racial exploitation in the "free" West.

56. "The Chinese form about one-eighths of the population. They exhibit a most grotesque appearance. Their 'unmentionables' are either exceedingly roomy or very close fitting. The heads of the males are shaved. With the exception of the top, the hair from which is formed into a plaited tail, resembling 'pig tail tobacco.' Their habits are filthy, and their features totally devoid of expression. The whites are greatly alarmed at their rapid increase. They are very badly treated here. Every boy considers them lawful prey for his boyish pranks. They have no friends, unless it is the colored people, who treat every body well, even their enemies." Nubia, "Progress of the Colored People."

57. Lapp, *Blacks in Gold Rush California*, 202–3.

58. Wong, "Comparative Racialization," 798; Jun, "Black Orientalism," 1056. On Williams's intervention into African American discourse on Chinese immigration to California, see Wong, "Comparative Racialization," 812. Knadler's treatment of Williams as a transnational figure is also instructive. See *Remapping Citizenship*.

59. Jun, "Black Orientalism," 1058.

60. *Frederick Douglass' Paper*, January 26, 1855.

61. *Frederick Douglass' Paper*, April 6, 1855.

62. Wong, "Comparative Racialization," 818.

63. For readings of this scene as an expression of Williams's deep ambivalence toward the law, see Knadler, *Remapping Citizenship*, 129, and Wong, "Comparative Racialization," 818.

64. In his reading of Williams as a "transnational figure," Knadler links Williams's narrative with the autobiographies of other African American westerners, Nat Love and Miflin Wistar Gibbs, arguing that "on the one hand, these writers 'accommodated' or adapted and fit their stories to a dominant racial uplift ideology among a middle-class aspiring African-American community. Yet, on the other hand, their stories reveal a more 'accommodating' citizenship, one that allows sufficient space for other kinds of competing and even contradictory identifications" (*Remapping Citizenship*, 120). Like Knadler, we contend that Williams's geographic mobility is central to his understanding of citizenship and results in the fragmentary nature of his narrative; however, we argue that Williams's ambivalence—and the narrative's fragmentation—is a response to the uneven opportunities offered a black independent actor in the mercantilist environment of the West, rather than the pressure exerted by a dominant racial uplift theory.

65. *Frederick Douglass' Paper*, September 28, 1855.

66. Turner, *Frontier in American History*, 33.

67. Wong, "Comparative Racialization," 818.

POSTSCRIPT

Creole Adjudication
Governing New Orleans and Regional Provisionality in the Long Nineteenth Century

John Funchion

THE ETYMOLOGY OF the term "region" haunts as much as it animates the study of regionalism. Genealogies of the concept attest that at its root, it refers to a realm or "an administrative division; a subdivision of a larger geographical or political unit, for economic, administrative, or cultural purposes."[1] "A region is a part of something beyond itself," Sandra A. Zagarell reminds us, and it is often seen as subordinate to powers that penetrate and supersede it.[2] By this account, the region is a site of governability. Regions emerge as disciplinary units that lend themselves to their study and administration. We conceive of them conventionally as knowable communities predicated on personal immediacy rather than on abstract imaginary bonds. They are often deemed rural, premodern, or primordial spaces. Temporally, they can appear to be asynchronous with the urban and the modern even when incorporated within a larger political entity. In contrast to the dynamics of global and national forces, regions appear stable and manageable even when manipulated or threatened by powers that exist beyond them. The semantics of the region help account for its tenuous and often maligned place in U.S. literary studies. As a body of writing moored to static spaces of preservation, it presumably lacks the qualities associated with generative literary material: complexity, ambiguity, ambivalence, and formal richness.

Mapping Region in Early American Writing calls for a more capacious understanding of regionalism. The multiplicity of methods and objects of study in this collection testify to the many regionalisms that have shaped U.S. literature, culture, and politics in the early nineteenth century. But this richness itself reveals something about the quality of the region that has implications extending beyond the historical parameters of most of the preceding essays. In their introduction, Edward Watts and Keri Holt establish how mapping works as a fluid process: it creates fictional possibilities but also actual lines of geopolitical contest. As Watts and Holt's invocation of David N. Cosgrove's theory of mapping illustrates, maps assume a set of spiritual and moral as well as political and cultural characteristics. Mapping, in other words, is an expansive concept coextensive but not always fully complicit with disciplinary division. While each contributor brings his or her own approach to bear on the region, mapping emerges as our animating trope. Its function is not unlike that of the ship that has long organized the work of Atlantic studies scholarship. Mapping, as it is used in our collection, requires a different vocabulary for comparative studies attending to the relationships and rivalries among regions. One of this volume's imperatives is to free regional literary and cultural studies from the binaries that historically have defined the field. Rather than imagining regions locked into either serving or opposing a larger geopolitical body, such as a nation, an empire, or a market, we see them as entities embedded within a network of localities scattered across the globe. Nation-states or empires may seek to annex particular regions, but they forge lines of political and cultural exchange that exist beyond these claims. The contestability of their content and form creates occasions for the literary in the broadest sense: completely new kinds of social, economic, and political affiliations become imaginable that transform and are transformed by the spaces they inhabit and the other localities connected to them.

While an artificial conclusion cannot be imposed on an essay collection that includes as wide an array of methods and objects of study as *Mapping Region in Early American Writing*, all of the contributors to our volume essentially concur on two crucial points. First, individually and in the aggregate, these essays provide us with a compelling regionally attuned cultural history that cannot be so easily squared, as Duncan Faherty especially stresses in his examination of early nineteenth-century New York literature, with either older nationalist or more recent transatlantic models of study. Second, every contributor underscores the fluidity of regions, their literatures, and transnational networks. For all, what defines these spaces is not their stability but their contestability, or what I will refer to as their regional provisionality. Descriptive accounts of these places and the people that inhabit them attempt to achieve their disciplinary aims but do not necessarily do so. Local peoples may oppose the nations and empires that seek to subsume them, but regional writing registers other lines of antagonism among indigenous peoples, migrants, settlers, and conquerors, too. In the process, it imagines new forms of affiliation among local communities and literatures across the globe.[3] Although this collection's essays focus predominantly on pre-1860 literature and culture, their alternative understandings of regionalism and their recognition of regionalism's centrality to early U.S. literature and culture necessarily invite us to revisit the way we apprehend postbellum regionalism. The secessionist discourse of the 1850s may have organized the nation's regions into two ruling sectional nationalisms, but local color writers working at the end of the nineteenth century, in fact, often directly drew on the antebellum writers, explorers, cartographers, and ethnographers that preceded them.

To chart this line of continuity between antebellum and postbellum regionalism in ways that mobilize this collection's operative concerns with mapping and regional contestability, I foreground one way of grappling with provisionality that surfaces throughout many of the preceding essays—even if it does not always figure centrally: legal regionalism. Specifically, I examine how Louisianan state law and literature envisaged regional affiliations across the globe that superseded those of the nation. The various economic, political, racial, and military conflicts borne out of the territorial disputes examined by many of the contributors to *Mapping Region in Early American Writing* had legal implications that extended well past the Civil War.

I specifically turn to George Washington Cable's writing on New Orleans as an instructive test case. In his work for the 1887 census and in his novel *The Grandissimes* (1880), Cable drew on early histories of the area to establish that the racial tensions and cultural challenges New Orleans faced in the years immediately after the Louisiana Purchase continued to haunt the city after Reconstruction. I maintain that Cable displays an acute awareness of the regional particularity of Louisiana's court system. Even as the state submitted to federal rule, its legal system remained Creolized insofar as it became the only state to base its court system on the Roman or civil-law practices of France and Spain rather than on the Anglo-Saxon common-law tradition that traced its roots back to England. Thus, while readers have long attended to the legal content of *The Grandissimes*, I am interested in how it uses civil legal logic to remedy the wrongs perpetrated in the text and to construct a narrative that romances neither sectionalism nor nationalism but imagines a translocal and more equitable Louisiana.

FROM PROVINCIAL TO PROVISIONAL REGIONALISM

The essays compiled for *Mapping Region in Early American Writing* address the challenge that everyone who studies local literatures of the long nineteenth century must tackle: how to prove that regions can be locally rooted without necessarily being homogeneous or culturally isolated. Regional fluidity has, in some measure, been addressed in previous scholarship on regionalism, but this collection extends and redirects this earlier work. Many of the contributors, for example, derive inspiration from Hsuan Hsu's idea of "regional production," which "involves not only the production of literature about regions but also the ways in which literary works 'produce,' reimagine, and actively restructure regional identities" in relation to larger national and global phenomena.[4] Hsu's approach, however, is not without precedent. Stephanie Foote too treats regionalism as more of a process or as a strategy rather than as a genre "*about* the representation of difference," which shaped responses to the cultural and economic changes of the late nineteenth century.[5] On this latter score, both Harry Brown's examination of the figure of William Apess and Keri Holt's study of Cherokee countermapping outline the contending ways in which American Indians were represented and represented themselves in relation to different spaces. To a degree, they flesh out the antebellum antecedents to the kinds of local color writing addressed in Foote's work.

Still others interested in regionalism turn to Gilles Deleuze and Felix Guattari's idea of *deterritorialization* to recast regions as sites of social dynamism rather than cultural preservation. Jonathan Elmer and Paul Giles have both persuasively appropriated this concept to account for how European ideologies became redefined during the colonization of the Americas and how "the national identity of the United States" became unsettled by the forces of globalization at the turn of the twenty-first century.[6] This concept itself, however, always casts locality or regionalism as the product of something beyond itself. Deleuze and Guattari explain that "States . . . *deterritorialize with one hand*" and "*reterritorialize with the other*" to create "neoterritorialities" that "are often artificial, residual, [and] archaic" even as they are also products of modernity. These territorialities then are "organized and created by the State, even though they might turn against the State and cause it serious problems (regionalism, nationalism)."[7] In his contribution to *Mapping Region in Early American Writing*, Andy Doolen powerfully develops the idea of territorialization to argue that it could be wed to competing narratives rather than just a singular national narrative, as in the case of Pike's liberal vision for the United States. In a similar vein, William V. Lombardi embraces the idea of the "rhizomatic West" to account for the porousness and inherent incompleteness of any attempt at territorial annexation. This term wonderfully accounts for how regions or localities become subject to redefinition or contestation. While the local remains a dynamic category in Doolen's and Lombardi's work, other scholarship indebted to the idea of territorialization, however, tends to cast the local as the finished product of this process. Michael Hardt and Antonio Negri, for example, insist that "local identities are not autonomous or self-determining but actually feed into and support the development of the capitalist imperial machine."[8] To insist on a version of the local or the region not always subordinate to or produced by something beyond itself is to indulge in the stuff of fantasy and romance.

While I also find territorialization to be an indispensable concept, I am much more invested in the notion of *provisionality*. Provisionality provides us with a way of apprehending regions as inherently conditional and translocal rather than as fixed and subnational sites. The term "provisional" bears several denotations that resonate with the claims advanced by the preceding essays in *Mapping Region in Early American Writing*, and it lays the groundwork for my analysis of the Territory of Orleans' legal regionalism and Cable's postbellum writing about it. On the one hand, it describes a "temporary" arrangement, entity, or border rather than referring to "something regular, permanent, or final."[9] The provisional is thus a geopolitical concept, demarking a semiautonomous space whose independent authority and legitimacy always remains tenuous. Provisionality, in other words, echoes what economists call regionalization: a concept that retains many of the attributes of deterritorialization but also "implies an activist element" in which a geographical space becomes reorganized around local and extralocal ideas of "culture, security, economic development and politics."[10] Localities, by this account, are not so much extirpated of their previous cultural and political content and then colonized as much as they undergo perpetual processes of reorganization and alteration.[11] Many of the essays found in *Mapping Region in Early American Writing* develop this line of thinking. Jennifer Schell, Martha Schoolman, and Steven Thomas all establish how slavery or its abolition could economically alter the cultural and political characteristics of particular localities.

If we see regions as inherently provisional, then we must study them as unsettled spaces populated with their own internal and external antagonisms. They are interstitial or what Peter Eisenman describes as "zones of undecidability."[12] Rather than lending themselves to administrative stability, they are places where "the struggle is up for grabs here—the struggle over who will appropriate them."[13] Previous work on regional writing registers this fundamental quality when it grapples with how a homogeneous place such as Sarah Orne Jewett's Maine still appears dynamic in several respects. The author who visits Dunnet Landing in *The Country of the Pointed Firs* (1896) represents this space and her position within it as one where she frets about joining a local funeral procession but remembers she "did not really belong" to this community.[14] These places exist as much outside as within a nation, empire, or global marketplace. Dunnet Landing may seem hermetically sealed away from the outside world, but it is also a place where people discuss the "painted savages" of the "South Sea Islands."[15]

Provisionality denotes a particular sense of temporality as well as spatiality. Thinking of regions provisionally means no longer deeming them sites of arrested development. Analepsis gives way to the timely and the ephemeral. Whatever meaning or set of cultural, economic, and political characteristics assigned to a region are "adopted for the time being."[16] As Watts's essay in this collection on the Madoc legend and other whitewashed accounts of pre-Columbian history makes clear, what specific pasts get sutured to particular regions contingently depend on the exigencies of the present. Robert Gunn's analysis of writing about the Old Southwest, moreover, shows how a locally rooted history might be used to serve aims of generating cultural consensus in the present. Provisionality, as it emerges out of the essays found in *Mapping Region in Early American Writing*, thus moves us away from nominative understandings of regionalism toward more performative apprehensions of regionalization.

This kind of critical outlook helps us make sense of the persistence of legal regionalism in the United States from the late eighteenth to the twenty-first century.

This collection already attests to the concomitant relationship between literary and legal regionalism, whether it be Janet Neary and Hollis Robbins's examination of how local courts deprived African Americans of the legal rights to property promised to them in California during the Gold Rush or Faherty's discussion of how *Rutgers v. Waddington* smothered local dissent in order to protect the interests of a nationally minded elite. As these phenomena already suggest, regional courts often occupy provisional positions and jurisdictions remain up for grabs in these spaces.

Accordingly, the aesthetics of regional writing, then, might be recast as one that does not aspire to eliciting a sense of totality but a provisional understanding of an interstitial space and its relationship to a wider network of other localities. My use of the term "aesthetics" is deliberate, as I would distinguish it from the more formally bound and categorically defined idea of genre. As the scholarship on late nineteenth-century local color writing suggests, regionalism is a catchall term that encompasses a range of forms and genres. Formally and generically, regional writing similarly lies inside and outside American literature. Readers of regionalism have alternatively cast the local as a vehicle for expressing literary nationalism or as apart from this tradition for being too idiosyncratic or provincial. Hamlin Garland, one of the most vocal advocates of late nineteenth-century regionalism, embraces both of these characterizations. For him, the literature of the West is wholly American but also one that eschews "strict conformity to accepted models."[17] The in-betweenness of regional writing, in other words, is essential to both its form and content. Regional writing appears so very bound to place, yet it is always, to borrow Judith Fetterley and Marjorie Pryse's titular phrase, "out of place" in U.S literature.[18] Here, then, aesthetics refers not to the activity of championing certain canons of taste or outlining a set of formal principles; it instead refers to art's capacity for imagining new social possibilities through the invention of new forms or the alteration of older ones.[19] Regional aesthetics undermines judgment in its most capacious sense; the body of writing associated with it puts rulings on matters of justice, politics, and taste all to the test.

UNCOMMON LAW:
REGIONAL TEMPORALITY AND SPATIALITY ON TRIAL

The conflicts between local and federal law, especially in Louisiana, point to an ambiguous legal environment that spanned the nineteenth century. The territory and state underwent two periods of legal drama that pitted its own local sovereignty against the authority of the federal courts: the years immediately after the U.S. acquisition of this territory and the years following the Civil War. Cable's work for the tenth census and *The Grandissimes* spans these two periods by providing accounts of the early incorporation of the Orleans and Louisiana Territories for a post-Reconstruction–era audience. Most general scholarship on the intersections between law and literature addresses the "especially vexed question" of personhood and "the natural right to property" in legal decisions involving Native Americans, blacks, and immigrants.[20] Many readings of Cable's work similarly attend to the instability of the term "Creole" in U.S. legal discourse when it applied to or excluded free people of color.[21] Even though its reliance on the Napoleonic black codes brutally regulated the behavior of slaves, French law accorded free people of color legal protections that U.S. law did not. But the scope of the legal conflict in New Orleans and Louisiana extended even beyond these important issues because, as a former French and Spanish possession, it has carried forth—even into the twenty-first century—the Roman or civil-law tradition while most of the United States operated under the customs of Anglo-American common law.

The Louisiana Purchase generated a number of thorny legal problems, drawing attention to the rest of the nation's regionally diffuse legal system.[22] The establishment of a federal constitution did not fully resolve these juridical conflicts, and it would take decades of Supreme Court rulings to trace out the limits of the federal government. These juridical differences became entrenched in the century before the Declaration of Independence, as three regional legal traditions took root in New England, the Middle Colonies, and the South. Anglo-Saxon common law allowed for the creation of multiple courts first in England and then later in the colonies.[23] Colonial and local (and eventually state) courts thus applied common-law precedents differently when hearing cases on a range of issues, including tort claims, property titles, and marital disputes. The most pronounced regional fissure dividing these localities stemmed from the trading and possession of slaves. Slave law was the most contentious of the many legal domains where comity among the states did not exist.[24] Made possible by the costly outcome of the Civil War, the ratification of the Thirteenth and Fourteenth Amendments brought an end to slavery and laid the groundwork for an even more powerful federal judiciary (though, as Thomas notes in his essay, the United States remained very much dependent on the slave labor of other regions). The dismantling of the Reconstruction Acts, however, returned power to the state legislatures and courts, as the rise of Jim Crow in the South made clear. Jurisdictional conflicts and uncertainties among the states and even within different localities in the states cast regions as sites of legal and political contest. And these tensions reverberated and were negotiated in regional literary works.

New Orleans and the Louisiana Territory uniquely exemplified the juridical and cultural contestability of the region throughout the nineteenth century. The area passed hands from one empire to another, from Spain to France to the United States. Its fluctuating political circumstances allowed piracy to thrive in the area, and the city quickly assumed a cosmopolitan character. Slavery was an institutional fixture, but under Spanish and French rule a number of people of African descent attained free-person status. These individuals occupied a legal category distinct both from whites and enslaved blacks, presenting a set of juridical problems. But what made New Orleans an especially vexing place in legal terms was its embrace of the Roman civil-law as opposed to the Anglo-Saxon common-law tradition. Both traditions emerge out of a network of translocal discourses that traverse national boundaries. One of the major challenges associated with the incorporation of the territory purchased from France was reconciling its laws with the rest of the nation it had just joined. Divided along the thirty-third parallel or roughly where the present-day northern boundary of the state of Louisiana lies, two separate territories were formed: Orleans to the south and Louisiana to the north. While the significantly larger Louisiana Territory immediately became subject to the common-law tradition, civil law would remain a part of Orleans.

When William Claiborne assumed the territorial governorship of Orleans, Jefferson hoped he would bring its court system in line with the rest of the nation.[25] In an important guide to criminal law in Orleans written to assist Claiborne with the administration of the area, Lewis A. Kerr insisted that "a similitude of laws seems in some degree essential to a sincere or permanent union between nations."[26] Claiborne would ultimately waffle. His reluctance to firmly import the common law gave rise to first a territorial and then a state legal system that adopted—sometimes to great confusion—parts of both legal traditions. One of the most fundamental distinctions between these two traditions concerned the doctrine of *stare decisis* or the custom of respecting the legal principles established by a preceding case ruling. This doctrine invested common-law judges with the power to shape the law on par with the legislature. Civil-law judges, by contrast, did not abide by the doctrine of *stare decisis*, criticizing it precisely for granting judges the ability to legislate. In common-law nations, the precedent of even a single case, especially when handed down by higher courts, must factor into rulings. Common-law judges are regarded as interpreters of the law, whereas civil-law judges are supposed to apply the law as clearly stipulated by a code of civil procedure. For this reason, in many civil-law countries apparent conflicts among laws or between a statue and the nation's constitution are referred back to the legislature rather than reconciled within the court system.

In the Territory of Orleans, the civil-law doctrine of *jurisprudence constante* created at least some basis for judges to exercise the discretion of their common-law counterparts. When following the parameters of *jurisprudence constante*, judges were not strictly bound by the preceding rulings of higher courts or single cases, but they could defer to previous decisions when they assumed a customary pattern. As the Supreme Court of Louisiana would later clarify, "when, by repeated decisions in a long line of cases, a rule of law has been accepted and applied by the courts, these adjudications assume the dignity of *jurisprudence constante*; and the rule of law upon which they are based is entitled to great weight in subsequent decisions."[27]

By redrafting and issuing their own version of the Napoleonic Code, the territory of Orleans and then the state of Louisiana created what we could accurately call an interstitial legal space. And even though the Judiciary Act of 1789 instructed the federal courts to abide by the state's own common- or civil-law tradition, *Swift v. Tyson* (1848) established that federal courts possessed the authority to create their own national common law until that decision was upended by what became the monumental *Erie* doctrine in 1938.[28] This created a peculiar set of problems for all state courts, especially Louisiana's civil-law legal system. But while much could be said about the legal contests that unfolded in the nineteenth century, I want to emphasize three features of this juridical conflict that have bearing on the literary and cultural study of regionalism and specifically Cable's work. First and most immediately, it poses problems for any strictly disciplinary account of local or regional writing and culture by casting Louisiana as a region of juridical instability rather than governability. The problem of governability, in this case, is also one that begins with the acquisition of the Louisiana Purchase and extends beyond the Civil War. Reconstruction uniquely contributed to this antagonistic discourse, but it did not usher in a new legal epoch. Second, it calls attention to the temporal discontinuities among regional spaces in ways that move beyond Johannes Fabian's influential study of the coeval and the allochronic in anthropological discourse. He argues that western ethnography imagined exotic sites of conquest as inhabiting various premodern stages of development.[29] Studies of U.S. regionalism sometimes enlist Fabian's work to suggest that localities in the South, West, and Midwest often appear as provincially backwater places existing allochronically out of step with the modernity of the Northeast or the western littoral. Taking up Lloyd Pratt's invitation to see "literary regionalism" instead as "contributing to time's division into several coeval temporalities," I see the contrast between *stare decisis* and *jurisprudence constante* as a struggle between two competing historiographical modes.[30] By using the principle of *jurisprudence constante*, Louisiana jurists were not applying a less contemporary understanding of justice but instead were imagining a different relationship between custom and modernity.[31] And third, the conflict between common and civil law points toward two different ways of networking localities globally. The common-law tradition created close ties among the Anglo-American world. Civil law bound Louisiana, on the other hand, to places in the Francophone and Hispanophone Caribbean and on the European continent.

This set of political conditions provided writers such as Cable with a fertile ground for their fiction. His census work and *The Grandissimes* present New Orleans as a zone of undecidability. Spain, France, and the United States all sought to regionalize New Orleans in their own terms, and Cable's census report should have assisted the federal government with this effort by offering a kind of anthropology of the region to its readers. Yet what emerges is a site defined by its perpetual unruliness. The bulk of his 1887 census report recounts a series of political upheavals from the early eighteenth century forward. During the area's early founding years, he notes, "gambling, dueling, and vicious idleness were indulged in to such a degree as to give the authorities grave concern."[32] While the Mississippi Company's charter compelled it to bring the region under greater control, this control would be challenged by skirmishes with the Natchez, Chouachas, and Chickasaw Indians and threatened by slaves who conspired with many of them with "the plan of striking for their own freedom" (48). Even though New Orleans and French control of the area endured through these threats, Cable insists that the culture of the city's early settlers soon assumed its own set of characteristics: "The new active element of New Orleans," he explains, "was now that new variety of French-speaking, but not French, people" (55). Here he draws attention to the unruliness of "Creole" identity itself, suggesting that who got to be counted as Creole and who got to control New Orleans remained consistently intertwined.[33] New Orleans figured as the flashpoint for the insurrection of 1768 against Spanish rule and the Burr conspiracy in 1805. These outbreaks of violence and intrigue took place in tandem with several transfers of national power. When Anglo rule finally came to New Orleans, Cable reports, the "proportion of American appointees into the new courts and the public offices" as well as "a supposed partiality for Americans in cases of law" contributed to the "serious degree of excitement" or discontent among the Creoles (112).

NARRATING JURISDICTIONAL PROVISIONALITY

The Grandissimes is set against the backdrop of this transfer to federal power. All of the events pivot around "the Cession," as the consequences of "American jurisdiction" bear directly on the fate of the Grandissimes' property holdings, the rights of free colored people, and the implications of *Code Noir* or the Napoleonic black codes.[34] Agricola Fusilier, Honoré Grandissime's uncle, suspects that federal control will not hold, proving to be "a mere temporary political manoeuvre" (51). Commentators have registered the sonorous and circumstantial similarities between cession and secession to attend to the text's status as a Reconstruction novel.[35] These parallels crucially link the provisional character of antebellum New Orleans with its post–Civil War circumstances. But the legal particularity of these linked moments can be more precisely tied to the contest between two legal traditions even if these allusions remain more indirect. When Governor Claiborne converses with Honoré about "the pure lawlessness" of Louisiana and about New Orleans's resistance to federal rule, the latter accuses Claiborne of thinking like "a true Anglo-Saxon" for not appreciating the degree to which the Creoles would go to protect their customs and laws (94). The novel also mentions two of the territorial legal architects by name: Edward Livingston and Daniel Clark. Agricola sees Livingston as a "great villain," even though the German American Joseph Frowenfeld recognizes him as a "great lawyer" (85). But while we receive two competing perceptions of Livingston, the narrator caustically refers to Clark as a man of intrigue who had begun "to amass those riches which an age of litigation has not to this day consumed" (79).

Clark and Livingston both curried favor with the Creoles by opposing the Breckenridge Act, which separated the Louisiana Territory into two and began the process of imposing the common-law tradition on both territories. In the territory of New Orleans, though, Livingston—along with other lawyers—successfully laid the groundwork for creating a mixed jurisdiction. Historian Mark Fernandez establishes that Livingston, as a Jeffersonian who wanted the elected legislative branch to retain the most power, "admired ... the civilian approach to law" because it followed the logic of codification and affirmed "the limited role of the jurists."[36] Given their roles in the "Creolization" of the Louisiana justice system, Clark and Livingston might more intuitively elicit feelings of appreciation as opposed to derision from Creole characters such as Agricola in Cable's novel.[37] Clark, however, proved an opportunist and had previously participated in an attempt to annex New Orleans before the Purchase, leading many Creoles to suspect his motives. The ambivalent, albeit brief, mention of Livingston is more complicated. Agricola, or the group he represents, would have assuredly respected his efforts to promote the civilian tradition in Louisiana. Writing from his vantage point at the end of the nineteenth century, though, Cable may have found it hard to extol Livingston for his defense of slavery in the territory. Indeed, one of the principal reasons behind his initial opposition to the Breckenridge Act was its interference with the slave trade in the Orleans Territory. Thus, while Livingston's efforts may have done much to ameliorate the tensions between the federal government and the Creoles, his defense of slavery sowed the seeds for disunion later in the century. Potentially in Cable's eyes, Livingston's legal legacy paved the way for both de jure and de facto racism in Louisiana.

Despite civilian law's complicity with legalized racism, Cable does not dismiss its tradition outright. In the essay that many literary critics maintain ended his literary career in the South, "The Freedman's Case in Equity" (1885), Cable appeals to the language of civil law. His call for "universal justice and equity" rather than for equality resonates with the Louisianan justice system.[38] As civilian judges should defer to the civil codes written by the legislature when rendering their decisions, they are granted only a few acceptable allowances for judicial discretion. One such allowance pertains to the principle of equity whereby the judge may "mitigate the harshness of strict application of a statute, or to allocate property or responsibility according to the facts of the individual case."[39] In other words, the principle of equity allows a judge to break with both statutory law and the custom of previous rulings (i.e., *jurisprudence constante*). The term is an apt one for Cable's purposes, as he aligns the prevailing de facto racism of the post-Reconstruction South with how the belief in the inequality of the races rested on the custom of the country. Slavery had made racial inequality "the corner-stone of the whole social structure."[40] To insist on the rights of all people, then, required a deviation from not just popular sentiment but also from tradition; justice in this case had to rest on a fair application of the law even if this meant abandoning the certainty of its past applications. Equity answers the power of custom by appealing to the knowledge of the present. It cognitively remaps an entire set of legal relations on the basis of an individual case. The result is not a new precedent that must be followed in future rulings, but the mere suggestion that custom and code may have given rise to social injustice can have profound implications.

Cable's decision to appeal to the terms of the civilian legal tradition in his essay on civil rights offers an important insight into *The Grandissimes*'s engagement with the law. Rather than just registering the jurisdictional instability of New Orleans, Cable salvages the principles of civil law, thereby retaining the cultural distinctiveness of Louisiana but arriving at a more just end. The novel essentially puts both the Grandissime property holdings and the legal rights of free persons of color on trial. There is an ongoing question, in fact, about whether "that great majority of Spanish titles derived from the concessions of post-commandants and others of minor authorities, hold good" (46). These concerns intersect with the novel's examination of the fairness of the *Code Noir*, which condemns Bras-Coupé, the African prince turned slave who famously appears in numerous stories within the novel, to "the death of a felon" for hitting his master when "a white offender" would have been only punished with "a small fine or a few days' imprisonment" (180). Imposing federal common law and judicial oversight might rectify the injustice of Bras-Coupé's fate, but it would almost certainly not recognize the legitimacy of a number of Spanish and French property titles. Cable also likely knew that the power accorded to judges by the common law could assuredly be used in the name of oppression as much as it could liberation. The Dred Scott decision had already established this fact, and, as Michael Germana notes, "four years after *The Grandissimes* was first published in *Scribner's* the U.S. Supreme Court decided the Civil Rights Cases of 1883."[41] This decision essentially overturned the Civil Rights Act of 1875 and curtailed the protections against racial discrimination promised by the Fourteenth Amendment. Both of these rulings confirm the fears voiced by many civil-law advocates because the Supreme Court essentially made binding laws without the consent of the people (i.e., Congress) to deprive part of the population of their universal rights.

Cable's novel promotes a form of legal and literary regionalism that neither cedes power entirely to the federal government nor reverts back to the ills of sectionalism. Instead, the novel appeals to equity and *jurisprudence constante* as ways to redress the wrongs in the text through the civilian tradition. Crucial to its narrative and juridical logic, then, is the often-vexing character of Joseph Frowenfeld. Described as a German American "immigrant" from the North, he seems to embody all the characteristics of the quintessential local color interloper when he first arrives and begins to set up shop as an apothecary (8). After residing in the city for some time, he eventually declares, "I am a Louisianan," a point that Honoré concedes but qualifies as distinct from what Creoles "call a Louisianan" (151). Frowenfeld's intermediary position compels him to map his surroundings, as he peruses volumes on New Orleans history and notes how streets such as "rue Enghien" became known as "Ingine street" (103). But more importantly, it places him into an adjudicating position. He looks on "this throng" of New Orleans inhabitants with a "far-away interest" or a sense of disinterestedness (81). In the backroom of his pharmacy, he presides over a discussion of property holdings and government appointments between Governor Claiborne and Honoré. He directly mentions to Honoré that he learned that "some of the titles under which your relatives hold their lands are found to be of the kind which the State's authorities are pronouncing worthless" (220). In each of these cases, Frowenfeld—along with the reader—weighs the law's merits. Frowenfeld, much like Livingston (whom he regards as a great lawyer), wishes to preserve many of the customs of New Orleans life but without perpetuating its past injustices and rigid caste structure.

Rather than outwardly challenging Creole culture and law, Frowenfeld repeatedly seeks out ways to make it more equitable. Two moments in the text stand out for best illustrating his use of what resembles civil legal reasoning. The first of these instances occurs after Frowenfeld hears three different accounts of the Bras-Coupé story. Learning that Agricola essentially "delivered Bras-Coupé to the law to suffer only the penalties of the crime he had committed against society by attempting to be a free man," Frowenfeld arrives at his own judgment of the incidents surrounding the slave's plight (191). While the Grandissimes lament the end he meets, they nevertheless honor the legal standing of the black codes. The apothecary reaches a different conclusion and implores his landlord and Honoré's half-brother, Honoré Grandissime, F.M.C. (free man of color), to take up the cause of his people. Honoré F.M.C. recoils initially because he insists that he "cannod be one Toussaint l'Ouverture," but Frowenfeld stresses he wants the landlord to work within the bounds of the law: "I can imagine a man in your place, going about among his people, stirring up their minds to a noble discontent, laying out his means, sparingly here and bountifully there, as in each case might seem wisest" (196). He further suggests appealing to the white Creoles who "have a spirit of fairness" to recognize "the rights of all" (196). While the context is not strictly a legal one, Frowenfeld advocates a form of judgment whereby cultural continuity is preserved by appealing to a conditionally qualified sense of fairness or equity. Rather than counseling Honoré F.M.C. to lay down a binding precedent to be applied to every wrong affecting blacks, he urges him to apply his reason when attending to the particulars of every case. He also bases his argument for the recognition of universal human rights on "fairness" as applied to a specific set of circumstances.

When it comes to the matter of property titles, Frowenfeld again displays a propensity for civilian legal thinking. At the heart of the novel lies the fate of the disinherited Nancanou mother and daughter. They lost the title to their estate when their late husband and father lost the deed to Agricola gambling. Honoré, who controls his family's property holdings, eventually decides to seek out Frowenfeld's advice on the matter. During the course of their conversation, Frowenfeld insists that "they have been deeply wronged" and believes "restitution should be made to them" (220). Honoré envies Frowenfeld for having the "easy part—the theorizing," but his thoughts clearly garner the respect of a wise judge (221). The apothecary reminds his companion that he "bade me study this community," and based on this understanding he has found "it may be the same with other communities . . . that just upon the culmination of the moral issue it turns and asks the question which is behind it, instead of the question which is before it" (220). Frowenfeld characterizes the wish to look backward as one of expediency and aligns the present question with the matter of deciding what is just. According to this line of reasoning, he concludes that the property must be returned to the Nancanou family, as expediency would sanction something egregiously unfair in this case. Frowenfeld again exhibits the legal reasoning of a civilian jurist by factoring in the customs of the community—what can be likened to *jurisprudence constante*—only to advise a course of action that applies narrowly to the plight of the Nancanous to satisfy the principle of equity. He does not imply that Honoré's actions in this regard should be considered a precedent to be followed in subsequent property disputes.

These critical acts of adjudication rest on a mapping of Louisiana law in relation to a set of competing legal customs inherited from other nations that can never fully be comprehended in their totality. That these judgments are rendered by a character associated with the federal North suggests that Cable believed the injustices pervading Louisiana could be best redressed by permitting federal rule but only if it respected the authority of the local legal system. What emerges, then, is a Louisiana neither aligned with the South and its sectionalist overtones nor fully allied with U.S. nationalism. This leaves the state within a realm of the provisional as an always shifting space—one where judgment remains in some manner contingent on a present set of circumstances. In the terms of the novel itself, Cable appears to want to preserve the Creole character of the justice system through the voice of Frowenfeld but in a way that "has been diluted and sweetened" (330).

The Grandissimes's embrace of the principle of equity and civilian legal logic means it produces a localized temporality at odds with the time of common law. Kunal Parker establishes how the common law is depicted as "immemorial" by tracing its origins to a time before the written record of the law when jurists sagaciously sought ways to protect the ancient liberties promised to Englishmen. "Freed from the strictures of a law that could be pinned down in chronological, historical time," Parker consequently contends, common-law judges could assert that the chronologically bound "acts of monarchs and legislatures . . . could never possess the wisdom of a law that embodied the wisdom of multiple generations going back into the mists of time."[42] Even though nineteenth-century common-law courts had to reconcile the immemoriality of the common law with nascent theories of teleological history, their authority rested on the claim that they could stand outside of historical time. The U.S. Supreme Court similarly presents itself as "immortal and therefore not temporally bound, and that claim of continuity typically extends to the product of that institution—namely, its rulings."[43] The consequence of the immemorial temporality inherent to the common law and the institution of the Supreme Court is what Alison L. LaCroix terms "temporal imperialism."[44] The court, by standing outside of historical time, can impose its own "narrative of continuity over time," dividing it into epochs to protect and exercise the power of its decisions in ways unavailable to the legislature.[45] It is hard for a literary critic not to discern a correlation between the way common-law jurists portray their legal tradition and the way champions of the literary canon used to define superior literary taste: both derive their power—legal and cultural, respectively—from a claim to timelessness. This kind of temporal power provided the federal courts with a rationale for overruling state law and later literary critics with a justification for sidelining regional literature for being artistically inferior and evanescent.

Cable accordingly composed a historical romance that creates a different kind of aesthetic and legal temporality. Although he treats a set of historical events, his regionally inflected literary and legal aesthetics underscores the importance of the timely. Frowenfeld earns respect for his judgment by repeatedly standing within instead of outside of time. When he first returned from Europe to New Orleans, Honoré acknowledges he found himself "accepting with the amiable, old-fashioned philosophy of conservatism, the sins of the community," but "contact with Frowenfeld had robbed him of his pleasant mental drowsiness" (279). Frowenfeld, in other words, compels Honoré to pursue two restitutions—the return of the Nancanou inheritance and his recognition of his half-brother Honoré F.M.C.—precisely because he inhabits the present, and his form of adjudication is one that accounts for customary patterns but refuses to see them as binding. As he explains to Agricola in a different context, bringing about justice does not require one to "overturn the government" but to overturn "conventionality" (229). Cable's historical romance is aesthetically moored to the present. While the events portrayed in the text have a relation to Cable's own historical moment, they do not constitute what Georg Lukács refers to as the "*necessary prehistory* of the present."[46] Nor does *The Grandissimes* indulge in the fantasy that its readers might be able to stand "outside of history" and be "immune to all versions of time" as the common law and, as Lloyd Pratt argues, many historical romances claim.[47] Instead, the temporality of the text remains indeterminate—temporally provisional. We occupy Frowenfeld's present, judging the events of the novel on principles of equity rather than deferring to the certainty and continuity offered by common-law precedent. Occasionally, though, Cable jolts his readers back into his present through the use of either parenthetical asides or direct parallels. He notes, for example, how the pervasive fear of blacks in antebellum New Orleans has not been overcome after the Civil War, asking, "what atrocities are we unconsciously perpetuating North and South now, in the name of mercy or defence . . . ?" (315). Moments like this one suggest not the promise of a progressive movement through time nor its cyclical repetition, but they instead instruct us to adjudicate the present in a manner that resonates with temporally specific legal acts as manifested either by the passage of statutes in the legislature or by the application of equity by the courts.

This temporality, which privileges the synchronic over the diachronic, then also underscores the need to right wrongs locally, as embodied by Frowenfeld's own sensitivity toward and admiration for Creole culture. But this culture and the civil law that remains a part of it did not emerge organically out of the bayous of Louisiana. It is a cultural and legal iteration of a mélange of Francophone and Hispanophone cultures that are themselves embedded within a complex web of rival social, racial, and political affiliations. Bras-Coupé and the *Code Noir* that deprives him of his just liberty both emerge out of an Atlantic world; the French and Spanish legal systems and cultures owe their development to not only their metropoles but also the places they colonized. This amalgam of cultural and juridical uncertainties is partly what gives regional writing and certainly Cable's work its character. Literary narratives bring some measure of coherence to these spaces, but what we receive is not a stable sense of social totality but a provisional map that gestures toward a global and local totality that it can never fully represent nor govern.

LETTERS OF THE LAW:
MAPPING GOVERNABILITY IN U.S. REGIONAL WRITING

What I hope this postscript illustrates is the power of the essays assembled in *Mapping Region in Early American Writing* to rewrite the way we study U.S. regionalism both before and after the Civil War. No doubt we could surely uncover many lines of continuity that I have left unaddressed. But the various ways writers mapped and contested local spaces in the early nineteenth century surely shaped the legal and literary debates transacted after the Civil War. The law regionalizes the United States in ways that both reproduce and challenge federalism and nationalism throughout the long nineteenth century. It sanctions forms of state sovereignty unknown in other nation-states, granting considerable power to local and state judges as interpreters and makers of the law. Many of these states also bear a transatlantic genealogy, borrowing from the common-law tradition of Britain and, in some states, the civil-law tradition of the European continent. These legal traditions remain intertwined with the legacies of European and U.S. imperialism. Their dynamism and ceaseless revision, however, also cast regionalism more as an ongoing process than as a discrete object. And this process and the conflicts among legal traditions and jurisdictions require forms of adjudication, interpretation, and narration.

While by no means exceptional, Louisiana's unruliness remained a fixture of the literature and later films and TV serials about it. It provided a space for Kate Chopin to contemplate the limitations and possibilities of womanhood; it emerged as an imperfect safe haven for African Americans at the conclusion to Pauline Hopkins's *Contending Forces* (1900); it served as an incubator for fascist tyranny in Robert Penn Warren's *All the King's Men* (1947); it animated the multiethnic and fragmentary world of John Kennedy Toole's *Confederacy of Dunces* (1980); and it now figures as a criminally rife and existentially unsettling place in Nic Pizzolatto's *True Detective* (2014). The closest contemporary reincarnation of *The Grandissimes*, though, may very well be David Simon's *Treme* (2010–13). In that TV series, New Orleans's interstitial qualities thwart its post-Katrina recovery, as neither the federal government nor the local authorities appear equipped or willing to rebuild the city effectively. Simon celebrates New Orleans's local traditions and music and travels down its transnational or translocal routes of cultural exchange, but he also suggests that it lies outside the national imagination in ways that prove detrimental to the people who live there. The entire series echoes one of the final sentiments expressed in *The Grandissimes*—that "To-day almost all the savagery that can justly be charged against Louisiana—strange to say—be laid at the door of the *Américain*" (329–30).

NOTES

1. "Region, n.," *OED Online*, October 2013, http://www.oed.com (accessed January 12, 2014).

2. Zagarell, "Region," 199.

3. Philip Joseph and Tom Lutz powerfully attest to regionalism's international character, but this comparative vocabulary cannot ever fully escape the language of nations. Cosmopolitanism imagines ethical relationships among strangers, but it builds on the abstract imaginary of the nation and the formal structure of the state. Approaching locality and region, as this volume of essays has done, requires a translocal or interlocal perspective that can describe phenomena neither necessarily opposed to nor complicit with nationalism and cosmopolitanism.

4. Hsu, *Geography*, 165.

5. Foote, *Regional Fictions*, 4.

6. Giles, *Global Remapping*, 14. See also Elmer, *On Lingering and Being Last*.

7. Deleuze and Guattari, *Anti-Oedipus*, 257, 258.

8. Hardt and Negri, *Empire*, 45.

9. "Provisional, adj. and n.," *OED Online*, June 2014, http://www.oed.com (accessed July 25, 2014).

10. Schulz, Söderbaum, and Öjendal, "Introduction," 5.

11. This postscript expands and extends the work of a previous essay in which I address the notions of regionalization and the translocal. See Funchion, "Reading Less Littorally," 63–66.

12. Eisenman, "Zones of Undecidability," 240.

13. Žižek, *Living in the End Times*, 266.

14. Jewett, *Country of the Pointed Firs*, 15.

15. Ibid., 64.

16. "Provisional, adj. and n."

17. Garland, *Crumbling Idols*, 121.

18. Fetterley and Pryse, *Writing Out of Place*, 1.

19. Here I evoke Jacques Rancière's idea of aesthetics. See Rancière, *Politics of Aesthetics*, 12–30; Rancière, "Politics of Literature," 152–68.

20. Wald, *Constituting Americans*, 30. Other examples of this scholarship include the following: Best, *The Fugitive's Properties*; Crane, *Race, Citizenship, and Law*; Dayan, *Law Is a White Dog*; Nabers, *Victory of Law*; and Brook Thomas, *Civic Myths*.

21. See Foote, *Regional Fictions*, 119–23.

22. While it lies outside the purview of my analysis, the Louisiana Remonstrance of 1804 also played a crucial role in establishing white Creole supremacy in the newly annexed region. For a fascinatingly thorough account of this document and its relevance to U.S. empire building, see Doolen, *Territories of Empire*, 29–31.

23. For a comprehensive survey of the regional legal tradition in the colonies and the early republic, see Konig, "Regionalism in Early American Law."

24. Sally Hadden addresses the fragmented history of slave law and the challenges it posed to the nation's legal system. See Hadden, "Fragmented Laws of Slavery."

25. It should be noted, though, that Jefferson, wishing to distance himself from the Anglophilia displayed by many of his Federalist contemporaries, advocated the introduction of codification modeled on the French legal system throughout the early republic. These codes, however, were still subject to the rulings of judges who adhered to the principles and precedents of common law.

26. Kerr, *Exposition*, 3.

27. Qtd. in Algero, "Value of Precedent in Louisiana," 91.

28. The Supreme Court overturned the *Swift v. Tyson* decision in *Erie Railroad Co. v. Tompkins*, ruling that the federal courts had to apply state common law when hearing cases that concerned state legal issues.

29. See Fabian, *Time and the Other*, 1–35. For an extended account of the uneven development of U.S. literary regionalism, see Bramen, *Uses of Variety*, 115–55.

30. Lloyd Pratt, *Archives of American Time*, 130.

31. Here I should clarify that I use "modernity" as conventionally used in literary and cultural studies. Legal historians associate modernity more closely with legal modernism, which was a mode of legal interpretation that did not arise until the twentieth century. See Luban, *Legal Modernism*, 51–92.

32. Cable, *New Orleans of George Washington Cable*, 42. Subsequent references will be cited parenthetically.

33. For two excellent accounts of race and Creole identity in Cable's work, see Gillman, "The Squatter, the Don, and *The Grandissimes*"; Jones, *Strange Talk*, 115–33.

34. Cable, *The Grandissimes*, 45–46. Subsequent references will be cited parenthetically.

35. See Greeson, "Expropriating the Great South"; Piep, "Liberal Visions of Reconstruction"; Edmund Wilson, *Patriotic Gore*, 563–87.

36. Fernandez, "Edward Livingston, America, and France," 273.

37. Ibid., 275.

38. Cable, "Freedman's Case in Equity," 418.

39. Merryman and Pérez-Perdomo, *Civil Law Tradition*, 49.

40. Cable, "Freedman's Case in Equity," 409.

41. Germana, "Real Change," 103.

42. Parker, *Common Law, History, and Democracy*, 15.

43. LaCroix, "Temporal Imperialism," 1332.

44. Ibid., 1329.

45. Ibid., 1372.

46. Lukács, *Historical Novel*, 61.

47. Lloyd Pratt, *Archives of American Time*, 123.

WORKS CITED

NEWSPAPERS

American Whig Review (August 1848)
Frederick Douglass' Paper (1851, 1855)
The National Era (Washington, D.C.; 1849–50)
The North Star (Rochester, N.Y.; 1849)
Spirit of the Times (1835–61)

PRIMARY AND SECONDARY SOURCES

Adams, John. "Letter to Samuel Osgood, 14 November 1775." In *Letters of Delegates to Congress, 1774–1789.* Ed. Paul H. Smith, Gerard W. Gawalt, Rosemary Fry Plakas, et al. Vol. 1. Washington, D.C.: Library of Congress, 1976–96. 342.

Adelman, Jeremy, and Stephen Aron. "From Borderlands to Borders: Empires, Nation-States, and the Peoples in Between in North American History." *American Historical Review* 104, no. 3 (1999): 814–41.

Alexander, Edward P. *Revolutionary Conservative: James Duane of New York.* New York: AMS Press, 1938.

Algero, Mary Garvey. "The Value of Precedent in Louisiana: A Contemporary Examination." *Loyola Law Review* 51 (2005): 87–100.

Anderson, Benedict. *Imagined Communities: Reflections on the Origin and Spread of Nationalism.* Rev. ed. New York: Verso, 1991.

Anderson, William Wemyss. "The British West Indies." *National Era*, October 25, 1849.

———. *A Description and History of the Island of Jamaica, Comprising an Account of Its Soil, Climate, and Productions, Shewing Its Value and Importance as an Agricultural Country, and a Desirable Place of Residence for Certain Classes of Settlers. Reprinted (it is believed for the first time) from the Great Work, "An Account of America, or the New World," by John Ogilby, Esq., Master of the Revels in Ireland; First Published in the Year 1671. With a Preliminary Chapter and Notes, to Connect the Work with Our Own Times.* New York: Stanford & Swords, 1851.

———. *Jamaica and the Americans.* New York: Stanford & Swords, 1851.

Andrew III, John A. *From Revivals to Removal: Jeremiah Evarts, the Cherokee Nation, and the Search for the Soul of America.* Athens: University of Georgia Press, 2007.

Andrews, William. *Slave Narratives after Slavery.* New York: Oxford University Press, 2011.

Apess, William. *On Our Own Ground: The Complete Writings of William Apess, A Pequot.* Ed. Barry O'Connell. Amherst: University of Massachusetts Press, 1992.

Appadurai, Arjun. *Modernity at Large: Cultural Dimensions of Globalization.* Minneapolis: University of Minnesota Press, 1996.
Appiah, Kwame Anthony. *The Ethics of Identity.* Princeton, N.J.: Princeton University Press, 2005.
Arac, Jonathan. *The Emergence of American Literary Narrative, 1820–1860.* Cambridge, Mass.: Harvard University Press, 2005.
———. "F. O. Matthiessen: Authorizing an American Renaissance." In *The American Renaissance Reconsidered.* Ed. Walter Benn Michaels and Donald Pease. Baltimore: Johns Hopkins University Press, 1985. 90–112.
Armitage, David. "Three Concepts of Atlantic History." In *The British Atlantic World, 1500–1800.* Ed. David Armitage and Michael J. Braddick. New York: Palgrave-Macmillan, 2002. 11–27.
Armstrong, Nancy, and Leonard Tennenhouse. "The Problem of Population and the Form of the American Novel." *American Literary History* 20, no. 4 (2008): 667–85.
Armstrong, Zella. *Who Discovered America? The Amazing Story of Madoc.* Chattanooga, Tenn.: Lookout, 1950.
Aron, Stephen. *American Confluence: The Missouri Frontier from Borderland to Border State.* Bloomington: Indiana University Press, 2006.
Asbury, Francis, and Thomas Coke. *The Doctrines and Discipline of the Methodist Episcopal Church in America.* Philadelphia: Henry Tuckniss, 1798.
Ashcroft, Bill. *Postcolonial Transformation.* New York: Routledge, 2001.
Axtell, James. *The Invasion Within: The Contest of Cultures in Colonial North America.* New York: Oxford University Press, 1985.
Ayers, Edward L., Patricia Nelson Limerick, Stephen Nissenbaum, and Peter S. Onuf. *All Over the Map: Rethinking American Regions.* Baltimore: Johns Hopkins University Press, 1996.
Baepler, Paul Michel, ed. *White Slaves, African Masters: An Anthology of American Barbary Captivity Narratives.* Chicago: University of Chicago Press, 1999.
Baker, Jennifer. *Securing the Commonwealth: Debts, Speculation, and Writing in the Making of Early America.* Baltimore: Johns Hopkins University Press, 2005.
Bakhtin, M. M. *The Dialogic Imagination: Four Essays.* Trans. Caryl Emerson. Austin: University of Texas Press, 1981.
Bancroft, George. *History of the United States from the Discovery of the North American Continent.* 10 vols. New York: Hart, 1854–78.
Bancroft, Hubert Howe. *History of Mexico, 1804–1824.* 4 vols. San Francisco: History Company, 1883.
Barone, Robert W. "Madoc and John Dee: Welsh Myth and Elizabethan Imperialism." *Elizabethan Review* 14 (1999), accessed September 21, 2012. http: www.elizreview.com/Dee.htm.
Barrett, Lindon. "African-American Slave Narratives: Literacy, the Body, Authority." *American Literary History* 7, no. 3 (Autumn 1995): 422–61.
The Bay of San Francisco: The Metropolis of the Pacific Coast and Its Suburban Cities: A History. Vol. 2. San Francisco: Lewis, 1892.
Belich, James. *Replenishing the Earth: The Settler Revolution and the Rise of the Anglo-World, 1783–1939.* New York: Oxford University Press, 2009.

Belknap, Jeremy. *American Biography; or, An Historical Account of Those People Who Have Been Distinguished in America.* 1794–98. 2nd ed. New York: Harper, 1851.

Bell, Michael Davitt. *The Development of American Romance: The Sacrifice of Relation.* Chicago: University of Chicago Press, 1980.

Bercovitch, Sacvan, ed. *The Cambridge History of American Literature, 1590–1820.* New York: Cambridge University Press, 1994.

Bernard, Donald R. *The Life and Times of John Manjiro.* New York: McGraw-Hill, 1992.

Best, Stephen. *The Fugitive's Properties: The Law and the Poetics of Possession.* Chicago: University of Chicago Press, 2004.

Bhabha, Homi K. *The Location of Culture.* London: Routledge, 1994.

———, ed. *Nation and Narration.* London: Routledge, 1990.

Bigelow, John. *Jamaica in 1850: Or, the Effects of Sixteen Years of Freedom on a Slave Colony.* Introduction by Robert J. Scholnick. Urbana: University of Illinois Press, 2006.

Biggs, J. *The History of Don Francisco De Miranda's Attempt to Effect a Revolution in South America.* Boston: E. Oliver, 1811.

Bloch, Ruth. *Visionary Republic: Millennial Themes in American Thought, 1756–1800.* New York: Cambridge University Press, 1985.

Blum, Hester. "American Graves, Pacific Plots." In Brückner and Hsu, *American Literary Geographies,* 149–70.

Bowen, Rev. Benjamin F. *America Discovered by the Welsh in 1170 AD.* London, 1873; reprint, Philadelphia: Lippincott, 1876.

Bown, Stephen R. *The Naturalists: Scientific Travelers in the Golden Age of Natural History.* New York: Barnes & Noble, 2002.

Brack, Gene M. *Mexico Views Manifest Destiny, 1821–1846: An Essay on the Origins of the Mexican War.* Albuquerque: University of New Mexico Press, 1975.

Brackenridge, Henry Marie. *Views of Louisiana, Together With a Journal of a Voyage up the Missouri River in 1811.* Pittsburgh, Pennsylvania: Cramer, 1814.

Bramen, Carrie Tirado. *The Uses of Variety: Modern Americanism and the Quest for National Distinctiveness.* Cambridge, Mass.: Harvard University Press, 2000.

Branch, Michael P. "John Kirk Townsend." In *Early American Nature Writers: A Biographical Encyclopedia.* Ed. Daniel Patterson, Roger Thompson, and Scott Bryson. Westport, Conn.: Greenwood, 2008. 373–80.

———, ed. *Reading the Roots: American Nature Writing before Walden.* Athens: University of Georgia Press, 2004.

Brathwaite, Kamau. *The Development of Creole Society in Jamaica, 1770–1820.* Oxford: Oxford University Press, 1971; Kingston, Jamaica: Ian Randle, 2005.

Breen, T. H. *Tobacco Culture: The Mentality of the Great Tidewater Planters on the Eve of Revolution.* 2nd ed. Princeton, N.J.: Princeton University Press, 2001.

Brenner, Neil, and Stuart Elden. "Henri Lefebvre on State, Space, Territory." *International Political Sociology* 3, no. 4 (2009): 353–77.

Brodhead, Richard H. *Cultures of Letters: Scenes of Reading and Writing in Nineteenth-Century America.* Chicago: University of Chicago Press, 1993.

Brooks, J. T. *Four Months among the Gold-Finders in Alta California: Being the Diary of an Expedition from San Francisco to the Gold Districts.* London: David Bogue, 1849.

Brooks, Timothy. *Vermeer's Hat: The Seventeenth Century and the Dawn of the Global World.* London: Bloomsbury, 2008.
Brown, Charles Brockden. *Edgar Huntly; Or, Memoirs of a Sleepwalker.* 1798. Ed. Norman S. Grabo. New York: Penguin, 1988.
———. "For the Literary Magazine. Southey's *Madoc.*" *Literary Magazine* 4, no. 26 (November 1805): 342–43.
Browne, Stephen Howard. *Jefferson's Call for Nationhood.* College Station: Texas A&M University Press, 2003.
Brückner, Martin. *The Geographic Revolution in Early America: Maps, Literacy, and National Identity.* Chapel Hill: University of North Carolina Press, 2006.
Brückner, Martin, and Hsuan L. Hsu. *American Literary Geographies: Spatial Practice and Cultural Production, 1500–1900.* Newark: University of Delaware Press, 2007.
———. eds. "Introduction," in Brückner and Hsu, 11–28.
Budd, Louis J. "Gentlemen Humorists of the Old South." *Southern Folklore Quarterly* 17 (1955): 232–40.
Buell, Lawrence. *The Environmental Imagination: Thoreau, Nature Writing, and the Formation of American Culture.* Cambridge, Mass.: Belknap Press of Harvard University Press, 1995.
———. *The Future of Environmental Criticism: Environmental Crisis and Literary Imagination.* Malden, Mass.: Blackwell, 2005.
Bullock, Steven C. *Revolutionary Brotherhood: Freemasonry and the Transformation of American Social Order, 1730–1840.* Chapel Hill: University of North Carolina Press, 1996.
Burder, George. *The Welch Indians: Or A Collection of Papers Respecting a People Whose Ancestors Emigrated from Wales to America, In the Year 1170, With Prince Madoc.* London, n.p. 1797.
Burke, Edmund. "Speech on Conciliation with America." In *Burke's Speeches: On American Taxation, On Conciliation with America, and Letter to the Sheriffs of Bristol.* Ed. F. G. Selby. Westport, Conn.: Greenwood, 1956. 64–134.
Burrows, Edwin G. *Forgotten Patriots: The Untold Story of American Prisoners during the Revolutionary War.* New York: Basic Books, 2008.
Burrows, Edwin G., and Mike Wallace. *Gotham: A History of New York City to 1898.* New York: Oxford University Press, 1999.
Burstein, Andrew. *America's Jubilee.* New York: Knopf, 2001.
Busch, Briton Cooper. *"Whaling Will Never Do for Me": The American Whaleman in the Nineteenth Century.* Lexington: University Press of Kentucky, 1994.
Bushnell, Horace. "The Age of Homespun." In *Work and Play*, 39–76. London: Alexander Strahan, 1864.
Butler, Pierce Mason. "Life and Manners in *Arkansas*, By and Ex-Governor of a Cotton-Growing State." In Porter, *The Big Bear*, 154–58.
———. "Western Life and Manners. By a New Arkansas Correspondent of the 'Spirit of the Times.'" *Spirit of the Times* 14, no. 3 (March 16, 1844): 25.
Cable, George Washington. "The Freedman's Case in Equity." *Century Magazine*, January 1885, 409–18.
———. *The Grandissimes: A Story of Creole Life.* 1880. New York: Penguin, 1988.

---. *The New Orleans of George Washington Cable: The 1887 Census Office Report*. Ed. Lawrence N. Powell. Baton Rouge: Louisiana State University Press, 2008.

Cady, Edwin. *The Light of Common Day: Realism in American Fiction*. Bloomington: Indiana University Press, 1971.

Calloway, Colin G., ed. *Our Hearts Fell to the Ground: Plains Indian Views of How the West Was Lost*. Boston: Bedford/St. Martin's, 1996.

Campbell, Neil. *The Cultures of the American New West*. Edinburgh: University of Edinburgh Press, 2000.

---. *Post-Westerns: Cinema, Region, West*. Lincoln: University of Nebraska Press, 2013.

---. *The Rhizomatic West: Representing the American West in a Transnational Global Media Age*. Lincoln: University of Nebraska Press, 2008.

Carlyle, Thomas. *Latter Day Pamphlets: Modern Prisons*. Boston: Phillips & Sampson, 1850. In *The Making of Modern Law*, Gale Digital Collections, 2014.

---. "Occasional Discourse on the Negro Question." *Fraser's Magazine* 40, 1849, 670–79.

---. *Occasional Discourse on the Nigger Question*. London: Thomas Bosworth, 1853.

Carney, Judith. *Black Rice: The African Origins of Rice Cultivation in the Americas*. Cambridge, Mass.: Harvard University Press, 2001.

Carver, Jonathan. *Travels through the Interior Parts of North America in the Years 1766, 1767, and 1768*. 3rd ed. London, 1781.

Cass, Lewis. "Documents and Proceedings Relating to the Emigration, Preservation, and Improvement of the Aborigines of America." *North American Review*, January 1830, 62–120.

Catlin, George. *Letters and Notes on the Manners, Customs, and Condition of the North American Indians*. Philadelphia: Lippincott, 1844.

Cayton, Andrew R. L., and Susan E. Gray, eds. *The American Midwest: Essays on Regional History*. Bloomington: Indiana University Press, 2001.

Chaplin, Joyce E. *An Anxious Pursuit: Agricultural Innovation and Modernity in the Lower South, 1730–1815*. Chapel Hill: University of North Carolina Press, 1993.

Chipman, Donald E. *Spanish Texas, 1519–1821*. Austin: University of Texas Press, 1992.

Chopra, Ruma. *Unnatural Rebellion: Loyalists in New York City during the Revolution*. Charlottesville: University of Virginia Press, 2011.

Clifford, James. *Routes: Travel and Translation in the Late Twentieth Century*. Cambridge, Mass.: Harvard University Press, 1997.

Comer, Krista. "Everyday Regionalisms in Contemporary Critical Practice." In Kollin, 30–58.

---. "Exceptionalism, Other Wests, Critical Regionalism." *American Literary History* 23, no. 1 (2011): 159–73.

---. *Landscapes of the New West: Gender and Geography in Contemporary Women's Writing*. Chapel Hill: University of North Carolina Press, 1999.

---. *Surfer Girls in the New World Order*. Durham, N.C.: Duke University Press, 2010.

Cooke, Ebenezer. *Sotweed Redivivus; or, the Planter's Looking Glass*. Annapolis, Md.: William Parks, 1730.

Coombes, Annie E., ed. *Rethinking Settler Colonialism: History and Memory in Australia, Canada, Aotearoa New Zealand, and South Africa*. Manchester, U.K.: Manchester University Press, 2012.

Cosgrove, Denis. *Mappings*. London: Reaktion, 1999.
Covici Jr., Pascal. "Mark Twain and the Humor of the Old Southwest." In *The Frontier Humorists: Critical Views*. Ed. M. Thomas Inge. New Haven, Conn.: Archon, 1975. 233–58.
Cox, Isaac Joslin. *The Early Exploration of Louisiana*. 2 vols. University of Cincinnati Press, 1906.
———. "The Louisiana-Texas Frontier, Part II." *Southwestern Historical Quarterly* 17, no. 1 (1913): 1–42.
Cox, James M. "Humor of the Old Southwest." In *The Comic Imagination in American Literature*. Ed. Louis D. Rubin Jr. New Brunswick, N.J.: Rutgers University Press, 1973. 101–12.
Craig, David Marcellus. *Robert Southey and Romantic Apostasy: Political Argument in Britain, 1780–1840*. London: Royal Historical Society, 2007.
Crane, Gregg D. *Race, Citizenship, and Law in American Literature*. New York: Cambridge University Press, 2002.
Creighton, Margaret S. *Rites and Passages: The Experience of American Whaling, 1830–1870*. New York: Cambridge University Press, 1995.
Crèvecoeur, J. Hector St. John. *Letters from an American Farmer and Sketches of Eighteenth-Century America*. Ed. Albert E. Stone. New York: Penguin, 1981.
Cronon, William. *Changes in the Land: Indians, Colonists, and the Ecology of New England*. New York: Hill & Wang, 1983.
———. "The Trouble with Wilderness; or, Getting Back to the Wrong Nature." In *Uncommon Ground: Rethinking the Human Place in Nature*. New York: Norton, 1996.
Cuffe Jr., Paul. *Narrative of the Life and Adventures of Paul Cuffe*. Vernon, N.Y., 1839.
Cushman, Robert. "Reasons and Considerations Touching the Lawfulness of Removing Out of England into the Parts of America." In *Mourt's Relation: A Journal of the Pilgrims at Plymouth*. 1626. Ed. Dwight B. Heath. Bedford, Mass.: Applewood Books, 1963. 88–99.
Dain, Bruce. *A Hideous Monster of the Mind: American Race Theory in the Early Republic*. Cambridge, Mass.: Harvard University Press, 2003.
Dainotto, Roberto M. *Place in Literature: Regions, Cultures, Communities*. Ithaca, N.Y.: Cornell University Press, 2000.
Dana, Richard Henry. *Two Years before the Mast*. 1840. New York: Penguin, 1964.
Davidson, Cathy N. *Revolution and the Word: The Rise of the Novel in America*. New York: Oxford University Press, 1986.
Dayan, Colin. *The Law Is a White Dog: How Legal Rituals Make and Unmake Persons*. Princeton, N.J.: Princeton University Press, 2013.
Deacon, Richard. *Madoc and the Discovery of America: Some New Light on an Old Controversy*. London: Muller, 1966.
de Graaf, Lawrence Brooks, Kevin Mulroy, and Quintard Taylor, eds. *Seeking El Dorado: African Americans in California*. Seattle: Autry Museum of Western Heritage, Univ. of Seattle Press, 2001.
Delano, Reuben. *Wanderings and Adventures of Reuben Delano, Being a Narrative of Twelve Years Life in a Whaleship!* Worcester, Mass., 1846.
Deleuze, Gilles, and Felix Guattari. *A Thousand Plateaus: Capitalism and Schizophrenia*. Tranlated by Brian Massumi. Minneapolis: University of Minnesota Press, 1987.

———. *Anti-Oedipus: Capitalism and Schizophrenia*. Trans. Robert Hurley, Mark Seem, and Helen R. Lane. Minneapolis: University of Minnesota Press, 1983.
Deloria, Philip J. *Playing Indian*. New Haven, Conn.: Yale University Press, 1998.
Deloria Jr., Vine. *Custer Died for Your Sins*. New York: Macmillan, 1969.
Denson, Andrew. *Demanding the Cherokee Nation: Indian Autonomy and American Culture, 1830–1900*. Lincoln: University of Nebraska Press, 2004.
De Voto, Bernard. *Mark Twain's America*. 1932. Lincoln: University of Nebraska Press, 1997.
Dolin, Eric Jay. *Leviathan: The History of Whaling in America*. New York: Norton, 2007.
Doolen, Andy. *Territories of Empire: U.S. Writing from the Louisiana Purchase to Mexican Independence*. New York: Oxford University Press, 2014.
Dorman, Robert L. *Revolt of the Provinces: The Regionalist Movement in America, 1920–1945*. Chapel Hill: University of North Carolina Press, 1993.
Douglass, Frederick. *My Bondage and My Freedom*. Ed. William L. Andrews. Urbana: University of Illinois Press, 1987.
———. *Narrative of the Life of Frederick Douglass, An American Slave, Written by Himself*. In *The Oxford Frederick Douglass Reader*. Ed. William L. Andrews. New York: Oxford University Press, 1996.
Drake, James D. *The Nation's Nature: How Continental Presumptions Gave Rise to the United States*. Charlottesville: University of Virginia Press, 2011.
Drayton, John. *A View of South-Carolina, as Respects Her National and Civil Concerns*. Charleston: W. P. Young, 1802.
Duck, Leigh Anne. *The Nation's Region: Southern Modernism, Segregation, and U.S. Nationalism*. Athens: University of Georgia Press, 2006.
Duckett, Alvin L. *John Forsyth: Political Tactician*. Athens: University of Georgia Press, 1962.
Dunn, Richard S. "The English Sugar Islands and the Founding of South Carolina." In *Shaping Southern Society: The Colonial Experience*. Ed. T. H. Breen. New York: Oxford University Press, 1976. 48–58.
———. *Sugar and Slaves: The Rise of the Planter Class in the West Indies, 1624–1713*. Chapel Hill: University of North Carolina Press, 1972.
DuVal, Kathleen. *The Native Ground: Indians and Colonists in the Heart of the Continent*. Philadelphia: University of Pennsylvania Press, 2006.
———. "Restructuring American Studies: Transnational Paradoxes, Comparative Perspectives." *Journal of American Studies* 28, no. 3 (1994): 335–58.
———. "Transnationalism and Classic American Literature." *PMLA* 118, no. 1 (2003): 62–77.
Eaves, Lucille. *A History of California Labor Legislation, with an Introductory Sketch of the San Francisco Labor Movement*. Berkeley: University Press, 1910.
Eddy, John, and Deryck Schreuder, eds. *The Rise of Colonial Nationalism: Australia, New Zealand, Canada, and South Africa First Assert Their Nationalities, 1880–1914*. Sydney: Allen & Unwin, 1988.
Edwards, Bryan. *The History, Civil and Commercial, of the British Colonies in the West Indies*. 5 vols. London: John Stockdale, 1793.
Egan, James. "The 'Long'd-for Aera' of an 'Other Race': Climate, Identity, and James Grainger's *The Sugar Cane*." *Early American Literature* 38, no. 2 (2003): 189–212.

Eisenman, Peter. "Zones of Undecidability: The Interstitial Figure." In *Anybody*. Ed. Cynthia Davidson. Cambridge, Mass.: MIT Press, 1997. 240–45.
Eliot, T. S. *Notes toward the Definition of Culture*. New York: Harcourt, Brace, 1949.
Elliott, Emory. "New England Puritan Literature." In Bercovitch, 171–306.
Elmer, Jonathan. *On Lingering and Being Last: Race and Sovereignty in the New World*. New York: Fordham University Press, 2008.
Emerson, Ralph Waldo. "Self-Reliance." In *Emerson: Essays and Lectures*. Ed. Joel Porte. New York: Library of America, 1983.
Eperjesi, John R. *The Imperialist Imaginary: Visions of Asia and the Pacific in American Culture*. Hanover, N.H.: Dartmouth University Press, 2005.
Evelev, John. *Tolerable Entertainment: Herman Melville and Professionalism in Antebellum New York*. Amherst: University of Massachusetts Press, 2006.
Fabian, Johannes. *Time and the Other: How Anthropology Makes Its Object*. 2nd ed. New York: Columbia University Press, 2003.
Faherty, Duncan. *Remodeling the Nation: The Architecture of American Identity, 1776–1858*. Hanover, N.H.: University of New England Press, 2007.
Fernandez, Mark. "Edward Livingston, America, and France." In *Empires of the Imagination: Transatlantic Histories of the Louisiana Purchase*. Ed. Peter J. Kastor and François Weil. Charlottesville: University of Virginia Press, 2009. 268–98.
Fetterley, Judith, and Marjorie Pryse. *Writing Out of Place: Regional Women's Writing and American Literary Culture*. Urbana: University of Illinois Press, 2003.
Filson, John. *The Discovery, Settlement, and Present State of Kentucky*. Wilmington, Del., 1784.
Finley, James B. *Life among the Indians; or, Personal Reminiscences and Historical Incidents Illustrative of Indian Life and Character*. Cincinnati: R. P. Thompson, 1857.
Fisher, James A. "The Struggle for Negro Testimony in California, 1851–1863." *Southern California Quarterly* 51, no. 4 (December 1969): 314–41.
Fisher, Philip. *Still the New World: American Literature in a Culture of Creative Destruction*. Cambridge, Mass.: Harvard University Press, 1999.
Fliegelman, Jay. *Prodigals and Pilgrims: The American Revolution against Patriarchal Authority*. New York: Cambridge University Press, 1982.
Flores, Dan L. *Jefferson and Southwestern Exploration: The Freeman and Custis Accounts of the Red River Expedition of 1806*. Norman: University of Oklahoma Press, 1984.
———. *Journal of an Indian Trader*. College Station, Tex.: Texas A&M University Press, 2006.
Foote, Stephanie. *Regional Fictions: Culture and Identity in Nineteenth-Century American Literature*. Madison: University of Wisconsin Press, 2001.
Forsyth, John. *The Speech of Mr. Forsyth of Georgia, on the Bill Providing for the Removal of the Indians*. Washington, D.C.: D. Green, 1830.
Franklin, Benjamin. An Edict by the King of Prussia. 1773. In *Franklin: The Autobiography and Other Writings on Politics, Economics, and Virtue*. Ed. Alan Houston. New York: Cambridge University Press, 2004. 302–6.
Franklin, Catherine. "The Welsh American Dream: Iolo Morganwg, Robert Southey, and the Madoc Legend." In *English Romanticism and the Celtic World*. Ed. Gerard Cauthers and Allen Rawes. New York: Cambridge University Press, 2003. 69–84.

Franklin, Wayne. *Discoverers, Explorers, Settlers: The Diligent Writers of Early America.* Chicago: University of Chicago Press, 1989.

Freehling, William W. *The Reintegration of American History: Slavery and the Civil War.* New York: Oxford University Press, 1995.

Fresonke, Kris. *West of Emerson: The Design of Manifest Destiny.* Berkeley: University of California Press, 2003.

Funchion, John. "Reading Less Littorally: Kentucky and the Translocal Imagination in the Atlantic World." *Early American Literature* 48, no. 1 (2013): 61–91.

Furtwangler, Albert. *Acts of Discovery: Visions of America in the Lewis and Clark Journals.* Urbana: University of Illinois Press, 1993.

Gale, Steven H., ed. *Encyclopedia of American Humorists.* New York: Garland, 1988.

Gardner, Eric. "Early African American Print Culture and the American West." In *Early African American Print Culture.* Ed. Lara Langer Cohen and Jordan Alexander Stein. Philadelphia: University of Pennsylvania Press, 2012. 75–92.

———. *Unexpected Places: Relocating Nineteenth-Century African American Literature.* Jackson: University Press of Mississippi, 2009.

Gardner, Jared. *The Rise and Fall of Early American Magazine Culture.* Urbana: University of Illinois Press, 2012.

Garland, Hamlin. *Crumbling Idols: Twelve Essays on Art Dealing Chiefly with Literature, Painting and the Drama.* 1894; Cambridge, Mass.: Harvard University Press, 1960.

Gaul, Theresa Strouth. "Editing as Indian Performance: Elias Boudinot, Poetry, and the *Cherokee Phoenix.*" In *Native Acts: Indian Performance, 1603–1832.* Ed. Joshua David Bellin and Laura L. Mielke. Lincoln: University of Nebraska Press, 2011. 281–305.

———. *To Marry an Indian: The Marriage of Harriett Gold and Elias Boudinot in Letters, 1823–1839.* Chapel Hill: University of North Carolina Press, 2005.

Germana, Michael. "Real Change: George Washington Cable's *The Grandissimes* and the Crime of '73." *Arizona Quarterly* 61, no. 3 (2005): 75–108.

Giles, Paul. *The Global Remapping of American Literature.* Princeton, N.J.: Princeton University Press, 2011.

———. "Reconstructing American Studies: Transnational Paradoxes, Comparative Perspectives." *Journal of American Studies* 28, no. 3 (1994): 335–58.

———. "Transnationalism and Classic American Literature." *PMLA* 118, no. 1 (2003): 66–77.

Gillman, Susan. "The Squatter, the Don, and *The Grandissimes* in Our America." In *Mixing Race, Mixing Culture: Inter-American Literary Dialogues.* Ed. Monika Kaup and Debra J. Rosenthal. Austin: University of Texas Press, 2002. 140–59.

Gilmore, John. *The Poetics of Empire: A Study of James Grainger's The Sugar Cane.* London: Athlone, 2000.

Gilroy, Paul. *The Black Atlantic: Modernity and Double Consciousness.* Cambridge, Mass.: Harvard University Press, 1993.

Gleijeses, Peter. "The Limits of Sympathy: The United States and the Independence of Spanish America." *Journal of Latin American Studies* 24, no. 3 (1992): 481–505.

Goebel Jr., Julius. *History of the Supreme Court of the United States: Antecedents and Beginnings to 1801.* New York: Macmillan, 1971.

Goetzmann, William H. *Exploration and Empire: The Explorer and the Scientist in the Winning of the American West.* New York: History Book Club, 2006.

Goldman, Anne. *Continental Divides: Revisioning American Literature.* New York: Palgrave, 2000.

Gonzalez-Day, Ken. *Lynching in the West: 1850–1935.* Durham, N.C.: Duke University Press, 2006.

Goudie, Sean X. *Creole America: The West Indies and the Formation of Literature and Culture in the New Republic.* Philadelphia: University of Pennsylvania Press, 2006.

Gould, Elija H. "Entangled Atlantic Histories: A Response from the Anglo American Periphery." *American Historical Review* 112, no. 5 (2007): 1415–22.

Gould, Philip. *Barbaric Traffic: Commerce and Anti-Slavery in the Eighteenth-Century Atlantic World.* New York: Cambridge University Press, 2003.

———. "Representative Men: Jeremy Belknap's *American Biography* and the Political Culture of the Early Republic." *Auto/biography* 9/10 (1994): 83–97.

Grainger, James. *The Sugar Cane.* In *Caribbeana: An Anthology of the West Indies, 1657–1777.* Ed. Thomas Krise. Chicago: University of Chicago Press, 1999. 166–260.

Grant, Susan-Mary. *North over South: Northern Nationalism and American Identity in the Antebellum Era.* Lawrence: University Press of Kansas, 2000.

Greenfield, Bruce Robert. *Narrating Discovery: The Romantic Explorer in American Literature, 1790–1855.* New York: Columbia University Press, 1992.

Greeson, Jennifer Rae. "Expropriating the Great South and Exporting 'Local Color': Global and Hemispheric Imaginaries of the First Reconstruction." In *Hemispheric American Studies.* Ed. Caroline F. Levander and Robert S. Levine. New Brunswick, N.J.: Rutgers University Press, 2008. 116–39.

———. *Our South: Geographic Fantasy and the Rise of a National Literature.* Cambridge, Mass.: Harvard University Press, 2010.

Grewal, Inderpal. *Transnational America: Feminism, Diasporas, Neoliberalisms.* Durham, N.C.: Duke University Press, 2005.

Grey, Susan E. *The Yankee West: Community Life on the Michigan Frontier.* Chapel Hill: University of North Carolina Press, 1996.

Griffith, John T. *Reverend Morgan John Rhys: The Welsh Baptist Hero of Civil and Religious Liberty of the 18th Century.* Lansford, Penn., n.p., 1899.

Gross, Robert A. "Reading for an Extensive Republic." In Gross and Kelley, 516–44.

Gross, Robert A., and Mary Kelley, eds. *A History of the Book in America. Vol. 2: An Extensive Republic: Print, Culture, and Society in the New Nation, 1790–1840.* Chapel Hill: University of North Carolina Press, 2010.

Grossberg, Michael, and Christopher Tomlins, eds. *The Cambridge History of Law in America.* New York: Cambridge University Press, 2008.

Grover, Kathryn. *The Fugitive's Gibraltar: Escaping Slaves and Abolitionism in New Bedford, Massachusetts.* Amherst: University of Massachusetts Press, 2001.

Gruenwald, Kim M. *River of Enterprise: The Commercial Origins of Regional Identity in the Ohio Valley, 1790–1850.* Bloomington: Indiana University Press, 2002.

Gruesz, Kirsten Silva. *Ambassadors of Culture: The Transamerican Origins of Latino Writing.* Princeton, N.J.: Princeton University Press, 2002.

Gura, Philip. "The Study of Colonial American Literature, 1966–1987." *William and Mary Quarterly* 45, no. 2 (1988): 310.
Gurney, Joseph John. *A Winter in the West Indies, Described in Familiar Letters to Henry Clay, of Kentucky*. London: John Murray, 1840.
Gustafson, Sandra M. "Histories of Democracy and Empire." *American Quarterly* 59, no. 11 (2007): 107–33.
Gutierrez, David G. "Significant to Whom? Mexican Americans and the History of the American West." In *A New Significance: Re-envisioning the History of the American West*. Ed. Clyde A. Milner and Allan G. Bogue. New York: Oxford University Press, 1996. 519–39.
Hadden, Sally E. "The Fragmented Laws of Slavery in the Colonial and Revolutionary Eras." In Grossberg and Tomlins, 253–87.
Hakluyt, Richard. *The Voyages, Navigation, Traffiques, and Discoveries of the English Nation*. London, n.p., 1582, 1589.
Haley, James L. *Passionate Nation: The Epic History of Texas*. New York: Free Press, 2006.
[Haliburton, Thomas Chandler, ed.]. *Traits of American Humor, by Native Authors*. 3 vols. London: Colburn, 1852.
Hallock, Thomas. *From the Fallen Tree: Frontier Narratives, Environmental Politics, and the Roots of the National Pastoral, 1749–1826*. Chapel Hill: University of North Carolina Press, 2003.
Hämäläinen, Pekka. *The Comanche Empire*. New Haven, Conn.: Yale University Press, 2008.
Hamilton, Alexander. *The Law Practice of Alexander Hamilton*. Ed. Julius Goebel Jr. New York: Columbia University Press, 1964.
Hancock, David. *Citizens of the World: London Merchants and the Integration of the Atlantic Community, 1735–1785*. New York: Cambridge University Press, 1997.
Hardt, Michael, and Antonio Negri. *Empire*. Cambridge, Mass.: Harvard University Press, 2000.
Harvey, David. *Cosmopolitanism and the Geographies of Freedom*. New York: Columbia University Press, 2009.
Hatch, Nathan O. *The Democratization of American Christianity*. New Haven, Conn.: Yale University Press, 1989.
Heflin, Wilson L. *Herman Melville's Whaling Years*. Ed. Mary K. Bercaw Edwards and Thomas Farel Heffernan. Nashville: Vanderbilt University Press, 2004.
Heise, Ursula K. *Sense of Place and Sense of Planet: The Environmental Imagination of the Global*. New York: Oxford University Press, 2008.
Herr, Cheryl Temple. *Critical Regionalism and Cultural Studies: From Ireland to the American Midwest*. Gainesville: University of Florida Press, 1996.
Hildreth, Richard. *The "Ruin" of Jamaica*. New York: American Anti-Slavery Society, 1855.
Hobsbawm, Eric, and Terence Ranger, eds. *The Invention of Tradition*. New York: University of Cambridge Press, 1983.
Holdredge, Helen. *Mammy Pleasant*. New York: Putnam's Sons, 1953.
Holley, Mary Austin. *Texas. Observations, Historical, Geographical, and Descriptive, in a Series of Letters Written during a Visit to Austin's Colony in 1831*. Baltimore: Armstrong & Plaskitt, 1833.

Holt, Thomas C. *The Problem of Freedom: Race, Labor, and Politics in Jamaica and Britain, 1832–1938*. Baltimore: Johns Hopkins University Press, 1991.

Houck, L. *The Spanish Régime in Missouri: A Collection of Papers and Documents Relating to Upper Louisiana*. Vol. 2. Chicago: R. R. Donnelley, 1909.

Howe, Daniel Walker. *Making the American Self: Jonathan Edwards to Abraham Lincoln*. Cambridge, Mass.: Harvard University Press, 1997.

———. *What God Hath Wrought: The Transformation of America, 1815–1848*. New York: Oxford University Press, 2007.

Hsu, Hsuan L. "Chronotopes of the Asian American West." In Witschi, 145–60.

———. *Geography and the Production of Space in Nineteenth-Century American Literature*. New York: Cambridge University Press, 2010.

———. "Literature and Regional Production." *American Literary History* 17, no. 1 (2005): 36–69.

Hudson, Angela Pulley. "'Forked Justice': Elias Boudinot, the U.S. Constitution, and Cherokee Removal." In *American Indian Rhetorics of Survivance: Word Medicine, Word Magic*. Ed. Ernest Stromberg. Pittsburgh: University of Pittsburgh Press, 2006. 50–65.

Hudson, Lynn M. *The Making of "Mammy Pleasant": A Black Entrepreneur in Nineteenth-Century San Francisco*. Chicago: University of Illinois Press, 2003.

Hulsebosch, Daniel J. *Constituting Empire: New York and the Transformation of Constitutionalism in the Atlantic World, 1664–1830*. Chapel Hill: University of North Carolina Press, 2008.

Hutcheon, Linda. *Irony's Edge: The Theory and Politics of Irony*. New York: Routledge, 1994.

Imlay, Gilbert. *A Topographical Description of the Western Territory of North America*. New York: Campbell, 1793.

Inge, Thomas, and Edward J. Piacentino. *The Humor of the Old South*. Lexington: University Press of Kentucky, 2001.

Irlam, Shaun. "'Wish You Were Here': Exporting England in James Grainger's *The Sugar Cane*." *English Literary History* 68, no. 2 (2001): 377–96.

Irving, Washington. *The History of New York from the Beginning of Time to the End of the Dutch Dynasty*. 1809. Rpt. in *Washington Irving: Tales and Sketches*. Ed. James W. Tuttleton. New York: Library of America, 1983. 363–729.

Irwin, Benjamin. *Clothed in Robes of Sovereignty: The Continental Congress and the People Out of Doors*. New York: Oxford University Press, 2011.

Jackson, Donald Dean. *Thomas Jefferson and the Stoney Mountains: Exploring the West from Monticello*. Urbana: University of Illinois Press, 1981.

Jackson, Jack. *Indian Agent: Peter Ellis Bean in Mexican Texas*. College Station: Texas A&M University Press, 2005.

Jackson, Robert. *Seeking the Region in American Literature and Culture: Modernity, Dissidence, Innovation*. Baton Rouge: Louisiana State University Press, 2005.

Jacobs, Harriet. *Incidents in the Life of a Slave Girl*. New York: Barnes & Noble, 2005.

Jameson, Fredric. *Postmodernism, or, the Cultural Logic of Late Capitalism*. Durham, N.C.: Duke University Press, 1991.

Janin, Hunt. *Claiming the American Wilderness: International Rivalry in the Trans-Mississippi West, 1528–1803*. Jefferson, N.C.: McFarland, 2006.

Jasanoff, Maya. *Liberty's Exiles: American Loyalists in the Revolutionary World.* New York: Vintage, 2012.
Jay, Gregory. *American Literature and the Culture Wars.* Ithaca, N.Y.: Cornell University Press, 1997.
Jebb, Richard. *Studies in Colonial Nationalism.* London: Arnold, 1905.
Jefferson, Thomas. *Notes on the State of Virginia.* In *The Portable Thomas Jefferson.* Ed. Merrill D. Peterson. New York: Penguin, 1985. 34–213.
———. *The Papers of Thomas Jefferson.* Vol. 1. Ed. Julian P. Boyd et al. Princeton, N.J.: Princeton University Press, 1950.
———. *Writings.* Ed. Merrill D. Peterson. New York: Library of America, 1984.
Jehlen, Myra. "The Literature of Colonization." In Bercovitch, 13–167.
Jewett, Sarah Orne. *The Country of the Pointed Firs and Other Stories.* 1896; New York: Norton, 1991.
Jones, Gavin. *Strange Talk: The Politics of Dialect Literature in Gilded Age America.* Berkeley: University of California Press, 1999.
Joseph, Philip. *American Literary Regionalism in a Global Age.* Baton Rouge: Louisiana State University Press, 2007.
Jun, Helen. "Black Orientalism: Nineteenth-Century Narratives of Race and U.S. Citizenship." *American Quarterly* 58, no. 4 (2006): 1047–66.
Justice, Daniel. *Our Fire Survives the Storm: A Cherokee Literary History.* Minneapolis: University of Minnesota Press, 2006.
Justus, James H. *Fetching the Old Southwest: Humorous Writing from Longstreet to Twain.* Columbia: University of Missouri Press, 2004.
Kaplan, Amy. *The Anarchy of Empire in the Making of U.S. Culture.* Cambridge, Mass.: Harvard University Press, 2002.
———. "Nation, Region, and Empire." In *The Columbia History of the American Novel.* Ed. Emory Elliott. New York: Columbia University Press, 1991. 240–66.
Karttunen, Frances Ruley. *The Other Islanders: People Who Pulled Nantucket's Oars.* New Bedford, Mass.: Spinner, 2005.
Kastor, Peter J. "'What Are the Advantages of the Acquisition?': Inventing Expansion in the Early American Republic." *American Quarterly* 60, no. 4 (2008): 1003–35.
Katchun, Mitch. *Festivals of Freedom: Memory and Meaning in African American Emancipation Celebrations, 1809–1915.* Amherst: University of Massachusetts Press, 2006.
Katz, Cindi. "Vagabond Capitalism and the Necessity of Social Reproduction." *Antipode* 33, no. 4 (2001): 709–28.
Keller, William F. *The Nation's Advocate: Henry Marie Brackenridge and Young America.* Pittsburgh: University of Pittsburgh Press, 1956.
Kelley, Wyn. *Melville's City: Literary and Urban Form in Nineteenth-Century New York.* New York: Cambridge University Press, 1996.
Kenny, Gale F. *Contentious Liberties: American Abolitionists in Post-Emancipation Jamaica, 1834–1866.* Athens: University of Georgia Press, 2011.
———. "Manliness and Manifest Racial Destiny: Jamaica and African American Emigration in the 1850s." *Journal of the Civil War Era* 2, no. 2 (June 2012): 151–78.

Kerkering, John D. *The Poetics of National and Racial Identity in Nineteenth-Century American Literature.* New York: Cambridge University Press, 2003.

Kerr, Lewis A. *An Exposition of the Criminal Laws of the Territory of Orleans.* New Orleans: Bradford, 1806.

Kerr-Ritchie, J. R. *The Rites of August First: Emancipation Day in the Black Atlantic World.* Baton Rouge: Louisiana State University Press, 2007.

Kip, Leonard. *California Sketches with Recollections of the Gold Mines.* Albany, N.Y.: Arastus H. Pease, 1850.

———. *The Volcano Diggings: A Tale of the California Bar.* New York: J. S. Redfield, 1851.

Klein, Milton, Richard D. Brown, and John B. Hench, eds. *The Republican Synthesis Revisited: Essays in Honor of George Athan Billias.* Worcester, Mass.: American Antiquarian Society Press, 1992.

Knadler, Stephen. *Remapping Citizenship and the Nation in African American Literature.* New York: Routledge, 2010.

Kollin, Susan, ed. *Postwestern Cultures: Literature, Theory, Space.* Lincoln: University of Nebraska Press, 2007.

Kolodny, Annette. *In Search of First Contact: The Vikings of Vinland, the Peoples of the Dawnland, and the Anglo-American Anxiety of Discovery.* Durham, N.C.: Duke University Press, 2012.

Konig, David Thomas. "Regionalism in Early American Law." In Grossberg and Tomlins, 144–77.

Konkle, Maureen. *Writing Indian Nations: Native Intellectuals and the Politics of Historiography, 1827–1863.* Chapel Hill: University of North Carolina Press, 2004.

Kovarsky, Joel. *The True Geography of Our Country: Jefferson's Cartographic Vision.* Charlottesville: University Press of Virginia, 2014.

Kramer, Lloyd. *Nationalism in Europe and America: Politics, Cultures, and Identities since 1775.* Chapel Hill: University of North Carolina Press, 2011.

Krupat, Arnold. *Ethnocriticism: Ethnography, History, Literature.* Berkeley: University of California Press, 1992.

LaCroix, Alison L. "Temporal Imperialism." *University of Pennsylvania Law Review* 158, no. 5 (2010): 1329–73.

A Lady of the State of New-York. *The Fortunate Discovery; or, The History of Henry Villars.* New York: Samuel Campbell, 1798.

———. *Moreland Vale; or, The Fair Fugitive.* New York: Samuel Campbell, 1801.

Lapp, Rudolph. *Blacks in Gold Rush California.* New Haven, Conn.: Yale University Press, 1977.

Larson, John Lauritz. "Pigs in Space; or, What Shapes America's Regional Cultures?" In Cayton and Grey, 69–77.

Lawson-Peebles, Robert. *Landscape and Written Expression in Revolutionary America.* New York: Cambridge University Press, 1988.

Lay, Bennett. *The Lives of Ellis P. Bean.* Austin: University of Texas Press, 1960.

Leary, John Patrick. "Detroitism." *Guernica*, January 15, 2011.

LeMenager, Stephanie. *Manifest and Other Destinies: Territorial Fictions of the Nineteenth-Century United States.* Lincoln: University of Nebraska Press, 2004.

———. "Trading Stories: Washington Irving and the Global West." *American Literary History* 15, no. 4 (2003): 683–708.

Levander, Caroline, and Robert S. Levine. "Hemispheric Literary History." *American Literary History* 18, no. 3 (2006): 397–405.

Levine, Robert S., and Samuel Otter. Introduction to *Frederick Douglass and Herman Melville: Essays in Relation*. Ed. Robert S. Levine and Samuel Otter. Chapel Hill: University of North Carolina Press, 2008. 1–16.

Lewis, James E. *The American Union and the Problem of Neighborhood: The United States and the Collapse of the Spanish Empire, 1783–1829*. Chapel Hill: University of North Carolina Press, 1998.

Lewis, Meriwether, and William Clark. *The Journals of Lewis and Clark*. Ed. Frank Bergon. 3rd ed. New York: Penguin, 2003.

Lewis, Nathaniel. *Unsettling the Literary West: Authenticity and Authorship*. Lincoln: University of Nebraska Press, 2003.

Limerick, Patricia Nelson. *The Legacy of Conquest: The Unbroken Past of the American West*. New York: Norton, 1987.

Linklater, Andro. *Measuring America: How an Untamed Wilderness Shaped the United States and Fulfilled the Promise of Democracy*. New York: Walker, 2002.

Littlefield, Daniel F. "Thomas Bangs Thorpe and the Passing of the Southwestern Wilderness." *Southern Literary Journal* 1, no. 1 (Spring 1979): 56–65.

Litwack, Leon. *North of Slavery: The Negro in the Free States*. Chicago: University of Chicago Press, 1965.

Long, Edward. *The History of Jamaica; or, General Survey of the Antient and Modern State of That Island*. London: Lowndes, 1774.

Loomis, Noel M. "Philip Nolan's Entry into Texas in 1800." In *The Spanish in the Mississippi Valley, 1762–1804*. Ed. John Francis McDermott. Urbana: University of Illinois Press, 1974. 120–32.

Loomis, Noel M., and Abraham P. Nasatir. *Pedro Vial and the Roads to Santa Fe*. Norman: University of Oklahoma Press, 1967.

Loshe, Lillie Deming. *The Early American Novel*. New York: Columbia University Press, 1907.

Loughran, Trish. *The Republic in Print: Print Culture in the Age of U.S. Nation Building, 1770–1870*. New York: Columbia University Press, 2007.

Luban, David. *Legal Modernism*. Ann Arbor: University of Michigan Press, 1994.

Lukács, Georg. *The Historical Novel*. Trans. Hannah and Stanley Mitchell. Lincoln: University of Nebraska Press, 1983.

Lutz, Tom. *Cosmopolitan Vistas: American Regionalism and Literary Value*. Ithaca, N.Y.: Cornell University Press, 2004.

Lynn, Kenneth S. *Mark Twain and Southwestern Humor*. Boston: Little, Brown, 1959.

Lyon, Thomas J. *This Incomparable Land: A Guide to American Nature Writing*. Minneapolis: Milkweed Editions, 2001.

Lytle, Thomas G. *Harpoons and Other Whalecraft*. New Bedford, Mass.: Old Dartmouth Historical Society, 1984.

Macy, Obed. *The History of Nantucket*. Boston, 1835.

Magness, Phillip W., and Sebastian N. Page. *Colonization after Emancipation: Lincoln and the Movement for Black Resettlement*. Columbia: University of Missouri Press, 2011.

Malone, Dumas. *Jefferson the President: Second Term, 1805–1809*. Boston: Little, Brown, 1974.

Mancall, Peter C. *Envisioning America: English Plans for the Colonization of North America, 1580–1640*. New York: Bedford, 1995.

———. *Hakluyt's Promise: An Elizabethan's Obsession for an English America*. New Haven, Conn.: Yale University Press, 2007.

Manjiro, John. *Drifting toward the Southeast*. Trans. Junya Nagakuni and Junji Kitadai. New Bedford, Mass.: Spinner, 2003.

Marksman, Peter. "The Indian Convert." In Richey et al., 253–56.

Matthiessen, F. O. *American Renaissance: Art and Expression in the Age of Emerson and Whitman*. New York: Oxford University Press, 1941.

McCoy, Drew R. *The Elusive Republic: Political Economy in Jeffersonian America*. Chapel Hill: University of North Carolina Press, 1980.

McCullough, Kate. *Regions of Identity: The Construction of America in Women's Fiction, 1885–1914*. Stanford, Calif.: Stanford University Press, 1999.

McCusker, John C. and Russel Menard. *The Economy of British America, 1607–1789*. Chapel Hill: University of North Carolina Press, 1985.

McFerrin, John B. "Cherokee Mission." In Richey et al., 216–17.

McGann, Jerome. "Washington Irving, *A History of New York*, and American History." *Early American Literature* 47, no. 2 (2012): 349–76.

McGill, Meredith. *American Literature and the Culture of Reprinting*. Philadelphia: University of Pennsylvania Press, 2003.

McKee, Kathryn, and Annette Trefzer. "Preface: Global Contexts, Local Literatures: The New Southern Studies." *American Literature* 78, no. 4 (2006): 677–90.

McKibben, Frank P. "The Stone Fleet of 1861." *New England Magazine* 24, no. 4 (1898): 484–90.

———. "The Whaling Disaster of 1871." *New England Magazine* 24, no. 4 (1898): 490–96.

McLoughlin, William. *Cherokee Renascence in the New Republic*. Princeton, N.J.: Princeton University Press, 1986.

Meinig, D. W. *The Shaping of America: A Geographical Perspective on 500 Years of History*. Vol. 2. New Haven, Conn.: Yale University Press, 1986.

Melville, Herman. *Moby-Dick or The Whale*. Ed. Harrison Hayford et al. Evanston, Ill.: Northwestern University Press, 1988.

Merchant, Carolyn. "Reinventing Eden: Western Culture as a Recovery Narrative." In *Uncommon Ground: Rethinking the Human Place in Nature*. Ed. William Cronon. New York: Norton, 1996. 132–70.

Merk, Frederick. *Manifest Destiny and Mission in American History: A Reinterpretation*. New York: Knopf, 1963.

Merryman, John Henry, and Rogelio Pérez-Perdomo. *The Civil Law Tradition: An Introduction to the Legal Systems of Europe and Latin America*. 3rd ed. Stanford, Calif.: Stanford University Press, 2007.

Miller, Angela. *The Empire of the Eye: Landscape Representation and American Cultural Politics, 1825–1875*. Ithaca, NY: Cornell University Press, 1993.

Miller, Charles. *Jefferson and Nature: An Interpretation*. Baltimore: Johns Hopkins University Press, 1988.

Miller, Robert T., ed. *Discovering Indigenous Lands: The Doctrine of Discovery in the English Colonies*. New York: Oxford University Press, 2010.

Morgan, Kenneth. "The Organization of the Colonial American Rice Trade." *William and Mary Quarterly* 52, no. 3 (1995): 433–52.

Morgan, Philip D. *Slave Counterpoint: Black Culture in the Eighteenth-Century Chesapeake and Lowcountry*. Chapel Hill: University of North Carolina Press, 1998.

Morse, Jedidiah. *Geography Made Easy*. Boston: I. Thomas and E. T. Andrews, 1794.

Moseley, Edward H. "The United States and Mexico, 1810–1850." In *United States–Latin American Relations, 1800–1850: The Formative Generations*. Ed. Thomas Ray Shurbutt. Tuscaloosa: University of Alabama Press, 1991. 122–96.

Motley, Warren. *The American Abraham: James Fenimore Cooper and the Frontier Patriarch*. Cambridge: Cambridge University Press, 1987.

Mulderink III, Earl F. *New Bedford's Civil War*. New York: Fordham University Press, 2012.

Mulford, Carla. "The New Science and the Question of Identity in Eighteenth-Century British America." In *Finding Colonial America: Essays in Honor of J. A. Leo Lemay*. Ed. Carla Mulford and David Shields. Newark: University of Delaware Press, 2001. 79–103.

Nabers, Deak. *Victory of Law: The Fourteenth Amendment, the Civil War, and American Literature, 1852–1867*. Baltimore: Johns Hopkins University Press, 2006.

Native American International Caucus. "The Sacred Circle of Life: A Native American Vision." In Richey et al., 658–61.

Neary, Janet. "Mining the African American Literary Tradition: James Williams's *Fugitive Slave in the Gold Rush* and the Contours of a 'Black Pacific.'" *ESQ: A Journal of the American Renaissance* 59, no. 2 (2013): 329–74.

Nellis, Eric. *An Empire of Regions: A Brief History of Colonial British America*. Toronto: University of Toronto Press, 2010.

Nelson, Dana D. "Representative/Democracy: The Political Work of Countersymbolic Representation." In *Materializing Democracy: Toward a Revitalized Cultural Politics*. Ed. Russ Castronovo and Dana D. Nelson. Durham, N.C.: Duke University Press, 2002. 218–47.

———. *National Manhood: Capitalist Citizenship and the Imagined Fraternity of White Men*. Durham, N.C.: Duke University Press, 1998.

Newlin, Keith. *Hamlin Garland: A Life*. Lincoln: University of Nebraska Press, 2008.

Newton, Wesley P. "Origins of United States–Latin American Relations." In *United States–Latin American Relations, 1800–1850: The Formative Generations*. Ed. Thomas Ray Shurbutt. Tuscaloosa: University of Alabama Press, 1991. 1–24.

Nichols, Peter. *Final Voyage*. New York: G. P. Putnam's Sons, 2009.

Nixon, Rob. *Slow Violence and the Environmentalism of the Poor*. Cambridge, Mass.: Harvard University Press, 2011.

Noll, Mark A. *America's God: From Jonathan Edwards to Abraham Lincoln*. New York: Oxford University Press, 2002.

Nordholt, Jan Willem Schulte. *The Myth of the West: America as the Last Empire*. Grand Rapids, Mich.: Eerdmans, 1995.

Nwankwo, Ifeoma Kiddoe. *Black Cosmopolitanism: Racial Consciousness and Transnational Identity in the Nineteenth-Century Americas*. Philadelphia: University of Pennsylvania Press, 2005.

O'Connell, Barry. "Literacy and Colonization: The Case of the Cherokees." In Gross and Kelley, 495–515.

Odum, Howard W., and Harry Estill Moore. *American Regionalism: A Cultural-Historical Approach to National Integration*. New York: Henry Holt, 1938.

Ogilvie, George. *Carolina; or, the Planter*, ed. David Shields. *Southern Literary Journal* 18, no. 1 (1986): 7–82, 102–12.

Oliva, Leo E. "Enemies and Friends: Zebulon Montgomery Pike and Facundo Melgares in the Competition for the Great Plains, 1806–1807." *Kansas History* 29, no. 1 (2006): 34–47.

Olson, Dana. *The Legend of Prince Madoc and the White Indians*. n.p., Jeffersonville, Ind., 1987.

Onuf, Peter S. *Jefferson's Empire: The Language of American Nationhood*. Charlottesville: University Press of Virginia, 2000.

Owsley, Frank Lawrence, and Gene A. Smith. *Filibusters and Expansionists: Jeffersonian Manifest Destiny, 1800–1821*. Tuscaloosa: University of Alabama Press, 1997.

Parker, Kunal. *Common Law, History, and Democracy in America, 1790–1900: Legal Thought before Modernism*. New York: Cambridge University Press, 2011.

Parkman, Francis. *France and England in North America*. 7 vols. Boston: Putnam, 1865–92.

Paton, Diana. "The Flight from the Fields Reconsidered: Gender Ideologies and Women's Labor after Slavery in Jamaica." In *Reclaiming the Political in Latin American History*. Ed. Gilbert M. Joseph. Durham, N.C.: Duke University Press, 2001. 175–204.

Pease, Donald E., ed. *Revisionary Interventions into the Americanist Canon*. Durham, N.C.: Duke University Press, 1994.

Peckham, George. *A True Report of the Late Discoveries*. London, 1583.

Perdue, Theda, ed. *Cherokee Editor: The Writings of Elias Boudinot*. Athens: University of Georgia Press, 1996.

Perkins, Bradford. *Prologue to War: England and the United States, 1805–1812*. Berkeley: University of California Press, 1961.

Phillippo, James M. *Jamaica: Its Past and Present State*. London: John Snow, 1843.

Piacentino, Ed. "Intersecting Paths: The Humor of the Old Southwest as Intertext." In *The Enduring Legacy of Old Southwest Humor*. Baton Rouge: Louisiana State University Press, 2006.

Piep, Karsten H. "Liberal Visions of Reconstruction: Lydia Maria Child's *A Romance of the Republic* and George Washington Cable's *The Grandissimes*." *Studies in American Fiction* 31, no. 2 (2003): 165–90.

Pike, Zebulon Montgomery. *Journals, with Letters and Related Documents*. 2 vols. Ed. Stephen Harding Hart and Archer Butler Hulbert. Norman: University of Oklahoma Press, 1966.

Pilton, James William. Newsletter, *San Francisco Negro Historical and Cultural Society*, October 1967. California History Series, Vol. 2, No. 2. Special Collections, San Francisco Public Library.

Pitts, Leonard. *The Decline of the Californios: A Social History of the Spanish-Speaking Californians, 1846–1890*. Berkeley: University of California Press, 1966.

Pizer, Donald. *Hamlin Garland's Early Work and Career*. Berkeley: University of California Press, 1960.
Pleasant, Mary Ellen. "Memoirs and Autobiography." *Pandex of the Press* 1, no. 1 (January 1902): 1–6.
Porter, William T. "To Correspondents." *Spirit of the Times: A Chronicle of Turf, Agriculture, Field Sports, Literature, and the Stage* 11, no. 28 (September 11, 1841): 325.
———. *The Big Bear of Arkansas, and Other Sketches, Illustrative of Characters and Incidents in the South and South-West*. Philadelphia: T. B. Peterson, 1846.
Power, Douglas Reichart. *Critical Regionalism: Connecting Politics and Culture in the American Landscape*. Chapel Hill: University of North Carolina Press, 2007.
Pratt, Lloyd. *Archives of American Time: Literature and Modernity in the Nineteenth Century*. Philadelphia: University of Pennsylvania Press, 2010.
Pratt, Mary Louise. *Imperial Eyes: Travel Writing and Transculturation*. London: Routledge, 1992.
Pryse, Marjorie, and Judith Fetterley. *Writing Out of Place: Regionalism, Women, and American Literary Culture*. Urbana: University of Illinois Press, 2005.
Rael, Patrick. *Black Identity and Black Protest in the Antebellum North*. Chapel Hill: University of North Carolina Press, 2002.
Rafinesque, Constantine Samuel. *New Flora and Botany of North America*. Philadelphia: Carey, 1836–38.
Rakove, Jack N. "Ambiguous Achievement: The Northwest Ordinance." In Frederick Williams, *Old Northwest*, 1–20.
Rancière, Jacques. *The Politics of Aesthetics: The Distribution of the Sensible*. Trans. Gabriel Rockhill. London: Continuum, 2004.
———. "The Politics of Literature." In *Dissensus: On Politics and Aesthetics*. Trans. and ed. Steven Corcoran. London: Continuum, 2010. 152–68.
Ransom, John Crowe. *Selected Essays of John Crowe Ransom*. Ed. Thomas Daniel Young and John Hindle. Baton Rouge: Louisiana State University Press, 1984.
Regis, Pamela. *Describing Early America: Bartram, Jefferson, Crevecoeur, and the Rhetoric of Natural History*. Dekalb: Northern Illinois University Press, 1992.
Renan, Ernst. "What Is a Nation?" In *The Poetry of the Celtic Races and Other Essays by Ernst Renan*. Ed. William G. Hutchison. London: Walter Scott, 1896. 61–83.
Report of the Committee to Whom Was Referred on the Sixteenth Instant, the Petition of Thirty-Six American Citizens Confined at Carthagena, in South America, under Sentence of Slavery, November 21, 1808. Washington, D.C.: U.S. House of Representatives, 1808.
Reséndez, A. "National Identity on a Shifting Border: Texas and New Mexico in the Age of Transition, 1821–1848." *Journal of American History* 86, no. 2 (1999): 668–88.
Reynolds, Charles. *Modes of Imperialism*. New York: St. Martin's Press, 1981.
Reynolds, David. *Beneath the American Renaissance: The Subversive Imagination in the Age of Emerson and Melville*. Cambridge, Mass.: Harvard University Press, 1988.
Rhys, Rev. Morgan. "An Oration on Liberty." In Griffith, 55–59.
Richey, Russell E., et al. *The Methodist Experience in America: A Sourcebook*. 2 vols. Nashville, Tenn.: Abingdon, 2000.
Rickels, Milton. *Thomas Bangs Thorpe: Humorist of the Old Southwest*. Baton Rouge: Louisiana State University Press, 1962.

Rodriguez O., Jaime E., and Virginia Guedea. "How Relations between Mexico and the US Began." In *Myths, Misdeeds, and Misunderstandings: The Roots of Conflict in U.S.-Mexican Relations.* Ed. Jaime E. Rodriguez and Kathryn Vincent Lepp. Wilmington, Del.: Scholarly Resources, 1997. 17–46.

Ronda, James P. *Finding the West: Explorations with Lewis and Clark.* Albuquerque: University of New Mexico Press, 2001.

———. *Lewis and Clark among the Indians.* Lincoln: University of Nebraska Press, 1988.

———. "'We Have a Country': Race, Geography, and the Invention of Indian Territory." *Journal of the Early Republic* 19, no. 4 (Winter 1999): 739–55.

Rothman, Adam. *Slave Country: American Expansion and the Origins of the Deep South.* Cambridge, Mass.: Harvard University Press, 2005.

Rothman, Sheila M. *Living in the Shadow of Death: Tuberculosis and the Social Experience of Illness in American History.* Baltimore: Johns Hopkins University Press, 1995.

Roughley, Thomas. *The Jamaica Planter's Guide; or, A System for Plantation and Managing a Sugar Estate, or Other Plantations in that Island, and through the British West Indies in General.* London: Longman, Hurst, Rees, Orme, and Brown, 1823.

Round, Philip. *Removable Type: Histories of the Book in Indian Country, 1663–1880.* Chapel Hill: University of North Carolina Press, 2010.

Rowe, John Carlos. *Literary Culture and U.S. Imperialism.* New York: Oxford University Press, 2000.

Rubin Jr., Louis D., ed. *I'll Take My Stand: The South and the Agrarian Tradition.* New York: Harper, 1962.

Rugemer, Edward Bartlett. *The Problem of Emancipation: The Caribbean Roots of the Civil War.* Baton Rouge: Louisiana State University Press, 2009.

Sadowski-Smith, Claudia. "Introduction: Comparative Border Studies." *Comparative American Studies* 9, no. 4 (2011): 273–87.

Sandiford, Keith. *The Cultural Politics of Sugar: Caribbean Slavery and Narratives of Colonialism.* New York: Cambridge University Press, 2000.

Scammon, Charles Melville. *The Marine Mammals of the Northwestern Coast of North America, Together with an Account of the American Whale-Fishery.* New York: Dover, 1968.

Schell, Jennifer. *"A Bold and Hardy Race of Men": The Lives and Literature of American Whalemen.* Amherst: University of Massachusetts Press, 2013.

Schoolman, Martha. *Abolitionist Geographies.* Minneapolis: University of Minnesota Press, 2014.

———. "Violent Places: *Three Years in Europe* and the Question of William Wells Brown's Cosmopolitanism." *ESQ* 58, no. 1 (Summer 2012): 1–35.

Schulten, Susan. *Mapping the Nation: History and Cartography in Nineteenth-Century America.* Chicago: University of Chicago Press, 2012.

Schulz, Michael, Fredrik Söderbaum, and Joakim Öjendal. "Introduction: A Framework for Understanding Regionalization." In *Regionalization in a Globalizing World: A Comparative Perspective on Forms, Actors and Processes.* London: Zed Books, 2001.

Seelye, John. *Beautiful Machine: Rivers and the Republican Plan, 1775–1825.* New York: Oxford University Press, 1991.

Shackleford, James Atkins. *David Crockett: The Man and the Legend.* Ed. John B. Shackleford. 1956; Lincoln: University of Nebraska Press, 1986.

Shapiro, Stephen. *Culture and Commerce of the Early American Novel: Reading the Atlantic World-System.* University Park: Pennsylvania State University Press, 2008.

Sheridan, Richard. *Doctors and Slaves: A Medical and Demographic History of Slavery in the British West Indies, 1680–1824.* New York: Cambridge University Press, 1985.

Shields, David. *Oracles of Empire: Poetry, Politics, and Commerce in British America, 1690–1750.* Chicago: University of Chicago Press, 1990.

Shoemaker, Nancy. *Living with Whales: Documents and Oral Histories of Native New England Whaling History.* Amherst: University of Massachusetts Press, 2014.

Shortridge, James R. *The Middle West: Its Meaning in American Culture.* Lawrence: University of Kansas Press, 1989.

Simms, William Gilmore. *Views and Reviews in History and Fiction.* 2nd series. New York: Wiley & Putnam, 1845.

Slaughter, Eric. "The Dividing Line of American Federalism: Partitioning Sovereignty in the Early Republic." In Brückner and Hsu, 61–88.

Sloane, David E. E. "Mark Twain and the American Short Story." In *A Companion to the American Short Story.* Ed. Alfred Bendixen and James Nagel. New York: Wiley-Blackwell, 2010. 78–99.

Slotkin, Richard. *The Fatal Environment: The Myth of the Frontier in the Age of Industrialization, 1800–1890.* 1985; Norman: University of Oklahoma Press, 1994.

Smelser, Marshall. *The Democratic Republic, 1801–1815.* New York: Harper & Row, 1968.

Smith, Anthony D. *National Identity.* Reno: University of Nevada Press, 1991.

———. *Nationalism and Modernism.* London: Routledge, 1998.

[Smith, Richard Penn]. *Col. Crockett's Exploits and Adventures in Texas, Written by Himself.* London: R. Kennet, 1837.

Smith, Thomas W. *A Narrative of the Life, Travels and Sufferings of Thomas W. Smith.* Boston, 1844.

Sobel, Mechal. *The World They Made Together: Black and White Values in Eighteenth-Century Virginia.* Princeton, N.J.: Princeton University Press, 1987.

Soja, Edward W. *Thirdspace: Journeys to Los Angeles and other Real-and-Imagined Places.* Malden, Mass.: Blackwell, 1996.

Southey, Robert. *Madoc: A Poem.* Boston: Monroe, 1805.

Spengemann, William C. *A New World of Words: Redefining Early American Literature.* New Haven, Conn.: Yale University Press, 1994.

"A Sporting Adventure in Arkansas. By an Officer of the U.S. Army." *Spirit of the Times* 12, no. 45 (January 7, 1843): 154.

Stagg, J. C. A. *Borderlines in Borderlands: James Madison and the Spanish-American Frontier, 1776–1821.* New Haven, Conn.: Yale University Press, 2009.

Steiner, George. "From Frontier to Region: Frederick Jackson Turner and the New Western History." *Pacific Historical Review* 64, no. 4 (1995): 479–501.

Sten, Christopher. "City of Hope and Fear: Douglass and Melville in the Nation's Capital." *Leviathan: A Journal of Melville Studies* 10, no. 2 (2008): 23–36.

Stephanson, Anders. *Manifest Destiny: American Expansion and the Empire of Right*. New York: Hill & Wang, 1995.
Stillman, Richard. *Spreading the Word: A History of Information in the California Gold Rush*. Lincoln: University of Nebraska Press, 2006.
Stoddard, Amos. *Sketches Historical and Descriptive of Louisiana*. Philadelphia: Carey, 1812.
Streeby, Shelley. *American Sensations: Class, Empire, and the Production of Popular Culture*. Berkeley: University of California Press, 2002.
Stuart, John A. "The Yankee That Couldn't Talk Spanish." In Porter, *Big Bear*, 140–42.
Sweet, Timothy. *American Georgics: Economy and Environment in American Literature*. Philadelphia: University of Pennsylvania Press, 2001.
Tang, Edward. "Writing the American Revolution: War Veterans in the Nineteenth-Century Cultural Memory." *Journal of American Studies* 32, no. 1 (April 1998): 63–80.
Tatum, Stephen. "Spectrality and the Postregional Interface." In Kollin, 3–29.
Taylor, Alan. *William Cooper's Town: Power and Persuasion on the Frontier of the Early American Republic*. New York: Vintage, 1996.
Taylor, Bayard. *El Dorado, or Adventures in the Path of Empire, Comprising a Voyage to California, Via Panama, Life in San Francisco and Monterey*. New York: Knopf, 1949.
Taylor, Quintard. *In Search of the Racial Frontier: African Americans in the American West, 1528–1990*. New York: Norton, 1998.
Tennenhouse, Leonard. *The Importance of Feeling English: American Literature and the British Diaspora, 1750–1850*. Princeton, N.J.: Princeton University Press, 2007.
Thomas, Brook. *Civic Myths: A Law-and-Literature Approach to Citizenship*. Chapel Hill: University of North Carolina Press, 2007.
Thomas, Steven W. "Doctoring Ideology: James Grainger's *The Sugar Cane* and the Bodies of Empire." *Early American Studies* 4, no. 1 (2006): 78–111.
———. "Taxing Tobacco and the Metonymies of Virtue: The Poetics of Thomson, Browne, Byrd, and Cooke." In *Global Economies: Cultural Currencies of the Eighteenth Century*. Ed. Michael Rotenberg-Schwartz. New York: AMS Press, 2012. 73–96.
Thome, James A., and J. Horace Kimball. *Emancipation in the West Indies. A Six Months' Tour in Antigua, Barbadoes, and Jamaica, in the Year 1837*. New York: American Anti-Slavery Society, 1838.
Thompson, John. *The Life of John Thompson, a Fugitive Slave*. n.p., Worcester, Mass., 1856.
Thornton, A. P. *Doctrines of Imperialism*. New York: Wiley, 1965.
Thorpe, Thomas Bangs. "The Big Bear of Arkansas." In Porter, *Big Bear*, 13–31.
———. "The Disgraced Scalp Lock." In *The Mysteries of the Backwoods; or, Sketches of the Southwest, including Character, Scenery, and Rural Sports*. Philadelphia: Carey & Hart, 1846.
———. *The Taylor Anecdote Book. Anecdotes of Zachary Taylor, and the Mexican War. By Tom Owen, the Bee-Hunter. Together with a Brief Life of General Taylor, and His Letters*. Philadelphia: Carey & Hart, 1848.
———. "Tom Owen, the Bee-Hunter. By a New Yorker in Louisiana." *Spirit of the Times* 9, no. 21 (July 27, 1839): 247.
Toulmin, Harry. *A Description of Kentucky in North America*. Ed. Thomas Clark. 1792; Lexington: University of Kentucky, 1945.

Townsend, John Kirk. *Narrative of a Journey across the Rocky Mountains, to the Columbia River, and a Visit to the Sandwich Islands, Chili, etc.* Ed. George A. Jobanek. 1839; Corvallis: Oregon State University Press, 1999.
Traxel, William L. *Footprints of the Welsh Indians: Settlers in North America before 1492.* New York: Algora, 2004.
Truett, Samuel, and Eliott Young. "Making Transnational History: Nations, Regions, and Borderlands." In *Continental Crossroads: Remapping U.S.-Mexico Borderlands History.* Ed. Samuel Truett and Eliott Young. Durham, N.C.: Duke University Press, 2004. 1–32.
Turner, Frederick Jackson. *The Frontier in American History.* Ed. Wilbur Jacobs. Tucson: University of Arizona Press, 1997.
Ulrich, Laurel Thatcher. *The Age of Homespun: Objects and Stories in the Creation of an American Myth.* New York: Knopf, 2001.
Van Alstyne, Richard Warner. *The Rising American Empire.* New York: Oxford University Press, 1960.
Vernon, Irene S. "The Claiming of Christ: Native American Postcolonial Discourses." *MELUS* 24, no. 2 (1999): 75–88.
Vertovec, Steven. "Conceiving and Researching Transnationalism." *Ethnic and Racial Studies* 22, no. 2 (1999): 447–62.
Vevier, C. "American Continentalism: An Idea of Expansion, 1845–1910." *American Historical Review* 65, no. 2 (1960): 323–35.
Wald, Priscilla. *Constituting Americans: Cultural Anxieties and Narrative Form.* Durham, N.C.: Duke University Press, 1995.
Waldron, Jeremy. "What Is Cosmopolitan?" *Journal of Political Philosophy* 8, no. 2 (2000): 227–43.
Walker, Cheryl. *Indian Nation: Native American Literature and Nineteenth-Century Nationalisms.* Durham, N.C.: Duke University Press, 1997.
Wallace, Robert K. *Douglass and Melville: Anchored Together in Neighborly Style.* New Bedford, Mass.: Spinner, 2005.
Warner, Michael. *The Letters of the Republic: Publication and the Public Sphere in Eighteenth-Century America.* Cambridge, Mass.: Harvard University Press, 1991.
Warren, Harris Gaylord. *The Sword Was Their Passport: A History of American Filibustering in the Mexican Revolution.* Baton Rouge: Louisiana State University Press, 1943.
Warrior, Robert. *The People and the Word: Reading Native Nonfiction.* Minneapolis: University of Minnesota Press, 2005.
Washington, George. *The Writings of George Washington.* 28 vols. Ed. John C. Patrick. Washington, D.C.: U.S. Government Printing Office, 1938.
Watson, Douglas S. "Spurious California: 'Four Months among the Gold-Finders': Henry Vizetelly's Confession to an Astounding Literary Hoax." *California Historical Society Quarterly* 11, no. 1 (March 1932): 65–68.
Watts, Edward. *An American Colony: Regionalism and the Roots of American Culture.* Athens: Ohio University Press, 2002.
———. "Exploring, Trading, Trapping, Travel, and Early Fiction, 1780–1850." In Witschi, 13–28.

———. "Settler Postcolonialism as a Reading Strategy." *American Literary History* 22, no. 2 (Summer 2010): 459–70.

Watts, Steven. *The Republic Reborn: War and the Making of Liberal America, 1790–1820.* Baltimore: Johns Hopkins University Press, 1987.

Weaks-Baxter, Mary. *Reclaiming the American Farmer: The Reinvention of a Regional Mythology in Twentieth-Century Southern Writing.* Baton Rouge: Louisiana State University Press, 2006.

Webb, Walter Prescott. *Divided We Stand: The Crisis of a Frontierless Democracy.* New York: Farrar & Rinehart, 1937.

Welburn, Ron. *Roanoke and Wampum: Topics in Native American Heritage and Literatures.* New York: Peter Lang, 2000.

West III, James L., ed. *Gyascutus: Studies in Antebellum Southern Humorous and Sporting Writing.* Amsterdam: Rodopi, 1978.

Weyler, Karen. *Intricate Relations: Sexual and Economic Desire in American Fiction, 1789–1814.* Iowa City: University of Iowa Press, 2004.

Whitaker, Arthur Preston. *The United States and the Independence of Latin America, 1800–1830.* Baltimore: Johns Hopkins University Press, 1941.

White, Ed. *The Backcountry and the City: Colonization and Conflict in Early America.* Minneapolis: University of Minnesota Press, 2005.

———. "Divided We Stand: Emergent Conservatism in Royall Tyler's *The Algerine Captive.*" *Studies in American Fiction* 37, no. 1 (2010). 5–27.

White, Richard. *The Middle Ground: Indians, Empires, and Republics in the Great Lakes Region, 1650–1815.* New York: Cambridge University Press, 1991.

Whitecar Jr., William B. *Four Years Aboard the Whaleship.* Philadelphia, 1860.

Wilentz, Sean. *The Rise of American Democracy: Jefferson to Lincoln.* New York: Norton, 2005.

Williams, David. "John Evans: The Welsh Indians." *American Historical Review* 54, no. 2 (January 1949): 277–95.

Williams, Frederick, ed. *The Old Northwest: Essays on Its Formulation, Provisions, and Legacy.* East Lansing: Michigan State University Press, 1988.

Williams, Gywn A. *Madoc: The Making of a Myth.* London: Methuen, 1979.

Williams, James. *Fugitive Slave in the Gold Rush.* Ed. Malcolm J. Rohrbough. Lincoln: University of Nebraska, 2002.

Williams, Raymond. *Keywords: A Vocabulary of Culture and Society.* Rev. ed. Oxford: Oxford University Press, 1983.

———. *Writing in Society.* New York: Verso, 1983.

Wilson, Edmund. *Patriotic Gore: Studies in the Literature of the American Civil War.* New York: Oxford University Press, 1962.

Wilson, Rob. *Reimagining the American Pacific: From South Pacific to Bamboo Ridge and Beyond.* Durham, N.C.: Duke University Press, 2000.

Witschi, Nicolas S., ed. *A Companion to the Literature and Culture of the American West.* Malden, Mass.: Wiley-Blackwell, 2011.

Wong, Edie. "Comparative Racialization, Immigration Law, and James Williams's *Life and Adventures.*" *American Literature* 84, no. 4 (2012): 797–826.

Wood, Peter. *Black Majority: Negroes in Colonial South Carolina, from 1670 through the Stono Rebellion.* New York: Knopf, 1974.

Woodworth, Steven E. *Manifest Destinies: America's Westward Expansion and the Road to the Civil War*. New York: Random House, 2011.

Worden, Daniel. *Masculine Style: The American West and Literary Modernism*. New York: Palgrave Macmillan, 2011.

Wright, Lyle. *American Fiction, 1774–1850: A Contribution toward a Bibliography*. San Marino, Calif.: Huntington Library, 1969.

Yates, Norris W. *William T. Porter and The Spirit of the Times*. Baton Rouge: Louisiana State University Press, 1957.

Yoakum, H. *History of Texas from Its First Settlement in 1685 to Its Annexation to the United States in 1846*. 2 vols. New York: Redfield, 1855.

Yokota, Kariann. *Unbecoming British: How Revolutionary America Became a Postcolonial Nation*. Cambridge, Mass.: Harvard University Press, 2011.

Young, Robert. *White Mythologies: Writing History and the West*. New York: Routledge, 2004.

Zagarell, Sandra A. "*Country*'s Portrayal of Community and the Exclusion of Difference." In *New Essays on The Country of the Pointed Firs*. Ed. June Howard. New York: Cambridge University Press, 1994. 39–60.

———. "Region." *Keywords for American Cultural Studies*. Ed. Bruce Burgett and Glenn Hendler. New York: New York University Press, 2007. 199–201.

Zerbe, Richard O., Jr., and C. Leigh Anderson. "Culture and Fairness in the Development of Institutions in the California Gold Fields." *Journal of Economic History* 61, no. 1 (March 2001): 115–31.

Žižek, Slavoj. *Living in the End Times*. London: Verso, 2010.

Zuck, Rochelle Rainere. "Cultivation, Commerce, and Cupidity: Late-Jackson Virtue in James Fenimore Cooper's *The Crater*." *Literature of the Early Republic* 1 (2009): 39–64.

CONTRIBUTORS

HARRY BROWN is associate professor of English at DePauw University in Greencastle, Indiana, where he teaches early American literature, Native American literature, and digital humanities. His book, *Injun Joe's Ghost*, examines the figure of the Native American mixed-blood in American writing. His most recent research involves environmental crisis narratives and Puritan gravestone verse.

ANDY DOOLEN is associate professor of English and American studies at the University of Kentucky and the author of *Territories of Empire: U.S. Writing from the Louisiana Purchase to Mexican Independence* (Oxford, 2014) and *Fugitive Empire: Locating Early American Imperialism* (Minnesota, 2005), in addition to articles in several leading journals.

DUNCAN FAHERTY is associate professor of English and director of American studies at Queens College and the CUNY Graduate Center. He is the coeditor of *Studies in American Fiction* and, along with Ed White, the cocurator of the *Just Teach One* digital humanities project housed at the American Antiquarian Society. He is the author of *Remodeling the Nation: The Architecture of American Identity, 1776–1858*, and his work has also appeared in *American Literature*, *American Quarterly*, *Early American Literature*, and *Reviews in American History*. He is currently at work on a book about U.S. literary production in the first two decades of the nineteenth century.

JOHN FUNCHION is associate professor of English and American studies at the University of Miami. He is also the author of the book *Novel Nostalgias: The Aesthetics of Antagonism in Nineteenth-Century U.S. Literature*.

ROBERT GUNN is associate professor of English at the University of Texas at El Paso, where he specializes in literatures of encounter, linguistic representations of race, and nineteenth-century networks of U.S. imperialism. He is the author of *Ethnology and Empire: Languages, Literature, and the Making of the North American Borderlands* in the NYU Press series America and the Long 19th Century.

KERI HOLT is associate professor of English at Utah State University. Her research and teaching focus on eighteenth- and nineteenth-century American literature and culture, with an emphasis on regionalism and the early American West. Her work has been published in journals such as *Western American Literature*, *Early American Literature*, and *Studies* in *American Fiction* and in edited collections such as *John Neal and Nineteenth-Century American Literature and Culture*, *William Gilmore Simms's Civil War*, and *Teaching Olaudah Equiano's Narrative*.

WILLIAM V. LOMBARDI is a doctoral candidate in the University of Nevada, Reno's Literature and Environment emphasis. His articles and reviews dealing with the nineteenth- and twentieth-century U.S. West and ecocriticism in global contexts have appeared in *Western American Literature*, *Interdisciplinary Studies in Literature and Environment*, and *Journal of American Studies*. His most recent work focuses on place making in narratives of the California Gold Rush.

JANET NEARY is assistant professor of English at Hunter College, City University of New York. Her research examines nineteenth-century African American narrative and visual culture, with a focus on slave narratives. She came to Hunter in 2009 after receiving her PhD in English from the University of California, Irvine, with emphases in feminism and critical theory. She is at work on two books on race and visual culture: a monograph, *Fugitive Testimony: Race, Representation, and the Slave Narrative Form*, and a collection of primary texts, *A More Perfect Likeness*, coedited with Sarah Blackwood. Recent essays have appeared in *MELUS* and *ESQ: A Journal of the American Renaissance*, and she has work forthcoming in *African American Review* and *J19*.

HOLLIS ROBBINS is director of the Center for Africana Studies at Johns Hopkins University and chair of the Humanities Department at the Peabody Institute, where she has taught since 2006. Her work focuses on the intersection of nineteenth-century American and African American literature and the discourses of law, bureaucracy, and the press. Robbins has edited or coedited four books on nineteenth-century African American literature as well as numerous journal articles, including "*Django Unchained*: Repurposing Film Music," *Safundi* 16, no. 3 (July 2015); "William Wordsworth's 'We Are Seven' and the First British Census," *ELN* 48, no. 2 (2010); and "Fugitive Mail: Henry 'Box' Brown and Antebellum Postal Politics," *American Studies* 50, no. 1/2 (2009).

JENNIFER SCHELL is currently associate professor of English at the University of Alaska Fairbanks. Her specialties include early American literature, Arctic writing, print and visual culture, transnational studies, and environmental humanities. Her book *"A Bold and Hardy Race of Men": The Lives and Literature of American Whalemen* was published in August 2013 by the University of Massachusetts Press. She has also published articles on J. Hector St. John de Crèvecoeur's *Letters from an American Farmer*, William Wells Brown's *Clotel*, Herman Melville's *Moby-Dick*, and the History Channel's *Ice Road Truckers*. She is currently working on a book project on Arctic extinction narratives.

MARTHA SCHOOLMAN is assistant professor of English at Florida International University in Miami. She is the author of *Abolitionist Geographies* (University of Minnesota Press, 2014) and coeditor with Jared Hickman of the essay collection *Abolitionist Places* (Routledge, 2013). She has also published essays on transcendentalism, antislavery literature, and literary geography in *Arizona Quarterly, Atlantic Studies, ESQ: A Journal of the American Renaissance*, and the essay collection *American Literary Geographies: Spatial Practice and Cultural Production* (University of Delaware Press, 2007).

STEVEN W. THOMAS is assistant professor of English and the director of the film and media minor at Wagner College in Staten Island, New York. He has published essays about the eighteenth-century Atlantic world focused on literature about cash crop economies. The essay included in this volume is part of that ongoing inquiry into literature's relationship to a political economy that compares different locations in the context of circum-Atlantic exchange. In addition, he has also published about contemporary theories of globalization in relation to popular cinema. Currently, he is writing a book that traces the history of Ethiopia's symbolic significance in American literature from the seventeenth century to the present.

EDWARD WATTS is professor of English at Michigan State University. His books include *Writing and Postcolonialism in the Early Republic* (1998), *An American Colony: Regionalism and the Roots of Midwestern Identity* (2002), and *In This Remote Country: Colonial French Culture in the Anglo-American Imagination, 1780–1860* (2006). He has edited or coedited four other books. He teaches courses in American literature and culture, Michigan literature, and writing from settler colonies.

INDEX

abolitionism, 85, 87–95, 95n11, 114, 160–65, 170–71, 176, 230, 236, 244, 247n54, 253
Adams, John, 12
Adams, John Quincy, 211, 220, 225n56
Adams, Sam, 144
aesthetics, 81–82, 99, 108, 110, 116, 249, 254, 263; Jacques Rancière's use of, 141, 157n1, 266n19
African-Americans, 11, 84, 134n2; in California, 14, 15, 18–19, 226–48, 254; in Jamaica, 87, 89, 90–95; in Louisiana, 265; in New England, 162, 165, 170–71, 176. *See also* free people of color; slavery and slaves
Africans, 84, 86, 87, 100, 107–8, 111, 112–14, 260. *See also* slavery and slaves
agrarian (and agrarianism), 12n18, 85, 89–90, 94, 100, 101, 105, 116, 131–32. *See also* agriculture; Agrarian movement; Jeffersonianism; yeoman
Agrarian movement (of 1930s), 106, 116–18
agriculture (and farming), 26, 29, 35, 37–38, 71, 133, 183, 196, 216, 217; plantation, 84–85, 87, 90–92, 101–3, 104, 111–12, 114. *See also* agrarian; yeoman
Alamo, the, 73
American studies, 10, 55, 61n46, 62, 84
American Whig Review, 76, 80n25
Anderson, Benedict, 10, 13, 21n30, 95n1, 146
Anderson, William Wemyss, 82, 88, 89–95, 95n15; *Jamaica and the Americans*, 89–95
Apache Indians, 131
Apess, William, 11, 18–19, 181–98, 252; *Eulogy on King Philip*, 182, 191; The *Experiences of Five Christian Indians*, 182, 193; *Indian Nullification*, 182; *A Son of the Forest*, 182, 190, 193–96
Appadurai, Arjun, 50
Arac, Jonathan, 7, 21n22, 79n7
Armitage, David, 100
Armstrong, Nancy, 158n25
Aron, Stephen, 44n42
Articles of Confederation, 12, 140
Asbury, Francis, 184, 187–88
assimilation, 7, 30, 183, 192, 196, 203–4, 224
Atlantic studies, 86, 99, 101–2, 119n33, 142, 157n12, 250, 264; circum-Atlantic, 100, 115, 146; cis-Atlantic, 100; relation to Caribbean, 103, 112, 115, 118; relation to Louisiana Purchase, 121, 132. *See also* black Atlantic; transatlantic; transnationalism
Audubon, John James, 54
Ayers, Edward L., 22n43
Aztecs, 27, 39–40

backwoods, 64–67, 70, 72–77, 181–84, 186–87, 189, 193–97, 244
Bakhtin, M. M., 117, 120n57
Ballou's Dollar Monthly Magazine, 161, 163, 168
Baltimore, Maryland, 129, 169, 171
Bancroft, George, 20n7
Baudrillard, Jean, 46
Belknap, Jeremy, 31–32, 34, 38, 42, 43n16
Bell, Michael Davitt, 20n11
Benjamin, Walter, 10

299

Best, Stephen, 266n20
Bhabha, Homi K., 20n4, 223n4
Bigelow, John, 89, 92–94, 95n9
black Atlantic, 121, 134n2. *See also* Atlantic studies; transatlantic
Black Atlantic, The, 71
borderlands. *See* empire, empire-building
Boudinot, Elias, 190, 199, 203–6, 208–10, 212, 217–20
Bowen, Benjamin, 42n3, 43n26, 43n35
Brackenridge, Henry Marie, 32, 43n21
Brackenridge, Hugh Henry, 32, 35
Bramen, Carrie Tirado, 266n29
Branch, Michael P., 46, 54, 60n36, 61n40
Breckenridge, John, 1
Breckenridge Act, 259
Brenner, Neil, 122, 134n8
Britain. *See* Great Britain
British Emancipation Act of 1863, 85, 87, 91
British West Indies. *See* Caribbean
Brown, Charles Brockden, 31, 143
Brown, Harry, 10–11, 18, 252
Brückner, Martin, 2, 6, 78n1
Bryant, William Cullen, 26
Buell, Lawrence, 59
Buffalo, New York, 89
Burr, Aaron (and Burr Conspiracy), 123–25, 128–29, 135n15, 143, 258
Bush, George W., 78
Butler, Pierce Mason, 70, 73, 75

Cable, George Washington, 19, 251–52, 255–60, 262–64; "The Freedman's Case in Equity," 259; *The Grandissimes*, 19, 251, 254, 257, 260–64, 267n33; *The New Orleans of George Washington Cable: The 1887 Census Office Report*, 251, 258
Cady, Edwin, 20n11
Caesar, Clarence, 246n32
Caleb, Hannah, 193–95
California, 15, 19, 61n51, 69, 72, 227–45, 246n19, 246n22, 246n32, 246n35, 246n39, 246–47n43, 247n49, 247n58

Campbell, Neil, 47, 60n12, 78n1
camp meetings, 184–87, 193–95, 197
Canada, 7, 66, 87, 89–91, 94, 182, 193
canon formation, 8–9, 14, 21n21, 47, 64, 141–45, 148–55, 158n22. *See also* Faherty, Duncan; literary history
capitalism, 8, 41, 55, 82–84, 92–94, 100–106, 115–18, 137n46, 146, 158n36, 164, 170, 252. *See also* trade
captivity, 124, 127–30, 135–36n26; Barbary, 124, 136, 148; Indian, 43n37, 127
Carey and Hart (publishers), 67
Caribbean, 81–95, 99–100, 102–3, 108, 111, 112–15, 162; Antigua, 84; Barbados, 85, 102; Jamaica, 17, 82–95, 108, 112, 113
Carlyle, Thomas, 87, 95n10
Carney, Judith, 111–12
cartographic texts, 3–5, 122. *See also* charting
cartography, 5–6, 17, 143
Carver, Jonathan, 27
Cass, Lewis, 211, 273
Catlin, George, 23, 52
charting, 2, 4, 6–7, 10, 15–17, 20, 22n45, 51, 146, 153, 186
Cherokee Indians, 11, 14, 19, 39, 70–72, 74, 185, 193, 197n11, 199–225, 242, 252
Cherokee Nation v. Georgia, 72
Cherokee Phoenix, 199–223
Childs, John, 35, 37
China, 56, 230, 233. *See also* globalization; labor
Christianity (and Christians), 4, 5, 8, 14, 18, 19, 21, 25, 88, 94, 242; and African Americans, 173–74; and colonization, 28–29, 32, 38; and Native Americans, 181–85, 189–97, 197n2, 198n17, 203, 217. *See also* conversion; Methodism; Methodist-Episcopal church; Missionaries; Quakers; Second Great Awakening
Civil War, U.S., 6, 8, 19, 84, 100, 117, 176n8, 251, 254–55, 257–58, 264. *See also* Confederacy
Claiborne, William, 256, 258, 267

Clark, William, 45–54, 57–59, 123, 131. *See also* Lewis and Clark
Clatsop, Fort, 57–58, 70
Clifford, James, 59, 116
Clinton, Dewitt, 40
Clinton, George, 143
coffee, 86, 91–92, 173
Coke, Thomas, 184, 197n10
Coleridge, Samuel Taylor, 42n4
colonialism, 6–8, 12–13, 17–19, 21n19, 25, 38–39, 46, 57, 72, 89–93, 101–3, 109, 119n33, 122, 146–47, 157n9, 165
colonization societies (Africa), 89
Columbia River, 17, 36, 47, 55–57, 134n20. *See also* Lewis and Clark
Columbus, Christopher, 25–27, 54, 127
Comanche Indians, 70, 126, 131, 135n22, 135n23
Comer, Krista, 59, 60n14, 78n1
commerce, 48–50, 52, 61n46, 71, 100, 104, 117, 125, 133, 143, 183, 196, 209, 230. *See* capitalism; commerce; mercantilism; trade
Conestoga Indians, 27
Confederacy (Confederate States of America), 8
constitution: California, 227–28, 237; Cherokee, 206–15, 224n15; Massachusetts, 170; U.S., 12, 90, 140, 147, 206–8, 212, 214–15, 219, 255–56; state, 140, 215; Virginia, 106
contact zones, 61n50, 117, 121
conversion, 29, 72, 88, 181–83, 185, 190–97, 203
Cooke, Ebenezer 100, 104–9, 112–13
Cooper, James Fenimore, 54–55, 68–69, 93, 101, 131, 144, 148, 157n20, 158n21; *The Prairie*, 54–55, 131
Cosgrove, Denis, 2, 4, 183, 196, 250
cosmopolitanism, 7, 11, 15, 20n11, 21n22, 117, 145, 265n3; in Maine, 83; in New England, 17–18, 160–65, 167–68, 170, 172–73, 176, 236; in New Orleans, 255; in the U.S. West, 47–48, 56–57, 59, 66

cotton, 94, 104, 109, 110, 116, 122, 169
countermapping, 16, 18–19, 202, 227, 252
Cox, Isaac Joslin, 135n21
Creole: Caribbean, 90, 103, 112, 115, 162; New Orleans, 255–64, 266n22, 267n33
Crevecouer, Hector St. John de, 5, 16, 30, 37–38, 42n12, 43n41, 127, 177n17
critical regionalism, 10, 13, 21n20, 106, 145, 158n23; and the U.S. West, 45, 47–48, 50, 53, 59, 60nn11–12, 60n14, 62, 78n1. *See also* provisionality; regionalism; regionalization; transregional
Crockett, David (Davy), 63, 65, 73–74, 78, 79n21
Cromwell, Oliver, 96n29
Cronon, William, 46, 59
Cushman, Robert, 28–29

Dainotto, Roberto M., 118
Dana, Richard Henry, 54–55
Davidson, Cathy N., 142–43, 157n15
Davidson, Donald, 116
Dayan, Colin, 266n20
Deacon, Richard, 42n6, 43n29, 44n45
Dee, John, 28–30
Delano, Reuben, 161, 166
Deleuze, Gilles, 61n53, 117, 252, 265n7. *See also* rhizome
Deloria, Philip J., 25–26, 42n1
democracy, 31, 130, 158n20, 183, 244, 267n42
Detroit, 95, 96n31, 177n14
DeVoto, Bernard, 79n4
Doctrine of Discovery, 28–30, 32–33, 35, 41
Dolin, Eric Jay, 162, 176n7
Doolen, Andy, 14, 17–18, 252, 266n22
Douglass, Frederick, 11, 18, 88, 90, 160–62, 168–73, 175, 176n1, 226, 231, 236, 242, 245, 246n35; *Frederick Douglass' Paper*, 90, 91, 227, 229, 231–32, 235, 237, 242; *My Bondage and My Freedom*, 160–62, 168–72, 176n1; *Narrative of the Life of Frederick Douglass*, 88, 166, 176n4, 177n23, 226–27

Drayton, John, 108, 110–12, 114
Dred Scott v. Sandford, 100, 260
Duane, James, 139, 140, 151, 156n6, 157n9, 158n31
DuVal, Kathleen, 49, 60n33

early American studies, 9–11, 46, 142–43
ecocriticism, 45, 47–48, 59, 60n14. *See also* nature writing
Edwards, Bryan, 113–14
Egan, James, 120n48
Elden, Stuart, 122, 134n8
Eliot, T. S. 116
Elliott, Emory, 20n9
Elmer, Jonathan, 252, 265n6
Emancipation Proclamation (U.S.), 84–85, 241
Emerson, Ralph Waldo, 7, 94
empire: Hardt and Negri's concept of, 130, 252; Spanish, 25, 35, 45, 50, 96n29, 124–30, 131, 133, 135n21, 135n22, 135n24, 135n26, 251; U.S., 23–25, 48–49, 62, 90–92, 130, 139, 142, 145. *See also* charting; empire-building; expansionism; Great Britain; Mexican-American War; Manifest Destiny; Monroe Doctrine
empire-building, 61n51, 75–78, 122–23, 126, 129–30, 132–34, 135n15, 135n21. *See also* filibustering
England. *See* Great Britain
Enlightenment, 2, 5, 16–17, 29, 31, 33, 46, 53
Erie Railroad Co. v. Tompkins (Erie doctrine), 257, 266n28
Evacuation Day, 138, 142
Evans, John, 34–35, 38, 43n29
exceptionalism, 5, 147. *See also* nationalism
expansionism, 1, 7, 16–19, 20n7, 43n16, 78, 84, 139, 141–42, 157n17, 243; and African Americans, 227; and agriculture, 101, 105; and humor, 63–66, 68–69, 71–73; and imperialism, 4–5, 14, 95n19; and Pike expedition, 123, 127, 129, 130–33, 134n5, 135n21, 136n32; and trans-Mississippi region, 47–52; and Welsh Indians, 26–28, 30–36, 41. *See also* empire; empire-building; Jeffersonianism
exploratory writing, 45–62, 121–37, 136n43

Faherty, Duncan, 14, 17–18, 141–42, 144–47, 155
farming. *See* agrarian; agriculture; yeoman
Faulkner, William, 64, 78
federalism, 130, 140–41, 264
Federalists, 1, 21n36, 28–31, 34–35, 37, 41, 43n16, 133, 144, 151, 153, 266n25
Fero, David, 127–29, 136n31
Fetterley, Judith, 8, 9, 10, 20n11, 254
filibustering, 123–26, 129, 133, 136n32
Filson, John, 27, 32, 35, 43n22
Fink, Mike, 63, 74–77
Finley, James B., 185–86, 193, 197n12
Fisher, Philip, 21n20
Flag of Our Union, 161, 163, 168
Fliegelman, Jay, 158n30
Flores, Dan L., 135n21, 135n24
Florida, 27–28, 39, 42n4, 135n21
Foote, Stephanie, 20n11, 21n22, 22n45, 251–52, 266n21
Forsyth, John, 210–11, 224n23, 224n25, 225n58
Fort Mandan, 45–46, 52, 53, 58
France (and French), 5, 32, 45, 49–50, 53, 58, 104, 132, 136n34, 231–34, 247n49; civil law, 251, 255–58, 260, 264, 266n25; expansion, 25, 26, 28
Franklin, Benjamin, 31, 43n37, 107, 127
Frederick Douglass's Paper. *See under* Douglass, Frederick
Freemasonry, 40–41, 235
free people of color, 19, 226–27, 229, 230–36, 239, 241, 243–45, 255, 258–61, 267n38, 267n40; in Jamaica, 85–87, 90, 94
Free Soil Party, 87, 89, 90, 92
free trade. *See* capitalism; trade

Index

Fresonke, Kris, 135n15
frontier. *See* West, the (U.S.)
Fugitive Slave Act, 87, 162, 227
Funchion, John, 19, 266n11

Gardner, Eric, 227, 229, 245n13, 245n14
Gardner, Jared, 155
Garland, Hamlin, 5, 21n3, 254
Gaul, Theresa Strouth, 223n7, 225n50
geography, 11, 78n1, 82, 121, 131–32, 134n2, 186, 190, 226–28, 246n38; national, 4, 6, 14–15, 50, 54, 143, 155; southern U.S., 104, 109, 111, 118
Georgia, 63, 72, 116, 200, 210, 211, 215, 219–20, 227. *See also* Lowcountry region
Georgic poetry, 103, 109, 113
Giles, Paul, 6, 11, 61n46, 252
Gillman, Susan, 267n33
Gilroy, Paul, 71–72, 116–18. *See also* Atlantic studies; black Atlantic
global, 2, 4, 18, 38, 99, 106, 117–18, 155, 249, 251–53, 257, 264; economics, 41, 45, 47–51, 53, 55–57, 59, 61n51, 82–83, 146, 161, 170, 176n7; literature, 7, 102; scholarship, 62; and U.S., 6, 16, 17, 20n7
globalization, 48–50, 55–57, 62, 118, 252
global South, 17, 87, 100, 118n2
gold rush, 15, 19, 226–34, 236–37, 244–45, 245n12, 245n17, 254
Goudie, Sean X., 103
Gould, Philip, 43n16
Grainger, James, 100, 113–15
Great American Desert. *See* Great Plains
Great Britain (England and British Empire), 45, 50, 65, 220–21, 235, 251, 255; and colonial North America, 25–28, 31, 33, 41, 105, 108, 115; and post-Revolutionary U.S., 132, 139–40, 148–49, 152, 157n9; and the West Indies, 87–89, 90–92
Great Plains, 131, 132
Greeson, Jennifer Rae, 20n15
Griffiths, Maurice, 32, 35–37
Guattari, Felix, 61n53, 117, 252, 265n7. *See also* rhizome

Gunn, Robert, 15–17, 253
Gustafson, Sandra M., 158n20

Hadden, Sally E., 266n24
Haiti, 85–86, 118, 246n39. *See also* Caribbean
Hakluyt, Richard, 28, 30, 38, 42n9
Hallock, Thomas, 2, 21n36, 122
Hamilton, Alexander, 139–40, 147, 151, 156nn6–7, 157n18
Hardt, Michael, 130, 252. *See also* empire
Harris, George Washington, 63
Harrison, William Henry, 76
Harvey, David, 163
Hatch, Nathan O., 182–86, 190, 192, 196
Hawaii, 55–58, 61n45, 229, 233. *See also* globalization; Pacific Islands; Pacific Ocean
hegemony, 61n50, 106, 117, 121, 131–32, 141
hemispheric studies, 7, 8, 55, 61n46, 62, 81–82, 85, 89–95, 99, 102, 121, 132
historiography, 5, 7, 20, 63, 89, 126, 134n2, 134n5, 142
Hobsbawm, Eric, 20n4, 33
Holt, Keri, 11, 14, 18, 19, 249–50, 252
Howe, Daniel Walker, 20n7, 168, 185–86, 192
Howells, William Dean, 5, 19
Hsu, Hsuan L., 4, 6, 50, 53, 61n45, 78n1, 81–84, 86, 88, 92, 251
Hudson's Bay Company, 57
humor, Old Southwest, 15, 17, 61–78, 79n2, 79n3

Imlay, Gilbert, 32
immigration (and immigrants), 8, 30–42, 94, 143–44, 227–42, 246n43, 247n58, 255. *See also* migration
imperialism. *See* empire
Indian removal. *See* removal, Indian
Indian tribes, 24–28, 30–31, 33, 75–79, 122, 185, 191, 193, 230, 232, 237, 258. *See also* Native Americans; *and specific tribes*
indigenous peoples. *See* Indian tribes; Native American; *and specific tribes*

industrialism (and industrialization), 2, 8, 9, 101, 102, 106, 163, 169, 185. *See also* labor; technology
interstitial, 155, 253, 254, 257, 265. *See also* provisionality
Irving, Washington, 31, 52, 54–55, 58, 61n46, 144, 157n19, 157n20
Irwin, John, 20n3, 22n42

Jackson, Andrew, 78, 200, 211, 219
Jay, Gregory, 21n21
Jay Treaty (1794), 27
Jefferson, Thomas, 1–2, 34, 38, 114, 125–26, 217, 220, 266n25; Lewis and Clark Expedition, 45, 48–52; *Notes on the State of Virginia*, 100, 104–5, 110, 259; southwestern U.S. expansion, 130, 132, 135n21, 256; *Summary View of the Rights of British America*, 38, 104
Jeffersonianism, 29–32, 33–36, 41, 100–101, 122, 132, 259. *See also* expansionism
Jehlen, Myra, 20n9
Jewett, Sarah Orne, 83, 84, 93, 253
Jim Crow, 100, 117, 255
Joseph, Philip, 11, 20n11, 21n22, 265n3

Kaplan, Amy, 142
Kendall, George Wilkins, 63, 66
Kentucky, 1, 28, 32, 37, 126. *See also* Crockett, David; Filson, John; Thorpe, Thomas Bangs
Kentucky Palladium, 35
Kerr, Lewis A., 256
Kerry, John, 78
Kirkland, Caroline, 6, 68, 93
Knadler, Stephen, 229, 244, 245n13, 245n14, 247n58, 247n63, 248n64
Kolodny, Annette, 26, 42n2
Konig, David Thomas, 266n23
Kramer, Lloyd, 28–29

labor, 87–88, 94, 99–118, 177n14, 232; agricultural, 84–85; Chinese, 229–30, 233–34, 236–37, 242–44, 245n15, 246n43, 247n50, 247n56, 247n58; conflict (class), 99, 100; free-labor, 87; indentured, 87, 107, 182, 187, 189; management of, 100, 107, 114, 115, 116; slave, 84, 86–92, 101, 103–6, 107, 117, 170, 255; wage, 85, 86, 114, 152, 162, 167, 169, 170, 172, 231. *See also* mining; slavery and slaves; whaling; working class; yeoman
Lady of the State of New-York, A, 14, 142, 147–48, 151, 152; *The Fortunate Discovery*, 142, 147–52, 153; *Moreland Vale*, 142, 147–48, 152–54, 158–59n38
Land Ordinance of 1784, 2, 3, 7
land speculation, 31, 101, 105
Lapp, Rudolph, 230, 236, 246n39
law: civil (Roman, civilian), 12–13, 251, 255–62, 264–65, 267n39; civil cases (U.S.), 6, 139, 156n6, 207, 209, 234; common (Anglo-American), 251–52, 255–57, 259–60, 262–65, 266n25, 266n28, 267n42; federal judiciary (and U.S. Supreme Court), 140, 156n6, 207, 255, 260, 263, 265, 266n28; Judiciary Act of 1789, 257; Napoleonic black codes (*Code Noir*), 255, 258, 261, 264. *See also* Fugitive Slave Act; property; slavery and slaves; *and specific court cases*
legal history, 139–41, 254–58. *See also* law
LeMenager, Stephanie 52, 60n33, 60n36, 131
Levine, Robert S., 61n46, 161
Lewis, Meriwether, 34, 45–53, 54, 59, 60n19, 61n38. *See also* Lewis and Clark
Lewis, Nathaniel, 46, 54
Lewis and Clark, 16–17, 34, 45, 47–48, 57, 58, 60n33, 123, 131, 134n10, 136n42; *Journals*, 47–53
liberalism, 29, 88, 107, 132–33, 137n46, 164, 171–72, 252
Liberator, 161, 169
Lincoln, Abraham, 138, 142, 156n4, 168
literary history, 7–12, 46, 63–64, 99–100, 141–47, 149, 158n22, 245n12, 249;

Cherokee, 199, 223; colonial, 103, 108, 115–18, 121. *See also* Canon formation; Faherty, Duncan; regionalism

Livingston, Edward, 258–59, 261

local (locality, localism), 1–2, 4–20, 21n26, 41, 55–56, 60n14, 72–73, 164, 250–57, 262, 264–65, 265n3; California, 226, 228, 232–33, 237, 242; Cherokee, 199–200, 202–5, 208–11, 214, 215–19, 221–23; Christian Indian communities, 183–85, 187–88, 190, 192–95; Jamaica, 86, 92; New York, 138, 141, 146, 152–53; southern colonies, 99; U.S. West, 49, 62–65, 68

local color, 8, 19, 63, 145, 250, 252, 254, 261

Locke, John, 110, 130

Lombardi, William V., 16–17, 252

London (England), 27, 56, 65, 89, 112, 163. *See also* Great Britain

Long, Edward, 108, 112–14

Longfellow, Henry Wadsworth, 26, 43n28

Longstreet, Augustus Baldwin, 63

Loshe, Lillie Deming, 158n22

Loughran, Trish, 10, 13, 21n30, 22n42, 95n1, 146

Louisiana, 63, 66, 251, 254–55, 256–57, 259, 260–65. *See also* Louisiana Purchase; Louisiana Territory; New Orleans; Territory of Orleans

Louisiana Purchase, 1, 2, 31, 35, 84, 123, 129, 251, 255, 257; and Pike expedition, 121, 130, 133, 135n21, 137n46; *See also* Jeffersonianism; Lewis and Clark; Louisiana Territory; Territory of Orleans

Louisiana Territory, 32, 35, 37, 123, 124, 127, 133, 255–56, 258, 259, 266n22. *See also* Territory of Orleans

Lowcountry region, 100, 101, 103, 107, 108–12, 113, 115, 116. *See also* Georgia; South Carolina

loyalists, British (Tories), 108, 138–59, 156n1, 156n6, 157n14, 158n31

Lukács, Georg, 263

Lutz, Tom, 20n11, 21n22, 265n3

Madison, James, 216–17

Madoc, Prince. *See* Welsh Indians

Maine, 79n2, 83, 93, 253

Mandan Indian, 25–27, 34–35, 41, 46, 52, 53

Manifest Destiny, 16, 20n9, 34, 53, 131

mapping (and maps), 1, 6, 10, 15–20, 62, 116, 249–51, 262; Cherokee, 199–200, 206, 214, 229; Denis Cosgrove, 2, 4, 183, 250; Pike expedition, 124–25, 135n21, 136n35. *See also* Cosgrove, Denis

Marshall, John, 72

Marx, Karl, 130

Maryland, 32, 103, 105, 116, 160, 169, 170, 226, 228. *See also* Baltimore, Maryland; Tidewater region

Mason, George, 30

Massachusetts, 5, 96n29, 143, 144, 163, 182, 233. *See also* New Bedford, Massachusetts

McCoy, Drew R., 132–33, 137n46

McCullough, Kate, 20n11

McFerrin, John B., 185–86, 193

McGann, Jerome, 157n19

McGill, Meredith, 21n38

McLoughlin, William, 223–24n10, 225n49, 225n59

Melville, Herman, 18, 116, 127, 160–61, 172

memorials, Indian, 212–15, 224n33, 225n52

mercantilism, 93, 101, 105, 132. *See also* trade

Methodism, 19, 181–89, 192–93

Methodist-Episcopal church, 173, 182–84, 187–89, 197

Mexican–American War, 60n33, 60n36, 64, 69, 72, 75–78, 80n25

Mexican Revolution. *See under* revolution

Mexico: government of, 69, 72–77, 128–29, 233; Mexican territory, 17, 122–31, 135n15; people, 125, 229, 233–34, 243

Midwest. *See* Great Plains

migration 17, 29, 50, 73, 89, 91, 93, 149, 163, 221, 235–36. *See also* immigration
mining, 231–34, 236, 239
Miranda, Francisco, 124–25
missionaries, 28, 57, 83, 93, 96n29, 184–85, 187–89, 197. *See also* Christianity
Mississippi River, 15, 30, 122–23, 126–29, 133
Mississippi Valley, 1–2, 26–27, 37, 45, 47, 75, 84, 126–29, 134n10
Missouri Compromise of 1850, 9, 100, 228
Missouri River, 26–27, 46, 50, 51. *See also* Lewis and Clark
Mitchel, Isaac, 147
Monroe Doctrine, 92
Monterrey, Battle of, 76
Morgan, Philip D., 102, 106
Morse, Jedidiah, 14
Mound Builders, 26, 39–41
Muscogee Indians, 73

Nabers, Deak, 266n20
National Anti-Slavery Standard, 161, 165
National Era, 95n15, 231, 236
nationalism (and nation), 5, 8–15, 19, 20n4, 21n30, 65, 81–82, 94, 99, 202–5, 210–12, 216, 220–23, 251, 252, 262, 264, 265n3; civil and romantic, 2, 26–35, 43n16; and literature, 130, 141, 143, 146, 148, 152, 254; and New Bedford, 164, 168, 174, 176; and the West, 45, 48–49, 51, 58, 60n33. *See also* exceptionalism
Native American, 18, 51, 56–58, 66, 69–75, 162, 229, 233–34, 242–43, 255; Methodist conversion, 181–98; Pike expedition, 121, 123, 128, 130; Southern British-American colonies, 109–10. *See also* Indian tribes; *and specific tribes*
Native American International Caucus, 197, 198n33
nature writing, 45–61. *See also* ecocriticism
Navigation Acts, 102
Neary, Janet, 10, 11, 14–15, 18–19, 254
Negri, Antonio, 130, 252. *See also* empire

Nelson, Dana D., 75–76, 128, 136n42
New Bedford, Massachusetts, 18, 160–77, 226, 236
Newby, William H. (pseud. Nubia), 227–29, 232–37, 246n35, 246n39, 424–44
New England, 7, 11, 17–18, 20n9, 26, 82–88, 92–95, 96n29, 143, 147, 236, 255; Native Americans, 182–83, 192; whaling, 160–61, 174. *See also specific states*
New Orleans, 19, 27, 126, 249–67. *See also* Territory of Orleans
New Orleans Picayune, 63
New York, 14, 72, 89, 90, 99, 129, 163, 172, 176n1, 182; Washington Irving, 31, 58; literature, 18, 138–59, 250; newspapers, 63, 65–67, 231, 236
New York Daily Times, 237
New York Evening Post, 89
New York Trespass Act, 139–41, 154, 156n6, 157n14
New York Tribune, 229, 236, 247n45
New Zealand, 7, 162
Nixon, Rob, 60n14
Nolan, Philip, 125–29, 135n2, 135n24, 135n26, 136n28
Norris, Frank, 83
North Carolina, 26, 27, 34, 103, 185, 186, 200, 211. *See also* Tidewater region
North Star, 230–31, 236
Northwest Ordinance, 7, 10, 30, 35, 84. *See also* Old Northwest
nostalgia, 8, 52, 73, 79n19, 83, 84, 103, 117, 118, 144, 168
Nubia. *See* Newby, William
Nuttall, Thomas, 55–56, 61n40
Nwankwo, Ifeoma Kiddoe, 168, 170

Odum, Howard W., 116–17,
Ogilby, William, 90. *See also* Anderson, William Weymss
Ogilvie, George, 100, 108–12, 115
Ohio, 27, 30, 34, 36–37, 41, 63, 185–86
Ohio River, 32, 41, 74, 126

Old Northwest, 2, 20n15
Onuf, Peter S., 20n2
Oregon Territory, 54, 56–57, 131. *See* Townsend, John Kirk
Osage Nation, 49, 131
Otter, Samuel, 161

Pacific Islands, 28, 52, 55–56
Pacific Northwest, 32, 55, 57
Pacific Ocean (and Pacific Rim), 131–32, 134n10, 160, 174
Paine, Thomas, 7
Panic of 1837, 65
Parker, Kunal, 262–63
Parkman, Francis, 20n7, 52
pastoral, 103, 108, 110, 113
Paulding, James Kirke, 68–69, 73
Pawnee, 131
Paxton Riots, 30
Pease, Donald, 21n21
Pendleton, John Kennedy, 6, 265
Pequot, 182–83, 186, 193, 195–96
Philadelphia, 50, 143, 145, 164, 167, 226, 229, 235
Phillips, Wendell, 88
Pike, Zebulon Montgomery, 14, 18, 123–37, 252
plantation. *See* labor; slavery and slaves
Pleasant, Mary Ellen, 226–29, 236, 245n2
Plessy v. Ferguson, 100, 118n2, 242
Porter, William T., 63–73
postfrontier, 47, 50, 59, 78n1
postwestern, 48, 52, 53, 55, 78n1
Powell, David, 38, 42n9
Powell, Douglas Reichart, 47, 145
Pratt, Lloyd, 257, 264
Pratt, Mary Louise, 61n50, 117, 134n2
print history (and culture), 4, 9–10, 63, 89, 155, 161, 176; Cherokee, 199–202, 218; and nationalism, 12–14, 21n30, 65, 78, 146–47
Proclamation Line of 1763, 25
property (property rights), 31, 85–86, 108, 113, 138–39, 144, 147–54, 156n6, 157n14, 207–10, 219, 227–28, 233, 235, 239–40, 254, 255, 258–62. *See also* law; New York Trespass Act; slavery and slaves
Protestant ethic, 94
provisionality (regional), 6, 200, 250, 251, 252–54, 257, 258, 262, 264
Pryse, Marjorie, 8, 10, 20n11, 21n23

Quakers, 162, 176, 177n12. *See also* Christianity

racial ideology (and racism), 11, 23–25, 31–36, 41, 43n25, 72, 181, 184, 186–89, 222–23, 230, 238–39, 240–44, 259–260
racialization, 11, 243, 245n13, 245nn14–15, 246n29, 247n43, 247n55, 247n58, 247n63. *See also* whiteness
Rancière, Jacques. *See under* aesthetics
Ranger, Terence, 20n4
Ransom, John Crowe, 116, 117
Reconstruction (U.S.), 84, 100, 117, 134n2, 234, 243–44, 251, 254–55, 257–58, 260, 267n35
regionalism, 19–20, 44, 47, 99, 145–47, 228, 249–54, 257, 260, 264–65; and British West Indies, 81–86, 89, 92; and literature, 8, 108, 115–18; and nation, 4, 7, 13–15, 62–64, 121, 141–42. *See also* critical regionalism; regionalization
regionalization (and regions), 1–13, 19, 26–28, 30–35, 39, 41, 46–59, 99, 162–63, 249–54, 255, 266n11; and African Americans, 226, 229–31, 234–43; and British West Indies, 81–85, 91–95; and literature, 62–69, 155, 257–58, 263–64; and nation, 71–78, 131, 132, 141, 143; and religion, 183–84, 186, 192, 195. *See also* critical regionalism; regionalism
removal, Indian, 18–19, 64, 69, 70, 72, 75, 183, 243–44; Cherokee, 199–200, 211–12, 214–15, 218–20, 223; Removal Act (1830), 191
Renaissance (American), 7, 144
Renan, Ernst, 95n1

republicanism (and republicans), 2, 25, 32–35, 40, 43n32, 44n42, 148
Republican Party. *See* Jeffersonians
republican synthesis, 34–41, 43n32, 141
Revere, Paul, 144
revolution: Haitian, 85–86; Mexican, 125, 130, 136n31, 137n49; postrevolutionary era, 27, 29, 30, 41, 104, 126, 138–59; U.S., 7, 102, 108, 133, 164, 200, 220
rhetoric, 7, 11, 20n9, 22n45, 38, 48, 60n36, 124, 130, 145, 149, 231; Cherokee, 200–203, 205, 223n4, 224n31, 225n57; imperialist, 46, 54–56; nationalist, 14, 26, 210–23
rhizome (rhizomatic), 47, 48, 53, 57, 59, 117, 252. *See also* Deleuze, Gilles; Guattari, Felix
rice, 99, 100, 101–2, 108–12, 115, 118, 119n33
Rio Grande, 76, 124
rivers, 26, 69–70, 124, 133, 230. *See also specific rivers*
Robbins, Hollis, 10, 11, 14–15, 18, 19, 254
romance (genre), 112, 147, 251, 252, 263–64
Romanticism (romantic nationalism), 2, 9, 32–35
Ronda, James, 48, 50, 59n1, 60n10, 223
Round, Philip, 218, 224n13
Rowe, John Carlos, 20n7, 55, 60n10
Rowlandson, Mary, 127
Rowson, Susannah, 143, 147
rum, 86, 99, 118, 191, 194
Rush, Benjamin, 32
Russia (Russian Empire), 27, 32, 45, 229
Rutgers v. Waddington, 139–41, 144, 147, 151, 156nn6–7, 157n18, 158n31, 254

Saint Louis, 37, 61n46, 63, 137n49
San Francisco, 226–29, 233–36, 240, 242, 245n2
satire, 31, 100, 104, 105, 112
Schell, Jennifer, 10, 18, 176n7, 177n12, 177n17, 236, 247n47, 253
Schoolman, Martha, 10, 14, 17, 95nn10–11, 253
Schulten, Susan, 4, 5

sea narratives, 55, 116, 127, 160, 165–86, 172–74, 177n21
Second Great Awakening, 181–82, 185–87, 189–92, 196
seduction narrative. *See* sympathy
Seelye, John, 4, 20n3
sentimentalism. *See* sympathy
settler colonialism, 25–28, 72
Shapiro, Stephen, 146
Shawnee Indians, 28, 35–38, 49
Shays' Rebellion, 30
Shelley, Percy Bysshe, 54
Shields, David, 108, 110
Simms, William Gilmore, 34, 43n28
Sioux Indians, 51, 57, 131. *See also specific tribes*
slavery and slaves, 65, 84, 137n46, 138, 146, 190, 240–43, 245n4, 246n35, 253; civil law, 255, 259–60, 266n24; fugitive slaves, 161–65, 168–71, 226–28, 231–36; Jamaica, 85–95; Philip Nolan, 127, 136n28; proslavery and antislavery newspapers, 161–65, 168–71, 177n13, 177n27, 177n30; southern British-American colonies, 100–105, 108–16; Venezuela filibuster, 124. *See also under* labor
Slotkin, Richard, 52, 73
Smith, Adam, 107
Smith, Anthony D., 20n4, 33, 35, 43n16, 43n27
Smith, Thomas W., 161, 166
Society for the Study of Midwestern Literature, 22n46
Society for the Study of Southern Literature, 22n46
South, the (U.S.), 6, 12, 13, 14–15, 17, 20n15, 84, 88, 184, 255–56, 257, 267n37; economic production, 91, 99, 100, 117; post-Reconstruction, 259–60, 262, 264; slavery, 87, 227–29, 236, 239–40, 243; the Southwest, 62–74, 79. *See also* Confederacy; *and specific states*
South Carolina, 70, 100, 101, 102, 103, 107, 108–12, 113, 115, 116, 118, 119n6, 119n35. *See also* Lowcountry region

Southern Literary Journal, 22n46
Southey, Robert, 27, 31, 39, 42n4
Southwest, the (U.S.), 15, 17, 62–80, 123, 130, 133, 253
sovereignty: Cherokee, 19, 72, 199–200, 204–8, 211–22; of the individual, 29, 55, 90–91, 129, 170–71, 182, 185–86, 188, 229, 244–45; and literature, 141, 148, 155; Native, 72; state, 122, 130, 264; territorial, 124, 254; U.S., 22n42, 122, 125, 130–33, 140, 211
Spanish Empire (and Spain). *See under* empire
Spirit of the Times. See Porter, William T.
Stoddard, Amos, 34, 37–42, 42n6, 44n42, 44n43
Stowe, Harriet Beecher, 84, 231
Stuart, John A., 69
sublime, 59, 185, 188
sugar, 85–87, 91–93, 99, 100, 101, 102, 103, 112–15, 116, 118. *See also* Walker, Kara
Sweet, Timothy, 103, 225n50
Swift v. Tyson, 257, 266n28
sympathy (seduction, sentimentalism), 75, 112, 128, 143, 146, 148–52, 154, 166, 188, 220, 231–32, 260

Tatum, Stephen, 50, 61n51, 78n1
Taylor, Bayard, 229, 236, 247n49
Taylor, Zachary, 76–78, 227
technology, 26, 37, 51, 69, 110, 111, 113, 114, 177. *See also* industrialism
temperance, 166, 191
temporality, 2, 62, 63, 84, 86, 106, 141, 215, 235, 253, 262–64, 266n29; deep time, 8, 34; emancipatory, 88–89
Tennenhouse, Leonard, 152, 158n25
Tennessee River, 27, 39, 207
territorialization, 121–23, 126, 129–31, 133, 134n6, 252–53
Territory of Orleans, 252, 256–58. *See also* Louisiana Territory; New Orleans
Texas, 20n15, 63, 73–75, 118, 124–26, 135n21, 135n24, 135–36n26, 136n28

Thomas, Steven W., 17, 119n18, 120n49, 253, 255
Thorpe, Thomas Bangs, 63, 65–71, 73–78, 79n19; *Big Bear of Arkansas*, 67–72, 74, 79n12, 79n13, 79nn16–17, "The Disgraced Scalp-Lock," 74–76. *See also* Porter, William T.
Tidewater region, 100, 101, 103–8, 109, 112–16. *See also* Maryland; North Carolina; Virginia
time. *See* temporality
tobacco, 51, 99, 100, 101, 102, 103–8, 109, 110, 115, 118, 247n56
Tocqueville, Alexis de, 130
Toulmin, Harry (also Henry), 35–39, 43n34
Townsend, John Kirk, 16, 47, 48, 52–59, 61n40, 61n46, 61n50
trade, 86, 91–92, 126, 129, 132–33, 136n34, 137n49, 146, 177n13, 191, 240, 255; colonial, 28, 61n51, 99–120; New Bedford, 160–76; U.S. West, 48–49, 50–58, 71, 72, 83, 123. *See also* capitalism; globalization; mercantilism; slavery and slaves
transatlantic, 88, 108, 118, 149, 151–52, 265; markets, 100–103, 111, 133; scholarship, 8, 62, 116, 117, 121, 250. *See also* Atlantic studies; black Atlantic
trans-Atlantic, the (as distinct from transatlantic), 100, 115. *See also* Atlantic studies; black Atlantic
translocal, 81, 251–52, 256, 265, 265n3, 266n11. *See also* transregional
transnationalism, 16, 47, 121, 124, 129–30, 132, 134n2, 158n36, 168, 173, 247n58, 250; exchange, 49, 50–51, 55–57, 118, 133, 265; scholarship 61n46, 62, 116, 134n3, 136–37n43; slavery and abolition, 81–87, 89, 94
transregional, 51, 57, 155. *See also* translocal
travel writing. *See* cartographic texts; charting
treaties, 71, 140; Indian, 212–20
Treaty, Jay (1794), 27
Treaty of Guadalupe-Hidalgo (1848), 227

Treaty of Paris (1784), 27, 138, 155n1
Truett, Samuel, 121–22
Trumbull, John, 36
tuberculosis, 91
Turner, Frederick Jackson, 6–8, 10, 21nn16–17, 117, 134n2, 244, 248n66
Tuscarora Indians, 27
Twain, Mark, 64, 78, 79n4
Tyler, Royall, 148

U.S.–Mexico War, *See* Mexican–American War

Van Buren, Martin, 143
Venezuela. *See* Miranda, Francisco
Vikings, 26, 34, 41
Virginia, 26, 39, 102–5, 106–8, 116, 118, 143. *See also* Tidewater region
virtue, 76–77, 108–9, 125, 128–29, 137n46, 146, 151, 154, 218; agrarian, 37, 101, 103, 105–6, 115

Wald, Priscilla, 255
Wales, 25, 27, 33, 38, 40. *See also* Welsh Indians
Walker, Cheryl, 191
Walker, Kara, 99–100, 118, 118n1
Wampy, Anne, 193–97
Warner, Michael, 10, 13, 21n30
War of 1812, 9, 26, 32, 34, 37, 40–41, 144
Washington, Booker T., 83
Washington, George, 76, 106, 138–42, 146–47, 151, 156n5, 216–18, 220, 224n37, 225n40, 251
Watts, Edward, 16, 17, 20n15, 46, 55, 60n10, 249–50, 253
Welsh Indians, 15, 16, 25–44
West, the, (U.S.) 9, 15, 17, 45–59, 61n45, 68–69, 83, 100, 134n2, 184, 190, 254; African Americans, 227, 229–244, 245n12, 246n43, 248n64; exploration, 45–59, 122–23; humor, 71–78; Madoc legend, 25, 26, 29, 31, 34; trade, 84, 99
Western American Literature, 22n46
Western Literature Association, 22n46
West Indies. *See* Caribbean
Weyler, Karen, 152–53
whaling, 160–62, 164–69, 172–76, 177n13, 177n17, 177n21
Whig Party, 65, 76, 142, 227
Whisky Rebellion, 23, 30
White, Ed, 20n3, 141, 144, 153
White, Richard, 22n42, 60n33
Whitecar, William, Jr., 161, 167, 175
whiteness, 25, 28, 31, 33–35, 37, 40–42, 73–77, 93, 108, 160
Whittier, John Greenleaf, 236, 247n49
Wilentz, Sean, 20n7
Wilkinson, James, 123, 124, 125–27, 129
Williams, Gwyn A., 27, 42n6, 42n9, 43n29, 44n45
Williams, James, 227–29, 232–44, 245n15, 246n29, 247n55, 247n58, 248n63
Williams, Raymond, 145, 152
Williams, William, 182, 186–88, 191
Wilson, Rob, 56, 61n45
Winthrop, John, 5
Wong, Edlie, 229, 242–44, 245nn13–15, 246n29, 247n45, 247n55, 247n63
working class, 114, 160, 169–70, 176. *See also* labor

Yale University, 90
Yankton Indians, 51, 57
Yates, Norris W., 65, 70, 79n5, 79n14
yeoman, 37, 93, 101, 104–7, 109, 115. *See also* agrarian
Young, Elliot, 121–22
Young, Robert J. C., 33. *See also* whiteness

Zagarell, Sandra A., 95n1, 249
Zerbe, Richard O., Jr., 233–34

www.ingramcontent.com/pod-product-compliance
Lightning Source LLC
Chambersburg PA
CBHW011754220426
43672CB00018B/2958